Peyton Gash

Peyton Gash

ROCK and GEM

RONALD LOUIS BONEWITZ
CONSULTANTS MARGARET CARRUTHERS, RICHARD EFTHIM

LONDON, NEW YORK, MUNICH,
MELBOURNE, AND DELHI

Senior Editors Angeles Gavira, Peter Frances
Senior Art Editor Ina Stradins
Designers Paul Drislane, Peter Laws
US Editor Chrisine Heilman
Production Controllers Melanie Dowland, Luca
Frassinetti, Kevin Ward
DTP Designer John Goldsmid

Managing Art Editor Philip Ormerod
Art Director Bryn Walls
Publishing Manager Liz Wheeler
Category Publisher Jonathan Metcalf

Produced for Dorling Kindersley by
Grant Laing Partnership
48 Brockwell Park Gardens,
London SE24 9BJ

Managing Editor Jane Laing
Managing Art Editor Christine Lacey
Art Editors Alison Gardner, Miranda Harvey
Designers Nick Avery, Vicky Short, Paul Ashby
Project Editor Jane Simmonds
Editors Frank Ritter, Helen Ridge
Picture Researcher Jo Walton
Proof Reader Becky Gee
Indexer Dorothy Frame
Specially Commissioned Photography
Linda Burgess and Gary Ombler
Crystal Illustrations Tim Loughhead,
Precision Illustration

Smithsonian Project Coordinators
Ellen Nanny, Katie Mann
Consultants Margaret Carruthers, Richard Efthim

First American Edition, 2005

Published in the United States by
DK Publishing, Inc.
375 Hudson Street
New York, New York 10014

05 06 07 08 09   10 9 8 7 6 5 4 3 2 1

Copyright © 2005 Dorling Kindersley Limited

A Cataloging-in-Publication record for this book is
available from the Library of Congress.

ISBN 0-7566-0962-3

Color reproduction by Colourscan, Singapore
Printed and bound in Hong Kong,
China by L. Rex

Discover more at
www.dk.com

CONTENTS

ORIGINS

EARTH HISTORY | COLLECTING SPECIMENS

THE FORMATION OF THE UNIVERSE

WHEN WE LOOK TODAY at rocks and minerals, and at the planet Earth formed from them, it is hard for us to imagine a time when none of this existed—a time even before there were chemical elements, the building blocks from which rocks and minerals are made. Yet between 13 billion and 15 billion years ago, the entire universe consisted of one tiny dot of primordial energy. Then, in an instant, the Big Bang set in motion a chain of events that resulted in the creation of atoms and, over millions of years, in the formation of galaxies and stars. It was only within stars that the elements were formed that would make minerals, rocks, and planets.

COSMIC BACKGROUND
This image shows the Cosmic Microwave Radiation Background, a faint heat radiation that emanates from all points in the sky. It is thought to be left over from the fireball-like conditions prevalent in the early universe.

THE BIG BANG

According to the most widely held theory of how the universe came into being, the physical universe and all within it emerged from an infinitely small point of pure energy in a highly compressed state and at an extremely high temperature. The rapid expansion of this point of energy through the Big Bang resulted in a relatively rapid drop in its density and temperature, and within a few seconds, a number of elementary particles such as electrons, photons, neutrons, and protons formed. This expanding mass of energy and particles was still far too hot for the formation of atoms, an event that required perhaps another 300,000 years of expansion and cooling. Only then did the first atoms appear, chiefly of hydrogen and helium.

PARTICLE TRACKS
Studying the tracks of subatomic particles in a particle accelerator gives scientists insight into the Big Bang's early stages.

EDWIN HUBBLE

American astronomer Edwin Hubble (1889–1953) is famous for proving that we live in an expanding universe. Hubble made his most important discoveries in the 1920s. He found that other galaxies exist beyond our own galaxy, the Milky Way. By analyzing changes in the wavelength of light from these other galaxies, he showed that they are moving away from the Milky Way, and that the farther away a galaxy is, the faster it recedes. As a result, Hubble concluded that the universe as a whole is expanding. His crucial observations led directly to the Big Bang theory.

AFTER THE BIG BANG
In the first few billionths of a second after the Big Bang, the universe consisted of a "soup" of enormously varied particles and radiation.

"Up" quark

"Down" quark

Electr

PROTON　　**NEUTRON**

QUARKS BIND
In the next seconds, quarks started binding to form protons and neutrons. One "down" and two "up" quarks made a proton, while one "up" and two "down" quarks made a neutron

Neutron

Energy released by collisions

Proton

Single proton

Electron

HYDROGEN ATOM

Electron

Helium nucleus, two protons and two neutrons

Nucleus

Electron

HELIUM AT

NUCLEI FORM
Between 1 and 180 seconds after the Big Bang, collisions between protons and neutrons formed the nuclei of light elements, mainly helium, though they did not yet capture electrons

ATOMS APPEAR
After about 300,000 years, helium nuclei began to capture pairs of electrons, forming helium atoms. Protons captured one electron each, forming hydrogen atoms

GALAXIES APPEAR

Hydrogen and helium gas, along with two other light elements, lithium and beryllium, were the only chemical elements in the universe for hundreds of millions of years. Eventually, variations in the density of matter in the expanding universe caused small regions of higher gravity to occur (the denser matter becomes, the more gravitational pull it exerts). Gas was drawn into these regions by the force of gravity, creating vast, coalescing clouds of hydrogen. Within each of these huge gas clouds, or nebulae, numerous even more dense areas formed, each drawing yet more gas into itself. Eventually, in the centers of the densest areas of gas, temperatures and pressures rose to such a point that hydrogen atoms began to fuse together to form helium. This nuclear fusion generated light and yet more heat—creating the first stars to light the newly formed universe. Each cloud of newborn stars constituted a galaxy.

NURSERY OF STARS
Nebulae are clouds of gas and dust that are the birthplace of stars. This nebula, known as the Keyhole Nebula, is glowing with color because of the hot young stars within it.

DOUBLE SPIRAL GALAXY
Galaxies exist in five basic shapes, one of which is a spiral. A typical single galaxy will contain around 100 billion stars.

CREATING THE FIRST MINERALS

Stars can be thought of as factories for making heavier elements from hydrogen. At the high temperatures and pressures in the cores of stars, nuclei can collide with such energy that they fuse together to become heavier elements. These heavier elements can then fuse with more hydrogen or with other freshly made nuclei to form heavier nuclei. In this way, oxygen, carbon, and most of the other elements up to the mass of iron are formed. Heavier elements than iron are made toward the end of the life of large stars by a process of adding neutrons to nuclei and radioactive decay. At the end of the life of large stars, the star will explode. Such an explosion is called a supernova. Minerals are found in meteorites that formed in the outflows of red giant stars and others around supernovae.

SUPERNOVA EFFECT
The blast from an ancient supernova heated this gas cloud in the constellation Cygnus, making it glow.

OPEN STAR CLUSTER
The Quintuplet cluster (shown here) is the largest cluster of stars inside our Milky Way galaxy. This group of young stars formed 4 million years ago and contains the brightest star in the galaxy, called the Pistol star.

GENERATIONS OF STARS

New stars are created from material spread through space by the explosion of other stars. Our own star, the Sun, is a third-generation star, containing elements that have been cycled through at least two other stages of star death. Although, like all stars, second-generation stars are mainly hydrogen, they incorporate elements formed in the first generation of stars and can use these as building blocks for new isotopes and elements. We can identify these second-generation elements and isotopes in the Sun and in the planets circling it, including Earth.

ULTRAVIOLET SUN
Our local star, the Sun, here photographed through an ultraviolet filter, is a third-generation star.

BIRTH OF THE SUN

Our solar system consists of the Sun, planets, moons, asteroids, comets, and assorted other debris left over from its formation. The solar system was formed out of a rotating cloud of interstellar gas and dust (known as the solar nebula) that was the remnant of two earlier generations of stars. It was located toward the edge of a galaxy we know as the Milky Way. Roughly 4.6 billion years ago, the nebula collapsed, possibly due to shock waves from a nearby exploding supernova. The collapse of the nebula caused its rate of rotation to increase, and the collapsing material flattened into a disk, known as the protoplanetary disk. Matter continued to be drawn from this disk toward the center. Energy from the collapse caused the temperature in the center to rise and the density to increase. Eventually, the temperature and density were high enough for hydrogen nuclei to start fusing to form helium and giving off energy in the form of heat and light. Our own star, the Sun, was born.

MILKY WAY
The Milky Way is a spiral galaxy. Its nucleus consists mainly of old red and yellow stars; younger, bluer stars form the arms, where our Sun is found.

SUN COMPOSITION
The Sun, the center of the solar system, is roughly 75 percent hydrogen and 25 percent helium. Other elements are present at levels less than 1 percent. These minor elements can only have been formed by processing through two generations of stars.

ORIGIN OF THE PLANETS

Not all of the material in the solar nebula ended up being dragged into the forming Sun by the force of gravity. Some gas and dust remained orbiting in the protoplanetary disk. Here, dust particles stuck together into larger and larger agglomerations. Some of these dust balls were melted to form tiny rocks smaller than marbles. Known as "chondrules," these were in turn accreted, sticking together in ever larger bodies until gravitational forces could take over and keep them together. These bodies are called planetesimals. Once the planetesimals grew to around half a mile in size, they started to attract other similar-sized objects due to gravitational attraction.

At this stage the process of accretion grew in efficiency. Many of the planetesimals continued to coalesce until they formed objects the size of Mercury or Earth. The whole process, starting from the initial collapse of the nebula and continuing through the various stages up to the formation of planets, may well have taken about 10 million years. Not all of the planetesimals were caught up in the formation of planets. Some of them were frozen at between approximately half a mile and a few dozen miles in size. Many of these bodies are preserved as asteroids orbiting in the asteroid belt between Mars and Jupiter.

FROM SOLAR NEBULA TO SOLAR SYSTEM
The solar system formed from a huge nebula (cloud) of gas and dust, which condensed into a spinning disk with the proto-Sun at its center. While the Sun further condensed and atomic fusion began, particles in the rest of the disk accreted, starting the process that led to the formation of planets.

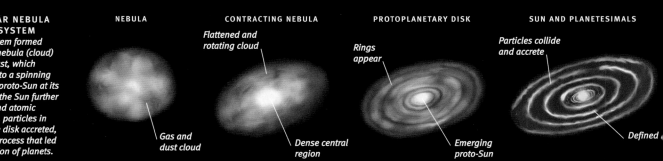

NEBULA
Gas and dust cloud

CONTRACTING NEBULA
Flattened and rotating cloud
Dense central region

PROTOPLANETARY DISK
Rings appear
Emerging proto-Sun

SUN AND PLANETESIMALS
Particles collide and accrete
Defined

INNER AND OUTER PLANETS

The protoplanetary disk became hotter closer to the Sun than farther out. In the hotter regions, ices evaporated. Also, gas was driven out toward the outer parts of the solar system, a movement helped by the solar wind, a stream of energetic particles emitted from the Sun. As a result, planets in the inner solar system—known as the terrestrial planets—are small and rocky. But in the cold outer regions, the rocky bodies accreted ice and, because of the cold and their greater mass, could also hold on to gases such as methane, ammonia, hydrogen, and helium. The result was the formation of giant gas planets. Pluto formed far out, along with many other similar frozen bodies. These remained small since they were sparsely distributed and so could not accrete efficiently. They also did not gain much ice and gas driven off from the inner solar system. Some astronomers do not consider Pluto a planet, but just one of many icy bodies beyond Neptune.

SMALL, STONY EARTH
The four inner planets, including Earth, are composed largely of metal and stone.

LARGE, GASEOUS JUPITER
Jupiter and the other large outer planets have rocky cores but are mostly made of frozen gases.

Sun Mercury Venus Earth Mars Jupiter Saturn Uranus Neptune Pluto

NEAR AND FAR
The distance line above gives a rough idea of each planet's distance from the Sun. The stony planets (Mercury, Venus, Earth, and Mars) cluster near the Sun, while the gas giants (Jupiter, Saturn, Uranus, and Neptune) orbit at greater distances.

ORBITS OF THE PLANETS
All of the inner planets circle the sun in elliptical orbits, in the same direction and roughly on the same plane. A portion of Pluto's orbit crosses Neptune's, and the orbits of comets (blue line) can extend beyond that of Pluto.

ASTROBLEME
Meteorite craters, such as the impressive Tswaing crater near Pretoria, South Africa, are known as "astroblemes."

ROCKS FROM SPACE

Meteorites—rocks that fall to Earth from space—are of particular interest in the study of the origin of the solar system. Nearly all meteorites are thought to be fragments of asteroids, rocky bodies that range from objects more than 560 miles (900 km) in diameter to particles of microscopic dust. Mostly orbiting in a belt between Mars and Jupiter, asteroids are thought to have aggregated from material in the solar nebula about the same time as Earth was formed. The larger asteroids are, in fact, planetesimals that have never accreted to form a planet. Collisions between them produce fragments called meteoroids, some of which are propelled into Earth-crossing orbits, falling to Earth as meteorites. Types of meteorites and their contribution to our understanding of the solar system are explored on pages 74–75.

Accreted rock

STONY-IRON METEORITE
Meteorites can be divided into three groups: stony, iron, and, as here, a stony-iron mix of silicates and nickel–iron alloy.

THE FORMATION OF EARTH

THE ROCKS AND MINERALS we observe on Earth today are the result of an ongoing series of processes that began with the initial formation of Earth from the solar nebula over 4.5 billion years ago, and will continue for at least as long into the future.

BULGING SPHERE
Earth is nearly a perfect sphere, but because of its rotation it bulges a little at the equator and is slightly flattened at the poles.

EARTH TAKES SHAPE

As with the other planets, Earth formed through the accretion process, sweeping up solid material from the disk of the solar nebula (see pp.10–11). As the mass of Earth increased, so did its gravity. Increasing gravity drew in ever–larger planetesimals and other meteoritic debris, accelerating the growth of the planet. Initially, the accreting planet was loosely consolidated—it did not form a coherent whole. But within a relatively short time, under the impact of collisions with meteorites and planetesimals, it consolidated and developed a differentiated structure. The shock of the impacts generated heat, causing rocks to melt. The molten Earth separated into liquid iron and silicate melt, the less dense silicate material floating on top of the higher–density metallic iron core. The silicate portion then also started to separate out into the higher–density mantle and the lower–density crust on the top. Accretion continues to this day as Earth sweeps up tons of space debris each year.

Small bodies and dust accrete to asteroid size

Asteroid-size body joins others of similar size

Larger object forms

THE ACCRETION OF EARTH
Matter from the solar nebula was drawn together to form asteroid-size bodies. These objects then accreted to form even larger bodies. Repeating the process over time formed Earth.

Lighter elements form mantle

Molten core

CORE AND MANTLE
As more and larger objects were drawn together, melting took place, with heavy elements migrating to the core. Lighter elements formed a mantle, which was surrounded by a rocky crust.

MODEST PLANET
Although it may seem large to us, Earth is a planet of medium size. With a diameter of 7,928 miles (12,756 km), it is the largest of the four rocky inner planets, but much smaller than any of the giant gas planets.

EARTH GAINS A SATELLITE

SURFACE OF THE MOON
The Moon's surface is scarred by impact craters. Some of these have been filled by flows of basaltic lava from beneath the Moon's crust, forming maria or seas.

According to the most widely accepted current theory, the Moon was formed as the result of an awesome collision early in Earth's history. Around 4.5 billion years ago, a very large planetesimal—probably an object about the size of Mars— hit Earth, penetrating far below the surface and splashing out a huge amount of debris. This Earth debris, along with material from the planetesimal itself, went into orbit around Earth. There, by the process of accretion, it formed the Moon. Studies of trace elements in lunar rocks show results similar to those obtained from Earth's mantle. This implies that at the time of the collision, the structure of Earth must have already differentiated into a lighter mantle and a denser core. Only the lighter mantle rocks were splashed out into orbit. Because lunar rocks have been dated to near the time when Earth was formed, scientists have concluded that planet formation must be a relatively rapid process. In the space of less than a hundred million years, it is likely that Earth formed, Earth's mantle developed, the awesome collision with the planetesimal occurred, and the splashed-out lunar material accreted to form the Moon.

MOON ROCK
The overall composition of rocks recovered from the Moon matches that of mantle rock on Earth.

Basalt from the Moon's surface

MOON STRUCTURE
Like Earth, the Moon has a mantle and a crust. It may also have an iron-rich core, but if such a core exists it is small. The Moon is less than half the size of Earth, with a diameter of 3,476 miles (5,562 km).

FORMATION OF THE MOON
The Moon was formed from material splashed out of Earth by the impact of a large planetesimal, along with a portion of the planetesimal itself. The debris of this massive collision was held in orbit by Earth's gravity and gradually cooled and coalesced. The process of accretion then formed Earth's natural satellite.

Mars-sized impactor

Earth

BOMBARDMENT OF EARTH

Earth

Debris begins to coalesce

DEBRIS ORBITS EARTH

Debris accretes to form the Moon

Earth

ACCRETION FORMS MOON

Pyroxene

CORE COMPOSITION
The composition of iron-nickel meteorites is thought to resemble that of Earth's core.

MOLTEN IRON
The outer portion of Earth's core is thought to be molten iron, as here created by human skill in a foundry.

CORE MINERALS FORM

Earth's core seems to have formed early on in the planet's development, as heavier elements sank toward the center. There is no way of obtaining samples of the core, at least not with current technology, but a range of ingenious methods has been used to determine the core's composition, including studies of Earth's magnetic field, of earthquake waves as they pass through Earth, of rock density, and of meteorites. These studies have led to the conclusion that Earth has a solid inner core surrounded by a liquid outer core. The core is probably composed mainly of iron with a small percentage of nickel, and a lighter element, possibly sulfur. Further refinements of the core's composition are probably still taking place as a result of chemical interaction with the lower mantle. The temperatures in the inner core are estimated to be close to those on the surface of the Sun. Exactly which iron minerals might form at such temperatures and pressures is not known.

13

MANTLE AND CRUST MINERALS

The intensity of the heat in the interior of the forming Earth encouraged chemical reactions between the iron–rich core and the surrounding material. Most of the elements that combine readily with iron formed denser minerals that accumulated in a thick shell around the core. This created what is known as the lower mantle. Lighter minerals were formed from elements with a greater affinity for oxygen than for iron. These combined as oxide compounds, predominantly silicates. Being lighter, these compounds rose upward to form the upper mantle and the crust, in effect floating on the denser lower mantle.

CORE, MANTLE, AND CRUST
Earth has three distinct layers: a core, consisting of a solid inner core and a fluid outer core, which together make up more than half the planet's diameter; the mantle, a layer of dense minerals making up most of the rest of Earth's diameter; and a thin crust composed of rocks and minerals chemically distinct from those of the core and mantle.

Core–mantle boundary, where liquid outer core and solid lower mantle meet

Plume of hot, upwelling mantle rock carries heat to surface

INNER CORE
Solid nickel-iron; down to 3,960 miles (6,370 km) below Earth's surface

Land surface made of continental crust

OUTER CORE
Liquid nickel-iron; down to 3,200 miles (5,150 km) below the surface

LOWER MANTLE
Solid, mostly silicates rich in magnesium; down to 1,860 miles (2,990 km) below the surface

UPPER MANTLE
Solid, primarily peridotite; down to 410 miles (660 km) below the surface

Continental shelf drops into ocean depths

CONTINENTAL CRUST
Solid, mixture of igneous, metamorphic, and sedimentary rocks; down to 45 miles (70 km) below the surface

Sea floor made of oceanic crust

OCEANIC CRUST
Solid, primarily basalt; down to 4 miles (7 km) below the surface

Ocean surface

Boundary between lower and upper mantle

MANTLE XENOLITH
Xenoliths are fragments of older rock incorporated in younger rock. In this xenolith from France, upper-mantle peridotite has been brought to Earth's surface in basaltic lava.

DATING EARTH

One of the earliest attempts to calculate the age of Earth was made in the 17th century, when Anglo-Irish Bishop Ussher, working from Biblical genealogy, estimated that Earth and the universe were created in October 4004 BC. The first accurate estimate was obtained in 1956 by physicist Claire Patterson (shown below) who compared radioisotope measurements from meteorites and Earth minerals to give an age of 4.55 billion years (more recently modified to 4.56 billion years). The oldest directly measured date is for zircon crystals taken from Mount Narryer, Western Australia, dating their formation to 4.4–3.9 billion years ago.

CLAIRE PATTERSON

OCEAN FLOOR ROCKS
Tectonic forces sometimes bring old ocean floor to the surface. These Newfoundland peridotites, thought to be similar to upper-mantle rocks, were once on the ocean bed.

CHEMICAL COMPOSITION

This bar chart illustrates the proportion of various chemical compounds that are found in the major layers of Earth.

- OTHERS
- NICKEL OXIDE
- MAGNESIUM OXIDE
- CALCIUM OXIDE
- IRON AND IRON OXIDES
- ALUMINUM OXIDE
- SILICON DIOXIDE

CONTINENTAL CRUST · OCEANIC CRUST · MANTLE · CORE

THE OXYGEN FACTOR

Although the core of Earth is denser than the mantle and crust, the distribution of the various chemical elements between the layers of Earth's interior was not necessarily determined by the density of the actual elements themselves. The tendency of various elements to interact either with iron or with oxygen could have been the principal determining factor. For example, uranium and thorium are very dense, heavy elements, yet they are concentrated in the crust, possibly because they both have a high affinity for oxygen. The importance of the role played by oxygen in Earth's crust is clearly illustrated by the fact that it makes up 50 percent of the crust by weight.

THE ATMOSPHERE AND THE OCEANS

The formation of the atmosphere and the oceans was directly connected to the formation of the crust. During the period of intense accretion, as Earth melted and recrystallized, water vapor and other gases were released to add to the gases from the solar nebula accumulated during the accretion process. This constituted Earth's first atmosphere. Then, 3.8 billion years ago, Earth and the Moon were subjected to intense meteorite bombardment that is thought to have stripped away the first atmosphere. Subsequent volcanic activity released nitrogen, carbon dioxide, and water vapor, which in turn were broken down by ultraviolet light into hydrogen, oxygen, and ozone. The water vapor collected to form oceans, where salts dissolved, increasing salinity. A second atmosphere formed, at first with little oxygen. As life developed in the oceans, oxygen was released, creating today's atmosphere.

WEATHER SYSTEM
Earth's atmosphere extends upward for a few hundred miles, but most weather systems occur in the bottom 10 miles (15 km).

FIRST ATMOSPHERE

Hydrogen released into space

Solar wind strips away atmosphere

Debris from space strikes Earth

Helium released

SECOND ATMOSPHERE

Hydrogen released to space

Carbon dioxide

UV light splits water into hydrogen and oxygen and ozone

Water

Oxygen and ozone

Nitrogen

ATMOSPHERIC CHANGE
Earth's first atmosphere, built up from gases (nitrogen, carbon dioxide, and water vapor) released by crystallization and from the solar nebula, was stripped away by meteorite strikes and the solar wind. The second atmosphere formed from volcanic gases modified by ultraviolet light.

ANCIENT LIFE
Formed by bacteria colonies, stromatolites in Shark Bay, Australia, are "living fossils." Stromatolite mounds like these formed in shallow seas more than 3 billion years ago.

EARTH'S CRUST

ONE OF THE MOST conspicuous features of Earth's surface is its division into continents and ocean basins. Both the oceanic and the continental crust lie on top of the mantle, but the two types of crust are significantly different. The lighter, thicker continental crust floats higher in the mantle than the denser, thinner oceanic crust. About two–thirds of Earth's surface is oceanic crust, but the continental crust has a far wider variety of rocks.

DRIFTING ROCKS
Earth's crust is fused with the upper mantle to form the lithosphere. This drifts on top of the asthenosphere.

Continental margin of thick sediments built up on ocean crust

Oceanic crust

Lithosphere

Asthenosphere

OCEANIC CRUST

The oceanic crust is much younger than the continental crust—even the oldest parts of the ocean floor are only 200 million years old. This is because oceanic crust is continually being recycled. It forms from mantle material rising within rifts and oceanic ridges, and spreading to either side of the ridge. This material returns to the mantle at the same rate in areas called subduction zones. The oceanic crust is composed of several layers, the topmost of which is a layer of sediments, primarily very fine muds overlying a layer of basalt. The lower layers are primarily gabbro, with increasing olivine content as the depth increases.

Abyssal plain

Continental slope

Continental crust made up of igneous, metamorphic, and sedimentary rocks

Boundary between crust and mantle, known as Mohorovicic discontinuity

Amygdule filled with zeolite

WIDESPREAD ROCK
This black rock is basalt that formed on land. Basalt is also the main component of the oceanic crust.

BLACK SMOKER
Associated with volcanic activity, black smokers are underwater hot springs, expelling mineral-rich water at temperatures up to 750°F (400°C). Most occur near mid-ocean ridges, where oceanic crust is formed.

JOHN TUZO WILSON

In the 1960s, Canadian geophysicist John Tuzo Wilson (1908–93) became one of the leading advocates of the theory that the sea floor is spreading from the ocean ridges. Wilson made a major contribution to the theory when he put forward the idea that volcanic mid-ocean island chains, such as Hawaii, form as a result of the sea floor's slow movement over the top of a "hot spot"—a fixed point where magma wells up inside the mantle.

ICELANDIC RIDGE
Oceanic crust and mid-ocean ridges are not often seen above sea level, but in Iceland the Mid-Atlantic Ridge rises out of the surrounding ocean.

CONTINENTAL CRUST

The continental crust covers about a third of Earth's surface, forming the main landmasses and the beds of the shallow seas that surround them. It is where most of the rocks and minerals discussed in this book are found.

The continental crust varies from 16 to 45 miles (25 to 70 km) in thickness, with the greatest thickness under the mountain ranges. At the heart of each continent is a stable mass of crystalline rocks from the Precambrian period (4.56 billion to 543 million years ago) covering thousands of square miles. This is known as the continental shield. Other rocks of the continental crust have more recently been subjected to the processes of the rock cycle (see pp.28–29), such as erosion, metamorphism, and sedimentation. It is this history of transformation over billions of years that accounts for their immense variety.

GRANITE OUTCROP
These granite rock pinnacles are in the Ahaggar Massif, Algeria. Composed of silica-rich minerals, such as quartz and feldspar, granite is found in large quantities in the continental crust.

Large feldspar crystal

Biotite

CRUSTAL ROCKS
Metamorphic rocks such as this gneiss are formed as a result of tectonic forces acting upon rocks of the continental crust.

AUSTRALIAN SHIELD
The central area of Western Australia is part of the ancient heart of the Australian continent—its stable continental shield.

FLOATING ROCK

Earth's crust behaves as if it were floating on the underlying denser, flexible rock of the mantle. This concept is known as "isostasy." The crust can be visualized as resembling an iceberg floating on water, and like an iceberg it extends downward into the medium on which it floats. Because Earth's crust is not all of the same density or thickness, different parts of it protrude into the mantle to different depths. Thus the crust extends deeper down into the mantle under tall mountain ranges, such as the Himalayas, than it does in low-lying areas, because it requires a deeper "root" to buoy up the mountain range's additional weight. About two-thirds of the thickness of the continental crust forms the root that supports the rest.

DEEP ROOTS
Everest is part of the Himalayas, a relatively young mountain range created by a collision of two continental plates. Mountains such as Everest have a "root" extending many miles into the mantle.

17

PLATE TECTONICS

The term "tectonics" refers to the building and movements of Earth's crust. According to the concept of plate tectonics, the solid, brittle lithosphere, which comprises the crust and a thin section of the uppermost mantle, rests on and is carried along by the underlying layer of hot and flowing mantle rock, the asthenosphere. The lithosphere is made up of both continents and ocean basins. It is divided into relatively rigid sections known as "plates," and the movement of these plates relative to one another results in the formation and the modification of Earth's major surface features.

PLATE BOUNDARIES
There are about a dozen large tectonic plates. Some of the plates consist of both continental and oceanic crust, while others are composed exclusively of oceanic crust.

Divergent or transform plate boundary

Convergent plate boundary

Deep-sea trench

Upper mantle

Lower mantle

Mantle plume rises from lower mantle to form hot spot

Plates move apart at oceanic rift

Plate dragged along by convection current

Motion of convection current

Subduction zone where tectonic plate descends into mantle

Core

PLATE MOTION
The force that drives the movement of tectonic plates is thought to be heat rising from the interior of the planet.

MOVING FORCE

The forces that drive the lithospheric plates across Earth's surface are as yet not fully understood, but the movement is thought to be caused by convection currents in the mantle, which are driven by heat within the planet. As the plates move relative to each other, diverging, converging, or moving past, major geological interactions take place along their boundaries. This is where many of the principal processes that shape Earth's surface happen—for example, earthquakes, volcanism, and the deformation of Earth's crust that builds up mountain ranges.

SEISMOGRAPH TRACE
The energy of tectonic movements creates vibrations in Earth's rocks that can be measured and recorded using a seismograph.

DIVERGENT BOUNDARIES

Where plates are moving away from each other along a divergent boundary—typically a mid-ocean ridge—magma (molten rock) wells up from below as the release of pressure produces partial melting of the underlying mantle. This magma, generally basaltic in composition, solidifies to create new, primarily oceanic crust. The accompanying plate movements generate a great deal of minor earthquake activity as the crust repeatedly fractures, heals, and fractures again.

BOUNDARY LINES
At divergent plate boundaries such as the Mid-Atlantic Ridge, new oceanic crust is created. Transform boundaries occur where plates pass one another.

Direction of plate movement

Spreading ridge

Transform boundary

Magma rising from mantle at mid-ocean ridge

Divergent plate boundary

Oceanic crust formed when magma cools and solidifies

OCEANIC RIFT
The divergent plate boundary of the Mid-Atlantic Ridge runs beneath the ocean from the Arctic to the Antarctic, except where it rises above sea level as a rift in Iceland.

CONVERGENT BOUNDARIES

A convergent boundary occurs where plates are moving toward each other. Where oceanic crust meets oceanic crust, one of the plates descends beneath the other—a process called subduction. The subducted crust is recycled into the mantle, compensating for the new crust being created continually at divergent plate boundaries. Subduction also happens where the oceanic crust of one plate meets the continental crust of another. The greater buoyancy of the continental crust prevents it from being subducted, so it is the plate carrying the oceanic crust that dives underneath. The subducted oceanic crust triggers melting at great depths and molten rock rises up through the crust, erupting to form explosive volcanoes. The numerous volcanoes found along the upper Pacific coast of the US, such as Mount St. Helens, are formed in this manner. If both plates meet along a continental edge, then neither can be subducted. The resulting collision causes the crust to crumple, pushing mountain ranges upward.

Mountain range formed by continental collision

Plateau behind mountain range

Overlying plate

Major fault

Continental crust attached to subducted sea floor

Subducted oceanic crust

Suture zone

COMPLEX COLLISION
An ocean–continent subduction zone can turn into a continent–continent collision zone once the subduction is complete.

UPWARD THRUST
The Himalayan mountain range, the highest on the planet, is still being thrust upward as the Eurasian and Indian-Australian tectonic plates collide.

TRANSFORM FAULTS

As well as divergent and convergent boundaries, there is a third type of plate boundary, where two plates move past each other without creating or destroying crust. This is called a transform boundary. Large earthquakes are caused by the continuous buildup and release of tension where the plates meet. California's San Andreas Fault and the North Anatolian fault system in Turkey are good examples of transform boundaries.

CALIFORNIA FAULT LINE
The San Andreas Fault in California is a transform boundary where the Pacific Plate and the North American Plate slide past one another.

RING OF FIRE
These volcanoes in Java are part of the "ring of fire" that surrounds the Pacific Plate. Subducted rock triggers melting, feeding volcanic activity at Earth's surface.

COLLECTING ROCKS AND MINERALS

THE WORLD OF ROCKS, minerals, gems, and fossils offers virtually endless possibilities for the hobbyist. Only a very small amount of specialized knowledge—little more than the ability to identify a few common minerals—is required to open a whole new world of enjoyment of some of nature's finest creations. Probably the most popular rock hobby is mineral collecting.

VESUVIUS ROCKS
Some collections are of finds from a single locality.

MAGNIFICATION
Collectors of small crystals need effective microscopes to examine and enjoy their minute specimens.

STARTING A COLLECTION

Most collectors begin by just accumulating rocks, minerals, and fossils. As their collection grows, they start being more selective, keeping only specimens with better color, better crystallization, or more interesting crystal forms. With widening experience, most collectors begin to specialize. Some minerals come in such a wide variety of crystal forms that a collection can be made of a single mineral; other collectors may focus on ore minerals, or on minerals from a particular locality. There are practical considerations that limit the scope of most collections. Some rare minerals are very expensive, and mineral collections can take up a huge amount of space. One solution is to collect tiny specimens called micromounts, whose form and beauty can only be seen under magnification.

FASCINATING FOSSILS
As well as minerals, fossils are a popular subject for specialized collections.

TREE CALCITE

SAND CALCITE

DOGTOOTH SPAR

CALCITE CRYSTALS
A mineral such as calcite, which exists in a rich variety of crystal shapes, provides suitable material for an interesting single-mineral collection.

FIELD EXPERIENCE
Rock collecting can be a hobby for a lifetime, as the collector develops knowledge and skills to enhance the activity.

COLLECTING SAFELY

While mineral collecting is generally a safe hobby, there are a few definite hazards that the collector needs to be aware of. The most dangerous collecting locality is around old mines and workings. Tunnels should never be entered—shoring timbers rot very quickly, and cave-ins and rockfalls are almost guaranteed to happen. In any case, there is often remarkably poor collecting inside old mines. If anything looked good, the miners usually dug it out. Mine dumps, by contrast, can be a good source of specimens, although be aware that they are often loosely piled and can be unstable. When collecting in locations such as beach cliffs, road cuttings, and rockfalls, attention must be paid not only to loose material underfoot but also to anything that may fall or roll from above. Collectors are injured every year by falling rocks. And, unless you absolutely know the locality to be safe, leave small children at home.

TEMPTING TUNNELS
Old mine shafts can be tempting, but are often highly dangerous places. Better specimens are usually found in the mine dumps outside.

HARD HAT

ROCK HAMMER

POCKET KNIFE

Trowel

Brushes for light cleaning

Sieve

LEATHER GLOVES

SAFETY KIT
Flying rock splinters and falling rocks cause injuries to collectors each year. Safety equipment and safe tools are a must.

SAFETY GOGGLES

Rubber or leather grip

SAFETY CHISELS

READY FOR ANYTHING
The experienced collector has a range of equipment for all collecting possibilities, from sieves and pans to various brushes and trowels. Most of these tools can be left in the car until they are needed.

ESSENTIAL EQUIPMENT

At first glance it might seem that any hammer would do for breaking rocks, but this is far from the case. Every year rock collectors are injured—even blinded—by using the wrong hammers. Geologist's hammers are made of special steels, and the striking ends are beveled to prevent steel splinters from flying off them. Special geological chisels are made for the same reasons. Wearing safety goggles is highly recommended when breaking or splitting stone. Access to some collecting localities requires safety equipment such as a hard hat and fluorescent vest. A cell phone is an important piece of safety equipment—with a fully charged battery. Carry it with you even if you are only going a short distance from the car. A fall into a ravine or other low spot may take you out of sight of potential help and add hours to the time it takes to find you. In desert country, an adequate supply of water is essential, and if you are in snake country, take an appropriate snake-bite kit. Clothing suitable to the weather and terrain is, of course, vital. Leave your low-cut shoes and tennis shoes at home. Leather boots offer better protection from snake bites, cactus spines, sharp stones, jagged metal, and rolling stones, and give much better traction.

DELICATE CHISEL
A collector uses a small hammer and chisel to chip away rock from an embedded fossil.

GEM PANNING
The gold pan is an essential piece of equipment for a collector. In addition to gold, many gemstones can be found by panning surface sediments.

The bank of a road cut through the pegmatite rock of the Black Hills in North Dakota reveals giant feldspar crystals (center left and below).

LEAF FOSSIL

FOSSIL HUNT
A rocky beach on the Isle of Wight, southern England, offers a rich hunting ground for fossil collectors.

WHERE TO LOOK

In many countries, guidebooks are available that give precise directions to localities where collectors can find rocks, minerals, and fossils. A search of the Internet can also yield good information. Specialist publications and websites keep collectors abreast of new localities. In some respects, collecting your own specimens has become more difficult in recent years. Working mines and quarries are constrained by legal liability as to whom they can permit on their premises; old mines are increasingly dangerous; old mine dumps have been picked over for decades by other collectors; and public access to land is often restricted. But some traditional sites for collecting, such as road cuts and eroded cliffs on shorelines, still provide excellent opportunities. There is also an increasing number of collecting localities open to the public on a fee-paying basis, and some clubs for enthusiasts have their own collecting sites. Those who do not wish to collect all their specimens personally can buy them from numerous dealers, many of whom offer interesting samples that become available as new localities are discovered or opened up.

LOOKING FOR GOLD
This mineral collector hopes to find gold nuggets by the time-honored method of panning through gravel sediment from a river bed.

CORUNDUM

ASSOCIATED ROCKS
The collector needs to know in which rocks the minerals he is seeking are found. For example, chromite is found in peridotite; corundum in recrystallized limestone.

GOLD NUGGET

CHROMITE CRYSTALS

OLD WORKINGS
This collector is looking for specimens in the waste rock of an old mineshaft in Cornwall, southwest England.

KEEPING BASIC NOTES

When they start out, new collectors often ignore the need to write down information about their finds. But experience soon shows that investing in a notebook and devoting the minimal amount of time it takes to keep at least basic notes is essential. It is especially important to make notes about exactly where specimens were found. A considerable time may go by before you revisit the locality, and by then, in the absence of notes, you will probably be unable to find the spot again. Even if in many cases memory can be relied on, the surroundings of the location cannot. Areas overgrow; trees fall; tracks and trails move; and seasons change. With the passage of time, it is amazing how different once-familiar landmarks can look. It is far from unknown for a collector to be standing virtually on the exact spot he or she is seeking, and not recognize it. Also, should you ever decide to sell specimens at a later date, precise information on where they were found will make them more valuable. Take notes about the collecting spot itself, any hazards there may be in the area, landmarks and distances for finding the locality, map references, and the names, addresses, and telephone numbers of any people from whom you have had to get permission to collect. All of these are things easily forgotten over time. Take your camera along as well. Photos are useful for jogging memories. Also keep all your old notebooks and delete nothing. You may want to retrieve information or revisit collecting spots 20 years later.

MAP AND COMPASS
A compass and a map are essential tools for finding collecting localities and relocating them at a later date. Note down map references for good locations.

DRAWING LOCATIONS
If you have the necessary skill, make drawings in your notebook of locations and the specimens that have come from them. It may be some time before you return.

GEOLOGICAL POTENTIAL
Geological maps—here being used near Colimas volcano, Jalisco, Mexico—are essential to find the rock types that have collecting potential.

LABELING SPECIMENS

It is a good idea to develop the habit of labeling specimens as they are collected. Labeling should go hand in hand with the keeping of basic notes. The simplest method of labeling is to stick a piece of adhesive tape on the specimen and write a number or other identifier on it. Then write down the identifier in the notebook. Most collectors keep a separate catalog of specimens, listing the contents of the collection itself. If you purchase specimens, carefully keep any information accompanying them. If you happen to acquire specimens from someone else's collection, save any and all labels that come with them. These may well have scientific and historical importance. In the beginning, all of this may not seem so important, but as a collection grows, so does the likelihood of mixing up specimens or forgetting the localities where they were found. Precise information enhances both the financial value of specimens and their scientific interest.

FROZEN NOTES
Keeping notes of locations and of specimens found is a necessary activity even under difficult conditions, as here in freezing Arctic weather.

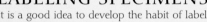

LABELED LINE
A collector hangs out bagged-up, recently found specimens on a line, each one clearly identified by a label for future reference.

TRANSPORTING SPECIMENS

The number of specimens destroyed or damaged in the course of the trip home can be disappointingly large. Wrapping of some sort is essential for most specimens, whether they are being carried in a backpack or a car. Some collectors use cloth or plastic specimen bags, but many specimens are resilient enough for newspaper to provide adequate protection. If you are using newspaper, though, also carry a few sheets of tissue paper in your backpack. Delicate specimens need to be wrapped first in tissue, and only then in newspaper. After wrapping them individually, place the specimens in your pack with crumpled paper between them to prevent them from damaging each other. If you find more specimens than you expect and run out of wrapping material, try leaves, grass, or pine needles as a natural alternative—they are better than nothing.

If specimens are wet when they are wrapped, unwrap them and let them dry as soon as you get home. Extremely delicate samples may deteriorate if left wet for long. Also, packing material that has gotten wet and then dried can be difficult to remove. Some materials are totally unsuitable for wrapping. Cotton balls should be kept away from specimens, since the fibers are almost impossible to remove. Cellulose wadding is not recommended, either. If it remains damp for any period, the cellulose can stick to specimens and may be difficult to get off.

IN THE BAG
A collector places a rock sample in a cloth specimen bag. More sensitive specimens can require elaborate wrapping to allow them to be transported safely.

CLEANING SPECIMENS

As a general rule, clean specimens as little as possible, starting with the gentlest methods. Try out your chosen cleaning method on your least valued specimen first to see what happens. Begin by using a brush to remove loose soil and debris, possibly aided by pointed tools. Hard rock specimens, such as gneiss or granite, are unlikely to be damaged by vigorous cleaning, but with delicate minerals, such as calcite crystals, it is essential to use a fine brush. Washing a specimen may seem an obvious recourse, but remember that some minerals dissolve or disintegrate in water. Never use hot water, since the heat may cause minerals to crack or shatter. Alcohol is often used to clean borates, nitrates, and sulfates, while certain acids are suitable for cleaning specific minerals. Weak hydrochloric acid, for example, is good for cleaning silicates. If you do use acids, seek specific information on their use from specialist books or from another collector, and always be aware of the risks involved. Aside from the serious hazard of acid burns, even the fumes released by some of them are toxic. Soaps should be avoided, but if you must use them, choose liquid dish-washing soaps rather than hand or bath soaps, which have additives that can penetrate specimens. The use of ultrasonic cleaners is not recommended, as they can shatter delicate specimens even at low intensities.

MUDDY ROCKS
Many specimens will be muddy or dirty when collected. Most dirt is more easily removed when it is dry.

WEAK HYDROCHLORIC ACID SOLUTION

CLEANING TOOLS

Dental pick

CLEANING UP
Removing rock with fine specialist tools is most often necessary when collecting fossils. The mineral collector, by contrast, is more likely to brush off dirt or to chisel out crystals.

PRESERVATION OF MINERALS

Once collected, some minerals are susceptible to physical and chemical effects that change or even destroy them. In some instances, they can also affect other minerals stored with them. Fortunately, these problems are well known, and preventative measures can be taken.

Deliquescence is the absorption of water from the atmosphere into the structure of the material, causing it to dissolve. The halide minerals, especially halite, carnallite, and sylvite, are prone to deliquescence. Specimens need dry storage. They may have to be placed inside a sealed polythene bag containing a small bag of silica gel to absorb any moisture.

Efflorescence is the loss of the water that is incorporated into the structure of certain minerals. The water evaporates, causing the specimen to discolor or disintegrate unless it is stored in humid conditions. Chalcanthite, borax, melanterite, and laumontite are examples of minerals prone to damage by efflorescence.

Effects of light: color changes. Certain minerals are noted for changing color under strong lighting. For example, colored topaz from Mexico and Utah eventually loses its color entirely if left exposed to light. Since many minerals may be affected by light to some degree, displayed specimens should be regularly examined with this in mind.

Effects of light: decomposition. Some minerals are strongly affected by light. Bright red realgar turns to golden-yellow, powdery orpiment. Other sulfides develop a surface tarnish that destroys their luster. These minerals are often bright, colorful, and attractive, so it is tempting to light them strongly. Place them in a display case that is generally dark, and only turn on lights when they are actually being admired.

Pyrite decay is probably the most difficult single problem. Pyrite and marcasite are both prone to deteriorate into a heap of powder. Sulfuric acid is released as a by-product, which can damage other specimens. The heat given off can even start a fire. Examine pyrite and marcasite specimens regularly for signs of deterioration. Dry storage is one of the best solutions.

BORAX

ROUGH SORTING
These fossil specimens have been roughly sorted, ready for further study and preparation for display.

White coating results from efflorescence

Powdered orpiment

ORPIMENT
When exposed to the light, specimens of the red-orange sulfide realgar turn into yellow, easily powdered orpiment.

STORAGE AND DISPLAY

Once specimens have been collected and cleaned, they need to be stored or, in the case of the most attractive pieces, displayed. For storage, many collectors like to put specimens in card trays inside shallow drawers. Every specimen should be accompanied by a label with as much information as is feasible. Some collectors also keep a catalog recording the complete history of the specimen, including its name, associates, exact locality, date of collection, and other relevant information. Each specimen is given a number corresponding to its listing in the catalog.

For display, use a sturdy, preferably glass-fronted cabinet or shelves that are well out of reach of children—they find colorful minerals irresistible. Many guests will wish to handle specimens. While their appreciation is welcome, they may not be aware that handling can damage delicate examples. It is always best if the collector hands specimens to guests, since he or she will know which ones are safe to handle. It is also a good idea to have carpet in the display area to minimize damage if specimens are dropped.

INFORMATIVE DISPLAY
Some collectors not only display their prize specimens, but provide museum-style information about them.

STORAGE BOXES
These specimens are stored in individual card trays. They can be numbered to link them to a catalog listing.

DISPLAY CABINET
A part of the impressive mineral collection of the Natural History Museum, London, is displayed under glass. The same principles govern the display of a private collection—specimens should be laid out simply and clearly in a secure cabinet.

ROCKS

IGNEOUS | SEDIMENTARY | METAMORPHIC

TYPES OF ROCK

A ROCK IS A NATURALLY occurring and coherent aggregate of one or more minerals—although there are a few rocks made from other substances, such as the decayed vegetation of which coal is composed. There are three major classes of rocks—igneous, sedimentary, and metamorphic—and each of these three classes is further subdivided into groups and types, principally based on differences in their mineral composition and texture.

IGNEOUS ROCKS

The magmas (molten rocks) from which igneous rocks are formed (see p.28) either solidify underground, creating intrusive rocks such as granite—known as "plutonic" rocks—or flow onto the surface of the land or ocean bed, forming extrusive rocks such as basalt. Igneous rocks vary in texture, depending on how rapidly the magma cooled. Rapid cooling creates tiny crystals and freezes the liquid to glass, while slower cooling forms coarse-grained rocks. The oceanic crust is primarily composed of igneous rocks, including volcanic basalts and the underlying gabbros.

Small crystals formed during rapid cooling after eruption

Large quartz crystal formed during slow cooling of magma before eruption

BASALT THIN SECTION

Fine-grained matrix

Crystals fill cavity (vug) left by gas bubble

BASALT WITH CRYSTAL-FILLED VUGS

ROCK FROM LAVA
Volcanic rocks, such as these on the Keanae Peninsula, Hawaii (right), are extrusive igneous rocks formed by cooled, solidified lava.

SIERRA GRANITE
The granite batholith of the Sierra Nevada range in California is an example of intrusive igneous rock.

PINK GRANITE SPECIMEN

Pink feldspar

Feldspar crystallized first in this slow-cooling magma

Mica fitted into spaces between feldspar crystals

Quartz formed last

GRANITE THIN SECTION

HAWAIIAN LAVA
Basaltic lava flows from Kilauea volcano, Hawaii. Volcanic material varies in composition—for example, basaltic lava contains a relatively low percentage of silica and flows easily.

SEDIMENTARY ROCKS

Sedimentary rocks are generally made of deposits laid down on Earth's surface by water, wind, or ice. These deposits are almost always laid down in layers or strata. The stratification survives compaction and cementation, and is a distinguishing characteristic of sedimentary rocks. They are also characterized by the presence of fossils, which are rarely found in any other type of rock. Some sedimentary rocks are formed by eroded fragments of other rocks in some way cemented together. They are classified by particle size, particle shape, and mineralogy. Some sedimentary rocks are of chemical origin, having been deposited in solid form from a solution, and some are of biochemical origin, composed predominantly of calcium carbonate. There are also organic deposits, such as coal, derived from the breakdown of the organic tissue of dead plants and animals.

Sand grain

Cement between grains

SANDSTONE THIN SECTION

Evidence of bedding

SANDSTONE SPECIMEN

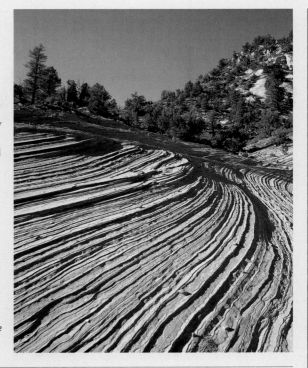

SEDIMENTARY LAYERS
This sandstone in Zion National Park, Utah, displays a typical layered structure. The highest layers are the youngest, while the deepest are the oldest.

METAMORPHIC ROCKS

Metamorphic rocks are formed when existing rocks are subjected to extreme temperatures or pressures (or both) that alter their mineralogical composition, texture, and internal structure. Quartzite, for example, is metamorphosed sandstone, and slate is metamorphosed mudstone or shale. Such changes typically occur deep within the crust, and may result from the deformation caused by plate tectonics. But metamorphic rocks can also form virtually at the surface of Earth under the impact of meteorites or near igneous intrusions, which create zones of high temperature around them. Metamorphic rocks include schists and gneisses, whose component minerals tend to segregate into separate bands, giving a layered appearance.

Biotite

GNEISS SPECIMEN

Quartz

Biotite

Feldspar

GNEISS THIN SECTION

ROCKY COAST
These coastal rocks near Cape Breton, Nova Scotia, Canada, are mainly schists and gneisses, but marked with pink granite that has been forced into cracks in the metamorphic rocks.

31

IGNEOUS ROCKS

VOLCANO VENT
A vent at Kilauea volcano, Hawaii, spews out lava that will cool to form igneous rock.

IGNEOUS ROCKS ARE DEFINED as extrusive or intrusive depending on whether or not the molten magma from which they were formed emerged at Earth's surface before crystallizing. Extrusive rocks form on the surface; intrusive rocks form below it. Intrusive rocks are categorized as plutonic if formed deep inside the crust and hypabyssal if formed at shallow depths. The silica content of the rocks is also a basis for classification. Felsic rocks have over 65 percent silica, intermediate rocks 55–65 percent, mafic rocks 45–55 percent, and ultramafic rocks less than 45 percent.

EXTRUSIVE ROCK

Extrusive igneous rocks are also known as volcanic rocks. The principal rock types in this category include basalt, obsidian, rhyolite, trachyte, and andesite. All of these generally form from lavas—the term for a magma that has flowed onto the surface, either on land or underwater. Other extrusive rocks, such as tuff and pumice, are formed in explosive volcanic eruptions. These "pyroclastic" rocks are porous because of the frothing expansion of volcanic gases when they formed. Basalt is the most common igneous rock, forming the floor of most oceans.

COOLING LAVA
Volcanic materials vary in chemical composition and temperature. Hot and low in silica, this basaltic lava flowing on Mount Etna, Sicily, has a rough texture as it cools and hardens.

BASALT COLUMNS
Basaltic magma, the type that forms most of the oceanic crust, has cooled to create these five-sided perpendicular columns near Aldeyarfoss, Iceland.

GRANITE PEAKS
Like all batholiths, the Sierra Nevada in California is made up of many smaller intrusions which, with erosion effects, give its peaks a varied appearance.

PLUTONIC INTRUSION

Plutonic intrusive rocks solidify deep within Earth's crust and are characterized by their large crystals. They occur as batholiths, plutons, and laccoliths. A batholith is a large igneous body with a surface exposure of at least 40 square miles (100 square km) and a thickness of about 6 to 9 miles (10 to 15 km). Batholiths form the cores of great mountain ranges, such as the Rockies and the Sierra Nevada in North America. They are generally composites of a number of smaller intrusions called plutons, each of which may consist of several different rock types.

Laccoliths are smaller-scale intrusions that create a characteristic dome-shaped structure, generally with a horizontal floor. Granite, diorite, peridotite, syenite, and gabbro are all plutonic igneous rocks.

DEVIL'S MARBLES

In Australia's Northern Territory, a dome of intrusive red granite has been exposed and weathered into rounded boulders.

Volcanic plug with radiating dikes

Ring dikes erode to form circular outcrop patterns

Dome-shaped laccolith

Sill forms between bedding planes

Dike forms vertically through rock strata

Massive batholith

"Swarm" of parallel dikes

TYPES OF IGNEOUS INTRUSION

Batholiths are the largest type of igneous intrusion. Like the smaller laccoliths, they are plutonic. Dikes, sills, and plugs are hypabyssal intrusions (see below).

HYPABYSSAL INTRUSION

Formed at shallow depths, hypabyssal intrusive rocks are characterized by fine crystallization. They are found in dikes, sills, volcanic plugs, and other relatively small formations. A dike is a sheetlike body that cuts vertically or at a steep angle to the surrounding rocks. Dikes range from less than half an inch to many yards in thickness, and can be hundreds of miles long. Sills are similar to dikes, except that they form parallel to the enclosing rocks, intruding between two strata. Plugs are formed from magma solidified inside volcanic vents.

DIABASE DIKE

A resistant dike of igneous diabase in Namibia projects above the surrounding rock.

VOLCANIC PLUG

The Devil's Tower in Wyoming is rock that cooled within a volcanic vent and has been exposed by erosion.

GRANITE TORS, HAYTOR
These weather-rounded granite boulders at a hilltop summit near an old granite quarry at Haytor, Devon, England, were once part of a mountain range.

GRANITE PEAKS
A sandstone arch frames this view of the massive granite batholith that is the Sierra Nevada mountain range.

GRANITE

THE MOST COMMON INTRUSIVE rock in Earth's continental crust, granite is familiar as a mottled pink, white, gray, and black ornamental stone. It is coarse- to medium–grained; rhyolite is its fine–grained equivalent (see p.46). Granite's three main minerals are feldspar, quartz, and mica, which occur as dark biotite and/or as silvery muscovite. Of the three principal minerals, feldspar predominates, and quartz usually accounts for more than 10 percent. The alkali feldspars are often pink (although they can also be white, buff, or gray), resulting in the pink granite often used as an ornamental stone for the facings of buildings and for floors.

Plagioclase feldspar also occurs in granite. The ratio between plagioclase and alkali feldspars has provided the basis for granite classifications, but if plagioclase greatly exceeds alkali feldspar, the rock is considered granodiorite. Granites from the eastern, central, and southwestern United States, southwest England, the Baltic Shield area, western and central France, and Spain tend be low in plagioclase, whereas in large regions of the western United States, granites in which plagioclase exceeds alkali feldspar are common. These granites in the western United States are part of a great series of batholiths—

EL CAPITAN, CALIFORNIA
A granite buttress, El Capitan rises 3,604 ft (1,098 m) from the valley floor of Yosemite National Park.

GRANITE'S DURABILITY

Granite has been a favorite stone for carving and for building structures for at least four millennia. Wherever it has been available, its strength and durability have made it a first choice for uses as exotic as temples and as mundane as millstones. Modern buildings are still faced with granite, both as an ornament and an acknowledgment of its agelessness as a building material.

Granite was highly favored by the ancient Egyptians for monumental carving, and for obelisks in particular. These needlelike spires were often dozens of yards tall and weighed many tons. The red granite was quarried near Aswan, site of the current hydroelectric dam across the Nile. Other colossal blocks were quarried for the interior chambers of the Great Pyramid, again weighing many tons. The King's Chamber alone is roofed by nine full-span granite blocks, each weighing more than 50 tons. Another single granite block in the pyramid weighs about 70 tons.

UNFINISHED OBELISK
A huge Egyptian obelisk lies unfinished in the granite quarry at Aswan.

MOUNT RUSHMORE
The 60-ft- (20-m-) high heads of four US presidents are carved from the granite of Mount Rushmore in South Dakota.

PINK GRANITE
In this specimen of pink granite, the three essential components of all granites can be seen: quartz, alkali feldspar, and mica. Pink granite is used as a building stone, and its extensive use in Aberdeen, Scotland, gives the city a notable pink hue. Aberdeen is the largest granite exporting area in Great Britain.

PROPERTIES

ROCK TYPE Felsic, plutonic, igneous

MAJOR MINERALS Potassium-feldspar, quartz, mica, sodium

MINOR MINERALS Sodium-plagioclase, hornblende

COLOR White, light gray, gray, pink, red

TEXTURE Medium to coarse

huge rock masses often hundreds or thousands of square miles in area—stretching from Alaska and British Columbia southward through Idaho and California into Mexico. Amphiboles and pyroxenes are minor essential minerals of granite, and many others occur as accessories.

FORMATION AND USES OF GRANITE

Granite crystallizes from silica-rich magmas dozens of miles deep in Earth's crust. Because it is formed at depth, the exposure of granite at the surface is evidence that the area has been uplifted and that the great thickness of rock overlying the granite has been eroded away. Many important mineral deposits are formed in the vicinity of crystallizing granite bodies from the hydrothermal solutions that are released by them. For example, pegmatite gemstones such as topaz, rock crystal, tourmaline, and aquamarine, as well as many metalliferous ores, including those of gold, silver, lead, and titanium, are deposited by these solutions.

The quarrying of granite was once a major industry due to demand for it as a building stone. Today, granite is used rather less, mainly as a veneer for commercial buildings and, to a lesser extent, to make tombstones and kitchen countertops. In some countries, granite is also quarried for use as curb stones.

GRANITE QUARRY
Towering blocks of granite stand in the Rock of Ages Quarry, a long-producing granite quarry in Barre, Vermont.

Gray quartz crystals

TRIUMPHAL ARCH
This triumphal arch in North Korea was recently constructed from granite.

Black biotite mica

THIN SECTION
An intergrowth of feldspar and quartz can be seen in this thin section of granite. Mica fits into the spaces between other crystals.

Mica

Feldspar

Quartz

AQUEDUCT
The aqueduct at Segovia, Spain, was built of Guadaramma granite during the reign of the Roman emperor Trajan (AD 98–117). It is 2,388 ft (728 m) long and is still in use.

Coarse crystallization

Pink feldspar

GRANITE VARIETIES
Of the numerous varieties of granite, some have names relating to their texture or the presence of minerals in addition to the three basic ones. Others have informal names based on color.

White orthoclase feldspar

Gray quartz

Feldspar phenocryst

Spherical phenocryst

Pink orthoclase feldspar

Pale orthoclase feldspar

Dark hornblende

WHITE GRANITE

PORPHYRITIC GRANITE

ORBICULAR GRANITE

GRAPHIC GRANITE

HORNBLENDE GRANITE

ANORTHOSITE

AN INTRUSIVE IGNEOUS ROCK, anorthosite is composed of at least 90 percent calcium-rich plagioclase feldspar—principally labradorite and bytownite. Olivine, pyroxene, garnet, and iron oxides make up the remaining 10 percent. Anorthosite is not a common rock on Earth, but where it does occur, it is found as immense masses, or as layers between mafic and ultramafic rocks such as gabbro and peridotite. There are large anorthosite-bearing rock bodies in New York State and Montana; eastern Canada; and South Africa. Many anorthosites have an interesting "cumulate" texture, where well-formed crystals appear to have settled out of the liquid magma, in a way similar to a sediment. Anorthosite is extremely common on the surface of the Moon, especially the far side. The ancient, rough, light-colored highlands of the Moon are made of anorthosite and similar rocks.

Pyroxene

Plagioclase crystals

THIN SECTION
A small amount of pyroxene is trapped between this accumulation of plagioclase crystals.

PROPERTIES

ROCK TYPE	Ultramafic, plutonic, igneous
MAJOR MINERALS	Calcium plagioclase
MINOR MINERALS	Olivine, pyroxene, garnet
COLOR	Light gray to white
TEXTURE	Medium to coarse

Light plagioclase feldspar crystals

Coarse grain size

COARSE ANORTHOSITE
This example of anorthosite from the Bushveld Complex of South Africa has a coarse texture.

ANORTHOSITE FROM THE MOON
Fine-grained anorthosite is thought to be the first rock that crystallized from the "magma ocean" that covered the Moon's surface early in its history.

SYENITE

SYENITES MAY BE VISUALLY SIMILAR to granite, and are often confused with it, but they can be distinguished from it by the absence or scarcity of quartz. A syenite is any one of a class of rocks essentially composed of an alkali feldspar or sodic plagioclase (or both), a ferromagnesian mineral—usually biotite, hornblende, or pyroxene—and little or no quartz. The alkali feldspars can include orthoclase, albite, or less commonly, microcline. Other minerals that can occur in small amounts in syenite include sphene, apatite, zircon, magnetite, and pyrite. When syenites contain quartz, they are quartz syenites. In the absence of quartz, feltspathoid minerals such as leucite, cancrinite, sodalite, or particularly nepheline, may be present.

PINK SYENITE
The pink coloring of syenite is due to the presence of alkali feldspar, which predominates in syenite.

Amphibole

PROPERTIES

ROCK TYPE	Intermediate, plutonic, igneous
MAJOR MINERALS	Potassium feldspar
MINOR MINERALS	Sodium plagioclase, biotite, amphibole, pyroxene, feldspathoids
COLOR	Gray, pink, or red
GRAIN SIZE	Medium to coarse

Orthoclase

Hornblende

THIN SECTION
Large, simple-twinned orthoclase crystals are present in this section, with hornblende and a little quartz.

Quartz

Feldspar

Coarse grain size

Gray feldspar crystals

LARVIKITE
This iridescent variety of syenite contains feldspar, pyroxene, mica, and amphibole.

DOLERITE

DOLERITE DIKE
A darker dike of dolerite cuts through a body of lighter granite.

DOLERITE IS EQUIVALENT to basalt and gabbro in composition, although it is intermediate between them in grain size. A fine- to medium-grained rock, dolerite is from one-third to two-thirds calcium-rich plagioclase feldspar, the remainder being principally pyroxene. It has a silica content of less than 55 percent, and its quartz content is usually less than 10 percent. Magnetite and olivine may be present: if olivine is present, the rock is called olivine-dolerite. Extremely hard and tough, it occurs in dikes and sills intruded into fissures in other rocks.

Plagioclase feldspars

Medium texture

DARK GRAY DOLERITE
Dolerite's medium texture and dark color can be seen in this specimen. It is one of the dark-colored rocks sold commercially as "black granite."

ANCIENT BUILDING STONE

The dolerite "bluestones" of the inner circle of Stonehenge were transported 240 miles (385 km) from Wales to Wiltshire, England. They were brought by sea, by river, and over land. Exactly what significance was attached by the builders to this particular stone is unknown, but it must have been considerable to justify the enormous effort required to get the bluestones to the site. Stonehenge was constructed in 3000–2000 BC.

STONEHENGE
The bluestone used for making the stone circle of Stonehenge originated at Carn Meini Quarry in Wales.

PROPERTIES

ROCK TYPE Mafic, plutonic, igneous
MAJOR MINERALS Calcium plagioclase , pyroxene
MINOR MINERALS Quartz, magnetite, olivine
COLOR Dark gray to black, often mottled white
TEXTURE Fine to medium

DOLERITE OUTCROPPING
The Tees River in northeast England forms waterfalls such as this one on the hard dolerite outcropping of Whin Sill.

GABBRO

GABBRO HILLS
The Black Cuillin Hills of the Isle of Skye are formed entirely from gabbro.

MEDIUM- OR COARSE-GRAINED rocks, gabbros consist principally of calcium-rich plagioclase feldspar and pyroxene, usually augite. They are low in silica—usually less than 55 percent—and quartz is rarely present. Gabbro is essentially the intrusive equivalent of basalt, but where basalt is often relatively homogeneous in mineralogy and composition, gabbros are highly variable. They are often found with layering of light and dark minerals (layered gabbro), with a significant amount of olivine (olivine gabbro), and with a high percentage of coarse crystals of plagioclase (leucogabbro). Gabbros are widespread, but not common, on Earth's surface. Commercially, they are sold as "black granite," although they owe their major economic significance to the ores contained within them. Some gabbros are mined for their nickel, chromium, and platinum content. Those containing magnetite and ilmenite are mined for their iron or titanium.

CHRISTIAN LEOPOLD VON BUCH (1774–1852)
Geologist von Buch, famed for creating the first geological map of Germany, named gabbro after a town in Italy.

THIN SECTION
This is an olivine gabbro (labradorite feldspar, augite, and olivine) from the Duluth Complex.

Olivine

Augite

PROPERTIES

ROCK TYPE Mafic, plutonic, igneous
MAJOR MINERALS Calcium plagioclase feldspar, pyroxene
MINOR MINERALS Olivine, magnetite
COLOR Dark gray to black
TEXTURE Medium to coarse

Light plagioclase feldspar

Dark pyroxene

LAYERED GABBRO
Alternating bands of light plagioclase feldspar and dark ferromagnesian minerals form this specimen.

COARSE GABBRO
This coarsely crystallized specimen of gabbro contains light-colored crystals of plagioclase and dark crystals of pyroxene.

39

PERIDOTITE

ONE OF THE MOST ECONOMICALLY important rocks, peridotite is the ultimate source of all chromium ore, and its variety kimberlite (see opposite) is the source of all naturally occurring diamonds. Fresh peridotite contains olivine, pyroxene, and chromite. Peridotite that has been altered by weathering becomes serpentinite, containing chrysotile, other serpentines, and talc. Formerly, peridotite was a major source of magnesite (see p.179), an important economic mineral. It is also the major source of chrysotile asbestos (see p.258), now of declining economic importance.

An intrusive igneous rock, peridotite is coarse-grained, dark-colored, and dense. It contains at least 40 percent olivine. It is related to the rock pyroxenite in that they form in similar environments and both are olivine-pyroxene rocks. Pyroxenite contains at least 60 percent pyroxene. Another related rock is dunite, a yellowish-green, intrusive igneous rock composed almost entirely of olivine. Like peridotite, dunite is an important source of the chromium ore chromite.

Peridotite is found interlayered with iron- and magnesia-rich rocks in the lower parts of layered, igneous rock bodies, where its denser crystals formed first through selective crystallization and then settled to the bottom

of still-fluid or semisolid crystallizing mushes. Within peridotite bodies, layers of chromite (the principal ore of chromium), an early crystallite and the first to settle, can reach several yards thick. Peridotite is also found in mountain belts as irregular, olivine-rich masses, sometimes with related gabbro, and in dikes (vertical or steeply inclined sheetlike bodies, which often cut existing rock structure). Garnet is often present as an accessory mineral, and weathered peridotites are commonly a source of nickel. Peridotite's other important occurrence is in volcanic pipes as kimberlite.

PERIDOTITE HILLS
The Semail ophiolite crops out of the mountain belt near Muscat, Oman. It is composed of layered peridotite and gabbro.

PROPERTIES

ROCK TYPE Ultramafic, plutonic, igneous
MAJOR MINERALS Olivine, pyroxene
MINOR MINERALS Garnet, chromite
COLOR Dark green to black
TEXTURE Coarse

EXPOSED PERIDOTITE
Gros Morne National Park in Newfoundland, Canada contains peridotite rocks from Earth's mantle.

GREEN PERIDOTITE
This specimen from Lanzarote in the Canary Islands takes its green coloring from the mineral olivine present within it.

THIN SECTION
This is harzburgite from New Zealand, with olivine and orthopyroxene visible.

Orthopyroxene

Olivine

EARTH'S MANTLE

Peridotite is a major structural component of Earth. It is the major component of the asthenosphere, the upper portion of the mantle upon which the plates rest. At depths of 40–125 miles (70–200 km), the mantle rocks are thought to exist at temperatures slightly above their melting point, and a small percentage may be molten. This gives the mantle the plasticity for continental movement.

LAVA FLOW
The deepest magmas originate in the upper layer of the mantle.

The basaltic magmas of the oceanic crust are generated in the astheno-sphere, their compositions determined to an extent by the mineral makeup of the peridotite.

MANTLE XENOLITH
Fragments of mantle peridotite are brought to the surface by deep-seated magmas.

Greenish coloring from olivine

DUNITE

Green olivine

Dark pyroxene

Coarse texture

PYROXENITE

RELATED ROCKS
Both pyroxene and dunite are related to peridotite. They are deep-seated in origin, and contain a large proportion of olivine.

KIMBERLITE PIPE
The mined-out diamond-bearing pipe at Kimberley, South Africa, has now filled with water. Kimberlite pipes do not have a great lateral extent, but they are very deep.

PROPERTIES

ROCK TYPE Ultramafic, volcanic, igneous

MAJOR MINERALS Olivine, pyroxene, mica

MINOR MINERALS Garnet, ilmenite, diamond

COLOR Dark gray

TEXTURE Fine to coarse/porphyritic

KIMBERLITE

THE MAJOR SOURCE OF DIAMONDS, kimberlite is a form of peridotite. It is mica-rich, often with well-formed crystals of brown phlogopite mica. Other abundant minerals include chromium- and pyrope-rich garnet and chrome-bearing diopside; lesser amounts of ilmenite, serpentine, pyroxene, calcite, rutile, perovskite, magnetite, and diamond can also be present.

Kimberlite occurs in pipes—intrusive igneous bodies roughly circular in cross section with vertical sides, and usually less than 3/4 mile (1 km) in diameter—and other igneous bodies that are also steep-sided and intrusive. These tend to be found in the uplifted centers of continental platforms, and appear to be roughly the same age, having formed during the Late Cretaceous Period (100 to 65 million years ago). It appears that the kimberlite was injected into zones of weakness in the crust as a relatively cool "mush" of crystals rather than as a liquid magma that crystallized within the pipes themselves, as there is usually little contact metamorphism of surrounding rocks. Xenoliths (fragments) of mantle rock are often brought to the surface in kimberlites, making them a valuable source of information about the mantle.

MINING KIMBERLITE

Diamonds were first discovered at De Kalk Farm on the banks of the Orange River, South Africa, in 1867, but the host rock was not discovered until two years later. At first, diamonds were extracted by panning from weathered kimberlite in open pits, but as the pits became deeper and the rock harder, it was necessary to mine underground. After the rocks have been blasted, they are brought to the surface and the diamonds are separated out. Wet, crushed kimberlite is passed across grease-covered tables: water does not stick to diamond, so the dry stones stick to the grease, while the kimberlite washes away (see p.107). The diamond crystals are scraped off. Now many of the mines are worked out and South Africa is no longer one of the top diamond-producing nations.

DRILLING
Drill-holes packed with explosives are blasted to break up the rocks.

ROUGH DIAMOND
Most gem-quality diamonds are found as octahedral crystals.

Diamonds need pressures of over 50,000 atmospheres to form. This corresponds to a depth below Earth's surface of at least 90 miles (150 km), well into the upper peridotite mantle. An examination of minute mineral grains trapped inside growing diamonds reveals that most diamonds formed one to three billion years ago. Once diamonds formed in the upper mantle, they remained there for millions of years before being blasted to the surface at supersonic speeds in devastatingly volatile eruptions. Fortunately, no kimberlite volcanoes are known to have erupted for over 60 million years.

Kimberlite is also called blue ground, a reference to its color. Weathered kimberlite is yellowish in color, and is called yellow ground. It is in areas of yellow ground that diamonds were first discovered in South Africa, and later in Arkansas, Colorado, and Wyoming.

Crystal of ferro-magnesian minerals

Dark matrix

Coarse texture

BRECCIATED KIMBERLITE
This dark, coarse-grained, heavy, and brecciated (fragmented) specimen is typical of kimberlite. The mineral is named after Kimberley in South Africa, the old center of the South African diamond industry.

Phlogopite

THIN SECTION
Larger, corroded crystals of phlogopite and pyroxene sit in a heavily altered matrix of olivine, calcite, and mica in this section of kimberlite from De Beers Mine, Kimberley.

Diamond

Altered pyroxene

WEATHERED KIMBERLITE
This heavily weathered specimen of kimberlite from Kimberley, South Africa, holds an octahedral diamond crystal.

BASALT

THIS VOLCANIC ROCK is the most common igneous rock at Earth's surface. However, most basalt is not seen because it forms the ocean floors. Volcanoes in the ocean basins eject basalt, and volcanic islands are made from it. On land, basalts have built enormous plateaus, such as in the Deccan of India, the Columbia River region of the northwestern US, and the Paraná Basin of South America. The large, dark maria on the Moon are basalt, and it is quite likely that the volcanoes on Mars and Venus are, too.

Dark in color and comparatively rich in iron and magnesium, basalts are mainly composed of plagioclase, pyroxene, and olivine. Most are very fine-grained and compact, even glassy, but it is also common for them to be porphyritic—having distinct crystals set in a fine-grained base or groundmass. The larger crystals are called phenocrysts, and commonly consist of olivine, augite, or plagioclase feldspar. Feldspathoids (see pp.242–48), such as nepheline and leucite, occur in many mafic basalts. Nepheline-basalts are fairly common in Germany, Libya, Turkey, and New Mexico. Leucite-basalts are principally found in Italy, Germany, eastern Africa, and Australia, and in Montana, Wyoming, and Arizona.

Basaltic lavas are frequently charged with water, the resulting froth making their rocks spongy. Basalts are very interesting to geologists because they form by partial melting of Earth's mantle. Unmelted fragments of the mantle (known as xenoliths) can be carried upward in basalts, giving geologists their only direct observation of the composition of the mantle.

COLUMNAR BASALT
This outcropping of basalt exposed by coastal weathering shows the columnar jointing that can occur as basalt cools and shrinks at different rates.

Fine matrix

BASALT

Fine matrix

Pyroxene phenocryst

PORPHYRITIC BASALT

Empty cavities

VESICULAR BASALT

VARIETIES OF BASALT
Several varieties of basalt are found, taking their names from their texture and crystallization.

BASALT PILLOWS
Pillow-basalt is formed when basaltic magma flows into water during underwater eruptions.

STUDYING LAVA FLOW
Volcanologists often take considerable personal risks in order to sample unadulterated lava.

AMYGDALOIDAL BASALT
Amygdules are the small, round cavities left by gas bubbles and filled with minerals. The steam cavities left in this specimen of basalt are filled with zeolite crystals.

Fine-grained matrix

Amygdule filled with zeolite

Mafic minerals

THE ROSETTA STONE

Made of black basalt, the Rosetta Stone was uncovered by Napoleon's troops in 1799 at Rosetta, near Alexandria, Egypt. Its identical inscriptions in three scripts—Egyptian hieroglyphs, demotic script (cursive hieroglyphs), and Greek—led to the decipherment of ancient Egyptian hieroglyphics by Jean-François Champollion of France. Carved in the reign of Ptolemy V Epiphanes (205–180 BC), it currently resides in the British Museum, London. It was acquired as war booty when Napoleon was defeated in Egypt by the British in 1801.

Egyptian hieroglyphs

Demotic script

Pigeonite crystal

Fine-grained base

Augite crystal

THIN SECTION
This section is of a lunar mare basalt collected from the edge of the Imbrium basin.

PROPERTIES

ROCK TYPE Mafic, volcanic, igneous

MAJOR MINERALS Sodium plagioclase, pyroxene, olivine

MINOR MINERALS Leucite, nepheline

COLOR Dark gray to black

TEXTURE Fine-grained to porphyritic

OBSIDIAN

A NATURAL VOLCANIC GLASS, obsidian forms when lava solidifies so quickly that mineral crystals do not have time to grow. The name obsidian simply refers to the glassy texture, and technically obsidian can have any chemical composition. However, most obsidian is similar in composition to rhyolite, and it is commonly found on the outer edges of rhyolite domes and flows. Like rhyolite, obsidian can show flow-banding. It is also found along the rapidly cooled edges of dikes and sills. Obsidian is typically jet-black, although the presence of hematite (iron oxide) produces red and brown varieties, and the inclusion of tiny gas bubbles can create a golden sheen.

FABERGÉ HORSE
This obsidian horse has gold hooves, ruby eyes, and an enameled bridle decorated with diamonds.

Tiny crystals of feldspar and phenocrysts (visible crystals) of quartz can also be present. Most obsidian is relatively young because volcanic glass devitrifies—minerals crystallize from the glass—over time. Spherical clusters of radially arranged, needlelike crystals called spherulites in snowflake obsidian can form through devitrification after the rock has cooled. Pitchstone obsidian has a resinous luster that forms as the rock absorbs water over time. Mount Hekla in Iceland, the Eolie Islands off the coast of Italy, and Obsidian Cliff in Yellowstone National Park, Wyoming, are all well-known occurrences of obsidian.

NEWBERRY CRATER
Obsidian is abundant in this crater in Oregon, resulting from numerous lava flows. Basalt, pumice, and rhyolite are also widespread in this huge area.

ANCIENT USES

Because obsidian is slightly harder than window glass and has a conchoidal fracture, allowing it to be chipped with razor-sharp edges, it was used by Americans Indians and many other ancient peoples to create weapons, tools, and ornaments. The Aztecs and Greeks used it for mirrors because it was so reflective. It was widely traded along ancient routes, and by studying the properties of obsidian artifacts, archaeologists can determine both the source of the material and the routes along which it was traded. It is still cut as a semiprecious stone today.

OBSIDIAN KNIFE BLADE
This image of a face from Mexico City, dating to 1325–1521, includes white flint and green obsidian.

ANCIENT ARTIFACTS
This obsidian Olmec mask and Aztec knife demonstrate two ancient methods of working obsidian to create a smooth and conversely, a razor-sharp finish.

PROPERTIES

ROCK TYPE Felsic, volcanic, igneous
MAJOR MINERALS Glass
MINOR MINERALS Hematite, feldspar
COLOR Black, brown, red
TEXTURE Amorphous

BLACK OBSIDIAN
This specimen of black obsidian clearly shows the excellent conchoidal fracture that made it perfect for chipping into tools. Its bright, vitreous luster shows why it was favored for mirrors.

Conchoidal fracture

Glass rather than mineral crystals

Flow-banding

Hematite crystals

OBSIDIAN WITH RED COLORING

White spherulites

SNOWFLAKE OBSIDIAN

VARIETIES OF OBSIDIAN
The presence of hematite (iron oxide) produces the red coloring in the thin section on the far left. The "snowflakes" in snowflake obsidian (left) are spherulites, spherical aggregates of needlelike crystals.

"APACHE TEAR"
Tumble-polished nodules of obsidian are sold as "apache tears."

43

JOINTED COLUMNS
The columnar jointing in the Causeway's basalt extends through the entire thickness of some of its component lava flows. The result of such effective jointing is columns extending up to a height of 80 ft (25 m).

THE GIANT'S CAUSEWAY

A PROMONTORY OF BASALT COLUMNS THAT JUT OUT OF A CLIFF FACE AS IF THEY WERE STEPS CREEPING INTO THE SEA, THE GIANT'S CAUSEWAY HAS BEEN INTENSIVELY STUDIED BY GEOLOGISTS SINCE THE 17TH CENTURY.

The Giant's Causeway extends along 4 miles (6 km) of the coast of County Antrim, Northern Ireland, about 25 miles (40 km) northeast of Londonderry. Formed 50 to 60 million years ago, it consists of about 40,000 stone pillars, each typically with five to seven irregular sides that vary from 15 to 20 in (40 to 50 cm) in diameter and measure up to 80 ft (25 m) in height.

ANCIENT BASALT FLOWS

Its structure is the result of successive surges of lava that flowed toward the coast and cooled when they met the sea. The basaltic lava that welled up through fractures in the local chalk beds can still be seen as dark bands jutting out into the sea where erosion has cut away the chalk. The layers of basalt formed columns that today have the appearance of a huge bundle of tightly standing hexagonal fenceposts. Each column exhibits "columnar jointing" which develops as the cooling lava contracts at different rates. Similar columnar jointing can be seen at the Devil's Tower, Wyoming (see p.48).

The tops of the columns form stepping stones that disappear under the sea. Its appearance led to the local legend that the Causeway was the creation of the giant Finn MacCoul, the ancient Ulster warrior. According to legend, he fell in love with a female giant on Staffa, an island in the Hebrides, and built this highway so that she could walk to meet him in Ulster.

In 1692 the Bishop of Derry made one of the first recorded visits to the Causeway, and a debate raged for nearly a century afterward about whether the Causeway was the work of giants, a natural occurrence, or human-made. It was not until 1774 that French volcanologist Nicolas Desmarest (1725–1815) proved that columnar basalts were formed by the cooling of molten lava.

CHIMNEY STACKS
In some areas of the Causeway, the basalt has eroded and weakened. Some of the columns have toppled, leaving a few columns still standing like chimney stacks.

GIANT'S CAUSEWAY HEAD
The distinctive jointed columns of the Causeway are very similar in appearance to those of Fingal's Cave on the Scottish island of Staffa. Most are hexagonal, although some have four, five, seven, or eight sides.

RHYOLITE

RHYOLITE MOUNTAIN
This mountainous outcrop in Snowdon, North Wales, is rhyolite.

A RELATIVELY RARE volcanic rock, almost exclusively confined to the interiors and margins of continents, rhyolite is the volcanic equivalent of granite (see p.34). Most rhyolites are porphyritic, with larger crystals (phenocrysts) in a fine-grained matrix of crystals too small to be seen with the naked eye, indicating that crystallization began before the lava flowed out onto the surface. The phenocrysts are most commonly quartz and sanidine, but can also include mafic minerals such as biotite, amphibole, and pyroxene. In banded rhyolites, there are few or no phenocrysts. Rhyolite commonly occurs with obsidian and pumice, and with intermediate volcanic rocks such as andesite.

Dark, larger crystals
Pale, fine-grained matrix of crystals

PORPHYRITIC RHYOLITE

PROPERTIES

ROCK TYPE Felsic, volcanic, igneous
MAJOR MINERALS Quartz, potassium feldspar
MINOR MINERALS Glass, biotite, amphibole, plagioclase
COLOR Very light to medium gray, light pink
TEXTURE Fine or porphyritic

Quartz
Flow-banding

THIN SECTION
Feldspar and quartz phenocrysts can be seen here.

Feldspar
Fine texture

RHYOLITE DOMES

Because rhyolitic lava is so silica-rich, it is also very sticky, or viscous, and rarely reaches Earth's surface. When it does, because it is so thick, the lava piles up over its vent without flowing away, and tends to form steep-sided domes rather than flows. Lava domes can be several hundred yards high, with a diameter of more than 3,000 ft (900 m). A lava dome is currently forming in the explosion crater at Mount St. Helens, Washington.

VOLCANIC RHYOLITE PLUG
Plugs such as this one at Church Rock, Arizona, are the solidified vents of ancient volcanoes, the surrounding cinder-cones of which have eroded away.

Flow-banding

BANDED RHYOLITE
In banded rhyolite, flow-banding, with swirling layers of colors and textures, is prominent.

ANDESITE

ANDES
Andesite is named for the Andes Mountains of South America, a subduction zone, and therefore a characteristic locality.

THE VOLCANIC EQUIVALENT of diorite (see p.37), andesite is fine-grained or porphyritic, and primarily consists of the plagioclase feldspars andesine and oligoclase, plus one or more of the dark, ferromagnesian minerals, such as pyroxene or biotite. Unlike rhyolites, andesites do not contain quartz. Amygdaloidal andesite occurs when the voids left by gas bubbles in the solidifying magma are later filled in, often with zeolite minerals. Porphyritic andesite occurs when larger phenocrysts of feldspar and pyroxene form in a fine-grained matrix. Andesite erupts from explosive volcanoes and is commonly found interbedded with volcanic ash and tuff. The steep-sided volcanoes of the Pacific Rim, the Caribbean, and the Mediterranean are composed in large part of andesites.

PROPERTIES

ROCK TYPE Intermediate, volcanic, igneous
MAJOR MINERALS Plagioclase feldspars
MINOR MINERALS Pyroxene, amphibole, biotite
COLOR Light to dark gray, reddish-pink
TEXTURE Fine, porphyritic

VOLCANOES

Andesitic volcanoes form on continental or ocean crusts above subduction zones where one oceanic plate is sinking beneath another. Ancient andesites can therefore be used to map ancient subduction zones. The Soufrière Hills in Montserrat, West Indies, Krakatau in Indonesia, Popocatépetl in Mexico, and Mt. Shasta, Mt. Hood, and Mt. Adams in the US have all expelled large quantities of andesitic rock.

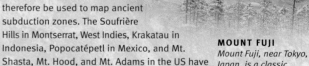

MOUNT FUJI
Mount Fuji, near Tokyo, Japan, is a classic andesitic volcano.

PORPHYRITIC ANDESITE
In this specimen, light phenocrysts are in a dark matrix.

Lighter-colored plagioclase crystals
Dark, fine-grained matrix

THIN SECTION
This andesite from Hakone volcano in Japan, shows large plagioclase and pyroxene crystals in a fine matrix.

Pyroxene
Plagioclase

FINE-GRAINED
This fine-grained andesite specimen contains small phenocrysts of light plagioclase feldspar.

PHONOLITE

CRIPPLE CREEK
Phonolite is found at Cripple Creek, In the Pike's Peak area of Colorado.

PHONOLITE IS A TYPE OF TRACHYTE (see below) that contains nepheline or leucite rather than quartz. They are commonly fine-grained and compact, and split into thin, tough plates, which make a ringing sound when struck, hence the rock's name. The principal dark-colored mineral is pyroxene, usually in the form of aegirine or augite. Phonolites are common in Europe, especially on the Eifel plateau and the Laacher See, Germany; in the Czech Republic; and in the Mediterranean area, particularly in Italy. In the US, phonolites are found in Colorado, and the Black Hills, South Dakota. The spectacular Devil's Tower, Wyoming, is probably phonolite's most famous occurrence (see p.48).

COMPACT PHONOLITE
This phonolite specimen shows characteristic fine grains.

Dark matrix crystals

PROPERTIES

ROCK TYPE Intermediate, volcanic, igneous
MAJOR MINERALS Sanidine, oligoclase
MINOR MINERALS Feldspathoids, hornblende, pyroxene, biotite
COLOR Medium gray
TEXTURE Fine to medium, porphyritic

TRACHYTE

TENERIFE
Trachytes are prominent and widespread on Tenerife, in the Canary Islands.

THE VOLCANIC EQUIVALENT of syenite, trachyte is commonly porphyritic. Some porphyritic trachytes contain phenocrysts of the mineral sanidine that are up to 2 in (5 cm) across. Dark, mafic minerals such as biotite, amphibole, and pyroxene can be present in small quantities. Trachyte is similar to rhyolite in color and occurrence, but contains very little or no quartz. Quartz-free trachytes, such as phonolite (see above), can contain feldspathoids such as leucite, nepheline, and sodalite. Unlike andesite, trachyte contains no phenocrysts of plagioclase feldspar. Trachyte has a characteristically rough texture, and its name comes from the Greek for "rough."

Trachyte occurs with other alkali-rich felsic, intermediate, and mafic volcanics on both continents and ocean islands. Localities include Ascension Island; Cripple Creek, Colorado, US; the Auvergne in France; and the Rhine district of central Europe.

USE IN PAVING

Tough and resistant volcanic rocks such as trachyte have been used for millennia as paving stones. In addition to trachyte, granite, basalt, and gabbro can still be found forming the surfaces of streets and roads. Individual stones may have been used and reused for centuries. In some places the cobbled surfaces of Roman roads still remain, grooved by the passage of countless wheels of all varieties. Although labor-intensive to mine and shape, the resulting surface has unsurpassed wear-resistance.

COBBLED STREET
The trachyte cobbles in this street have been polished smooth by years of wear.

Larger crystals visible within matrix

Dark matrix crystals

Sanidine

Dark matrix crystals

THIN SECTION
The typical texture of aligned sanidine crystals is seen here. The larger crystals show simple twinning.

GRAY TRACHYTE
A fine- to medium-grained and fairly uniform structure can be seen in this trachyte specimen.

PROPERTIES

ROCK TYPE Intermediate, volcanic, igneous
MAJOR MINERALS Sanidine, oligoclase
MINOR MINERALS Feldspathoids, quartz, hornblende, pyroxene, biotite
COLOR Off-white, gray, pale yellow, pink
TEXTURE Fine to medium, porphyritic

DEVIL'S TOWER

THE NECK OF AN ANCIENT VOLCANO, THIS STRIKING STRUCTURE STANDS HIGH ABOVE THE GREAT PLAINS OF WYOMING. IT IS KNOWN TO MANY AS THE LANDING STRIP USED BY THE SPACESHIP IN STEVEN SPIELBERG'S CLOSE ENCOUNTERS OF THE THIRD KIND.

VERTICAL STRIATIONS
As the phonolite remaining in the volcanic neck cooled and solidified, it developed vertical jointing. It is this that gives the Tower its vertically striated appearance today.

Located in northeastern Wyoming, 9 miles (14.5 km) south of the town of Hulett, the Devil's Tower is the neck, or "throat," of an ancient volcano, the pipelike conduit through which magma flowed to the surface. After the volcano erupted, much of the magma remained in the underground plug. The magma cooled and solidified, eventually forming into uniform columns. Over millions of years, the cone of the volcano and the sedimentary rock layers around it were removed by weathering and the Belle Fourche River, which meanders around the base of the Tower, leaving the neck exposed.

The Tower is composed of phonolite, a type of silica–deficient rhyolite magma (see p.47).

Phonolites are rich in nepheline and potash feldspar, and are typically fine-grained and compact. They split into thin, tough plates

AERIAL VIEW
The top of the Tower stands 1,267 ft (386 m) above the level of the Belle Fourche River and 5,115 ft (1,560 m) above sea level.

that make a ringing sound when struck, giving the rock its name. The principal dark-colored mineral in the Devil's Tower phonolite is the pyroxene aegirine.

The name "Devil's Tower" was given to the structure in 1875 by Colonel Richard Dodge. He was escorting a scientific team through the area, looking for gold, even though this was a violation of Indian treaty rights. Dodge translated one of the names given by the Indians to the area, meaning "Bad God's Tower," as "Devil's Tower." The most common American Indian name used for the Tower today is Mateo Tepee or "Bear Lodge." This name is derived from a Kiowa legend in which seven girls playing in the woods were chased by bears and found refuge on the Tower. The bears tried to climb up after them, but failed, leaving their claw marks (the vertical striations of the jointing) down the sides. It is still a sacred site of worship for many American Indians today.

NATIONAL MONUMENT
The Devil's Tower was proclaimed a National Monument by President Theodore Roosevelt on September 24, 1906. It has become a favorite among serious rock climbers, who enjoy climbing the long crack-lines in the rock.

CAVE FORMATIONS
The evaporation of lime-bearing waters dripping into caves can produce a dramatic assortment of cave formations. These include stalactites, which grow downward from the roof of a cave, and stalagmites, which grow upward from the floor.

LAVA IN A TUBE
Molten lava continues to flow through this lava tube on Kilauea Volcano, Hawaii. The lava is visible through a hole in the roof of the tube at a weak point in the crust.

INSIDE A STALACTITE
Stalactites build up a layer at a time, and resemble tree rings in cross section. Differences in mineral content on deposition can cause color banding.

Calcite stained with iron oxide

Unstained calcite layer

CAVES AND CAVERNS

CARVED OUT OF ROCK BY NATURAL FORCES, CAVES ARE AMONG THE MOST SPECTACULAR OF EARTH'S GEOLOGICAL FEATURES.

Naturally formed subterranean cavities, caves form as a result of many geological processes. The largest and most common caves are called solution caves. These are formed by chemical reaction between circulating ground water and underlying soluble or otherwise easily eroded rock. Other types of caves include lava tubes and marine grottos. A cave consists of either a single chamber or an extensive system of many chambers connected by smaller passageways.

SOLUTION CAVES

Solution caves are generally formed by dissolution of limestone (see p.54), and, in some cases, dolomite (see p.54). Limestone contains calcium carbonate (calcite), which is slightly soluble in the weak acid known as carbonic acid (H_2CO_3), which is formed as carbon dioxide dissolves in ground water. This acidic water percolates down through the overlying soils. Some collects in sinkholes that are already dissolved out of the underlying limestone or dolomite, and some trickles down through cracks in the rock. As dissolution continues, conduits expand to become interconnected drains for the movement of underground water.

Solution caves are simply parts of this underground drainage system. Some are completely water-filled, while others are dry passages left behind by streams that went on to cut through to lower levels or disappeared entirely. The longest known solution cave is Mammoth Cave in Kentucky, which extends more than 300 miles (500 km).

VOLCANIC CAVES

Volcanic (or lava) caves are tubes or hollows formed when a stream of lava flows over the ground. The surface of the flowing lava cools as it makes contact with the air and solidifies into rock. Beneath this solid crust, molten lava continues to flow. When the supply of lava ceases, the remaining molten material drains out, leaving long, cylindrical tunnels called lava tubes.

HARRISON'S CAVE
An underground stream flows through this spectacular solution cave in Barbados, filled with still-forming stalagmites and stalactites.

THE TERRA-COTTA ARMY

THE SHAPING OF CLAY EVOLVED FROM UTILITARIAN NEED INTO AN ART FORM THOUSANDS OF YEARS AGO. NOWHERE HAS THIS BEEN MORE SPECTACULARLY EXPRESSED THAN IN THE TERRA-COTTA ARMY OF THE FIRST CHINESE EMPEROR, QIN SHIHUANGDI.

In 1974 some farmers digging a well near Xi'an, China, discovered what would prove to be three pits containing over 7,000 life-size clay warriors and horses adjacent to the burial tomb of the first Chinese Emperor. The first pit held over 6,000 soldiers and a few horses and chariots; the second pit housed 1,400 soldiers and cavalry; and the third pit contained 68 officers. They were interred as part of the mausoleum of Qin Shihuangdi, who died in 210 BC. An empty fourth pit was also discovered, apparently unfinished due to Qin's untimely death.

Qin Shihuangdi was a hated tyrant who sacrificed thousands of lives on his personal projects. His tomb, constructed by 700,000 forced laborers and not yet discovered, was said to have a ceiling inlaid with pearls, a stone floor forming a map of the Chinese kingdom with 100 rivers of mercury flowing across it, and vast quantities of treasure protected by deadly booby traps. The discovery of high levels of mercury in the soil surrounding the site suggests that there may be some truth to the tale.

SOLDIERS AND HORSES
Each warrior stands to attention, as if awaiting the command to attack. Many weapons were also found in the tomb: bows and arrows, spears, and swords, as well as bronze and leather bridles, silk, linen, jade, and bone artifacts, and iron farm implements.

CREATING THE ARMY

Each of the otherwise hollow statues carved out of clay stood unaided on solid legs. This had never been achieved before. The remaining hollow body parts were made from a variety of molds, and then assembled. Pieces such as ears, beards and armor were modeled separately and attached. The entire figure was coated with thin layers of clay, and the final details, giving each soldier a unique appearance and personality, were sculpted. The whole figure was fired at a high temperature and then painted and coated with lacquer.

For two millennia the clay figures lay buried in water-soaked soil. The moment the figures were unearthed, their water-soaked glaze started to dry out, and the lacquer, with its colored pigments, began to flake and fall off. However, a chemical treatment developed recently at the University of Munich promises to preserve the crumbling warriors for future generations.

CONSERVATION
To preserve the figures, each one is being bathed in a solution containing hydroxyethyl methacrylate (HEMA), which is able to penetrate tiny pores in the glaze. It is then bombarded with electrons in a particle accelerator, converting the liquid into a strong polymer that bonds the lacquer together from the inside without altering the figure's appearance.

63

NAVAJO SAND PAINTING
This contemporary sand painting of a yei (holy person) was created by a Navajo medicine man. Sand painting is an art form designed to heal the sick. The patient lies on top of the sand painting and the medicine man rubs sand over him. At the end of the healing ceremony, the sand painting is destroyed, destroying the illness at the same time.

THE PAINTED DESERT

ONE OF THE MOST DRAMATIC AND COLORFUL EXPOSURES OF SEDIMENTARY ROCK ON EARTH IS FOUND IN THE HIGH DESERT AREA OF NORTH AMERICA. IT IS KNOWN AS THE PAINTED DESERT.

Government explorer Lieutenant Joseph C. Ives named the high desert area in the State of Arizona the Painted Desert in 1858. He thought it aptly described the rainbow of colorful layers of sedimentary rock exposed in the stark desert landscape.

The Painted Desert is a narrow, crescent-shaped arc, about 150 miles (240 km) long and varying in width from 10 miles (16 km) at its northern end near the Grand Canyon to 50 miles (80 km) at its southern end near Holbrook. Elevations within the Painted Desert range from 4,500 to 6,500 ft (1,370 to 1,980 m). The land is arid, with only 5 to 9 in (125 to 230 mm) of annual rain, and temperature extremes of –25 to 105°F (–31 to 41°C). It is sparsely vegetated, and very heavily eroded in parts. Within the Painted Desert at the very southern tip is the Petrified Forest National Park (see pp.334–35).

THE CHINLE FORMATION

The rock exposed in the Painted Desert is the Chinle Formation, of the Late Triassic Period (200–250 million years ago), composed of sandstones, mudstones, and shales. During the Triassic Period, northeastern Arizona was located near the equator. About 60 million years ago, after the Chinle Formation had been deeply buried by younger strata, the region was uplifted as part of the massive Colorado Plateau, through which the Colorado River eroded the Grand Canyon. Other erosion also took place, exposing the rocks that are now seen in the Painted Desert.

The varied colors of the formation are a result of the varying mineral content in the sediments when they were laid down, and the rate of their deposition. With slow deposition, oxides of iron and (hematite) aluminum are concentrated in the sediment, creating the red, orange, and pink colors seen at the north end of the Desert. In the southern portion of the Desert, deposition was rapid, leading to removal of oxygen from the sediment, and resulting in blue, gray, white, and lavender layers.

The most heavily eroded areas of the Painted Desert contain many deep, tortuous gullies with intervening sawtooth divides, combined with flat-topped mesas and buttes. These areas are known as badlands, and are the result of periodic torrential rains during thunderstorms and flash flooding. The soft mudstone erodes rapidly, creating gullies, while hills capped with sandstone or shale are more resistant, causing the development of hills and buttes with a steplike profile.

MULTICOLORED LAYER CAKE
Blue, gray, lavender, and white sedimentary layers run through the eroded rock in the southern portion of the Painted Desert. These colored rocks have been compared to a multicolored layer cake.

White horizontal lines of mudstone strata run through red and orange sandstone formations in the Wilderness area alongside the Blue Canyon in the Painted Desert of Arizona.

MARBLE

MARBLE IS A GRANULAR METAMORPHIC rock derived from limestone or dolomite (see p.54). Marbles are formed under the influence of heat and pressure, and consist of a mass of interlocking calcite or dolomite grains. The latter are called dolomitic marbles. Marbles rich in serpentine minerals are known as ophicalcites.

Marbles form in two ways: as a result of the deep burial of limestone in the older layers of Earth's crust with consequent heat and pressure from the thick layers of overlying sediments; and as a result of contact metamorphism near igneous intrusions. Pure marble is nothing but calcite; impurities in the original limestone often recrystallize during metamorphism to give mineral impurities in the marble. The most common impurities are quartz, mica, graphite, iron oxides, and small pyrite crystals. Silicates of lime or magnesia are found in other marbles, and can include diopside, tremolite, labradorite, albite, anorthite, garnet, vesuvianite, spinel, zoisite, epidote, tourmaline, and sphene. Many of these will be present in sufficient amounts to give a characteristic texture or color (or both) to the marbles in which they occur.

SCOTTISH MARBLE
From Ledmore North Quarry, Assynt, Sutherland, this marble source is one of only a few in a country better known for its quarrying of granite.

MARBLE QUARRY
Huge blocks of sparkling white marble are sliced from the rock face at Carrara, Italy, and removed by heavy machinery.

SWITCHBACKS
The haulage road at the Carrara marble quarry in Italy climbs back and forth across the steep rock face.

VARIETIES OF MARBLE

Pure marble is white. Some other marbles take their common names from their color or mineral impurities. Because the impurities were originally layers of other minerals thinly interbedded in the original limestone, they sometimes occur as bands in the marble. Impurities of serpentine, tremolite, brucite, and olivine may all impart a greenish tinge. Gray marble usually forms from relatively pure limestone and contains few mineral impurities. Small amounts of graphite color

HAZRATBAL MOSQUE
This mosque, with its distinctive dome and minaret, is on the shores of Lake Dal in Kashmir. It is made of white marble.

Marble fragment

ARCH OF CONSTANTINE
This marble arch, in Rome, Italy, was built in the 4th century AD. It is the model for many modern arches, including London's Marble Arch.

"The marble not yet carved can hold the form of every thought the greatest artist has."

MICHELANGELO

some gray marbles; some black marbles have higher graphite concentrations. Brown marble is colored by garnet and vesuvianite. Veined and patterned marbles are often created when an existing marble is cracked or shattered, and the spaces between the marble fragments filled in with calcite or other minerals. In marbles that have not been fully metamorphosed, fossils from the original limestone can sometimes still be seen. Marbles from Carrara, Italy, and Bergen, Norway, are examples of these. Where complete recrystallization has taken place, all fossil remains are completely obliterated.

PROPERTIES

ROCK TYPE Regional or contact metamorphic
TEMPERATURE High
PRESSURE Low to high
STRUCTURE Crystalline
MAJOR MINERALS Calcite
MINOR MINERALS Diopside, tremolite, actinolite
COLOR White, pink
TEXTURE Fine to coarse
PROTOLITH Limestone, dolomite

CARVING IN MARBLE

Michelangelo notwithstanding, the golden age of marble sculpture was arguably in the Classical Period of ancient Greece, from about 480 to 330 BC. Two sculptors epitomize the age: Praxiteles and Phidias. The statues of Praxiteles transformed the detached, majestic style of his immediate predecessors into his own, expressing gentle grace and sensuous charm. His most famous work was the *Aphrodite of Cnidus*, celebrated by the Roman author Pliny the Elder as the finest statue in the world. In this statue, the goddess is depicted naked, a bold innovation at the time, which prompted his model to exclaim, "Alas, where did Praxiteles see me naked?" Phidias undertook marble sculpture on a grand scale: he was the artistic director of the construction of the Parthenon in Athens. Phidias and his assistants also carved the marble figures that ornamented the Parthenon frieze. Most of the remains of these—often called the Elgin Marbles—are in the British Museum.

DAVID
Michelangelo's David (created 1501–04) was carved from marble from Carrara, Italy.

SCULPTOR AT WORK
The fine grain and flawless coloring of some marble allows intricate carvings, such as this example by a Vietnamese sculptor.

Iron oxide cement

Hematite vein

Limonite vein

MARBLE BRECCIA
From the Isle of Skyros, Greece, this specimen of marble has been cracked and shattered, the veins infilled, and fragments recemented with iron-rich calcareous cement. Color variations in the veining are a result of the decomposition products of mineral impurities in the original marble, such as reddish hematite, brown limonite, and pale green talc.

THIN SECTION
This is forsterite marble (forsterite and calcite), a typical, high-grade metamorphic marble from South Africa.

Calcite

Forsterite

Forsterite

TYPES OF MARBLE
The many variations in coloring of marble are determined by the other mineral impurities that are enclosed within it.

Color from graphite traces

Color from olivine

Visible olivine grains

Color from serpentine or tremolite

Color from diopside

GRAY MARBLE

OLIVINE MARBLE

GREEN MARBLE

POLISHED SLAB OF BLUE MARBLE

PIETRA DURA
Precious and semiprecious stones were meticulously cut and shaped into tendrils and floral arabesques, and then set in rows in the white marble.

LOVING COUPLE
Shah Jahan was heartbroken when his favorite wife, Mumtaz Mahal, died giving birth to their 14th child. It is said that he locked himself in his rooms and refused food for eight days. When he finally emerged, observers noted that his black beard had turned white.

THE CENOTAPHS
The central chamber of the mausoleum houses the public tomb of Mumtaz Mahal (below right), which rests beneath the center of the dome and in line with the entrance to it. The tomb of Shah Jahan was later squeezed in beside it.

THE TAJ MAHAL

A MARBLE MAUSOLEUM IN AGRA, INDIA, THE TAJ MAHAL WAS BUILT FOR THE MOGUL EMPEROR SHAH JAHAN TO MEMORIALIZE HIS FAVORITE WIFE, MUMTAZ MAHAL, WHO DIED IN CHILDBIRTH IN 1631.

Renowned as the finest example of Mogul architecture, the Taj Mahal combines symmetry and balance between all parts of the building with superb delicacy of detail in ornamentation. The chief architect was probably an Indian of Persian descent, Ustad Ahmad Lahawri.

Building began around 1632, with more than 20,000 workers employed from India, Persia, the Ottoman Empire, and Europe. Construction of the mausoleum complex spanned 22 years and cost between four and five million rupees. The central mausoleum itself was completed by about 1639, the adjunct buildings by 1643, and the decoration work in 1647.

MAKRANA MARBLE

The mausoleum itself is built of unusual white marble called Makrana marble, which changes hue according to the intensity of sunlight or moonlight. It rests on a plinth 25 ft (7 m) high, with four nearly identical facades, each with a wide central arch that rises to 110 ft (33 m). Each of the four corners is slanted, and incorporates smaller arches. The central dome reaches a height of 240 ft (73 m). It is surrounded by four lesser domes. The superb acoustics inside the main dome cause the single note of a flute to resound five times.

The interior is organized around an octagonal marble chamber, which is ornamented with low-relief carvings and hard-stone inlay called *pietra dura*. Within this are the cenotaphs of Mumtaz Muhal and Shah Jahan, both of which are inlaid with semiprecious stones. They are enclosed by a finely carved filigree marble screen. The true sarcophagi lie beneath, at garden level.

TAJ MAHAL, INDIA
Framed by four tall minarets, the central mausoleum is set at the north end of a formal garden quartered by long pools of water in which the building is reflected.

SLATE

A FINE-GRAINED metamorphic rock, slate has a characteristic "slaty cleavage," allowing it to be split into relatively thin, flat sheets. True slates split along the foliation planes formed during metamorphism rather than along the original sedimentary layers. Its cleavage is a result of microscopic mica crystals that have all grown oriented in the same plane. Slate forms when mudstone, shale, or felsic volcanic rocks are buried and subjected to low temperatures and pressures. Common around the world in regionally metamorphosed terrains, such as the Appalachians, the Rhenish mountains, western Germany, and the Taihang mountains, Hebei Province, China, slate occurs in a number of colors, depending on the mineralogy and oxidation conditions of the original sedimentary environment. Black slate, for example, forms in a very oxygen-poor environment; red in an oxygen-rich environment. Many slates are mottled or spotted. Fossils of plants and animals can be preserved in slate. Slate is quarried in large pieces for use in electrical panels, countertops, blackboards, and flooring, and in smaller pieces for roofing.

SLATE QUARRY
This slate quarry in Dinorwic, Wales, produced blue-gray slate until 1969.

PROPERTIES

ROCK TYPE Regional metamorphic
TEMPERATURE Low
PRESSURE Low
STRUCTURE Foliated
MAJOR MINERALS Quartz, mica, feldspar
MINOR MINERALS Pyrite, graphite
COLOR Various
TEXTURE Fine
PROTOLITH Mudstone, siltstone, shale, or felsic volcanics

THIN SECTION
This slate contains a folded band of coarser silt. The slaty cleavage crosses the bedding at a high angle.

Band of silt | Slaty cleavage

Fine grain size

Foliated structure

Fissile splitting

WELSH SLATE
This specimen is from Wales, Great Britain's principal source of slate. In the US, slate is quarried in Pennsylvania and Vermont.

SLATE ROOFING

The fissile nature of slate—its ability to split into thin sheets with parallel faces—makes it ideal as a durable roofing material. Slate quarrying and preparation was once a huge industry, now largely supplanted by modern materials. Fissile limestones are also used as roofing slates and known as "slate," though they are not true slates.

PIEDMONT SLATES
Local slates, such as these in Italy, are often part of a region's typical architecture.

PHYLLITE

LIKE SLATE, PHYLLITE is a fine-grained metamorphic rock that forms when fine-grained sedimentary rocks, such as mudstones or shales, are buried and subjected to relatively low temperatures and pressures for a long period of time. It has a similar tendency to split into sheets or slabs because of the parallel alignment of mica minerals, but its grains are larger than those of slate. Phyllite also has a shinier sheen than slate because of its larger mica crystals.

Many phyllites have a scattering of large crystals called porphyroblasts, which grow during metamorphism. Tourmaline, cordierite, andalusite, staurolite, biotite, and pyrite are all minerals that are commonly found as porphyroblasts in phyllites. Phyllite occurs in regionally metamorphosed terrains, in both young and old eroded mountain belts. It is sometimes used as a paving stone.

PERU
Many phyllites can be found in the Peruvian Andes, a vast mountain chain.

THIN SECTION
This section shows the dense mat of aligned muscovite that gives rise to the sheen on the specimen's surface.

Muscovite

Sheen on surface

PROPERTIES

ROCK TYPE Regional metamorphic
TEMPERATURE Low to moderate
PRESSURE Low
STRUCTURE Foliated
MAJOR MINERALS Quartz, feldspar, muscovite mica, graphite, chlorite
MINOR MINERALS Tourmaline, analusite, cordierite, pyrite, magnetite
COLOR Silvery to greenish-gray
TEXTURE Fine
PROTOLITH Mudstone, shale, siltstone, or felsic volcanics

GEOLOGICAL INDICATOR
Phyllite has little economic use, except as a paving stone, but it is a valuable indicator of geological conditions.

Wavy foliation

SCHIST

FOLDED SCHISTS
This schist outcrop is in the Austrian Alps.

SCHISTS ARE foliated metamorphic rocks with visible mineral crystals. They commonly show distinct layering of light- and dark-colored minerals. Most schists are composed largely of platy minerals such as muscovite, chlorite, talc, biotite, and graphite. Schist's characteristic schistose fabric (it splits easily along planes) is a result of the parallel orientation of these minerals. There are a number of different schists. For example, greenschist is a schist rich in the green minerals chlorite, actinolite, and epidote; blueschist is rich in blue glaucophane. The specific mineral composition of schist depends both on its original rock (protolith) and on its metamorphic environment. The mineral assemblage can thus be used to help determine both the environment in which the original rock formed and its metamorphic history.

Garnet
Kyanite
Muscovite

THIN SECTION
This typical garnet-mica schist comes from the Austrian Alps.

MUSCOVITE SCHIST
The silvery appearance of muscovite schist is due to the abundance of muscovite mica.

Silvery mica

PROPERTIES

ROCK TYPE Regional metamorphic
TEMPERATURE Low to moderate
PRESSURE Low to moderate
STRUCTURE Foliated
MAJOR MINERALS Quartz, feldspar, mica
MINOR MINERALS Garnet, actinolite, hornblende, graphite, kyanite
COLOR Silvery, green, blue
TEXTURE Medium
PROTOLITH Mudstone, siltstone, shale, or felsic volcanics

Wavy foliation
Garnet porphyroblast

Biotite
Bladed blue kyanite

GARNET SCHIST

KYANITE SCHIST

SCHIST VARIETIES
Many schists contain porphyroblasts: large crystals of minerals such as garnet that grow during metamorphism.

GNEISS

DOMES OF GNEISS
These granitic gneiss domes are in South Africa.

GNEISS BOWL
This Egyptian diorite-gneiss bowl dates from the period 2890–2686 BC.

DISTINCT BANDS of minerals of different colors and grain sizes characterize this metamorphic rock. In most gneisses the bands are folded, although the folds may be too large to see in a hand specimen. Gneiss is medium- to coarse-grained, and differs from schist in that its foliation is well developed, but it has little or no schistosity (tendency to split along planes). Most gneisses contain abundant quartz and feldspar, with porphyroblasts of metamorphic minerals such as garnet. They form at very high temperatures and pressures from sedimentary or granitic rocks, and make up the cores of mountain ranges. Pencil gneiss has rod-shaped individual minerals or aggregates of minerals. Being crystalline, gneisses do not split easily and are a popular building and facing stone. In the building industry, they are classified as granites.

ABRAHAM WERNER
Mineralogist Werner (1749–1817) adopted and popularized the use of the ancient terms gneiss and schist.

PROPERTIES

TYPE Regional metamorphic
TEMPERATURE High
PRESSURE High
STRUCTURE Foliated, crystalline
MAJOR MINERALS Quartz, feldspar
MINOR MINERALS Biotite, hornblende, garnet, staurolite
COLOR Gray, pink, multi-colored
TEXTURE Coarse
PROTOLITH Granite, shale, granodiorite, mudstone, siltstone, or felsic volcanics

Biotite
Quartz

THIN SECTION
Alternating bands of light and dark minerals give this granodioritic gneiss from the Hohe Tauern, in the Austrian Alps, its gneissic texture.

Feldspar

Alternate light and dark layers

FOLDED GNEISS

Eye- ("augen"-) shaped patches

BIOTITE GNEISS
Biotite is one of the minerals that form under metamorphic conditions, and occurs in quantity in biotite gneiss.

AUGEN GNEISS

Biotite
Pale feldspar

GNEISS VARIETIES
Gneisses can have a huge range of forms and mineral characteristics, and are named for them.

83

AMPHIBOLITE IN SCHIST
Layers of amphibolite run through schist in the Austrian Alps.

AMPHIBOLITE

SCHISTOSITY AND FOLIATION are well developed in most amphibolites. Made up predominantly of amphibole minerals, such as actinolite (see Tremolite, p.279), many samples contain microscopic grains of feldspar, pyroxene, and calcite. Some also contain macroscopic crystals of minerals such as garnet, diagnostic of regional metamorphic rocks formed under low to moderate temperatures and pressures. Amphibolites form from the metamorphism of mafic igneous rocks such as gabbros, and can also form from sedimentary rocks such as graywacke.

MINERAL COMPOSITION
Amphibolite comprises mainly amphibole minerals, but may also contain feldspar, garnet, pyroxene, and epidote.

Amphibole crystals

Coarse texture

PROPERTIES

ROCK TYPE Regional metamorphic
TEMPERATURE Low to moderate
PRESSURE Low to moderate
STRUCTURE Foliated, crystalline
MAJOR MINERALS Hornblende, actinolite
MINOR MINERALS Feldspar, calcite, pyroxene
COLOR Gray, black, greenish
TEXTURE Coarse
PROTOLITH Basalt, graywacke, dolomite

ROAD-BUILDING

Amphibolite is used in road-building and in other aggregates where a high degree of strength and durability is required. It is also sawn into sheets for use as ornamental stone in the facings of buildings, as flagstones, or as flooring. It is sometimes sold for use as countertops and for ornamental purposes under the name of "black granite."

HIGH-GRADE AGGREGATE
When crushed, amphibolite makes a high-grade aggregate for road-building.

Plagioclase

THIN SECTION
This finely banded amphibolite is from the Lewisian Complex in Achmelvich, Scotland.

Hornblende

PRECAMBRIAN HORNFELS
These hornfels are in Chamwood Forest, England.

HORNFELS

HORNFELS FORMS BY contact metamorphism close to igneous intrusions at temperatures as high as 1,300°–1,450°F (700°–800°C). Hornfels can form from almost any parent rock, and its composition depends on both that rock and the exact temperatures and fluids to which the rock is exposed. It is notoriously difficult to identify. The rock is usually dense, hard, very fine grained, relatively homogeneous, and has a conchoidal, flintlike fracture. It may be banded.

Hornfels is often categorized by the mix of minerals present in the sample. Garnet hornfels, for example, is characterized by porphyroblasts (large crystals set into a rock matrix) of garnet. Dark hornfels is easily confused with basalt.

Dark pyroxene crystals

Rhombic chiastolite

Bladed chiastolite

Fine-grained texture

PYROXENE HORNFELS

CHIASTOLITE HORNFELS

CORDIERITE HORNFELS

HORNFELS VARIETIES
Varieties of hornfels take their names from the presence of porphyroblasts of various minerals in the rock, such as pyroxene hornfels, chiastolite hornfels, and cordierite hornfels.

Garnet porphyroblasts

Hornblende and plagioclase

GARNET HORNFELS
The red color of this specimen of garnet hornfels is a result of the number of garnet crystals present in the rock.

Cordierite

Spinel

Biotite

PROPERTIES

ROCK TYPE Contact metamorphic
TEMPERATURE Moderate to high
PRESSURE Low to high
STRUCTURE Crystalline
MAJOR MINERALS Hornblende, plagioclase, andalusite, cordierite, and others
MINOR MINERALS Magnetite, apatite, titanite
COLOR Dark gray, brown, greenish, reddish
TEXTURE Microcrystalline to fine
PROTOLITH Almost any rock

THIN SECTION
This rock was a mudstone heated to very high temperature adjacent to an intrusion.

QUARTZITE

QUARTZITE CAP
The peak of Stob Ban in Scotland is capped with white quartzite.

THE QUARTZ-RICH ROCK is formed by the burial, heating, and squeezing of sandstone. The name quartzite can also refer to rock formed by precipitation of cement in pore spaces. Such rock contains rounded quartz grains. Quartzite is very hard and brittle, and shows conchoidal fracture.

PROPERTIES

ROCK TYPE	Regional metamorphic
TEMPERATURE	High
PRESSURE	Low to high
STRUCTURE	Crystalline
MAJOR MINERALS	Quartz
MINOR MINERALS	Mica, kyanite, sillimanite
COLOR	Almost any
TEXTURE	Medium
PROTOLITH	Sandstone

Crystalline quartz

METAQUARTZITE
The metamorphic variety of quartzite is a crystalline rock with over 90 percent quartz.

GRANULITE

FAULT BLOCK
The Tetons in Wyoming contain granulite.

GRANULITE IS THOUGHT to form at very high temperatures and pressures near the base of the crust. It usually has a high concentration of pyroxene, with diopside or hypersthene, garnet, calcium plagioclase, and quartz or olivine. Granulites are tough, massive, and coarse-grained. The "granulite facies" is one of the major divisions in the classification of metamorphic rocks.

PROPERTIES

ROCK TYPE	Regional metamorphic
TEMPERATURE	High
PRESSURE	High
STRUCTURE	Crystalline
MAJOR MINERALS	Feldspar, quartz, garnet
MINOR MINERALS	Spinel, corundum
COLOR	Gray, pinkish, brownish, mottled
TEXTURE	Medium to coarse
PROTOLITH	Felsic igneous and sedimentary rocks

Pale crystals   *Fine matrix*

UNFOLIATED ROCK
Unlike many other regionally metamorphosed rocks, granulite is characterized by a lack of foliation.

FULGURITE

LIGHTNING
As lightning strikes sand in the desert, some of the sand fuses into a fulgurite.

NAMED AFTER the Latin for "thunderbolt," fulgurites form when lightning strikes. They form either as crusts or as tubes, some of which branch out like trees. The tubes are lined with fused sand, or glass, with partially melted sand on the outside. In theory, fulgurites can form in any type of easily melted rock, but most are found in desert regions where sand has been melted, and the surrounding loose material has since eroded away. The largest fulgurite ever recorded was about 16 ft (5 m) long. Fulgurites have no practical use, although they are decorative.

Empty core where sand was vaporized by lightning

Partially melted sand

PROPERTIES

ROCK TYPE	Contact metamorphic
TEMPERATURE	Very high
PRESSURE	Low
STRUCTURE	Glassy (amorphous)
MAJOR MINERALS	Amorphous silica
MINOR MINERALS	Various
COLOR	Gray, white
TEXTURE	Glassy to sandy
PROTOLITH	Usually sand

SAND FULGURITE
Sand fulgurites occur as tubes of fused sand, whereas rock fulgurites are glassy crusts.

MIGMATITE

MIXED ROCK
The granitic rock is light against the dark bands of schist or gneiss.

MIGMATITE, MEANING "mixed rock," consists of schist or gneiss interlayered, streaked, or veined with granite rock. The bands may be tightly folded. Migmatites often occur in areas of high-grade metamorphism. The granite streaks are the result of partial melting of the parent rock, at temperatures below the melting point of the schist or gneiss. Migmatites also form near large intrusions of granite when some of the magma has intruded into surrounding metamorphic rocks.

PROPERTIES

ROCK TYPE	Regional metamorphic
TEMPERATURE	High
PRESSURE	High
STRUCTURE	Foliated, crystalline
MAJOR MINERALS	Quartz, feldspar, mica
MINOR MINERALS	Various
COLOR	Banded light and dark gray, pink, white
TEXTURE	Coarse
PROTOLITH	Various, including granite and gneiss

Light quartz and feldspar

Dark gneissose component

MIXED ROCK
Folds of granite are interlayered with gneiss in this sample of migmatite.

BANDED MIGMATITE
The interlayering of schist and gneiss with lighter-colored granite is visible in this specimen.

85

MINERALS

MORE THAN 350 OF EARTH'S MINERALS

WHAT IS A MINERAL?

QUARTZ GEODE

MINERALS ARE THE STUFF of which Earth's rocks are made. A mineral is defined as a naturally occurring solid with a specific chemical composition and a distinctive internal crystal structure. Minerals are usually formed by inorganic processes, although there are organically produced substances, such as hydroxylapatite in teeth and bones, that are also considered minerals. Certain substances, including opal and glass, resemble minerals in chemistry and occurrence but do not have a regularly ordered internal arrangement. These are known as mineraloids.

WHAT ARE MINERALS MADE OF?

Most minerals are chemical compounds, composed of two or more chemical elements, although copper, sulfur, gold, silver, and a few others occur as single "native" elements. A mineral is defined by its chemical formula and by the atomic arrangement of its crystallization. For example, iron sulfide has the chemical formula FeS_2 (where Fe is the element iron, and S is sulfur). It can crystallize in two different ways. When it crystallizes in the cubic crystal system (see p.100), it is called pyrite; but when instead it crystallizes in the orthorhombic crystal system (see p.101), it becomes a different mineral, marcasite.

COPPER DUCK

NATIVE ELEMENT
Native copper was probably the first metal used by humankind, either hammered into tools or cast into artifacts. This copper duck's head was made in North Africa about 1,900 years ago.

MARCASITE

PYRITE

IRON SULFIDES
Pyrite and marcasite have exactly the same chemical composition—they are both iron sulfide—but their different crystal structures make them different minerals.

ELECTRICAL CHARGE

A mineral compound is based on an electrical balance between a positively charged part, often a metal, and a negatively charged part. These charged particles are known as ions. In many minerals the negative electrical charge is carried by a "radical" which is a combination of atoms, rather than by single atom. For example, the sulfur in pyrite is present as the disulfide (S_2) group, with two sulfur atoms, which has a negative charge the same as the positive charge of an iron (Fe) ion. The sulfur radical balances the iron ion and the formula for pyrite is FeS_2. To take another example, one atom of carbon (C) and three atoms of oxygen (O) combine to give the CO_3 radical, which acts as a single, negatively charged unit. The element or elements that carry the negative electrical charge determine which chemical group a mineral is assigned to (see p.90). For example, minerals formed with two sulfur atoms are known as sulfides, those formed with oxygen alone are oxides, those made with the carbon and oxygen ion are called carbonates, and those formed with silicon and oxygen are silicates.

Carbon atom

Oxygen atom

CARBONATE
Carbonates are formed with one carbon atom and three oxygen atoms.

NATIVE SULFUR
Sulfur is mined at Kawah Ijen, Java. Volcanic gases escaping from small openings in the ground (fumaroles) carry dissolved sulfur to the surface, where it deposits as a yellow crust.

VOLCANIC RHYOLITE
The Rhyolite Hills in Iceland are, as their name suggests, formed of rhyolite, a silica-rich rock produced as a result of volcanic activity.

Each silicon atom is bonded to four oxygen atoms that form a tetrahedral shape

Silica tetrahedra join at the corners to form a helix

Crystal face

QUARTZ CRYSTAL

QUARTZ STRUCTURE
Silica tetrahedra link to form quartz and other silicate minerals.

COMMON MINERALS

There are more than 4,000 known minerals, but only about 100 of these are common. Silicon and oxygen are by far the most abundant elements in Earth's crust. They make up about three-fourths of the crust by weight, and silicates, such as quartz, feldspar, and olivine, are by far the most common minerals in rocks, making up about 90 percent of the rocks at Earth's surface. Carbonates are important in forming sedimentary rocks such as limestone. Many sulfides, including pyrite and galena, and oxides, such as hematite, are also relatively common. So are some of the native elements, such as copper.

HIGH SIERRA
The peaks of the Sierra Nevada, California, are made of granite, a rock typically composed of about 70 percent silica.

SYNTHETIC GEMS
Emeralds and rubies that are grown synthetically are not classified as minerals.

SYNTHETIC RUBY BOULE

MINERAL OR NOT?

The term mineral is commonly applied to certain organic substances, such as coal, oil, and natural gas (as when referring to a nation's mineral wealth), although these particular materials are more accurately referred to as hydrocarbons. Gases and liquids are not, in the strict sense, minerals. Although ice, the solid state of water, is considered a mineral, liquid water is not. Nor is liquid mercury, which is sometimes found in mercury ore deposits. Synthetic equivalents of certain minerals, such as emeralds and diamonds, are produced in the laboratory, but these are not minerals, in that they do not occur naturally.

SYNTHETIC GILSON EMERALD

The "minerals" referred to when talking of foods are also not minerals in the geological sense, as they refer to single elements, such as calcium, zinc, or iron.

CRUDE OIL
Although called a "mineral" in economic terms, oil is classed as a hydrocarbon.

ICEBERG
The crystallized water that forms an iceberg is a mineral, but the liquid water it floats in is not.

89

IDENTIFYING MINERALS

EVEN FOR EXPERTS, MINERAL IDENTIFICATION is often far from easy. But there are certain physical properties—determined by the crystalline structure and chemical composition of the mineral—that can help with identification without requiring the use of expensive equipment. Some of these properties, such as hardness and density, can be measured objectively, while others, such as color and luster, demand a more subjective assessment. Where minerals are found as distinct crystals, there is an additional set of properties that can be used for identification (see pp.98–103).

COLOR

Some minerals have characteristic colors and others do not. The bright blue of azurite, the yellow of sulfur, and the green of malachite allow an almost instant identification. At the other end of the scale, fluorite occurs in virtually all colors, so it can only be identified by observing other properties.

Color in minerals is caused by the absorption or refraction of light of particular wavelengths. This can happen for a number of reasons. One is the presence of foreign atoms—atoms not part of the chemical makeup of the mineral—in the crystal structure. These are called trace elements. As few as three or four atoms per million can absorb enough of certain parts of the visible light spectrum to give color to a mineral. The color produced by a particular trace element varies according to the mineral it inhabits. For example, chromium is the coloring element in both red ruby and green emerald. Color can also result from the absence of an atom or ionic radical from a point that it would normally occupy in a crystal. These types of defects are called vacancies, and their result is called a color center. The violet color of some fluorite is produced by a vacancy.

The structure of the mineral itself, without any defects or foreign elements, may also cause color. For example, opal is composed of minute spheres of silica that diffract light, while the color and sheen of moonstone is determined by the thin interlayering of two different feldspars. In some crystals, light vibrates in different planes within the crystal, with the result that, whatever the initial cause of its color may be, it appears as different colors when observed along different axes. This is called pleochroism.

GREEN FLUORITE

YELLOW FLUORITE

PURPLE FLUORITE

COLOR RANGE
These specimens show only a few of the many colors that can occur in fluorite. Different coloration depends on a range of factors, such as the presence of traces of hydrocarbons.

COLOR VARIATION
The multiplicity of colors in opal (above) is produced by the arrangement of microscopic spheres of silica in its structure. An image made using an electron microscope (left) shows the opal's fractured surface.

LUSTER

A mineral's luster is the general appearance of its surface in reflected light. There are two broad types of luster: metallic and nonmetallic. Metallic luster is that of an untarnished metal surface, such as gold, steel, or copper. Minerals with metallic luster are opaque to light, even on thin edges. By contrast, minerals with nonmetallic luster are generally lighter in color, and show some degree of transparency or translucency, even though this may only be on a thin edge. There are a number of terms that describe nonmetallic lusters: vitreous, having the luster of a piece of broken glass; adamantine, having the brilliant luster of diamond; resinous, having the luster of a piece of resin; pearly, having the luster of pearl or mother-of-pearl; greasy, appearing to be covered with a thin layer of oil; silky, appearing as the surface of silk or satin; dull, producing little or no reflection; and earthy, having the nonlustrous appearance of raw earth. With practice, the main types of luster can be distinguished easily by eye, but the difference between them cannot be precisely quantified.

METALLIC
The sulfide galena has a metallic luster and a distinctive pattern of cleavage.

VITREOUS
Many silicate minerals, such as this quartz crystal, have a vitreous luster and appear similar to glass surfaces.

GREASY
Orpiment can have a greasy or a resinous luster. Making the distinction requires a subjective judgment.

RESINOUS
Crystals of native sulfur are transparent or translucent with a resinous luster.

SILKY
The borate ulexite exhibits a silky luster, having the surface sheen of a bolt of satin.

DULL
A dull luster, such as that of this sample of hematite, is nonreflective, but not as granular as earthy luster.

EARTHY
Minerals with an earthy luster, such as this fine-grained calcite, have the look of freshly broken, dry soil.

DIAGNOSTIC STREAK

A streak is the color of the powder produced when a specimen is drawn across a surface such as a piece of unglazed porcelain—the back of a kitchen tile, for example. This technique is an extremely useful diagnostic because a mineral's streak is far more consistent than its color, which tends to vary from specimen to specimen. It can allow you to distinguish between minerals that are otherwise easily confused. For example, the iron oxide hematite gives a red streak, whereas magnetite, another oxide of iron, gives a black streak. If a mineral is too hard to mark a streak plate, the color of its powder can be determined by filing or crushing a small sample.

ORPIMENT

CINNABAR

CROCOITE

CHALCOPYRITE

HEMATITE

MOLYBDENITE

CONSISTENCY
The streak of a mineral is consistent from specimen to specimen, as long as you test an unweathered surface.

CLEAVAGE

Cleavage is the ability of a mineral to break along flat, planar surfaces. It occurs at places within the mineral's crystal structure where the forces bonding atoms are weakest. Cleavage surfaces are generally smooth and reflect light evenly. Cleavage is described by its direction relative to the position of crystal faces (using the terms cubic, prismatic, and basal) and by the ease with which it is produced. If cleavage produces smooth, lustrous surfaces with great ease, it is called perfect. Terms for lesser degrees of ease include distinct, imperfect, and difficult, while some minerals have no cleavage at all. A mineral can have cleavages in different directions, each of which may be of a different quality. For example, one may be perfect, another may be imperfect. Cleavage is a consistent property and thus useful for identification.

BERYL CLEAVAGE
Under a microscope, a beryl crystal shows structural breaks, which coincide with its potential cleavages. The direction of cleavages and the angles between them offer clues to aid identification.

CLEAR BREAKS
The parallel cleavage planes of this barite crystal are clearly visible. Barite has perfect cleavage.

Cleavage plane

PERFECT SHAPE
When Iceland spar calcite (left) is broken along its cleavage planes, a perfect rhombic shape results. Iceland spar is also identified by its transparency and double refraction (see opposite).

FRACTURE

Some minerals will break in directions other than along cleavage planes. These breaks are known as fractures and may also help in mineral identification. For example, hackly fractures, with jagged edges, are often found in metals, while shell-like conchoidal fractures are typical of quartz. Other terms for fractures include even (rough but more or less flat), uneven (rough and completely irregular), and splintery (with partially separated fibers).

Irregular surface

Hackly fracture surface

Conchoidal fracture

CONCHOIDAL
This Bronze Age chert ax shows conchoidal fracture, with cavities shaped like a bivalve seashell.

HACKLY
This gold nugget shows hackly fracture, involving sharp edges and jagged points.

UNEVEN
This specimen of chalcopyrite shows uneven fracture. Its broken surface is rough and irregular, with no pattern evident.

TENACITY

Tenacity is a term used for a set of physical properties—such as malleability, ductility, or brittleness—that depend on the cohesive force between atoms in mineral structures. Gold, silver, and copper are good examples of malleable minerals, capable of being flattened without breaking or crumbling. Acanthite is sectile, able to be smoothly cut with a knife. Talc is flexible, bending easily and staying bent after the pressure is removed. Other terms used include ductile (capable of being drawn into a wire), brittle (showing little resistance to breakage), and elastic (capable of being bent or pulled out of shape but returning to the original form when relieved).

WORKING SILVER
High malleability is one of the distinguishing characteristics of silver. It is exploited in the making of silverware.

HARDNESS

Testing hardness is an extremely useful aid to mineral identification. The hardness of a mineral is the relative ease or difficulty with which it can be scratched. A harder mineral will scratch a softer one, but not vice versa. Any mineral can be allotted a number on the Mohs scale, which measures hardness relative to ten minerals of increasing hardness, from 1 (as soft as talc) to 10 (as hard as diamond). Hardness should not be confused with toughness or strength. Very hard minerals (including diamond) can be quite brittle. There is a general link between hardness and chemical composition. Most hydrous minerals—that is, minerals containing water molecules—are relatively soft, as are halides, carbonates, sulfates, phosphates, and most sulfides. Most anhydrous oxides—those not containing water molecules—and silicates are relatively hard (above 5 on the Mohs scale).

THE MOHS SCALE OF HARDNESS

Hardness	Mineral	Other materials for hardness testing
1	Talc	Very easily scratched by a fingernail
2	Gypsum	Can be scratched by a fingernail
3	Calcite	Just scratched with a copper coin
4	Fluorite	Very easily scratched with a knife but not as easily as calcite
5	Apatite	Scratched with a knife with difficulty
6	Orthoclase	Cannot be scratched with a knife, but scratches glass with difficulty
7	Quartz	Scratches glass easily
8	Topaz	Scratches glass very easily
9	Corundum	Cuts glass
10	Diamond	Cuts glass

TESTING METHODS
Specialist tools are available to test hardness, but you can use a fingernail (scratches a mineral less than 2^1/$_2$ on the Mohs scale) or a knife blade (scratches under 5^1/$_2$).

FINGERNAIL TEST

Hardness point

SPECIALIST TOOLS

REFRACTIVE INDEX

When light passes through a transparent or translucent mineral, it changes velocity and direction. The extent of this refraction is measured by the refractive index, the ratio of the velocity of light in air to its velocity in the crystal. A high refractive index is linked to the dispersion of the light into its component colors, which gives minerals such as diamond their fire. For the amateur, refractive indices can be found using special liquids or with relatively inexpensive equipment.

Rhombohedral calcite

Twin image due to double refraction

DOUBLE REFRACTION
A calcite rhomb refracts light to two different degrees, thus creating a double image.

LIGHT INDEX
A refractometer is used to determine the refractive index of an unknown mineral.

SPECIFIC GRAVITY

Specific gravity (SG) is a measure of the density of a substance. It is the ratio of the mass of the substance to the mass of an equal volume of water. A mineral with an SG of 2 is twice as heavy as water of the same volume. Specific gravity can be determined by the use of special balances or by employing liquids formulated to allow minerals of below a given SG to float. Bromoform, for example, can be used to distinguish quartz from topaz—quartz floats in it while topaz sinks. With experience, you will find that the "feel" of a specimen begins to relate instinctively to its specific gravity. For example, quartz, with an SG of 2.6, feels "normal," galena, SG 7.6, feels "very heavy," and so on.

GALENA

QUARTZ

LIGHT BUT HARD
Although quartz is much harder than the sulfide galena, it has a much lower specific gravity.

FLUORESCENCE

Some minerals are characterized by fluorescence. This means that they emit visible light of various colors when subjected to ultraviolet radiation. To test for fluorescence, all that is needed is an ultraviolet light, which can be readily obtained from dealers selling lapidary and collectors' equipment. On its own, fluorescence is generally one of the less reliable indicators of a mineral's identity because it lacks consistency. Some specimens of a mineral will exhibit fluorescence while others do not, even where the specimens are from the same location and appear identical. Fluorescence is discussed further on pages 160–61.

FLUORESCENT GYPSUM
This white gypsum specimen is fluorescing rose-pink when lit by ultraviolet light. It contains layers of other nonfluorescent minerals.

MINERAL ASSOCIATIONS

MINERALS NORMALLY OCCUR TOGETHER in groups or "associations." The study of how different minerals came to be associated with each other provides important information on how rocks were formed. Just as fossils give a record of life on Earth, mineral associations hold a record of Earth's geological history. Patterns of association or assemblage can also help with the identification of minerals.

Apophyllite

Stilbite

LOCAL ASSOCIATIONS

Some minerals are consistently found together over large areas because they are found in the same rock type (see mineral assemblages, opposite). Other associations occur less extensively in veins, cavities, encrustations, or thin layers. Most such localized associations have built up through geologic time—the associated minerals were not formed simultaneously. For example, within a hollow left by a gas bubble in solidified lava (a geode), you may find agate, amethyst, and calcite. First, dissolved silica was deposited as an agate lining on the inside of the bubble. Later, other manganese-bearing silica solutions deposited the layer of amethyst, followed at yet another time by carbonate-rich waters, which deposited the calcite. By studying such associations, it is possible to build up a picture of a region's geological history.

IDENTIFICATION

The fact that certain minerals are likely to be found together can help with both discovery and identification of minerals. For those in search of metals, it is useful to know that lead and zinc ore minerals, such as galena and sphalerite, are often associated with calcite and barite, while gold is frequently found in association with quartz. Also, if you have difficulty identifying a mineral but recognize another that it is associated with, this can offer a valuable clue to its identity. For example, bertrandite is an obscure silicate that may be hard to identify, but it is found in association with the more familiar beryl. Again, if you have identified one mineral as a zeolite, it is likely that an associated mineral will be a zeolite, too.

ZEOLITE ASSOCIATES
Minerals belonging to the zeolite group of silicates, such as apophyllite and stilbite, are often found in association with one another.

Barite

Smoky quartz

CRYSTAL ORDER
Associations can be used to determine in which order minerals crystallized. In this specimen, the barite must have formed after the smoky quartz.

COPPER DEPOSIT

Important mineral ores, such as this copper deposit in Bingham, Utah, are often discovered through their associated minerals. In the case of copper, the original (primary) ore minerals—for example, chalcopyrite—are oxidized near or at Earth's surface into secondary minerals, such as malachite or azurite. When prospectors find these secondary minerals on the surface, they know that they will lead to a rich concentration of copper ore below. Similarly, vivianite forms near or at the surface from the alteration of iron or manganese ores and indicates their presence at greater depth.

Calcite

Amethyst

AMETHYST GEODE
The amethyst in this geode, a cavity in volcanic rock, was deposited by manganese-bearing silica solutions. Calcite was deposited later by carbonate-rich waters.

MINERAL ASSEMBLAGES

An association of minerals that forms more or less simultaneously and is usually present in a specific rock type is called an assemblage. For example, the association of orthoclase, albite, quartz, and biotite is a mineral assemblage for granite, while plagioclase, augite, olivine, and magnetite is an assemblage for gabbro. The minerals present in any specific rock vary depending on the forces present when it was formed. A shale formed at relatively low temperature, for example, will have the assemblage muscovite-kaolin-dolomite-quartz-feldspar; another shale formed at a higher temperature will have the assemblage garnet–sillimanite–biotite–feldspar. This effect is especially striking in metamorphic rocks. A basalt that is metamorphosed at high pressures and low temperatures recrystallizes into a rock containing glaucophane and albite. These minerals have a bluish coloration and the resulting rocks are known as blueschist. The same rock type metamorphosed at more moderate pressures and temperatures would contain abundant chlorite and actinolite, both of which are green, giving this rock the name greenschist.

SEDIMENTARY SHALE
Shale is an example of a sedimentary assemblage. It is a mixture of clay minerals, quartz, feldspar, and mica.

Feldspar

Quartz

Biotite mica

GRANITE ASSEMBLAGE
Granite is characterized by the familiar assemblage of quartz, feldspar, and mica.

Mica gives silvery sheen

Garnet

METAMORPHIC MIX
The assemblage of garnet, quartz, and mica in this specimen tells geologists that this metamorphic rock formed under conditions of relatively moderate pressure and relatively low temperature.

SCHIST EXPOSURE
Greenschist, as seen in this exposure on the Tibetan Plateau, is a metamorphic rock formed at moderate pressures and temperatures.

WHAT IS A CRYSTAL?

ALL MINERALS ARE CRYSTALLINE. A crystalline material is a solid in which the component atoms are arranged in a particular, repeating, three–dimensional pattern. This is expressed externally as flat faces arranged in geometric forms. Some crystals are large enough to see, even reaching dimensions measured in yards, and others are so small they can be seen only with the most powerful microscopes. But from the tiniest to the largest, crystals of the same mineral are built to the same atomic pattern. Crystallography—the study of the geometric properties and internal structure of crystals— is a fundamental part of mineralogy.

STRUCTURE OF GOLD
The highly magnified image (far right) shows the individual atoms that make up the specimen of gold (right).

MAGNIFIED GOLD

GOLD SPECIMEN

Gold plates

ATOMIC STRUCTURE

Unit cells combine to form lattice

Atom

CELL LATTICE
A lattice is the three-dimensional representation of the crystal's internal structure.

Bonding energy

CRYSTAL STRUCTURE
"Stick-and-ball" diagrams show how each atom in the structure of a crystal is bonded.

Atom

A crystal is built up of individual, identical, structural units of atoms or molecules called unit cells. A crystal can consist of only a few unit cells, or billions of them. The unit cell is reproduced over and over in three dimensions, constructing the larger scale internal structure of the crystal, which is called the lattice. The shape of the unit cell and the symmetry of the lattice determine the position and shape of the crystal's faces. The crystals of many different minerals have unit cells that are the same shape but are made of different chemical elements. The final development of the faces that appear on any given crystal is determined to a large extent by the geological conditions at the time that the crystal is forming. Certain faces may be emphasized, while others disappear altogether. The final form a crystal takes is known as its habit (see pp.102–103).

Iron atom flanked by two smaller sulfur atoms

UNIT CELLS

STRUCTURE OF MARCASITE
Marcasite crystals are created from repeating unit cells of one atom of iron flanked by two atoms of sulfur.

MARCASITE CRYSTALS

Chalk groundmass

CRYSTAL SYMMETRY

Symmetry axes

CUBIC SYMMETRY
All cubic crystals, such as those of halite (right), have four, threefold axes of symmetry.

Rock groundmass

HALITE

Because a crystal is built up of repeating geometric patterns, all crystals exhibit symmetry. Patterns of crystal symmetry fall into six main groups, called crystal systems (see pp.100–101). The first of these is the cubic system in which all crystals exhibit cubic symmetry. The characteristics of cubic symmetry may be explained as follows. If opposite points of a cube-shaped cubic crystal (such as halite) are held between the thumb and index finger and the crystal is rotated through 360 degrees, it will appear identical three times as the different faces and edges come into view. All cubic crystals have four axes of threefold symmetry. They all have other axes of symmetry, but these differ among classes within the cube system. For example, halite has three axes of fourfold symmetry, in addition to its four axes of threefold symmetry.

Cubic halite crystals

Sodium atom

Chlorine atom

HALITE LATTICE
This diagram shows the cubic arrangement of sodium and chlorine atoms in the halite lattice.

TWIN CRYSTALS

When two or more crystals of the same species, such as gypsum or fluorite, form a symmetrical intergrowth, they are referred to as twinned crystals. Twins can form by contact or by interpenetration. Penetration twinning may occur with the individual crystals at an angle to one another, as in the staurolite cross, or parallel to one another, as in the Carlsbad twin of orthoclase. If a twin involves three or more individual crystals, it is referred to as a multiple, or repeated, twin. Albite often forms multiple twins. Many minerals form twins, but they are particularly characteristic of some species (a group of minerals that are chemically similar), such as the "fishtail" contact twins of gypsum, or the penetration twins of fluorite.

Center twinning

Twin plane

Area of intergrowth

ALBITE CONTACT TWIN

CARLSBAD PENETRATION TWIN (ORTHOCLASE)

ST. ANDREW'S CROSS
Staurolite commonly forms two types of penetration twin, both of which resemble crosses: a St. Andrew's Cross (left), and a 90-degree cross.

CYCLIC TWIN
A group of crystals that forms radially from a common center, as in this cerussite specimen, is called a cyclic twin.

Center of twinning

FISHTAIL TWIN
The selenite variety of the mineral gypsum sometimes forms "fishtail" contact twins.

Twin plane

FLUORITE TWINS
Many of the cubic crystals of fluorite in the cluster shown here are penetration twinned.

CRYSTAL SYSTEMS

CRYSTALS ARE CLASSIFIED INTO SIX DIFFERENT SYSTEMS according to the maximum symmetry of their faces. The systems are cubic, tetragonal, hexagonal and trigonal (regarded as a single system), monoclinic, orthorhombic, and triclinic. Each system is defined by the relative lengths and orientation of its three crystallographic axes (indicated by the letters a, b, and c if they are all of different lengths). These axes are imaginary lines that pass through the center of an ideal crystal. Crystal systems, and subgroups called classes, are also defined by the crystals' axes of symmetry (see pp.98–99). Crystals in any single crystal system can assume a variety of shapes. One shape is shown for each system below.

HESSONITE
The individual crystals of hessonite garnet in this cluster are in the cubic system.

CUBIC

Cubic crystals have three crystallographic axes at right angles and of equal length (a_1, a_2 and a_3), and four threefold axes of symmetry. The main forms within this system are: cube, octahedron, and rhombic dodecahedron. Minerals that crystallize in the cubic system include halite, copper, gold, silver, platinum, iron, fluorite, leucite, diamond, garnet, spinel, pyrite, galena, and magnetite. The cubic system is also sometimes known as the isometric system.

a_3 axis
a_1 axis
a_2 axis

Cubic habit

PYRITE CUBES
Pyrite crystals form commonly as cubes, but can also be found as pentagonal dodecahedra and octahedra, or combinations of all three forms.

TETRAGONAL

Tetragonal crystals have three crystallographic axes at right angles—two are equal in length (a_1 and a_2), and the third (c) is longer or shorter. They have one principal, fourfold axis of symmetry. Tetragonal crystals have the look of square prisms. Some of the minerals that crystallize in the tetragonal system are rutile, calomel, cassiterite, zircon, chalcopyrite, and wulfenite.

c axis
a_2 axis
a_1 axis

Pyramid face
Prism face

ZIRCON
Zircon forms tetragonal crystals. The terminations of this specimen are pyramidal.

Pyramid face

HEXAGONAL AND TRIGONAL

Some crystallographers consider that there are seven crystal systems rather than six, separating the hexagonal from the trigonal crystals. Both hexagonal and trigonal crystals have three crystallographic axes of equal length (a_1, a_2, and a_3) set at 120 degrees to one another, and a fourth (c), perpendicular to the plane of the other three axes. They differ from one another in that trigonal crystals have only threefold symmetry, whereas hexagonal crystals have sixfold symmetry. Minerals that crystallize in the hexagonal system include beryl (emerald and aquamarine) and apatite. Some of the minerals that crystallize in the trigonal system are calcite, quartz, and tourmaline.

c axis
a_1 axis
a_2 axis
a_3 axis

Hexagonal prism

APATITE
Apatite forms hexagonal-shaped prisms, and its overall symmetry is hexagonal.

TOURMALINE
Minerals in the tourmaline group form trigonal prisms.

MONOCLINIC

Monoclinic crystals have three crystallographic axes of unequal length. One (c) is at right angles to the other two (a and b); these two axes are not perpendicular to each other, although they are in the same plane. The crystals have one twofold axis of symmetry. More minerals crystallize in the monoclinic system than in any other. The term "monoclinic" means "one incline." Minerals that crystallize in the monoclinic system include gypsum, borax, orthoclase, muscovite, clinopyroxene, jadeite, azurite, malachite, orpiment, and realgar.

c axis
a axis
b axis

ORTHOCLASE
Crystals of orthoclase are common, usually with prismatic habit and often formed as twins as in this specimen.

Twinned crystal

Termination face at end of crystal

Prism face

GOLDEN BARITE
These orthorhombic crystals of golden barite are from the Barrick Goldstrike Mine in Elko, Nevada.

ORTHORHOMBIC

Crystals in the orthorhombic system have three crystallographic axes (a, b, and c) at right angles, all of which are unequal in length. The crystals have three twofold axes of symmetry. The name "orthorhombic" means "perpendicular parallelogram." Minerals that crystallize in the orthorhombic system include olivine, aragonite, topaz, marcasite, and barite.

c axis
a axis
b axis

Prismatic crystal

TOPAZ
Topaz often forms beautiful prismatic crystals, terminated by bipyramids or other prisms.

TRICLINIC

Triclinic crystals have the least symmetrical shape of all crystals. They have three crystallographic axes of unequal length (a, b, and c), which are inclined at angles of less than 90 degrees to one another. The orientation of a triclinic crystal is arbitrary. Minerals that crystallize in the triclinic system include albite, anorthite, kaolin, kyanite, and microcline.

c axis
a axis
b axis

KYANITE
Kyanite is an important triclinic mineral that often forms masses of blue, bladed crystals.

Bladed crystals

CRYSTAL HABITS

A COMPLETE DESCRIPTION of the external shape of a crystal is known as its habit. This description includes all the crystal's visible characteristics. It incorporates the names of the crystal's faces (for example, prismatic or pyramidal) and the name of its form (for example, cubic or octahedral). It also includes more general descriptive terms, such as bladed or dendritic. The description of crystal habit can relate to a single crystal, or to an assemblage of intergrown crystals, known as an aggregate. Various terms are used to describe aggregates, such as massive or radiating.

GLOBULAR
Aggregates of calcite crystals with a globular habit rest on top of tiny quartz crystals in this specimen.

NAMING CRYSTAL FACES
This example shows all three types of crystal faces and their relationship to the c axis.

c axis

Pinacoid face

Pyramid faces

Prism face

CRYSTAL FACES

There are three types of crystal faces: prism, pyramid, and pinacoid, which are determined by their relationship to the crystallographic axes. Prism faces are those parallel to the c axis; pyramid faces cut through the c axis at an angle; and pinacoid faces are at right angles to the c axis. A crystal may have numerous sets of pyramid faces, each at a different angle to the c axis, as well as major and minor prism faces, with edges parallel to each other. However, in most crystals some faces are more developed than others. As a crystal grows, the faces that grow most quickly eventually eliminate themselves, while those that grow more slowly become prominent. Where prism faces predominate in a crystal, the crystal habit may be described as prismatic; where pyramid faces predominate, it may be described as pyramidal; and where pinacoid faces predominate, the habit is described as platy. A face at the end of a crystal is called a termination face.

Prism face

Long prismatic habit

Pyramid face

Dipyramidal habit

Platy habit

PRISMATIC
In this long specimen of beryl, prism faces predominate. Its habit can therefore be described as long prismatic.

PYRAMIDAL
If pyramid faces dominate in both directions, as in this specimen of sapphire, the habit is dipyramidal.

PLATY
These yellow wulfenite crystals could be described as having a platy habit.

Wulfenite crystals

CRYSTAL FORMS

Some crystal habits derive their names purely from their crystal forms: for example, cubic, crystallizing in the form of cubes; dodecahedral, crystallizing in the form of dodecahedrons; and rhombohedral, crystallizing in the form of rhombohedrons. If crystals of one system crystallize in forms that appear to be the crystals of another system, the habit name is preceded by the word "pseudo." For example, if cyclic twins of orthorhombic aragonite appear to form hexagonal prisms, they are described as pseudohexagonal. If the terminations (end faces) of the crystal are different from each other, the habit is known as hemimorphic.

Cube face

Crystal forms as cube, with 6 plane faces

CUBIC
Crystals that form in the cubic system can take the form of perfect cubes, as in this pyrite specimen.

Crystal forms as octahedron, with 8 plane faces

OCTAHEDRAL
This magnetite specimen has crystallized as an octahedron, and can be described as having an octahedral habit.

Octahedron face

Garnet crystal

Crystal forms as dodecahedron, with 12 plane faces

DODECAHEDRAL
These garnets on schist have crystallized as dodecahedrons, and can be described as having a dodecahedral habit.

FIBROUS

A fibrous aggregate, such as this tremolite, consists of slender, parallel or radiating fibers.

Fibrous strands

AGGREGATES

Aggregates are groups of intimately associated crystals. They differ from clusters in that in crystal clusters there are a number of individuals growing together, but there is not an intimate intergrowth as in aggregates. The type of aggregation is often typical of the particular mineral species. Terms used to describe aggregates include: granular, fibrous, radiating, botryoidal, stalactitic, concentric, geode, oolitic, and massive.

STALACTITIC

Stalactitic minerals, such as this rare green aragonite from a cave in France, form in cylinders or cones resembling icicles.

BOTRYOIDAL

This hematite has formed in globular aggregates, resembling a bunch of grapes, and is described as botryoidal.

Globular

Radiating crystals

GEODE

A geode is a partially filled rock cavity lined by mineral material, such as agate or amethyst.

Aragonite crystal

CONCENTRIC

This rhodochrosite is a concentric aggregate, forming roughly spherical layers around a common center.

Concentric layers

RADIATING

The crystals of this malachite specimen radiate from a common center. Malachite can sometimes form starlike groups.

Massive habit

MASSIVE

A mass of crystals that cannot be seen individually makes up this massive specimen of dumortierite.

CRYSTAL APPEARANCE

Some crystal habits are descriptions of the general appearance of a crystal. For example, tabular is used to describe a crystal with predominantly large, flat, parallel faces; bladed describes elongated crystals flattened like a knife blade; and stalactitic describes crystal aggregates that have grown in the shape of a stalactite.

Lenticular crystals

Fernlike shape

LENTICULAR

The crystals of this selenite rose have formed in lens shapes, and are described as being lenticular.

LAMELLAR

These mica crystals are described as lamellar. They are flat, platelike individual crystals arranged in layers.

Layered crystals

DENDRITIC

Dendritic aggregates, such as this silver, form in slender, divergent, somewhat plantlike branches.

Long, thin crystals

BLADED

These kyanite crystals are elongated and flattened like knife blades. They have a bladed habit.

Flat crystals

ACICULAR

This mass of slender, radiating mesolite crystals can be described as acicular, meaning needlelike.

103

WHAT IS A GEMSTONE?

THE DEFINITION OF A GEMSTONE is broad: the term can be used to describe any mineral that is highly prized for its beauty, durability, and rarity. A gem is a mineral enhanced in some manner by altering its shape, usually by cutting and polishing. Most gems begin as crystals of minerals (such as diamonds or sapphires), or as aggregates of crystals (such as malachite or jadeite). A limited number of noncrystalline materials of organic origin (such as pearl and amber) are also classified as gemstones, and are usually referred to as organic gems.

ANTIQUE BROOCH
This finely made gold antique brooch is set with faceted diamonds and rubies, both precious gems.

STRING OF PEARLS
These beautiful and lustrous pink pearls were cultured in fresh water over several years before being polished and threaded into this lovely necklace.

THE BEAUTY OF GEMS

The prime requisite for a gem is that it must be beautiful. A gemstone can owe its beauty to various properties: its depth of color or transparency; its color pattern, as seen in opal or agate; the intensity of its brilliance; or the pattern light makes within it, as seen in star sapphires or cat's-eye chrysoberyl. It must also remain beautiful, withstanding wear and preserving its polish or other finish.

A number of otherwise beautiful gemstones are too soft or too brittle to wear, and are cut only for collectors. More than 4,000 minerals have been identified, but fewer than 100 are used as gemstones. Of these, only a minority are of major importance: diamond, corundum (sapphire and ruby), beryl (emerald and aquamarine), chrysoberyl, feldspars (sunstone, moonstone, and labradorite), garnets, jadeite and nephrite (jade), lazurite (lapis lazuli), olivines (peridot), opal, aragonite (pearl), quartz (in all its varieties), spinel, topaz, tourmalines, turquoise, and zircon. Gems are usually divided into two categories: precious and semiprecious. Diamond and the two color varieties of corundum, sapphire and ruby, are considered precious, as is the deep green variety of beryl, emerald.

HINDU WEDDING
Conspicuous display in the form of gem-encrusted jewelry is an essential part of the Hindu wedding ritual.

MOONSTONE EARRINGS
These contemporary earrings are set with moonstone cabochons, which exhibit a blue schiller or sheen.

SAPPHIRES
Although it is normally thought of as blue, the variety of corundum known as sapphire actually forms in a wide range of colors.

EARLY USES OF GEMS

The use of gemstones goes far back in human history: people were adorning themselves with shells, pieces of bone, teeth, and pebbles by at least the Upper Paleolithic period (25,000–12,000 BC). Bright colors or beautiful patterns drew people initially, and when the shaping of stones for adornment began, the stones chosen were opaque and soft. As the techniques of shaping improved— in essence, the first gem cutting—other, harder stones were employed. Carnelian and rock crystal beads, both varieties of quartz, which is relatively hard, were fashioned at Jarmo in Mesopotamia (now Iraq) in the 7th millennium BC.

The next technical leap in cutting also took place in Mesopotamia, with the engraving of cylinder seals: finger-sized, engraved stone cylinders used as a means of identifying goods. When the seal was rolled on damp clay, a unique imprint resulted. The cylinder seals were also valued as adornment and possibly a symbol of status. Records of the time are the first indicating the belief that stones themselves have a "mystic" value—beliefs that persist today in the wearing of birthstones and in New Age uses. The Egyptians, Babylonians, and Assyrians all believed that colored stones had healing properties. The choice of stones and other healing materials was dictated by the colors that the disease under treatment caused in the body: yellow jaundice, blue lips, or fever-red skin, for example. Other colored materials, such as plants, were considered equally effective, but stones retained their colors over time.

QUARTZ BEADS
These roughly shaped quartz beads from Ghana were threaded on a necklace and used by traders as a form of currency.

SUMERIAN EARRINGS
These gold and lapis lazuli earrings are from one of the graves in the Royal Cemetery of Ur, Iraq, and date from about 2500 BC.

FRESCO AT SIGIRIYA
The beautiful 6th-century frescoes in the temples of the fortress city of Sigiriya in central Sri Lanka illustrate some of the sumptuous jewels created during that period.

IRAQI CARNELIAN NECKLACE
This necklace comes from what is now Iraq and was made in about 2500 BC from lapis lazuli, carnelian, and etched carnelian.

SEAL AND IMPRINT
In ancient Mesopotamia, intricate cylinder seals (right) were carved from semiprecious stones, such as serpentine and amethyst. When rolled on damp clay (far right), the seal made an imprint that identified the owner.

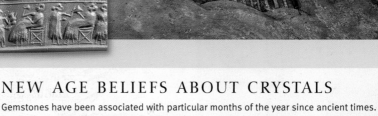

NEW AGE BELIEFS ABOUT CRYSTALS

Gemstones have been associated with particular months of the year since ancient times. In astrology, each of the 12 signs of the zodiac is associated with one or two gemstones, which are thought to resonate with the essential character of the person born under that sign, and consequently to bring the person luck. A hugely contentious subject between scientists and New Age practitioners is that of "crystal healing." Crystal healers claim that certain crystals—particularly quartz—give off "healing energy" when placed on the body, a claim contested by mineralogists, who recognize the impossibility of this given the minutely bound and intricately balanced energies that create a crystal in the first place. Yet anecdotal evidence from many sources suggests that when patients are treated by crystal healers, healing does occur in many instances. A new field of medical research suggests that the state of the immune system (and hence the state of health) is profoundly influenced by both conscious and unconscious mental and emotional factors. Perhaps it is the belief that the crystal will heal the body that causes it to heal, rather than the crystal itself.

JANUARY GARNET	FEBRUARY AMETHYST	MARCH AQUAMARINE	APRIL DIAMOND
MAY EMERALD	JUNE PEARL	JULY RUBY	AUGUST PERIDOT
SEPTEMBER SAPPHIRE	OCTOBER OPAL	NOVEMBER TOPAZ	DECEMBER TURQUOISE

BIRTHSTONES
The particular birthstones associated with each month vary from country to country and from one decade to the next. A modern European set of associations is shown here.

HEALING CRYSTALS
New Age practitioners believe that crystals have healing powers when placed against the body. This belief can be traced back to the ancient Egyptians, Babylonians, and Assyrians.

GEM MINING

MINING TECHNIQUES AND OPERATIONS have varied little over the millennia until very recent times. In common with other types of mining, gems are recovered in one of two ways: from the rocks in which they formed; and in weathered rock debris where they have been released from their original rock. The first type is often called "hard–rock" mining; the second is called placer mining. Gemstone mining of both kinds can be done by an individual or by huge corporations. Many gem mines have consisted of no more than a few individuals working cooperatively.

MOUNT MICA
The tourmaline deposit at Mount Mica, Maine, has produced thousands of carats of gem tourmaline (see p.288).

HARD–ROCK MINING

Gemstone deposits form in several different geological environments. Perhaps the best known are the "pipes" of kimberlite from which most diamonds are recovered (see p.41). Solid kimberlite is mined by the usual hard-rock methods of drilling and blasting. The rock is then crushed, and the diamonds extracted, sorted, and graded.

Diamonds are also found in lamproite pipes. The first commercial extraction of diamond from lamproite rock was at the Argyle Mine in Western Australia. Diamonds found in nearby placer deposits in 1979 led to the discovery of the lamproite pipe, and the mine opened in 1985. Argyle is an open-pit operation producing more diamonds than any other operation in the world. Placer deposits there are almost exhausted, and most diamonds are extracted from the solid rock. About 5 percent are gem quality, and they include 90–95 percent of the world's natural pink diamonds. These are sold by tender for as much as $100,000 per carat.

Many other gems are also sufficiently concentrated in their original rock to be mined economically. Among these are various quartz varieties, tourmaline, topaz, opal, emerald, aquamarine, some sapphire and ruby, turquoise, lapis lazuli, and chrysoberyl. Few of these require—or are valuable enough to justify—the extensive and expensive methods of mining diamond pipes. Even the largest pegmatite deposits, which are a rich source of gemstones and other valuable minerals, rarely warrant highly mechanized extraction operations, such as the one used to extract tourmaline at Mount Mica (see above). Most are worked by hand using basic tools. Drilling and blasting are avoided for most gems, because they are shock-sensitive. Additionally, many gem veins are in deteriorated rock, and the veins are often deteriorated themselves. In these deposits, mining is done with little more than a pick and shovel.

DRILLING KIMBERLITE PIPES
Kimberlite that has not deteriorated through weathering is a hard rock that has to be drilled and blasted. Vast quantities of rock are processed in the search for diamonds.

SIBERIAN DIAMOND MINE
The kimberlite in this Siberian diamond pipe is deeply weathered, permitting open-pit mining operations.

PLACER MINING

Because many gemstones are hard, dense, and impervious to chemical weathering, once released by weathering they can be carried considerable distances by water to concentrate in river beds, beaches, and on the ocean floor. These concentrations are called placer deposits.

Placer mining uses techniques that mimic the creation of the placer in the first place: the separation of the denser minerals—including the gemstones—in running water. The simplest method is panning (see right). In sieving, the separated denser minerals end up in the center of the sieve, and the gemstones are hand-sorted from this concentrate. Another method is to run gravel through a trough of flowing water with baffles on the bottom. The lighter material is washed away, and the denser gemstones are retained by the baffles. Jade and some quartz gemstones can be found by people simply walking up

SAPPHIRE GRAVELS
These sapphires were recovered from stream gravels in Montana by placer mining.

PANNING
In Sri Lanka and Laos, rubies and sapphires are mined by scooping up gravel in pans or baskets and hand-washing it to separate out the gems.

and down river beds or across deserts and picking up material from the surface. Some of the most productive diamond placers occur where diamond-bearing gravels have been dumped into the sea at the mouths of rivers, and then redistributed by wave action along beaches. Within recent decades, new underwater mining techniques have permitted the large-scale exploitation of sea-floor diamond deposits (see p.123).

SAND SHIFTING, NAMIBIA
In large-scale operations, such as the beaches of Namibia, earth-movers shift millions of tons of sand, recovering tens of thousands of carats of diamonds from the bedrock.

SORTING AND GRADING

After drilling and crushing rock containing diamonds, the diamonds are recovered using grease tables. Crushed kimberlite is wetted and made to flow in water across a sloping table covered with thick grease. The wet rock particles do not stick, but the dry diamonds do (water does not stick to diamonds). Periodically, the diamond-covered grease is scraped from the table, and the grease is removed from the diamonds before they are sent for sorting and grading.

Grease tables are sometimes used in the recovery of placer diamonds as well. In the simplest placer operations, the gemstones are first concentrated by placer mining methods, and then picked out by eye.

GREASE TABLE
The table is coated with grease, to which only the dry diamonds stick.

ROUGH DIAMONDS
Uncut diamonds such as these are graded according to their properties, such as color and clarity.

AFGHANISTAN
The mountains of Afghanistan have been producing gemstones for at least 7,000 years.

ANCIENT MINING

The mining of precious stones has a long history: lapis lazuli was mined at Badakhshan, Afghanistan, up to 7,000 years ago, and turquoise mining on the Sinai Peninsula began around 5,000 years ago. At about the same time, the Egyptians were mining emeralds near Aswan. Gemstones were widely valued commodities and were traded over long distances: for example, lapis lazuli from Badakhshan reached Egypt before 3000 BC, and China, India, and Greece by 2500 BC. Baltic amber was traded all around the Mediterranean, and Egyptian emeralds are found in Roman jewelry. With the conquests of Alexander the Great (356–323 BC), trade from the East increased, as did the number of gemstones available. In North and South America, turquoise was extensively mined in pre-Columbian times.

MINING AND CUTTING TECHNIQUES

Ancient miners were far from inefficient—some of their methods are still used today. Panning and basket-sieving of stream gravels have changed little. Digging into decomposed gem veins differs only in the tools used: antler picks were used in ancient times rather than steel. When copper and bronze tools came into use in the 2nd century BC, true hard-rock mining was possible. Emeralds were mined at Cleopatra's mines from 1500 BC (see p.293). Gem cutting differed little in principle from cutting today: the gem was abraded on a series of stones of greater and greater hardness, becoming ever finer in grain size.

EGYPTIAN GOLDSMITHS
Goldsmiths weigh and smelt gold, and present jewelry in this wall painting in the tomb of sculptors Nebamun and Ipuky (c. 1390–36 BC).

ANCIENT MASTERPIECE
This scarab pectoral from the tomb of Tutankhamun (c. 1361–52 BC) is inlaid with gold, lapis lazuli, carnelian, and other semiprecious gems.

MEGAGEMS

THE SMITHSONIAN INSTITUTION'S NATIONAL GEM COLLECTION CONTAINS SOME OF THE LARGEST, FINEST, AND MOST BEAUTIFUL GEMSTONES EVER FOUND. THEY ARE HOUSED AT THE NATIONAL MUSEUM OF NATURAL HISTORY IN WASHINGTON, DC.

The term "megagem," although not an official one, nonetheless represents a group of gemstones that stand out from others of their type in size and beauty. Many gems in the Smithsonian's National Gem Collection take their names from people who donated them to the collection, or who once figured in their histories. Some have no name, but are no less remarkable.

But what makes a gem a megagem? The first consideration for many is the gem's size, but in the case of very common materials, such as fluorite or calcite, large gems may also be commonplace. In such instances, the megagems are large but also particularly high-quality examples that best represent their type of mineral. The second consideration in defining a megagem is the gem's value, which may not be governed by size. The Blue Heart Diamond (see right) is small in comparison with the fluorite or the calcite gems also shown, but it is thousands of times more valuable. Rarity is a key factor. Intensely blue diamonds are seldom found, and those attaining the size, and also the shape, of the Blue Heart are much rarer still. Thus a relatively small stone cut from a very rare material is a megagem, whereas a larger stone cut from a more common material still may not be. All the stones illustrated here are highly prized, and therefore valuable, megagems in that they represent superb examples, both in size and quality, of their respective gemstone species.

Diamond consists of almost pure carbon

Cut draws out gem's natural heart shape

AMERICAN GOLDEN TOPAZ
At 22,892.5 carats, this 10.1-lb (4.6-kg) topaz (center) was cut from a Brazilian cobble in the late 1980s. Alongside it are two of the largest high-quality topaz crystals ever found, also from Brazil.

Pear-shaped cut

GROSSULAR GARNET
Just one of 15 minerals known as garnet, grossular may be pink, orange, red-orange, yellow, brown, or green. This 30-carat specimen was found in Sri Lanka in 1991.

Iron causes green coloring

Many facets

Beveled square cut

Fine facets

PERIDOT
This 311.8-carat peridot from Zabargad, Egypt, is one of the largest peridot gems known. Peridot is the gem variety of the mineral forsterite. The green coloring is caused by iron; the more iron, the deeper the color.

HELIODORE
The common name for heliodore is golden beryl. There are larger known examples than this 216-carat stone, but few can rival the beauty of its color or the brilliance of its cut. It came from Minas Gerais, Brazil.

HOOKER EMERALD
Weighing 75.47 carats, the Hooker Emerald is unusually flawless for an emerald of its size. Mined in Colombia and taken to Europe in the 17th century by the conquistadores, it was donated by Mrs. J. A. Hooker in 1977.

CALCITE
The normally soft and fragile structure of calcite restricts its use as a gemstone. Originating in Balmat, New York, this specimen weighs 1,800 carats and is probably the world's finest calcite gem.

Composition
of silicon and
oxygen makes
sphere
colorless

QUARTZ SPHERE
Fashioned in China in 1923–24 from a crystal probably found in Burma, this is the world's largest known flawless quartz sphere. It is 13 in (33 cm) in diameter.

Boron atoms impart
blue coloring

FLUORITE
A magnificent stone, this blue fluorite gem weighs 3,965.3 carats and was found in Hardin County, Illinois. No larger fluorite gem is known to exist.

Light from base
of gem

BLUE HEART DIAMOND
At 30.82 carats, the Blue Heart Diamond is somewhat smaller than the 45.52-carat Hope Diamond (see pp.124–25), but it has a unique character. It was cut in Paris in 1909–10, probably having originated in South Africa. Like the Hope Diamond, it owes its blue color to the presence of a tiny percentage of boron atoms.

Gem-quality
crystal

Trace vanadium
imparts violet-blue

Bright band

IMPERIAL TOPAZ
The 93.6-carat imperial topaz (below) is from Ouro Preto, Brazil. Topaz is famous for its ability to grow huge crystals of gem quality. The large crystal at left, also from Ouro Preto, weighs 875.4 carats.

TANZANITE
The gem variety of the mineral zoisite, this stone from Tanzania weighs 122.7 carats. A mirror shows its strong pleochroism—that is, its quality of presenting different colors when viewed from different directions.

MAHARANI CAT'S EYE
Found in Sri Lanka, the Maharani Cat's Eye weighs 58.2 carats. Cat's eye is a variety of chrysoberyl and is named after the bright, vertical band of many specimens, caused by light reflecting off titanium oxide crystals.

WITWATERSRAND, SOUTH AFRICA
Witwatersrand means "ridge of white waters." Its fabulously rich gold deposits occur in conglomerate beds.

MIXTEC PENDANT
This gold pendant of a Mexican deity was crafted by the Mixtecs of ancient Mexico.

ALFRED JEWEL
Made for Alfred the Great in the 9th century AD, the Alfred Jewel is a reading pointer of gold, enamel, and rock crystal.

SNAKE ARMLET
This pure gold armlet was found in the ruined Roman city of Pompeii, Italy. It was crafted between the 1st century BC and the 1st century AD.

GOLD

THROUGHOUT HUMAN HISTORY, gold has been the most prized of metals. Its color and brightness are highly attractive, it is extremely malleable, and it is usually found in nature in a relatively pure form—all qualities that have made it exceptionally valuable. It is also remarkably inert, and neither bonds nor reacts with most chemicals, so resists tarnishing. People have been using gold for at least 6,000 years, since the civilizations of ancient Egypt and Mesopotamia. In ancient times, gold was almost exclusively recovered from river and stream gravels—placer deposits—where particles of gold weathered from its original rock were concentrated.

SOURCES OF GOLD

Gold is rarely found in well-formed octahedral and dodecahedral crystals, but more commonly it occurs as dendritic growths, and as grains and scaly masses. Crystals about 1 in (2.5 cm) across have been found in California, and masses of over 200 lb (90 kg) have been recovered in Australia. Virtually all igneous rocks contain gold in low concentrations, where it occurs mostly as invisible, disseminated grains. Within Earth's crust, its abundance is estimated at about 0.005 parts per million. Because gold does not easily bond with other elements, there are only a few relatively rare gold-bearing minerals, in which it combines with tellurium and selenium.

One unusually rich concentration of these gold minerals was discovered at the famous gold-rush town of Cripple Creek, Colorado. Large masses of rock rich enough to mine only for the gold are rare, but fall into two

EGYPTIAN AMULET
This ancient Egyptian amulet in the form of the eye of Horus is crafted from gold, lapis lazuli, and enamel.

EGYPTIAN GOLD
Gold was a highly valued metal in ancient Egypt, worked with great skill. This relief (right) from the Tomb of Rekhmire depicts workers engraving and polishing gold and silver vases (c. 1567–1320 BC).

SCALES OF GOLD
This specimen of native gold is from Baita, Transylvania, Romania. The gold has formed as thin plates set in a groundmass of quartz. Gold is also often found in association with sulfides.

Scaly gold

GOLD RUSHES

PANNING FOR GOLD
The gold pan is a prospector's tool. Panning is a slow but thorough method.

The enormous gold discoveries in the western US and Australia in the 1840s and 1850s—aside from creating more destitution than wealth among the miners in general—poured so much gold into the world marketplace that all but a few countries decided to use their gold reserves to back their currencies. Concerning the situation of the average miner and prospector, two sayings emerged: "more money goes into the ground than ever comes out," and "the way to make a small fortune in mining is to start with a large one"! Two positive benefits (except perhaps for the native inhabitants of gold rush areas) were that the population shifts that accompanied the gold rushes opened new areas for agriculture, and that other valuable minerals were discovered aside from gold.

GOLD GRAINS
Most gold recovered from river and stream placers is in the form of scales and grains.

NEVADA GOLD RUSH
In 1902 a major gold rush occurred in Nevada after discoveries were made at a place later called Goldfield.

Massive quartz

types: hydrothermal veins, where it is associated with quartz and pyrite (fool's gold); and placer deposits. Some placer deposits are unconsolidated, and the gold there can be recovered by panning. Smaller quantities of gold often occur in copper and lead deposits, where it is recovered as a byproduct in the refining of those metals.

The principal ancient sources of gold were southern Egypt and Nubia (Sudan). Major sources in Europe during the Middle Ages were the mines of Saxony and Austria. The largest single gold-ore body known to the modern world is in South Africa's Witwatersrand. Half the planet's known gold reserves are in South Africa, with other large deposits in Russia, Brazil, Canada, Australia, and the US.

THE COLOR OF GOLD

In its native state, gold is always golden-yellow, but it is too soft in its pure state to wear well. To increase its hardness for use in jewelry, gold is alloyed with other metals. Pale or white gold results when silver, platinum, nickel, or zinc are added. Copper yields red or pink gold, and iron gives a blue tinge. The purity of alloyed gold is expressed as its carat (Ct) value, defined as the proportion of pure gold metal present. Twenty-four carats equates to 100 percent gold. So a piece of gold jewelry labeled "9-carat" is 9 parts out of 24 (37 percent) pure gold.

GOLD IN INDUSTRY

By far the most popular use of gold is in jewelry, but it has important industrial applications as well. It has high electrical conductivity (71 percent that of copper) and is chemically inert, so it finds an important application in the electronics industry for plating contacts, terminals, printed circuits, and semiconductor systems. The salvaging of obsolete computer electronics for their gold content has become a major recycling enterprise. Thin films of gold no more than a single atom thick reflect up to 98 percent of incident infrared radiation. These have been employed on satellites to control temperature and on space-suit visors to afford protection. Large office buildings often have their windows similarly coated, reducing the need for air-conditioning. Gold compounds also have important uses. Sodium aurichloride is used in the treatment of rheumatoid arthritis, and gold mercaptide compound is used for decorating china and glass articles.

GOLD WINDOWS
A thin gold coating on window glass in hot climates reduces the need for air-conditioning.

SATELLITE
Gold coatings on satellite components are vital for temperature control.

"What do you not drive **human hearts** into, cursed **craving** for **gold**!"

VIRGIL, AENEID

HABITS OF GOLD
Gold occurs in several habits: as crystalline masses, as flat plates, and as nuggets and grains recovered from stream and river placers.

GOLD CRYSTALS

FLAT GOLD PLATES

PROPERTIES

GROUP	Native elements
CRYSTAL SYSTEM	Cubic
COMPOSITION	Au
COLOR	Golden-yellow
FORM/HABIT	Octahedral, dodecahedral, dendritic
HARDNESS	2½–3
CLEAVAGE	None
FRACTURE	Hackly
LUSTRE	Metallic
STREAK	Golden-yellow
SPECIFIC GRAVITY	19.3
TRANSPARENCY	Opaque

Other mineralization in quartz

Actual size of nugget

LARGE GOLD NUGGET IN SMITHSONIAN COLLECTION

EGYPTIAN GOLD

A SYMBOL OF THE SUN IN A CULTURE THAT WORSHIPED THE SUN GOD RA, GOLD WAS HIGHLY PRIZED BY THE ANCIENT EGYPTIANS, WHO USED IT FOR ADORNMENT IN LIFE AND DEATH.

TUTANKHAMUN'S SECOND GOLD COFFIN
Each of the three gold coffins is inlaid with lapis lazuli, turquoise, and carnelian, and shows Tutankhamun in the form of Osiris, god of the dead.

GOLDEN THRONE
Tutankhamun's wooden throne is overlaid with gold and inlaid with lapis lazuli, carnelian, and turquoise. Depicted on the back of the throne is Queen Ankhesenamun as she adjusts the king's clothing.

VULTURE COLLAR
Found around the neck of Tutankhamun's mummy, this gold collar contains 250 inlaid segments of glass and obsidian. Each claw grasps a "shen," a symbol of totality.

In 1924 English archeologist Howard Carter (1874–1939) lifted the lid of the last shrine in the burial chamber in the tomb of Tutankhamun. He removed the layers of linen shrouds and "a golden effigy of the young boy-king of most magnificent workmanship, filled the whole interior of the sarcophagus!" This coffin proved to be the outermost of three. The third and final coffin was made of 243 lb (110 kg) of solid gold. Within this final coffin lay the mummy of Tutankhamun, his face covered with a superb mask of gold inlaid with lapis lazuli and colored glass. The tomb as a whole contained the greatest treasure ever discovered by an archaeologist.

The ancient Egyptians had prized gold and deeply colored precious stones long before the reign of Tutankhamun (18th dynasty—539–1292 BC). They probably first came across nuggets of gold in the waters of the Nile, where they had been washed downstream from the mountains of Nubia (modern Sudan). Gold, silver, and copper artifacts were discovered in the predynastic graves of Naqada near Nubt, which was a trading center for gold from about 3100 BC. *Nub* is the Egyptian word for "gold." From the beginning of the Old Kingdom (2575–2134 BC), pharaohs sent expeditions to Nubia to mine the quartz lodes there for gold. They sank deep shafts into the rock and lit fires around the quartz to shatter it. Then they crushed it, extracting the gold within. The mines were exhausted by the late 18th dynasty, and the Egyptians were then forced to mine the much harder rocks of the eastern desert for gold.

Virtually indestructible and highly malleable, gold was either hammered into shape while cold or melted and then cast. Goldsmiths' workshops were strictly controlled by the vizier on behalf of the pharaoh, and any gold objects made there belonged to him. By the fourth dynasty (c. 2575–2465 BC), gold was worked into vessels, furniture, and funerary equipment, and sophisticated jewelry, such as settings, chains, chokers, and armlets, was created. Precious stones such as lapis lazuli, turquoise, and carnelian were favored for inlay work, beads and cabachons, which were mounted in gold settings. Broad collars and earrings were made from the Middle Kingdom (2040–1640 BC) onward. Elaborate and heavy pectorals were created in the New Kingdom (1550–1070 BC). Worn by men as well as women from this time, earrings were stud-mounted for use in pierced ear lobes.

TUTANKHAMUN'S GOLD FUNERARY MASK
The magnificent gold funerary mask of Tutankhamun was inlaid with strips of lapis lazuli and colored glass. The gold symbolized Ra, the sun god, and the lapis lazuli represented the god Horus, who, it was believed, guided the dead through the underworld.

HOPE DIAMOND

WEIGHING 45.52 CARATS, THE HOPE DIAMOND IS AN EXCEEDINGLY RARE GEMSTONE. IT ALSO HAS A FASCINATING AND MYSTERIOUS HISTORY.

The Hope diamond was probably discovered at the Kollur Mine in the Golconda area of India. Precisely when it was found is not known, but a French gem merchant, Jean-Baptiste Tavernier, sold a 112-carat blue diamond from India to King Louis XIV of France in 1668. It was recut from its original Indian-style cut to a 67-carat, more brilliant heart shape in 1673. In 1749, Louis XV had the stone—now known as the French Blue—set into a piece of ceremonial jewelry for the Order of the Golden Fleece, a decoration worn only by the King.

During the French Revolution in 1792, the Hope diamond disappeared. Then, in 1812, a London jeweler, John Francillon, noted a 44-carat (45.5 modern metric carats) blue diamond in the possession of London diamond merchant Daniel Eliason. This diamond was probably cut from the French Blue.

MARIE ANTOINETTE
In this portrait of Marie Antoinette (1750–93), the wife of Louis XVI may be wearing the French Blue on her bust.

FROM FRENCH BLUE TO HOPE

The diamond again mysteriously disappeared until 1820, when it was bought by the British King George IV. In the King's possession at the time of his death in 1830, it was purchased by a London banker and gem collector, Henry Philip Hope, whose name it bears today. After Hope's death in 1839, the diamond passed through several hands, until bought in 1909 by Pierre Cartier. He in turn sold it to Evalyn Walsh McLean in 1910 for $180,000. He told her that the diamond brought bad luck to anyone who wore it, but this was probably because she had told him that she felt objects that were bad luck for others were good luck for her. Mrs. McLean wore the Hope diamond everywhere she went. Two years after her death in 1947, her entire collection of jewelry was purchased by New York jeweler Harry Winston. On November 10, 1958, he presented the diamond to the Smithsonian Institution as the foundation of a National Gem Collection. It arrived in a plain brown package by registered mail, insured for $1 million. The diamond has remained on continuous exhibition there ever since.

White cushion-cut diamond

Antique brilliant-cut blue diamond

FRONT AND BACK
The Hope diamond measures 1 in (25.6 mm) long by 4/5 in (21.8 mm) wide. An asymmetrical cushion antique brilliant cut, it is a fancy diamond with 58 facets plus two extra facets on the pavilion and additional facets on the girdle.

OLD DIAMOND IN A NEW SETTING
The Hope diamond's present-day setting was designed by Pierre Cartier in 1920. The gem is in a platinum setting surrounded by 16 pear-shaped and cushion-cut diamonds, and suspended from a chain of 45 diamonds.

1

SULFIDES

SULFIDE MINERALS ARE THOSE in which sulfur is combined with one or more metals. They tend to have simple structures, highly symmetrical crystal forms, and many of the properties of metals, including metallic luster and electrical conductivity. Many of the sulfides are brilliantly colored, and most have low hardness and high specific gravity. They are the ore minerals of most metals used by industry, such as antimony, bismuth, and copper, and are also an important source of gold, silver, and platinum. Sulfides occur in all rock types, and most are quite common. Related mineral families are the selenides, tellurides, antimonides, and arsenides. In these families, selenium, tellurium, antimony, and arsenic, respectively, combine with metals or semimetals. These mineral families tend to occur in association with sulfide minerals, and most are relatively rare.

Sulfur atom

Copper or iron atom

BORNITE CRYSTAL STRUCTURE
Bornite is a compound of copper, iron, and sulfur. The copper, iron, and sulfur atoms combine to form tetrahedra. The copper and iron atoms take the same places in the structure in relation to the sulfur atoms. Their ratio can vary widely in different specimens.

ACANTHITE

ZACATECAS
Acanthite is found in this Mexican state.

ACANTHITE TAKES ITS NAME from the Greek *akantha*, meaning "thorn," a reference to the spiky appearance of some of its crystals. It is a form of silver sulfide. Above 350°F (177°C), silver sulfide crystallizes in the cubic system, and it used to be assumed that cubic silver sulfide—known as argentite—was a separate mineral from acanthite. It is now known that they are the same mineral, with acanthite crystallizing in the monoclinic system at lower temperatures. Acanthite is the most important ore of silver. It forms in hydrothermal veins with native silver, pyrargyrite, proustite, and other sulfides such as galena. It also forms as a secondary alteration product of primary silver sulfides. It occurs in most silver deposits, including the Harz Mountains, Germany; and Kongsberg, Norway.

SILVER FEATHER
This modern American Indian piece features a silver feather with turquoise beads.

COMSTOCK LODE

The Comstock Lode was an immensely rich silver deposit that was discovered in Nevada in June 1859. It was so rich that a branch of the US mint was established at nearby Carson City to coin its output. However, by 1882, the deposit was exhausted, and its pit was flooded. The lode was formed by a shallow type of hydrothermal deposit, known as an epithermal deposit. As well as acanthite, other important silver-bearing minerals, stephanite and pyrargyrite, were found there.

COMSTOCK MINE
The mine was named for Henry Comstock, part-owner of the property on which it was discovered.

Metallic luster

Uneven fracture

Darkened, weathered surface

SILVER BUCKLE
This silver belt buckle has a central turquoise surrounded by a design stamped in the silver.

PSEUDOMORPH
This specimen is an argentite pseudomorph with the outward form of cubic symmetry.

Pseudomorphic cubic form

PROPERTIES

GROUP	Sulfides
CRYSTAL SYSTEM	Monoclinic
COMPOSITION	Ag_2S
COLOR	Black
FORM/HABIT	Pseudocubic
HARDNESS	2–2½
CLEAVAGE	Indistinct
FRACTURE	Subconchoidal, sectile
LUSTER	Metallic
STREAK	Black
SPECIFIC GRAVITY	7.2–7.4
TRANSPARENCY	Opaque

CHALCOCITE

ONE OF THE MOST important ores of copper, chalcocite is usually massive, but on rare occasions, it occurs in short prismatic or tabular crystals, or as pseudohexagonal prisms formed by twinning. The name chalcocite is derived from the Greek word for copper. Old names for chalcocite are chalcosine, copper glace, and redruthite (an allusion to its occurrence at Redruth, Cornwall, England), but all are now obsolete.

Chalcocite belongs to a group of sulfide minerals formed at relatively low temperatures, often as alteration products of other copper minerals such as bornite (see p.128). Concentrated in secondary alteration zones, it can yield more copper than the element's primary deposits. These alteration zones are often hydrothermal veins with minerals such as bornite, quartz, calcite, covellite, chalcopyrite, galena, and sphalerite in addition to chalcocite.

CORNWALL, ENGLAND
Cornwall has been a storehouse of minerals that have been mined for three millennia. Excellent chalcocite crystals were extracted and used here.

Lead-gray color

Indistinct cleavage

Metallic luster

INDUSTRIAL USES OF COPPER

Most copper is used for electrical applications. The windings of massive electrical generators are made of copper, as are the millions of miles of transmission lines. Most telephone calls worldwide still go through copper wires. Massive copper-alloy propellers drive ships, and aircraft are made from duralumin, an aluminum-copper alloy. Copper is also used in smaller but important applications such as roofing and cladding, brewer's vats, water and gas valves, copper-alloy fittings for water and gas pipes, and often for the pipes themselves. It would not be an exaggeration to say that the modern industrial age would be virtually impossible without copper. Copper also has many domestic uses (see p.128).

COPPER WIRE
Most copper goes for electrical applications.

COPPER ROOFING
Copper's malleability allows it to be used for curves.

SMELTING COPPER
Sparks fly in a foundry in Krasnoyarsk, Russia, during the smelting of copper.

PROPERTIES

GROUP	Sulfides
CRYSTAL SYSTEM	Monoclinic
COMPOSITION	Cu_2S
COLOR	Blackish lead-gray
FORM/HABIT	Short prismatic, thick tabular
HARDNESS	$2\frac{1}{2}$–3
CLEAVAGE	Indistinct
FRACTURE	Conchoidal
LUSTER	Metallic
STREAK	Blackish lead-gray
SPECIFIC GRAVITY	5.5–5.8
TRANSPARENCY	Opaque

Chalcocite itself alters to native copper and other copper ores. Superbly crystallized specimens have come from the Ural Mountains of Russia, and Cornwall, England. The Cornish deposits have been worked since the Bronze Age. Valuable ore deposits occur in the US in Ely, Nevada, Morenci, Arizona, and Butte, Montana; and excellent crystals are found in Bristol, Connecticut. Chalcocite is also found in Australia, Chile, the Czech Republic, Norway, Peru, Russia, and Spain.

MASSIVE CHALCOCITE
This specimen of typically massive chalcocite is from Khusib Springs Mine, Otavi, Namibia.

Prismatic crystal

Metallic luster

Pseudohexagonal crystals

Dolomite groundmass

LONG PRISMATIC CRYSTALS

CHALCOCITE CRYSTALS
These specimens show two forms of relatively rare chalcocite crystals.

SHORT PRISMATIC CRYSTALS

127

BORNITE

ONE OF NATURE'S MOST COLORFUL minerals, bornite is a copper iron sulfide, and a major ore of copper. It can show iridescent purple, blue, and red splashes of color on broken, tarnished faces, resulting in its common name, "peacock ore." Its formal mineral name comes from the Austrian mineralogist Ignaz von Born (1742–1791). Other informal names are "purple copper ore" and "variegated copper ore."

Bornite crystals are relatively uncommon, but when found they are pseudocubic, dodecahedral, or octahedral, frequently with curved or rough faces, although bornite is more often compact, granular, or massive. Its natural color can be coppery red, coppery brown, or bronze. It alters readily upon weathering to chalcocite (see p.127) and other copper minerals. Bornite forms principally in hydrothermal veins, with minerals such as quartz, chalcopyrite, marcasite, and pyrite. It also forms in some silica-poor intrusives, pegmatite veins, and contact metamorphic zones. Major deposits of bornite occur in Tasmania, Chile, Peru, Kazakhstan, Canada, and in Arizona and in Butte, Montana. Good-quality crystals are found in deposits in England.

TASMANIA
The large island of Tasmania, which lies off the southeastern coast of Australia, is a source of numerous minerals, including bornite.

PROPERTIES

GROUP Sulfides

CRYSTAL SYSTEM Tetragonal

COMPOSITION Cu_5FeS_4

COLOR Coppery red, brown

FORM/HABIT Usually massive

HARDNESS 3

CLEAVAGE Poor

FRACTURE Uneven to conchoidal, brittle

LUSTER Metallic

STREAK Pale grayish-black

SPECIFIC GRAVITY 5.1

TRANSPARENCY Opaque

BORNITE CRYSTALS
This group of well-developed bornite crystals shows both curved and rough crystal faces.

Iridescent surface

Massive habit

Purple oxidation

DOMESTIC USES OF COPPER

Copper and its alloys surround us in our everyday lives. It is highly durable, can be easily formed by casting, drawing, pressing, and forging, and is an unsurpassed conductor of heat and electricity. At home, our electricity flows along copper wires, and water flows through copper pipes and out through copper-alloy faucets. Water heaters have coils made from copper, and most are copper lined. Most domestic appliances have copper somewhere in their construction. Pots and pans made entirely of copper or with a copper base provide even heating. Many of the coins in our pockets are made of copper or copper alloy. Gold jewelry usually has copper alloyed with the gold to give it durability. Even getting into your house relies on copper—most keys and locks are made of copper alloys. Copper is also widely used in industry (see p.127).

RADIATOR COIL
Copper is an unseen component of many domestic appliances.

BRACELET
Copper bracelets are worn by many to relieve the pain of arthritis.

"Gold is for the mistress—silver for the maid— **Copper** for the craftsman, cunning at his **trade**"

RUDYARD KIPLING,
"COLD IRON"

MASSIVE BORNITE
This specimen of massive, tarnished bornite with yellow chalcopyrite, found in Russia, shows the rich oxidation colors that give it the names "purple copper ore" and "peacock ore."

Uneven fracture

SPHALERITE

SPHALERITE TAKES ITS NAME from the Greek *sphaleros*, meaning "treacherous," referring to its tendency to occur in a number of forms, which can be mistaken for other minerals, especially galena (see p.130). Red or reddish-brown transparent crystals are sometimes called ruby zinc or ruby blende, and opaque black crystals have sometimes been referred to as black jack. Although these are not formal mineral names, they can still be seen on labels in old collections. Sphalerite is also called blende from the German word for "blind," a name alluding to the fact that sphalerite does not yield lead.

Well-crystallized specimens are common in most zinc deposits. Iron may also be present in sphalerite, and can make up a quarter of its metallic content. Sphalerite is the most common zinc mineral and the principal ore of zinc; it is found associated with galena in most important lead-zinc deposits. It occurs in hydrothermal vein deposits, contact metamorphic zones, and high-temperature replacement deposits, where it is also associated with chalcopyrite and pyrite. Sphalerite is also found in minor amounts in meteorites and lunar rock. There are important deposits in the Mississippi River valley and in Canada, Mexico, Spain, and Russia.

Sphalerite is cut only as an unusual collectors' stone since it is notoriously difficult to cut into faceted gems because of its softness and tendency to cleave.

MISSISSIPPI RIVER VALLEY
One of the most abundant deposits of sphalerite is found where the states of Missouri, Arkansas, and Kansas meet.

PROPERTIES

GROUP Sulfides

CRYSTAL SYSTEM Cubic

COMPOSITION ZnS

COLOR Brown, black, yellow

FORM/HABIT Tetrahedral, dodecahedral

HARDNESS 3–4

CLEAVAGE Perfect in six directions

FRACTURE Conchoidal

LUSTER Resinous to adamantine, metallic

STREAK Brownish to light yellow

SPECIFIC GRAVITY 3.9–4.1

TRANSPARENCY Opaque to transparent

R.I. 2.36–2.37

Resinous luster

MASSIVE SPHALERITE

Pale dolomite and rock groundmass

Sphalerite crystals

CRYSTALLINE SPHALERITE

Sphalerite crystals

CRYSTALS IN MATRIX

SPHALERITE VARIETIES
Sphalerite is found in a variety of different habits and colors, including a red "ruby blende" (right).

Dark red crystals

RUBY BLENDE SPHALERITE

Quartz

Sphalerite crystal

Resinous luster

SPHALERITE CRYSTALS
These superbly formed sphalerite crystals, with pyrite and quartz, are from Casapalca, Lima, Peru.

Pyrite

Quartz

USES OF ZINC

Sphalerite is the principal ore of zinc. Zinc is used mainly for galvanizing iron and steel, in alloy with copper to make brass, and in alloys to make die casts (metal molds). Zinc oxide is used in the production of phosphors for TV tubes and fluorescent lamps, in cosmetics, plastics, paints, and printing inks, and as a catalyst in the manufacture of synthetic rubber.

DIE PRODUCTION
Zinc is a major metal used in die-cast components of numerous items.

BRILLIANT
This yellow-brown sphalerite has been faceted into a round brilliant cut. Its high fire shows rainbow colors.

OVAL
This oval cut shows off the golden-brown color of sphalerite. Such stones are cut for collectors.

EMERALD
Faceting this yellow-green sphalerite in an emerald cut is a supreme test of lapidary skill.

GALENA

GALENA MINE, IDAHO
The Galena Mine is one of several in the Coeur d'Alene area in Shoshone County, Idaho. Lead, silver, zinc, and gold are all mined here.

PROPERTIES

GROUP	Sulfides
CRYSTAL SYSTEM	Cubic
COMPOSITION	PbS
COLOR	Lead-gray
FORM/HABIT	Cubes, cubo-octahedrons
HARDNESS	2½
CLEAVAGE	Perfect
FRACTURE	Subconchoidal
LUSTER	Metallic
STREAK	Lead-gray
SPECIFIC GRAVITY	7.6
TRANSPARENCY	Opaque

THERE ARE MORE THAN 60 known minerals that contain lead, but by far its most important ore is galena, or lead sulfide. It is possible that galena was the first ore to be smelted to release its metal: lead beads found in Turkey have been dated to around 6500 BC. Smelting required nothing more complex than heating the galena in the embers of a campfire and retrieving the metal from beneath it when it cooled.

In addition to lead, galena often contains small amounts of silver, zinc, copper, cadmium, arsenic, antimony, and bismuth. Galena can contain so much silver that it is the principal ore of that metal in a particular locality, and it can also be a source of the other metals it may contain. The Romans efficiently separated the silver from smelted lead—some Roman ingots bear the inscription *ex arg*, indicating that they are made of lead from which the silver has been removed. Galena's name comes from the Latin, and means "lead ore," or "dross from melted lead."

Galena forms cubic crystals, predominantly cubes and cubo-octahedrons. Crystals exceeding 1 in (2.5 cm) are common. It weathers easily to form secondary lead minerals, such as cerussite, anglesite, and pyromorphite. Banded nodules of anglesite and

Cubic crystal cut by octahedral faces

Metallic luster

GALENA CRYSTALS
Galena is usually found in cube-shaped crystals, but the crystal shape sometimes also incorporates the faces of octahedrons, as in this specimen.

USES OF LEAD

Mystic associations are connected to lead rather than galena: the metal was associated with Saturn in alchemical practice, and efforts to transmute lead into gold were as much about symbolic personal transformation from the base into the pure as creating one metal from the other—although no one would have been disappointed if that had actually occurred. Lead was widely used in ancient times for everything from water pipes to cooking pots. In some localities such as the hot springs in Bath, England, Roman lead pipes are still in place and carry water exactly as they did 1,600 years ago.

ANCIENT USES
This Roman ingot (top) and papal bulla (document seal) are made of lead.

MODERN USES
Now supplanted by electronic technology, lead was until recently used to make metal type (above). It is still used in car batteries.

cerussite with a galena core are frequently found. Galena occurs in many different types of deposits: in hydrothermal veins, which contain the highest silver values; as replacements of limestone or dolomite; and in deposits of contact-metamorphic origin. In the extensive Mississippi River valley deposits, where 90 percent of US production is mined, galena occurs in brecciated (fractured) zones in limestone and chert. It occasionally occurs as a replacement of organic matter, and sometimes appears in coal beds. It is commonly found in association with sphalerite, pyrite, and marcasite. Its occurrences are widespread, but major deposits occur in Canada, Mexico, Germany, England, Serbia, Italy, Russia, Australia, and Peru.

Accessory dolomite

Metallic luster

CUBIC CRYSTALS

PENTLANDITE

NAMED IN 1856 for the Irish scientist Joseph Pentland, its discoverer, pentlandite is a nickel and iron sulfide. It principally has a massive or granular habit, and its crystals cannot be seen with the naked eye. Pentlandite occurs in silica-poor, intrusive igneous rocks, and has also been found in meteorites. It is almost always accompanied by pyrrhotite, and commonly with other sulfides such as chalcopyrite and pyrite. Pentlandite is the chief source of nickel. It is relatively widespread, but commercial deposits are scarce. The major ones are at Sudbury, Ontario, Canada; Lillehammer and Bodø, Norway; the Kola Peninsula of Russia; the Bushveld Complex of South Africa; and Stillwater, Montana.

KOLA PENINSULA
This part of Russia is a major commercial source of pentlandite.

PROPERTIES

GROUP	Sulfides
CRYSTAL SYSTEM	Cubic
COMPOSITION	$(Ni, Fe)_9S_8$
COLOR	Bronze-yellow
FORM/HABIT	Massive
HARDNESS	$3\frac{1}{2}$– 4
CLEAVAGE	None
FRACTURE	Conchoidal
LUSTER	Metallic
STREAK	Bronze-brown
SPECIFIC GRAVITY	4.6–5.0
TRANSPARENCY	Opaque

CANADIAN NICKEL
This monument celebrates the Canadian five-cent piece, made from nickel.

NICKEL SMELTING
Nickel ores require extensive refining and smelting to release the metal. This smelting plant is in Russia.

HOT NICKEL
Molten nickel pours into ingot molds at this nickel smelter.

MASSIVE PENTLANDITE
This typically massive specimen of pentlandite also contains pyrrhotite.

Massive habit

Uneven fracture

COVELLITE

BUTTE
This mineral-rich area of Montana is a key source of covellite.

COVELLITE IS COPPER SULFIDE, named in 1832 for the Italian Nicolas Covelli, who first described the mineral. It is generally massive and foliated in habit. When crystals form, they occur as thin, tabular, hexagonal plates, which, when thin enough, are flexible. Its color is indigo-blue, often tinged with purple iridescence. Covellite fuses very easily when heated, producing a blue-colored flame. It typically occurs as an alteration product of other copper sulfide minerals such as chalcopyrite, chalcocite, and bornite, and is a primary mineral in some places. It rarely occurs as a volcanic sublimate, as on Mount Vesuvius, where Nicolas Covelli collected it. Occurrences include Dillenburg, Germany; Bor, Serbia; Moonta, South Australia; Alghero, Sardinia; Butte, Montana; and at numerous copper mines in Arizona. Covellite is a minor ore of copper in some localities.

PROPERTIES

GROUP	Sulfides
CRYSTAL SYSTEM	Hexagonal
COMPOSITION	CuS
COLOR	Indigo-blue to black
FORM/HABIT	Foliated
HARDNESS	$1\frac{1}{2}$–2
CLEAVAGE	Perfect basal
FRACTURE	Uneven
LUSTER	Submetallic to resinous
STREAK	Lead-gray to black, shiny
SPECIFIC GRAVITY	4.6–4.7
TRANSPARENCY	Opaque

Iridescence

Foliated habit

Tabular crystals

Oxidized material

TABULAR COVELLITE CRYSTALS

IRIDESCENT COVELLITE
This spectacular, massive covellite specimen showing purple iridescence is from the Leonard Mine in Butte, Montana.

MOUNT VESUVIUS
Covellite was first collected and identified at Mount Vesuvius, near Naples, Italy.

PYRARGYRITE

FREIBERG
Pyrargyrite occurs in this part of Saxony, Germany.

ALSO CALLED DARK RUBY SILVER, pyrargyrite takes its name from the Greek words *pyros*, "fire," and *argent*, "silver," an allusion to its color and its silver content. Its dark red color becomes darker when exposed to light. Pyrargyrite forms in relatively low-temperature hydrothermal veins with other silver minerals, such as proustite (also called, confusingly, ruby silver) as well as galena, sphalerite, tetrahedrite, and calcite. Some of the best crystallized specimens are from St. Andreasberg in the Harz Mountains and from Freiberg, Saxony, both in Germany; from Colquechaca, Bolivia; Guanajuato, Mexico; near Silver City, Idaho, and the Comstock Lode, Nevada, in the US.

PROPERTIES

GROUP	Sulfosalts
CRYSTAL SYSTEM	Hexagonal/trigonal
COMPOSITION	Ag_3SbS_3
COLOR	Deep red
FORM/HABIT	Prismatic, scalenohedral
HARDNESS	$2^1/_2$
CLEAVAGE	Distinct
FRACTURE	Conchoidal to uneven
LUSTER	Adamantine
STREAK	Purplish-red
SPECIFIC GRAVITY	5.8
TRANSPARENCY	Translucent

Twinned crystals

SILVER ORE
This specimen exhibits good prismatic crystals and twinning. Named in 1831, pyrargyrite is an important source of silver.

Adamantine luster

BOURNONITE

CORNWALL
Bournonite is one of many minerals found in Cornwall, south-west England.

NAMED IN 1805 for the French mineralogist Count J. L. de Bournon, bournonite is a lead copper antimony sulfide. It occurs as heavy, dark crystal aggregates and masses, as well as the interpenetrating cruciform twins that give it its informal name of cogwheel ore. Bournonite is widespread, found in medium-temperature hydrothermal veins and associated with galena, sphalerite, chalcopyrite, and pyrite. Particularly prized specimens come from the Harz Mountains of Germany, where a few crystals exceed 1 in (2.2 cm) in diameter; Herodsfoot Mine, Cornwall, England; and localities in Italy, France, Bolivia, Peru, Canada, Australia, Romania, Greece, Japan, and Utah.

Quartz groundmass

HARZ MOUNTAINS

The Harz Mountains, which are located in Saxony, central Germany, have been a source of minerals, including bournonite, for centuries. The town of Goslar was founded in AD 922 to protect the rich silver mines nearby, and silver, lead, and iron deposits are found in a number of other localities. Smaller mineral deposits dot the mountains, and many new minerals were discovered there. A number of its mines can be visited by the public today.

NATIONAL PARK
Mines in the Harz Mountains now have protected status.

Metallic luster

PROPERTIES

GROUP	Sulfosalts
CRYSTAL SYSTEM	Orthorhombic
COMPOSITION	$PbCuSbS_3$
COLOR	Steel-gray
FORM/HABIT	Short prismatic to tabular
HARDNESS	$2^1/_2$–3
CLEAVAGE	Indistinct
FRACTURE	Subconchoidal to uneven
LUSTER	Metallic
STREAK	Steel-gray
SPECIFIC GRAVITY	5.8
TRANSPARENCY	Opaque

Prismatic crystals

COGWHEEL ORE
This specimen shows the shape of the prismatic, orthorhombic crystals that give bournonite its nickname "cogwheel ore."

BOULANGERITE

HARZ MOUNTAINS
These German mountains contain boulangerite.

BOULANGERITE WAS NAMED in 1837 for French mining engineer Charles Boulanger. It forms flexible, prismatic to needlelike crystals, and is also fibrous or massive. Boulangerite occurs in hydrothermal veins and other environments. It is widespread in small amounts, and found in Germany, Canada, Mexico, Sweden, France, the Czech Republic, and the US.

PROPERTIES

GROUP	Sulfosalts
CRYSTAL SYSTEM	Monoclinic
COMPOSITION	$Pb_5Sb_4S_{11}$
COLOR	Bluish-lead-gray
FORM/HABIT	Long prismatic to acicular
HARDNESS	$2\frac{1}{2}$–3
CLEAVAGE	Good
FRACTURE	Uneven, brittle
LUSTER	Metallic
STREAK	Brownish-gray to gray
SPECIFIC GRAVITY	6.2
TRANSPARENCY	Opaque

SLENDER CRYSTALS
This matted mass of fine acicular crystals in quartz comes from Peru.

Boulangerite crystals

PROUSTITE

CZECH REPUBLIC
The Czech Republic is a source of proustite.

AN IMPORTANT SOURCE of silver, proustite is light-sensitive, turning transparent scarlet to opaque gray in strong light. Crystals are prismatic, rhombohedral, or scalenohedral. It is also massive and compact. It forms in fairly low-temperature hydrothermal veins, with other silver minerals, galena, and calcite. Notable localities are Chañarcillo, Chile; and Saxony, Germany.

PROPERTIES

GROUP	Sulfosalts
CRYSTAL SYSTEM	Hexagonal/trigonal
COMPOSITION	Ag_3AsS_3
COLOR	Scarlet, gray
FORM/HABIT	Prismatic to short prismatic
HARDNESS	2–$2\frac{1}{2}$
CLEAVAGE	Distinct rhombohedral
FRACTURE	Conchoidal to uneven, brittle
LUSTER	Adamantine to submetallic
STREAK	Vermilion
SPECIFIC GRAVITY	5.8
TRANSPARENCY	Translucent

Prismatic crystals

Striated crystal face

CRYSTALLINE PROUSTITE
Due to its color, proustite is also called ruby silver.

JAMESONITE

MEXICO
Jamesonite is found in Mexico's Sierra Tarahumara.

FOUND AS ACICULAR TO FIBROUS crystals, jamesonite can also be massive and plumose. A lead iron antimony sulfide, it occurs in hydrothermal veins with other sulfosalt minerals; and in quartz with carbonate minerals, such as rhodochrosite, dolomite, and calcite. Jamesonite is widespread in small amounts, with the best specimens coming from Mexico, Serbia, Romania, England, and Bolivia.

ROBERT JAMESON
Jamesonite was named for a Scottish mineralogist, Robert Jameson, in 1825.

PROPERTIES

GROUP	Sulfosalts
CRYSTAL SYSTEM	Monoclinic
COMPOSITION	$Pb_4FeSb_6S_{14}$
COLOR	Steel-gray to dark lead-gray
FORM/HABIT	Acicular, fibrous
HARDNESS	2–3
CLEAVAGE	Good
FRACTURE	Uneven to conchoidal
LUSTER	Metallic
STREAK	Grayish-black
SPECIFIC GRAVITY	5.5–6.0
TRANSPARENCY	Opaque

FIBROUS JAMESONITE
This specimen shows fibrous crystallization, which is common in this mineral.

Metallic luster

Rock groundmass

Fibrous crystals

ZINKENITE

HARZ MOUNTAINS
Zinkenite occurs in these German mountains.

ZINKENITE, A LEAD TIN SULFIDE, was named in 1826 for J. K. L. Zinken, a German mineralogist. It forms acicular crystals in columnar and radiating aggregates. It is often massive or forms thick mats of hairlike fibers. Zinkenite usually occurs in quartz associated with other sulfosalts. The best specimens are found in St. Pons, France; Oruro, Bolivia; and Harz, Germany. It also occurs in Canada, England, Australia, Romania, and Colorado and Nevada.

ZINKENITE CRYSTALS
This specimen of striated, acicular zinkenite crystals in quartz is from Wolfsberg, Lower Saxony, Germany.

PROPERTIES

GROUP	Sulfosalts
CRYSTAL SYSTEM	Hexagonal
COMPOSITION	$Pb_9Sb_{22}S_{42}$
COLOR	Steel-gray
FORM/HABIT	Fibrous, massive
HARDNESS	3–$3\frac{1}{2}$
CLEAVAGE	Indistinct
FRACTURE	Uneven, brittle
LUSTER	Metallic
STREAK	Steel-gray
SPECIFIC GRAVITY	5.3
TRANSPARENCY	Opaque

Acicular crystals

Metallic luster

Quartz groundmass

CORUNDUM: SAPPHIRE

IT WAS NOT UNTIL the 18th century that it was clearly established that sapphires and rubies are, in fact, the same mineral—corundum, natural aluminum oxide. The name corundum is probably derived from the Sanskrit *kuruvinda*, meaning "ruby," the name given to red corundum (see pp.150–51). When it is found in other colors, it is called "sapphire." Next to diamond, corundum is the hardest mineral on Earth. It crystallizes in the hexagonal system, forming dipyramidal or rounded barrel-shapes.

MISSOURI RIVER
An unusually large placer deposit of gem-quality sapphire is found by the Missouri near Helena, the capital of Montana.

THE COLORS OF SAPPHIRE
Although popularly thought of as being blue, sapphire can also be colorless, green, pink, and a wide range of other hues. Rare pink-orange stones are called padparadscha, and sapphire that appears blue in daylight and reddish or violet in artificial light is called alexandrine or alexandrite sapphire. Sapphires are commonly pleochroic—that is, they appear to be differently colored when viewed from different directions.

All sapphires apart from blue ones are identified by the term "sapphire" preceded by the color: "pink sapphire," "yellow sapphire," and rare, colorless "white sapphire." All colored sapphires other than blue or deep red ones are collectively known as fancy sapphires. Technically, these names are reserved for gem-quality stones, but generally they are simply used for stones of the right color. When blue, sapphire is colored by trace titanium and iron, when pale green, yellow, or brown it is colored by iron, and when pink by very small traces of

LOGAN SAPPHIRE
The 423-carat Logan Sapphire was mined in Sri Lanka and may be the world's largest blue sapphire. It is about the size of a hen's egg.

SAPPHIRE RING
A natural, uncut sapphire crystal is mounted in a contemporary-style silver ring.

SAPPHIRE CRYSTAL
This water-worn crystal demonstrates the color zoning that is commonly seen in sapphires.

Color zoning

THE LORE OF SAPPHIRE
Because the term "sapphire" was applied only to blue corundum before the 19th century, all historic references relate to this color. In ancient Greece, and later in the Middle Ages, there was a belief that sapphires cured eye diseases and set prisoners free. Medieval alchemists related it to the element air, and sapphires were also believed to be an antidote against poisons and endowed with a power to influence the spirits at that time. In the 11th century the French bishop Marbodius described blue sapphire: "Sapphires possess a beauty like that of the heavenly throne; they denote the hearts of the simple, of those moved by a sure hope and of those whose lives shine with their good deeds and virtuousness." In the East, the sapphire is regarded as a powerful charm against the evil eye.

SAPPHIRE BUDDHA
This Buddha representation is carved from a superb single sapphire crystal.

chromium. With increasing amounts of chromium, pink sapphire forms a continuous color range with ruby. Vanadium, nickel, and cobalt can also alter colors. Most corundum contains nearly 1 percent iron oxide. Much sapphire is unevenly colored, with concentric zones of color; for example, green sapphire is often found to be alternating bands of yellow and blue, but skillful cutting of unevenly colored stones yields gems with a uniform appearance. The color and transparency of sapphire can both be changed by heating it or subjecting it to radiation. The somewhat milky stones from the Missouri River in Montana are clarified by heat treatment, as are many Sri Lankan stones.

From medieval times until the end of the 19th century, green sapphire was referred to as "Oriental peridot" and yellow sapphire as "Oriental topaz." In ancient literature, the term "sapphire" appears to have mostly referred to lapis lazuli, although blue corundum has itself been prized since at least 800 BC. One of the oldest sapphires is St. Edward's sapphire, set in the finial cross of the British Imperial State Crown (see p.157), and believed to date from Edward the Confessor's coronet in AD 1042. Blue sapphire was widely used in the jewelry of the medieval kings of Europe, and was considered the stone most fitting for ecclesiastical rings.

SAPPHIRE GRAVELS
These 1/8–1/4-in (3–5-mm) uncut sapphires from Phillipsburg, Montana, show the wide range of colors to be found in corundum.

GEMS OF ALL COLORS
Corundum comes in rainbow colors. All the colors are known as sapphire except red, which is known as ruby.

SOURCES AND USES OF SAPPHIRE
Corundum is most abundant in metamorphic rocks, and in silica-deficient igneous rocks such as nepheline syenites (see p.38). Large deposits are rare, however. Most sapphires and rubies are mined from alluvial deposits, where their higher density concentrates them when weathered from their original source. Myanmar, Sri Lanka, Nigeria, and Thailand are famous gemstone sources, but there are also deposits in Australia, Brazil, Kashmir, Cambodia, Kenya, Malawi, Colombia, and the US. Some of the richest deposits of non-gemstone corundum occur in India, Russia, Zimbabwe, South Africa, and Nigeria. Transparent sapphire is most commonly faceted, while star sapphire and other nontransparent varieties are cut *en cabochon*. Some sapphire is even carved or engraved despite its hardness. Non-gemstone corundum is used as an abrasive for grinding optical glass and for polishing metals, and has been made into sandpapers and grinding wheels; when naturally mixed with magnetite, it forms emery. It is also used in high-temperature ceramics because of its high melting point (3,700°F/2,050°C). It has been synthesized in industrial quantities since the 1920s, and synthetic sapphire has almost entirely replaced the natural material in most applications.

PROPERTIES

GROUP Oxides
CRYSTAL SYSTEM Hexagonal – trigonal
COMPOSITION Al_2O_3
COLOR Occurs in most colors
FORM/HABIT Pyramidal, prismatic barrel-shape
HARDNESS 9
CLEAVAGE None
FRACTURE Conchoidal to uneven
LUSTER Adamantine to vitreous
STREAK Colorless
SPECIFIC GRAVITY 4.0–4.1
TRANSPARENCY Transparent to translucent
R.I. 1.76–1.77

SINGLE CRYSTAL

TWIN CRYSTAL

CRYSTAL FORMS
These corundum crystals from Madagascar show superb crystal forms. The single crystal is 1 in (2.5 cm) long and has the classic corundum prismatic shape, with a triangular termination.

"**Kissing** your hand may make you feel very very good but a diamond and a **sapphire** bracelet lasts forever"

ANITA LOOS
GENTLEMEN PREFER BLONDES

STAR CABOCHON
When sapphire containing rutile needles oriented along the growth directions of the crystal is cut en cabochon, a star appears.

BRILLIANT
A brilliant cut is usually used for transparent sapphire to enhance its color.

GROWING SAPPHIRES
This laboratory technician in the United States is watching sapphire crystals grow in a crystal grower. The crystals are used in sodium vapor lamps.

Correct orientation

Growth axis

ORIENTING THE GEM
For a star stone to appear, a gem must be cut with a precise orientation to the rutile inclusions, which always align perpendicular to the length of the crystal. There is only one possible orientation that will produce a star stone in the finished gem.

Sawn to rough shape

Cut to profile

Domed top

CUTTING THE GEM
Once the gem is oriented, it is sawn into the rough shape required. It is then rounded in profile, and finally the top is cut into a smooth dome.

STAR STONES AND CAT'S EYES

THE APPARENT PRESENCE INSIDE A GEMSTONE OF A SINGLE BAND OF LIGHT, OR A NUMBER OF INTERSECTING LIGHT BANDS, CAN GIVE IT AN ETHEREAL, EVEN MAGICAL QUALITY. FOREMOST AMONG SUCH GEMS, BOTH IN BEAUTY AND IN VALUE, ARE STAR STONES AND CAT'S EYES.

Star stones and cat's eyes are not the names of specific mineral gem varieties. They are certain types of gemstones that exhibit a property called chatoyancy. Chatoyancy is the reflection of light from microscopic inclusions of other minerals within the gemstone. It is best observed when light from a single source, such as the Sun, is directed at the stone; under multiple light sources, the single or intersecting bands of light appear ill-defined or may disappear altogether. A single band is called a cat's-eye effect; intersecting stars are known as asterism.

A common cause of chatoyancy is the presence of the mineral rutile (titanium oxide). Corundum crystals, for example, grow during the metamorphism of clay-rich limestone. As the corundum (pure aluminum oxide) crystals grow, they incorporate atoms of titanium. As each crystal cools, the titanium atoms bond with oxygen atoms to form minute needlelike crystals of rutile (titanium oxide) within the corundum crystal. The rutile crystals are forced to align, forming sets of parallel crystals. In star sapphires, microscopic inclusions of rutile orient themselves in three bands lying horizontally at 120 degrees to each other. Viewed from above, the bands intersect as a star. Star sapphires (and other star stones) are cut *en cabochon* so that the dome of the cabochon is oriented to coincide with the point of intersection with the rutile crystals (see left). If oriented in any other direction, no star appears.

Gems that produce star stones include sapphire and ruby, quartz (which produces six- or twelve-rayed stars), garnet (four-, six-, or eight-rayed stars), spinel (both four- and six-rayed stars), and rarely, kornerupine (four-rayed stars). In every case, the gemstone must be cut in such a way that the optical effect is made visible, and the intersecting sets of light-reflecting, tiny, hollow tubes or fibrous crystals appear as bright bands. The most valuable star stones have well-centered stars with straight arms of equal intensity, as well as excellent background color.

CAT'S EYES

The simplest form of chatoyancy is the cat's eye, in which the needlelike inclusions are oriented in only one direction, producing a single band of light—reminiscent of the narrow, vertical pupil in the eye of a cat. When a cat's-eye stone is to be cut, the cabochon is oriented along the direction of the inclusions, perpendicular to the length of the crystal. Often, a jeweler making a brooch from a cat's eye will center the single line of light that appears so that it bisects the stone. In many smaller pieces the band of inclusions may be allowed to appear to the side of the gem.

Cat's-eye effect

Gem is cut with the line of inclusions set off-center

CAT'S-EYE CROSS
This pendant is composed of 12 chrysoberyl chatoyant gems set in the form of a cross. All of the gems are cut en cabochon *to highlight the cat's-eye effect. For dramatic effect, the central, largest gem is set so the cat's eye is horizontal, while the surrounding 11 gems are set so the cat's-eye effect appears vertically.*

STAR OF INDIA
In addition to the rutile bands in this 563-carat star sapphire, rutile crystals throughout give it a milky appearance.

ROSE QUARTZ
The relative depths of the three bands of inclusions may be seen inside this beautiful rose quartz.

BLACK SAPPHIRE
In a diamond and platinum ring setting, this 70.8-carat black sapphire from Sri Lanka shows a rare 12-rayed star.

STAR OF ASIA
Weighing 330 carats, this star sapphire originated in Burma. It is famous for its size, color, and sharply defined star.

Titanium oxide reflects light

ROSSER REEVES STAR RUBY
This 138.7-carat gem from Sri Lanka is probably the world's finest star ruby. In an earlier incarnation, it weighed 140 carats, but it was recut in the mid-20th century to center the star.

STAR OF BOMBAY
This striking star sapphire from Sri Lanka weighs 182 carats. Movie star Douglas Fairbanks gave it to his wife, Mary Pickford, who bequeathed it to the Smithsonian Institution in Washington, DC.

ART DECO STAR
Actually part of a platinum necklace in the Smithsonian's National Gem Collection, this 60-carat sky-blue star sapphire from Sri Lanka is mounted in a diamond-encrusted setting produced in the Art Deco style. Unlike the Star of India (above left), also in the Collection, the bands of microscopic inclusions are not uniform in their intensity.

YELLOW CHRYSOBERYL
This smooth cat's-eye gem is cut in a double cabochon (hollowed on both sides). Chrysoberyl is composed of beryllium aluminum oxide with iron and chromium, and ranges in color from yellow to brown.

RED-BROWN CHRYSOBERYL
The reddish-brown of this dark chrysoberyl double cabochon makes all the more dramatic the stripe of light reflecting from its microscopic inclusions. For jewelers, the term "cat's eye" refers to a chrysoberyl gem unless it is qualified by the name of another mineral.

High transparency

Broad band of rutile

Iron causes brown color

HAWK'S EYE QUARTZ

PALE QUARTZ

ENSTATITE CAT'S EYE
A magnesium silicate stone, enstatite ranges in color from white to gray to light brown or pale green. Heating can produce a deeper green. One bronze-colored variety, called "bronzite," often contains inclusions of hematite or goethite that give a cat's-eye effect.

CAT'S-EYE QUARTZ CABOCHONS
The three different varieties of quartz shown here all contain inclusions of crocidolite (blue asbestos), which create a cat's-eye effect when the gems are cut en cabochon. Chatoyant quartz is found in Sri Lanka, India, Brazil, Australia, and the US.

TIGER'S EYE QUARTZ

153

ICE

ALTHOUGH LARGELY ABSENT at lower latitudes, ice is still the most abundant mineral exposed at Earth's surface. Yet, in spite of being so common, ice is rarely seen in museums and virtually never in private collections. Water is not classified as a mineral because it has no crystalline form.

The name "ice" originates from the Middle English word *iis*, and also from the Dutch *ijs* and the German *eis*. As snow, it forms crystals that seldom exceed ¹/₄ in (7 mm), although as massive aggregates in glaciers, individual crystals may reach 18 in (45 cm). Other forms include dendritic frost, frost as skeletal, hopper-shaped prisms, and rounded polycrystalline bodies with concentric structures (hailstones and icicles). Crystals are generally colorless, but larger, massive bodies can be light blue. Ice's common white color is due to gaseous inclusions of air. There are at least nine polymorphs—different crystalline forms—of ice, each forming under slightly different pressure and temperature conditions.

The hardness of ice varies with its crystal structure, purity, and temperature. Ice exists only at temperatures below 32°F (0°C). At –47°F (–44°C), which is not unusual in arctic or high-alpine conditions, ice has a hardness of 4 on the Mohs scale, which is the same as fluorite (see pp.172–73). At –106°F (–77°C), a temperature still within reach in arctic or high-alpine conditions, it has the hardness of feldspar—about 6. At this temperature, it is hard enough to erode stone when windblown. If ice

exists on any of the planets or moons in the outer solar system, it could be even harder than this.

The classification applied to rocks can also be used for ice, dividing it into three types: igneous, when it crystallizes from liquid water; sedimentary, when it falls as snow; and metamorphic, when it is in glaciers under tremendous pressure, deforming and recrystallizing. Large crystals of hoar ice, 4 in (10 cm) long, are often found in caves, old mines, and glacial crevasses where they have crystallized directly from the air. Natural ice has declined in economic value, but as a medium for playing winter sports, it is only marginally supplanted by the artificial form.

DIFFERENT FORMS OF ICE
Ice occurs in rock form as glaciers (above), permafrost, and icebergs in the Arctic and Antarctic, and seasonally as snow or as ice covering lakes or rivers.

HOMEMADE ICE
Homemade or synthetic ice is not a mineral, just as synthetic gemstones are not regarded as minerals.

SNOWFLAKE
Each snowflake is made up of platy, hexagonal crystals of ice.

Airborne snow

Snow
(85–90% air)

Granular ice
(30–85% air)

Firn
(20–30% air)

Blue ice
(less than 20% air, as bubbles)

ICE-SHEET FORMATION
Ice sheets form through the gradual accumulation, compaction, and recrystallization of fallen snow.

PRESERVING FOOD

Once the preservative properties of chilling were discovered, the harvesting and storing of ice for use as a refrigerant became a major winter occupation in parts of Europe and North America. The Chinese are said to have stored ice in caves as early as the 8th century BC. The first icehouse in Great Britain was built in the early 17th century, and by the 18th century an icehouse was a usual part of a large estate. Some were built as pits, others at ground level. They were usually insulated with straw, both in the walls and around the ice blocks. Some had a capacity of hundreds of tons. An ice crop could last for up to three years, but many did not last the entire summer, so it was an unreliable method of long-term food preservation. With the advent of modern refrigeration and the production of artificial ice, natural ice is no longer an important product as a refrigerant.

PRIVATE ICEHOUSE
This icehouse on the Holkham Estate, Norfolk, was typical of the 18th-century English icehouse.

HARVESTING ICE
In 1900, workers cut sheets of ice from the surface of Canneaut Lake, Pennsylvania. The ice was then floated to an icehouse.

ICE-CORE RESEARCH

THIN SECTION
This section comes from an ice-core sample taken from the ice sheet in Greenland.

Cores of ice recovered from holes bored deep into glaciers and ice sheets have provided important information about past atmospheric conditions, including temperature, pollutants, and the presence of dust particles (which can bring about climate change). An ice sheet preserves the entire history of its accumulation, in some cases extending back more than 300,000 years. Actual samples of ancient atmospheres are trapped in air bubbles within the ice, as are records of snow accumulation, air temperature, and fallout from volcanic, terrestrial, marine, cosmic, and human-made sources.

SNOW CORING
These scientists are examining a newly extracted snow core, useful in avalanche research and for studying ice-sheet formation.

PROPERTIES

GROUP Oxides
CRYSTAL SYSTEM Hexagonal
COMPOSITION H_2O
COLOR Colorless
FORM/HABIT Platy, prismatic, dendritic, massive
HARDNESS Varies
CLEAVAGE Perfect, difficult
FRACTURE Conchoidal, brittle
LUSTER Vitreous
STREAK White
SPECIFIC GRAVITY 1.0
TRANSPARENCY Transparent to translucent

"In skating over thin ice, our safety is in our speed."

RALPH WALDO EMERSON,
"PRUDENCE," 1941

ICE HOTEL
This chapel of ice is part of the Ice hotel in Jukkasjarvi, Sweden. At the start of every winter, the hotel is constructed from 20,000 tons of snow and 3,000 tons of ice. During the winter months, tourists can stay in this hotel and others in Sweden, Greenland, Alaska, and Canada.

INTERIOR OF THE PEDERSON GLACIER
Deep within a glacier, such as this one in Alaska, ice often looks blue. This is because ice absorbs other colors in the spectrum, but reflects blue.

IGLOO
Igloos are built from fine-grained, compact snow cut into blocks. They provide temporary winter homes or dwellings on hunting grounds for Inuit from Greenland and Canada.

CUPRITE

A MAJOR ORE OF COPPER, cuprite is named from the Latin *cuprum*, meaning "copper." It can turn superficially dark gray on exposure to light. Cuprite typically has cubic crystals. In the variety called chalcotrichite or plush copper ore, the crystals are fibrous and found in loosely matted aggregates. It can also be massive and earthy. Cuprite is a secondary mineral, formed by the oxidation of copper sulfide veins. Fine specimens come from Namibia, Australia, Russia, France, and the US.

PROPERTIES

GROUP	Oxides
CRYSTAL SYSTEM	Cubic
COMPOSITION	Cu_2O
COLOR	Shades of red to nearly black
FORM/HABIT	Octahedral
HARDNESS	$3\frac{1}{2}$–4
CLEAVAGE	Distinct
FRACTURE	Uneven, brittle
LUSTER	Adamantine, submetallic
STREAK	Brownish-red, shining
SPECIFIC GRAVITY	6.1
TRANSPARENCY	Transparent to almost opaque

CUPRITE CRYSTALS
Cuprite crystals are cubic, octahedral, or rarely dodecahedral.

Adamantine luster on crystal faces

STEP CUT
Cuprite is extremely rare in faceted stones, and is cut for collectors only, here in a rectangular step cut.

ZINCITE

RED OXIDE OF ZINC is another name for zincite. Natural crystals are rare; it is usually massive and granular. When crystals do occur, they are hollow pyramidal. Some so-called natural crystals of zincite in the collector's market are, in fact, smelter products. Zincite is found mainly as an accessory mineral in zinc ore deposits. Crystals are found only in secondary veins or fractures. The key localities are Franklin and Sterling Hill, New Jersey, where it is an ore of zinc. Tsumeb, Namibia, is another important source.

MASSIVE ZINCITE
This massive specimen of zincite is from Sterling Hill, New Jersey.

Massive habit

Deep red zincite

PROPERTIES

GROUP	Oxides
CRYSTAL SYSTEM	Trigonal
COMPOSITION	ZnO
COLOR	Orange-yellow to deep red
FORM/HABIT	Massive
HARDNESS	4
CLEAVAGE	Perfect
FRACTURE	Conchoidal
LUSTER	Resinous
STREAK	Orange-yellow
SPECIFIC GRAVITY	5.7
TRANSPARENCY	Almost opaque

MAGNETITE

MAGNETITE IS HIGHLY MAGNETIC: it will attract iron filings and deflect a compass needle. An iron oxide in the spinel group of minerals, it usually forms octahedral crystals, although it is sometimes found in highly modified dodecahedrons. Magnetite can also be granular, occurring as disseminated grains and as concentrations in black sand. It is similar in appearance to hematite, but hematite is non-magnetic and has a red streak. Magnetite is one of the most widespread of the oxide minerals, and is found in a wide range of geological environments. It is a high-temperature accessory mineral in igneous and metamorphic rocks and in sulfide veins.

A major ore of iron, it forms large ore bodies in Norway; Kiruna, Sweden; and New York State. Excellent crystals are found at Binntal, Switzerland; Traversella, Italy; Zillertal, Austria; Värmland, Sweden; Durango, Mexico; and in New York and Vermont. The most strongly magnetic material is found in the Ural Mountains of Russia and Mount Elba, Italy.

Magnetite is said to be named for the Greek shepherd boy Magnes, who noticed that the iron ferrule of his staff and the nails of his shoes clung to a magnetite-bearing rock.

CRYSTAL
This magnetite crystal shows the mineral's classic octahedral habit.

Iron filings

MASSIVE MAGNETITE
This specimen of magnetite is covered with iron filings, an illustration of the strength of its intrinsic magnetism.

Magnetic field

PROPERTIES

GROUP	Oxides
CRYSTAL SYSTEM	Cubic
COMPOSITION	Fe_3O_4
COLOR	Black to brownish-black
FORM/HABIT	Octahedral
HARDNESS	$5\frac{1}{2}$–6
CLEAVAGE	None
FRACTURE	Conchoidal to uneven
LUSTER	Metallic to semi-metallic
STREAK	Black
SPECIFIC GRAVITY	5.2
TRANSPARENCY	Opaque

SPINEL

QUEENSLAND, AUSTRALIA
Spinel and sapphire are found together in this region.

SPINEL IS BOTH a mineral name and the name of a group of mostly rock-forming minerals, all of which are metal oxides, and all of which have the same crystal structure. Members of the group include gahnite (see p.162), franklinite (see p.158), and chromite (see p.158). Spinel minerals are usually found as glassy, hard octahedrons, grains, or masses. The spinel group contains the mineral spinel. The red variety is often called "ruby spinel" because of its blood-red color, although it is also found in green, blue, brown, and black. It is frequently cut as a gemstone because, as a member of the aluminum spinels, it is harder and more transparent than the iron or chromium spinels. Its name comes from the Latin *spinella*, meaning "little thorn," a reference to the sharp points on the octahedral crystals. Its red color is due to chromium.

Spinel is found in mafic igneous rocks, aluminum-rich metamorphic rocks, and contact metamorphosed limestones. Classic occurrences are the gem gravels of Myanmar, Sri Lanka, and Madagascar. Gem-quality stones are also found in Afghanistan, Pakistan, Brazil, Australia, Sweden, Italy, Turkey, Russia, and the US. The earliest known gem spinel dates from 100 BC and was found in a Buddhist tomb near Kabul, Afghanistan. Red spinel was known to the Romans at the same time. Blue spinels from the Roman period (51 BC–AD 400) have been found in England.

PROPERTIES

GROUP	Oxides
CRYSTAL SYSTEM	Cubic
COMPOSITION	$MgAl_2O_4$
COLOR	Red, yellow, orange-red, blue, green, brown, black
FORM/HABIT	Octahedral
HARDNESS	$7\frac{1}{2}$–8
CLEAVAGE	None
FRACTURE	Conchoidal to uneven
LUSTER	Vitreous
STREAK	White
SPECIFIC GRAVITY	3.6
TRANSPARENCY	Transparent to translucent
R.I.	1.71–1.73

SPINEL "RUBIES"

Many historic "rubies" were actually spinel. Two are part of the British Crown Jewels: the Timur Ruby and the Black Prince's Ruby. The Timur Ruby is inscribed with the names and dates of six of its owners—the earliest of whom is Shah Jahgagir, 1612, and the latest Ahmad Shah Durrani, 1754. The superb spinel known as the Black Prince's Ruby was supposedly given to Edward, the Black Prince (son and heir apparent of Edward III) by Pedro the Cruel, king of Castille, after the victory of Najera in 1367. It was later mounted in the British Imperial State Crown. Henry V wore and nearly lost it at the Battle of Agincourt in 1415. It has been passed down through the English, and later British, royal families.

TIMUR RUBY NECKLACE
Belonging to Queen Elizabeth II of England, the Timur ruby is in fact a spinel.

Sapphire in finial cross

BLACK PRINCE'S RUBY
Mounted above the Cullinan II diamond, this "ruby" is in reality a 170-carat spinel from Badakhshan, Afghanistan.

Diamond

Spinel

CUSHION MIX
The transparency of spinel makes possible brilliant, fiery gems. Here, brilliant-cut crown facets are combined with step-cut pavilion facets.

OCTAGONAL MIX
Although spinel is often thought of as a red gemstone, other spinel colors also produce superb gems.

BRILLIANT OVAL
This faceted brilliant oval shows the red coloration commonly associated with spinel and sometimes known as ruby spinel.

STAR CABOCHON
Star spinels are rare but, when found, show a four- or six-rayed star. Here, a six-rayed star is brought out by the cabochon cut.

Spinel crystal

Gahnite crystal

BLUE CRYSTALS IN CALCITE

BROWN CRYSTALS IN QUARTZ

AGGREGATE CRYSTALS

SPINEL CRYSTALS
The blue spinel crystals in calcite (far left) are from Lake Baikal, Russia. Brown spinel-group crystals (center) are known as gahnite, a zinc-rich variety of spinel. The ruby-red spinel crystals (left) have formed together into a crystal aggregate.

Octahedral crystal

Vitreous luster

Stream-rounded crystal

SPINEL CRYSTALS
These crystals are typical of those recovered from the gem gravels of Myanmar, Sri Lanka, and Madagascar.

FLUORESCENT MINERALS

VIEWED UNDER ULTRAVIOLET LIGHT, SOME CRYSTALS EMIT VISIBLE LIGHT IN REMARKABLE COLORS, LENDING THEM AN EERIE, PSYCHEDELIC APPEARANCE. FIRST NOTED IN FLUORITE, THE PHENOMENON IS CALLED FLUORESCENCE.

Fluorescence is the ability of some minerals to emit visible light of various colors when exposed to ultraviolet light (also known as "black light"). This particular kind of luminescence was first identified in 1824 by German mineralogist Friedrich Mohs (1773–1839), who also developed the Mohs scale of hardness. He observed that some fluorites, when viewed under ultraviolet light, appeared a completely different color than when viewed in daylight.

Ultraviolet light can be produced in both short and long waves, and some minerals fluoresce only in one or the other; still others fluoresce in both. There is an unpredictability to fluorescence: some specimens of a mineral will manifest it, while other specimens will not. For example, willemite from the Franklin district of New Jersey may show brilliant fluorescent colors, while willemite from other localities may show none whatsoever. More surprisingly, specimens that are apparently identical and come from the same locality may or may not fluoresce. Also, the color and intensity of the fluorescence can vary significantly, depending on the wavelengths of ultraviolet light used.

WHY MINERALS FLUORESCE

Fluorescence occurs when certain atoms within the structure of a mineral move into a different, higher-energy state when exposed to ultraviolet light. These atoms absorb energy from the ultraviolet light and become "excited." They stay in this excited state for no more than tiny fractions of a second; then, as they move back into their "unexcited" state, termed their "ground" state, the energy they absorbed is released as fluorescent light. The atoms that cause fluorescence are often trace elements (see pp.92). Trace elements are prone to "excitation" because they are already in an electronically unstable situation as a result of not fitting perfectly into the crystal structure that contains them.

Another phenomenon related to the "excitation" of a mineral's atoms is phosphorescence. This is a continued emission of light as an afterglow following the removal of the "exciting" light source. Willemite, for example, can phosphoresce as well as fluoresce.

Fluorescence is exploited in mineral science in several ways: in some minerals, it serves as a means of identification—ultraviolet is used to find minerals that fluoresce; and, in the extraction of ore minerals that fluoresce, ultraviolet verifies whether extraction processes are effective. Fluorescence is also used in the microscopic examination of small-scale structures in crystals.

Fluorescence from manganese

Calcite cluster

MANGANOAN CALCITE
This manganese-bearing calcite specimen is from Arizona. Manganoan calcite fluoresces scarlet-pink. Many calcites fluoresce.

Adamite

Rock groundmass

Other fluorescent

ADAMITE
Adamite fluoresces bright green. This specimen is from Ojuela Mine, Mapimi, Durango, Mexico. The brilliant fluorescence of adamite makes it a popular choice for most fluorescent collections.

Nonfluorescent mineral

Red-orange fluorescence

Aragonite crys

ARAGONITE
From Sicily, Italy, this specimen of aragonite is fluorescing salmon-pink. Aragonite can also fluoresce yellow, bluish, and greenish.

FLUORITE ON QUARTZ

Fluorite fluoresces violet-blue. This specimen is from Redburn Mine, Weardale, Durham, England. Blue fluorescence in fluorite is often caused by traces of erbium.

Fluorite

Quartz

Rock groundmass

Scapolite

SCAPOLITE

This scapolite specimen is from Quebec, Canada. It fluoresces yellow. Some scapolites fluoresce, others do not, depending on individual specimens.

Willemite

Calcite

Columnar calcite

Concentrated fluorescent material

CALCITE

The columnar crystals of this calcite specimen fluoresce white. Trace elements in calcite can produce other fluorescent colors.

WILLEMITE AND CALCITE

This specimen is from Franklin, New Jersey. The willemite is fluorescing green and the calcite is fluorescing red.

Gypsum

Nonfluorescent mineral

Sodalite

Rock groundmass

GYPSUM

From Montmartre, Paris, France, this gypsum fluoresces a rich yellow. Fluorescence is rare in gypsum, although it can be caused by foreign molecules.

SODALITE

This Indian sodalite, from Kishangarh, Madhya Pradesh, is fluorescing orange. Sodalite specimens may also fluoresce orange-red fading to yellow-white.

CASSITERITE

A TIN OXIDE, cassiterite is named for the Greek *kassiteros*, "tin." It can form heavily striated prisms and pyramids, and twinned crystals are quite common. It is also massive, and occurs as a botryoidal fibrous variety (wood tin) or water-worn pebbles (stream tin). Cassiterite forms in hydrothermal veins associated with granitic rocks, with tungsten minerals such as wolframite, and with molybdenite, tourmaline, and topaz. Durable and relatively dense, it becomes concentrated in sediments when eroded from its primary rocks. Many of the most productive tin ores are placer deposits. Fine crystals come from Portugal, Italy, France, the Czech Republic, Brazil, and Myanmar.

PROPERTIES

GROUP	Oxides
CRYSTAL SYSTEM	Tetragonal
COMPOSITION	SnO_2
COLOR	Medium to dark brown
FORM/HABIT	Short prismatic
HARDNESS	6–7
CLEAVAGE	Indistinct
FRACTURE	Subconchoidal to uneven
LUSTER	Adamantine to metallic
STREAK	White, grayish, brownish
SPECIFIC GRAVITY	7.0
TRANSPARENCY	Transparent to opaque
R.I.	2.0–2.1

OVAL BRILLIANT
The characteristic golden-orange color of this gem is transparent with a resinous luster.

CRYSTALS
Originating from Pingwu, Sichuan, China, this specimen on a muscovite groundmass includes twinned cassiterite crystals.

Muscovite

MINING AND USING TIN

There are few tin minerals; cassiterite is almost the sole source of the metal. Massive alluvial (river) deposits occur in Malaysia, Thailand, and Indonesia. It is also worked from primary deposits underground in Bolivia. Tin lodes have been worked in southwest England, including Cornwall, since pre-Roman times, although there is virtually no production today. Tin from Cornwall was traded across the Mediterranean world by the Phoenicians, and then alloyed with copper from Cyprus and elsewhere to make bronze.

TIN INGOT

CORNISH TIN MINE
An abandoned pump house marks the site of a pre-Roman tin mine on the Cornish coast.

Varlamoffite crystals

Short prismatic crystal

Rock groundmass

VARLAMOFFITE CASSITERITE

CASSITERITE VARIETIES
The varlamoffite specimen was found at Gunheath Pit, Cornwall. The fibrous, botryoidal variety is known as wood tin cassiterite.

WOOD TIN CASSITERITE

GAHNITE

SALIDA, CO
This area of Colorado produces fine gahnite crystals.

A ZINC ALUMINUM OXIDE, gahnite is a member of the spinel group, forming octahedral crystals. It is also found as irregular grains and masses. Gahnite crystals are usually dark green or blue to black and striated. It was named in 1807 for the Swedish chemist J. G. Gahn. Gahnite is found in schists and gneisses, in granite pegmatites, and in contact metamorphosed limestones. Good crystals come from the US, Sweden, Finland, Australia, Brazil, and Mexico.

PROPERTIES

GROUP	Oxides
CRYSTAL SYSTEM	Cubic
COMPOSITION	$ZnAl_2O_4$
COLOR	Dark green or blue
FORM/HABIT	Octahedral
HARDNESS	7½–8
CLEAVAGE	Indistinct
FRACTURE	Conchoidal
LUSTER	Vitreous
STREAK	Grayish
SPECIFIC GRAVITY	4.6
TRANSPARENCY	Translucent to nearly opaque

Octahedral crystal

Rock groundmass

BLUE GAHNITE
This specimen of octahedral crystals is from Franklin, New Jersey. Other localities in the US are Colorado and Maine.

PYROLUSITE

LAKE SUPERIOR
Pyrolusite is found in this part of Michigan.

A COMMON MANGANESE mineral, pyrolusite is the primary ore of manganese. It rarely forms crystals, and is usually found as light gray to black massive aggregates, metallic coatings, crusts, fibers, and nodules. Pyrolusite forms under highly oxidizing conditions as an alteration product of other manganese minerals such as rhodochrosite. It has also been found in bogs, lakes, shallow marine environments, and on the ocean floor. Rare crystals are found in Canada and the Czech Republic.

PROPERTIES

GROUP	Oxides
CRYSTAL SYSTEM	Tetragonal
COMPOSITION	MnO_2
COLOR	Steel-gray to black
FORM/HABIT	Massive
HARDNESS	6–6½
CLEAVAGE	Perfect
FRACTURE	Uneven, brittle, splintery
LUSTER	Metallic to earthy
STREAK	Black or bluish-black
SPECIFIC GRAVITY	4.4–5.1
TRANSPARENCY	Opaque

MASSIVE HABIT
This dark gray specimen of massive pyrolusite has an uneven fracture.

PROPELLERS
Manganese-bronze is used to make ships' propellers.

Dull luster

ANATASE

SWISS ALPS
Crystals found in the Swiss Alps are up to ³/₄ in (2 cm) in diameter.

FORMERLY KNOWN AS OCTAHEDRITE, anatase, along with rutile and brookite, is a polymorph of titanium oxide. It is found as brilliant crystals, which can be brown, indigo-blue, green, gray, and black. Anatase forms in veins in metamorphic rocks such as schists and gneisses, and in pegmatites. It is found in sediments and can be concentrated in placer deposits. Notable vein deposits occur widely in the Alps. Other localities for fine crystals are Brazil, Norway, and Colorado.

ANATASE CRYSTAL

BLACK CRYSTALS
This schist from Le Bourg-d'Oisans, Isère, France is scattered with tiny black anatase crystals.

Adamantine luster

PROPERTIES

GROUP Oxides
CRYSTAL SYSTEM Tetragonal
COMPOSITION TiO_2
COLOR Various shades of brown, or black, indigo-blue
FORM/HABIT Pyramidal
HARDNESS 5¹/₂–6
CLEAVAGE Perfect
FRACTURE Subconchoidal
LUSTER Adamantine to metallic
STREAK White to pale yellow
SPECIFIC GRAVITY 3.9
TRANSPARENCY Transparent to nearly opaque

BROOKITE

MINAS GERAIS
Brookite occurs in Minas Gerais, a famous mining area of Brazil.

NAMED IN 1825 FOR English crystallographer H. J. Brooke, brookite typically occurs as brown metallic crystals. The orthorhombic polymorph of titanium oxide, it is found in veins in gneisses and schists and, more rarely, in zones of contact metamorphism. It generally occurs with rutile, anatase, and albite. Because it is relatively dense, it gets concentrated in placer deposits. Fine crystals are found in the same Alpine deposits as anatase; they are also found in Brazil, Norway, Wales, and Colorado.

PROPERTIES

GROUP Oxides
CRYSTAL SYSTEM Orthorhombic
COMPOSITION TiO_2
COLOR Various shades of brown
FORM/HABIT Tabular, elongated
HARDNESS 5¹/₂–6
CLEAVAGE Indistinct
FRACTURE Subconchoidal to uneven
LUSTER Metallic to adamantine
STREAK White, grayish, yellowish
SPECIFIC GRAVITY 4.1
TRANSPARENCY Opaque to transparent

TABULAR CRYSTAL
This transparent tabular brookite crystal rests on a mass of albite crystals.

Striated brookite crystal face

Albite

RUTILE

CAROLINA
North Carolina is one of several US states that produce rutile crystals.

TAKING ITS NAME FROM the Latin *rutilis*, "red" or "glowing," rutile is a form of titanium oxide. It ranges from reddish-brown to red, although some specimens are nearly black, and the rutile in quartz is usually pale golden-yellow. Crystals are generally prismatic, but they can also be slender and acicular. Prism faces often have vertical striations. Multiple twinning is common, and may form latticelike structures. Other twinning also occurs. Rutile is a frequently occurring minor constituent of granites, pegmatites, gneisses, and schists. Good crystals are found in Sweden, Italy, France, Austria, Brazil, and in Pennsylvania, Arkansas, Georgia, North Carolina, California, and Virginia.

Rutile commonly forms microscopic, oriented inclusions in other minerals, and produces the asterism shown by some rose quartz, rubies, and sapphires. Quartz containing long, translucent rutile needles is known as rutilated quartz, and has been used as an ornamental stone since ancient times.

PROPERTIES

GROUP Oxides
CRYSTAL SYSTEM Tetragonal
COMPOSITION TiO_2
COLOR Reddish-brown to red
FORM/HABIT Slender prismatic
HARDNESS 6–6¹/₂
CLEAVAGE Good
FRACTURE Conchoidal to uneven
LUSTER Adamantine to sub-metallic
STREAK Pale brown to yellowish
SPECIFIC GRAVITY 4.2
TRANSPARENCY Transparent to opaque
R.I. 2.62–2.90

Metallic luster

Vertical striations

USES OF TITANIUM

Titanium is one of the most important metals in modern times. It has high strength, low density, and excellent corrosion resistance. It is used in aircraft, spacecraft, missiles, and ships. Since it is nonreactive with organic tissues, it is used to make artificial joints for hip replacements, and other prosthetic devices. Another important use of titanium oxide is as a white pigment.

HARRIER JUMP JET
The use of titanium alloys in jet engines and airframes has made aircraft like the Harrier possible.

SINGLE CRYSTAL
This large, semitransparent, single crystal of rutile originates from Val di Vizze, Trentino-Alto Adige, Italy.

CLEAR QUARTZ
Needlelike rutile inclusions intersect at an angle of 60° in this polished, clear quartz cabochon.

ROSE QUARTZ
Microscopic needles of rutile create three intersecting lines of light in this rose quartz star stone.

163

URANINITE

A MAJOR ORE OF URANIUM, uraninite was named in 1792 for its composition—it is uranium oxide. It is highly radioactive and must be handled and stored with care. Uraninite occurs commonly in massive (known as pitchblende), botryoidal, or granular habits, and less commonly as octahedral or cubic crystals. It is black to brownish-black, dark gray, or greenish. Uraninite is found as crystals in granitic and syenitic pegmatites along with other uranium-bearing minerals and rare-earth minerals. It also forms in high-temperature hydrothermal veins with cassiterite and arsenopyrite, and in medium-temperature hydrothermal veins as pitchblende. In addition, it occurs as small grains in sandstones and conglomerates, where it has often weathered into secondary uranium minerals. Fine crystals are found in Córdoba, Spain; Saxony, Germany; Chihuahua, Mexico; and Topsham, Maine.

PROPERTIES

GROUP Oxides
CRYSTAL SYSTEM Cubic
COMPOSITION UO_2
COLOR Black to brownish-black, dark gray, greenish
FORM/HABIT Octahedral
HARDNESS 5–6
CLEAVAGE None
FRACTURE Uneven to subconchoidal
LUSTER Submetallic, pitchy, dull
STREAK Brownish-black
SPECIFIC GRAVITY 6.5–11.0
TRANSPARENCY Opaque

Botryoidal habit

Dull to submetallic luster

BOTRYOIDAL HABIT
This specimen of uraninite has a botryoidal habit, which is common in this mineral.

THE POWER OF URANIUM

Uraninite is the principal source of uranium. This is a dense, hard, silvery-white metal that is ductile and malleable. Until nuclear fission was discovered, uranium was used in very small amounts in the coloring of ceramics and as a specialized catalyst. Uranium metal is recovered from uraninite by first converting it to uranium tetrafluoride, and then by further reducing the uranium tetrafluoride with magnesium to release metallic uranium. The risks of the use of uranium—mainly for generating power and in nuclear weapons—are controversial and under intense debate. Many claim that it is unsafe, no matter how it is stored, used, and disposed of, and may remain so for hundreds or even thousands of years.

NUCLEAR REACTOR
Uranium is essential for the operation of nuclear reactors for generating electricity.

MARIE CURIE
In exploring the properties of pitchblende, Marie Curie (1867–1934) made numerous discoveries about radiation.

FERGUSONITE

THERE ARE SEVERAL MINERALS called fergusonite, named for the Scottish mineralogist Robert Ferguson. The most common is fergusonite-(Y), which is rich in yttrium. Its crystals are prismatic to pyramidal, and it is black to brownish-black in color. Fergusonite-(Y) is found in granitic pegmatites associated with other rare-earth minerals. Localities include Hakatamura, Japan, and Ytterby, Sweden.

SWEDISH FERGUSONITE
This specimen of fergusonite crystals in feldspar is from Ytterby, Sweden.

PROPERTIES

GROUP Oxides
CRYSTAL SYSTEM Tetragonal
COMPOSITION $YNbO_4$
COLOR Black to brownish-black
FORM/HABIT Prismatic to pyramidal
HARDNESS $5^{1/2}$–$6^{1/2}$
CLEAVAGE Poor
FRACTURE Subconchoidal, brittle
LUSTER Vitreous to submetallic
STREAK Brown, yellow-brown, greenish-gray
SPECIFIC GRAVITY 4.2–5.7
TRANSPARENCY Opaque

Feldspar

Fergusonite

SAMARSKITE

NAMED IN 1847 for Russian mining engineer Vasili Samarski-Bykhovets, samarskite is a complex oxide of yttrium, iron, niobium, tantalum, and uranium. Its radioactive crystals are prismatic, with a rectangular cross-section. They are found in granitic pegmatites, often associated with columbite, monazite, and garnet. Localities include its place of discovery at Miass, Russia; and Divino de Uba, Brazil.

PROPERTIES

GROUP Oxides
CRYSTAL SYSTEM Orthorhombic
COMPOSITION $(Y,Fe,U)(Nb,Ta)O_4$
COLOR Black
FORM/HABIT Prismatic
HARDNESS 5–6
CLEAVAGE Indistinct
FRACTURE Conchoidal, brittle
LUSTER Vitreous to resinous
STREAK Dark reddish-brown to black
SPECIFIC GRAVITY 5.7
TRANSPARENCY Translucent to opaque

IRIDESCENT SHEEN
This specimen of samarskite exhibits an iridescent sheen on some surfaces.

Indistinct cleavage

ROMANÈCHITE

CORNWALL
Romanèchite is mined in this area of southwest England.

ONE OF THE MINERALS formerly known as psilomelane, romanèchite is named after its type locality, Romanèche-Thorins, France. Commonly massive or botryoidal, romanèchite can also be earthy. It is formed as an alteration product of other manganese minerals, and is an ore of manganese. Other localities include Tekrasni, India; Parral, Mexico; Cornwall, England; and Sodaville, Nevada.

MASSIVE ROMANÈCHITE

Dull luster

Submetallic luster

BOTRYOIDAL ROMANÈCHITE

PROPERTIES
GROUP Hydrous oxides
CRYSTAL SYSTEM Orthorhombic
COMPOSITION $(Ba,H_2O)Mn_5O_{10}$
COLOR Iron-black to steel-gray
FORM/HABIT Massive, botryoidal
HARDNESS 5–6
CLEAVAGE None
FRACTURE Uneven
LUSTER Submetallic to dull
STREAK Brownish-black, shining
SPECIFIC GRAVITY 4.7
TRANSPARENCY Opaque

BRAUNITE

MINAS GERAIS
This area of Brazil is a good source of braunite.

BRAUNITE IS CLASSIFIED as both an oxide and a silicate. It was named in 1831 for K. W. Braun, a German mineralogist. Crystals are pyramidal in habit, with striated faces; braunite can also be granular and massive. It is a major ore of manganese. Localities include Autlàn de Navarro, Mexico; Nombre de Dios, Panama; Ilmenau, Germany; Ouro Prêto, Brazil; and Nordmark, Sweden.

PROPERTIES
GROUP Oxides
CRYSTAL SYSTEM Tetragonal
COMPOSITION Mn_7SiO_{12}
COLOR Brownish-black to steel-gray
FORM/HABIT Pyramidal
HARDNESS 6–6½
CLEAVAGE Perfect
FRACTURE Uneven to subconchoidal, brittle
LUSTER Submetallic
STREAK Brownish-black to steel-gray
SPECIFIC GRAVITY 4.8
TRANSPARENCY Translucent to opaque

RAILROAD TRACKS
Manganese is added to the steel used to make railroad tracks, which reduces its brittleness.

CRYSTAL HABIT
This braunite crystal from Maharashtra, India, shows a classic pyramidal habit.

Pyramidal crystal

COLUMBITE

MADAGASCAR
Large crystals of columbite occur in Madagascar.

THREE DISTINCT COLUMBITE minerals are recognized: the more common ferrocolumbite and manganocolumbite, and the rarer magnesium–rich magnocolumbite. Columbite is an iron, manganese niobium tantalum oxide. When tantalum becomes significantly dominant over niobium in the structure, it becomes the mineral tantalite. Columbite and tantalite are found together in granite, granitic pegmatites, and placer deposits. Ferrocolumbite is an important ore of both tantalum and niobium. Localities include Greenland; Germany, Italy, France, Sweden, and Greece; and the pegmatite regions of Zimbabwe, South Africa, and Uganda.

PROPERTIES
GROUP Oxides
CRYSTAL SYSTEM Orthorhombic
COMPOSITION $(Fe,Mn)(Nb,Ta)_2O_6$
COLOR Iron-black to brown-black
FORM/HABIT Short prismatic
HARDNESS 6–6½
CLEAVAGE Distinct
FRACTURE Subconchoidal to uneven
LUSTER Metallic
STREAK Dark red to black
SPECIFIC GRAVITY 5.2–6.8
TRANSPARENCY Translucent to opaque

Tabular crystal

Metallic luster

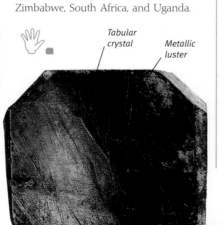

FERROCOLUMBITE
This opaque, tabular crystal of ferrocolumbite exhibits a metallic to resinous luster.

PYROCHLORE

COLORADO
This mineral-rich state is a source of pyrochlore.

PYROCHLORE TAKES ITS NAME from the Greek for "fire" and "green"—some specimens turn green after heating. It is a complex niobium sodium calcium oxide, an important niobium ore. It forms octahedral crystals, often twinned, and irregular masses. It is found in felsic igneous rocks and associated pegmatites, and in contact metamorphic zones. Localities include Miass, Russia; Oka, Quebec, Canada; and Conakry, Guinea.

PROPERTIES
GROUP Oxides
CRYSTAL SYSTEM Cubic
COMPOSITION $(Na,Ca)_2Nb_2(O,OH,F)_7$
COLOR Brown to black
FORM/HABIT Octahedral
HARDNESS 5–5½
CLEAVAGE Distinct
FRACTURE Subconchoidal to uneven
LUSTER Vitreous to resinous
STREAK Light brown, yellowish-brown
SPECIFIC GRAVITY 4.5
TRANSPARENCY Translucent to opaque

RELATED MINERALS
Microlite (below) contains tantalum in place of the niobium in pyrochlore (right).

Dull luster

Twinned octahedra

165

SWISS ALPS
The Alps on the borders of France and Switzerland are the foremost locality for rare pink octahedral fluorite crystals.

FLUORITE

OCCURRING IN WELL-FORMED CRYSTALS of many different colors, fluorite is calcium fluoride. Violet, green, and yellow are the most common colors, although it is colorless and transparent when free of trace elements—as much as 20 percent yttrium or cerium may replace the calcium in the composition of fluorite. Colors can occur in distinct zones within the same crystal, following the contour of the crystal faces. Fluorite crystals are widely found in cubes; octahedrons, which are often twinned, are much less common. Fluorite can also be massive, granular, or compact.

The phenomenon of fluorescence—the emission of visible light on exposure to ultraviolet light (see pp.160–61)—was first observed in fluorite and takes its name from it. The name fluorite comes from the Latin *fluere*, meaning "to flow," a reference to the ease with which it melts when used as a flux in the smelting and refining of metals. An old name for fluorite is fluorspar; this is now used only in industry to refer to the bulk stone.

USES OF FLUORITE

Fluorite finds many industrial uses: as a flux in the manufacture of steel, in the production of hydrofluoric acid, and as a catalyst in the manufacture of high-octane fuels. It used in the manufacture of artificial cryolite (see p.174) for the refining of aluminum, lead, and antimony, in the formation of opalescent glass (see panel, below), and in iron and steel enamelware. Clear, optical-quality fluorite, with its low refractive index and low dispersion, is used for apochromatic lenses for microscopes, which eliminate distortion of color. Fluorite is also a source of fluorine, which is used

PURPLE FLUORITE CRYSTALS

FLUORITE WITH GALENA

YELLOW FLUORITE CRYSTALS

GREEN FLUORITE

BLUE JOHN

COLORS OF FLUORITE
Fluorite has the widest color range of any mineral. It can be colorless, white, or various shades of purple, green, blue, yellow, or rarely, pink and red. Coloration is controlled by various trace elements substituting in its structure. Several colors can occur in the same specimen.

RECTANGULAR STEP
This rectangular step-cut has been faceted from purple fluorite.

YELLOW EMERALD
This specimen is a yellow, emerald-cut fluorite. Faceted fluorites are made only for collectors.

PINK EMERALD
This emerald cut has been carefully faceted from a specimen of delicate pink fluorite.

GREEN BRILLIANT
Fluorite's modest refractive index means that faceted stones can lack sparkle.

OPALESCENT GLASS

Fluorite plays an important part in the manufacture of glazed tiles and opalescent glass, a semi-opaque pressed glass, tinged with blue and having a milky iridescence. The color is produced by the slower cooling of the molten glass in those parts which are thick, causing some crystallization inside the glass. American artist John LaFarge first developed and patented opalescent glass in 1879, but it was Louis Comfort Tiffany who created the most striking and colorful Art Nouveau opalescent glass designs. During the 1920s and 1930s, many French companies made beautiful opalescent Art Deco vases, bottles and lampshades. Among the best known were those made by René Lalique.

PLAFONNIERE
This shallow, circular, opalescent glass bowl by Mark Sabino features a design of veil-tailed fish against blue. It is fixed to the ceiling by three metal chains.

OPALESCENT GLASS BOTTLE
Dating from 1911, the milky white sections of this Chinese opalescent glass bottle are painted with fish swimming among fronds.

PINK FLUORITE
This superb octahedral specimen of rare pink fluorite is perched on a cluster of smoky quartz crystals. It is from the Alps, the world's largest source of pink fluorite.

PROPERTIES

GROUP	Halides
CRYSTAL SYSTEM	Cubic
COMPOSITION	CaF_2
COLOR	Occurs in most colors
FORM/HABIT	Cubic, octahedral
HARDNESS	4
CLEAVAGE	Perfect octahedral
FRACTURE	Flat conchoidal
LUSTER	Vitreous
STREAK	White
SPECIFIC GRAVITY	3.0–3.3
TRANSPARENCY	Transparent to translucent
R.I.	1.43

for the fluoridation of water and in Teflon coating,, where the fluorine helps to provide the "nonstick" surface on Teflon cooking pans.

Fluorite's wide range of intense colors, the frequent occurrence of more than one color in a single stone, and the zoning or patchy distribution of color would make it a popular gemstone were it not for its softness and its fragility due to its perfect octahedral cleavage. Stones are sometimes faceted for collectors. The ancient Egyptians used fluorite in statues and to carve scarabs, and the Chinese have used it in carvings for more than 300 years. There has even been an attempt to pass off Chinese fluorite carvings as jade, but their softness provides a ready means of identification. In the 18th century, powdered fluorite was added to water to relieve the symptoms associated with kidney disease.

OCCURRENCE OF FLUORITE

Fluorite occurs as a vein mineral, often associated with lead and silver ores; it also occurs in pegmatite cavities, sedimentary rocks, and in hot-springs areas. It is found in numerous localities worldwide, but more important ones include Canada, the US, South Africa, Mexico, China, Mongolia, Thailand, Peru, Poland, Hungary, the Czech Republic, Norway, England, Spain, and Germany.

Fluorite octahedron

BANDED FLUORITE

The banded, purple and white or yellow variety of fluorite is popularly known as Blue John. The name may be a corruption of the French bleu jaune, "blue yellow," colors that are often interbanded in Blue John. A major source of this color-zoned fluorite is Castleton in Derbyshire, England, where it is found in at least 14 differently patterned veins. It was first mined there during Roman times and used to make vessels. The Romans particularly prized fluorite vessels because of the special flavor given to the wine drunk from them. This flavor was actually the result of the resin used to help hold the crystals together during manufacture.

BLUE JOHN RING
This 20th-century silver ring is set with a cabochon of Blue John from Castleton, England.

BLUE JOHN MINES, DERBYSHIRE
This open vein at the Odin Mine, Castleton, Derbyshire, is part of the Blue John Mines in the hillside of Treak cliff, which were worked by the Romans.

REDISCOVERY OF THE MINES

At the beginning of the 18th century, two miners—John Kirk and Joseph Hall—followed a vein of Blue John and stumbled into the old Roman mines. They and others went on to work the mines for the banded fluorite, which craftsmen, including Matthew Boulton (1728–1809), an early pioneer of steam power, used to fashion vases, ornaments, and jewelry. The mines are still worked today for the same purposes. Because of the brittleness of the mineral, it is often bonded with resins to increase its durability.

ROMAN CUP
This one-handled cup was carved in the 1st century AD from a single piece of fluorite, which is richly veined with purple, green, yellow, and white. It is decorated with a low-relief panel of vine tendrils.

Smoky quartz

CHIHUAHUA
Notable deposits of smithsonite are found in the Chihuahua area of Mexico.

SMITHSONITE

Rounded masses showing botryoidal habit

ALTHOUGH SMITHSONITE rarely forms crystals, spectacular examples—more than 1 in (2 cm) long—come from Tsumeb, Namibia. A zinc carbonate, smithsonite is most commonly found as botryoidal or stalactitic masses, or as honeycombed aggregates called "dry-bone" ore. Rhombohedral crystals of smithsonite generally have curved faces. It is a fairly common mineral found in the oxidation zones of most zinc ore deposits, and in adjacent calcareous rocks. There are significant deposits in Italy, Germany, Mexico, Zambia, and Australia, and fine specimens come from Colorado and New Mexico. Smithsonite is occasionally cut as ornaments, and *en cabochon* as gems. Frequently mined as an ore of zinc, it may have provided the zinc component of brass in ancient metallurgy.

Pearly luster

BLUE SMITHSONITE
This botryoidal mass of translucent blue smithsonite shades into green toward the bottom of the specimen.

Green smithsonite

Botryoidal smithsonite

WHITE SMITHSONITE

CABOCHON
Pieces of smithsonite that are of a sufficient thickness can be cut and polished as cabochon gems.

JAMES SMITHSON
Smithsonite is named for the English founder of the Smithsonian Institution.

PROPERTIES

GROUP Carbonates
CRYSTAL SYSTEM Hexagonal/trigonal
COMPOSITION $ZnCO_3$
COLOR White, blue, green, yellow, brown, pink, colorless
FORM/HABIT Botryoidal, rhombohedral, scalenohedral
HARDNESS 4–4½
CLEAVAGE Perfect rhombohedral
FRACTURE Uneven to conchoidal
LUSTER Vitreous to pearly
STREAK White
SPECIFIC GRAVITY 4.4
TRANSPARENCY Translucent to opaque
R.I. 1.62–1.85

SIDERITE

CORNWALL
Siderite is one of many minerals found in this part of south-west England.

AN IRON CARBONATE, siderite takes its name from the Greek *sideros*, "iron." Formerly known as chalybite, siderite has a calcite structure and can form rhombohedral crystals, often with curved surfaces, or scalenohedral, tabular, or prismatic crystals. It is more commonly massive or granular, and sometimes botryoidal or globular. Siderite is widespread, located in sedimentary, igneous, and metamorphic rocks. In sedimentary rocks it occurs in concretions and in thin beds with shale, clay, and coal seams. Well-formed crystals are found in hydrothermal veins and in some granitic and syenitic pegmatites. Single crystals up to 6 in (15 cm) are found in Quebec, Canada, and at the Morro Velho Mine in Brazil. Fine specimens have been found in Devon and Cornwall, England.

PROPERTIES

GROUP Carbonates
CRYSTAL SYSTEM Hexagonal/trigonal
COMPOSITION $FeCO_3$
COLOR Yellowish- to dark brown
FORM/HABIT Rhombohedral
HARDNESS 3½–4
CLEAVAGE Perfect rhombohedral
FRACTURE Uneven or subconchoidal
LUSTER Vitreous to pearly
STREAK White
SPECIFIC GRAVITY 3.9
TRANSPARENCY Translucent

MASSIVE SIDERITE
Numerous acicular quartz crystals coat this specimen of massive siderite.

IRON SMELTING

Siderite is a local, but not a major, source of iron. The smelting of iron from ores began in about 2000 BC in Anatolia and Persia, but it did not take place in China until as late as 600 BC. Iron proved a superior metal to bronze in almost every way, and its use led ultimately to the Industrial Revolution. Precisely where siderite as an ore fitted into these developments is yet to be determined.

RHOMBOHEDRAL SIDERITE
This mass of rhombohedral siderite crystals, many twinned, rests on a quartz groundmass.

Twinned crystals

Quartz groundmass

RUSTY IRON TONGS
This pair of hand-forged iron tongs, found in Norfolk, England, dates from the 1st century BC.

BOTRYOIDAL SIDERITE

MAGNESITE

BAHIA
The area of Bahia in Brazil is a rich source of magnesite.

DISTINCT CRYSTALS OF MAGNESITE are rare, but when found are rhombohedral or prismatic. Magnesite is generally massive, lamellar, fibrous, or granular. A carbonate of magnesium, magnesite takes its name from its composition. Most commonly white or light gray, it can be yellow or brownish when iron substitutes for some of the magnesium. Magnesite forms principally as an alteration product in magnesium-rich rocks, such as peridotites, and through the action of magnesium-containing solutions upon calcite. It also occurs as a primary mineral in limestones and talc or chlorite schists and is found in some meteorites. Localities include Australia and Brazil. It fizzes in warm hydrochloric acid.

PROPERTIES

ROCK TYPE Carbonates
CRYSTAL SYSTEM Hexagonal/trigonal
COMPOSITION $MgCO_3$
COLOR White, light gray, yellowish , brownish
FORM/HABIT Massive
HARDNESS 4
CLEAVAGE Perfect rhombohedral
FRACTURE Conchoidal, brittle
LUSTER Vitreous
STREAK White
SPECIFIC GRAVITY 3.0
TRANSPARENCY Transparent to translucent

RHOMBOHEDRAL CLEAVAGE
This cleavage mass of magnesite is with associated phlogopite and serpentine.

Phlogopite   *Serpentine*

Perfect rhombohedral cleavage

INDUSTRIAL USES OF MAGNESIUM

A source of magnesium, magnesite is used as a refractory material, as a catalyst and filler in the production of synthetic rubber, and in the preparation of magnesium chemicals and fertilizers. Magnesium is alloyed with aluminum, zinc, or manganese to give it structural strength for use in aircraft, spacecraft, road vehicles, and household appliances (see p.181).

FURNACE LINING
Magnesite is virtually impossible to melt, making it ideal for lining furnaces.

RHODOCHROSITE

HOKKAIDO
Rhodochrosite crystals are found in this area of Japan.

THE CLASSIC COLOR OF rhodochrosite is rose-pink, although it can also be brown or gray. It was named in 1800 from the Greek *rhodokhros*, "of rosy color." A manganese carbonate, most samples have some calcium and iron substituting for manganese; some also contain magnesium. It is found in hydrothermal ore veins formed at moderate temperatures, in high-temperature metamorphic deposits, and as a secondary mineral in sedimentary manganese deposits. In Butte, Montana, it is so abundant that it is mined as an ore of manganese. Other noted localities are in Romania, Gabon, Mexico, Russia, Japan, and the Sweet Home Mine, Colorado.

PROPERTIES

GROUP Carbonates
CRYSTAL SYSTEM Hexagonal/trigonal
COMPOSITION $MnCO_3$
COLOR Rose-pink, brown or gray
FORM/HABIT Rhombohedral
HARDNESS $3^{1}/_{2}$–4
CLEAVAGE Perfect rhombohedral
FRACTURE Uneven
LUSTER Vitreous to pearly
STREAK White
SPECIFIC GRAVITY 3.6
TRANSPARENCY Transparent to translucent
R.I. 1.6–1.8

ORNAMENTAL USE

Gem-quality crystals occur in several mines in Colorado and in Hotazel, South Africa. These are sometimes cut for collectors, but the more common, fine-grained, banded, stalactitic rock is the one normally used for decoration. Rhodochrosite is both soft and very fragile: faceted stones are rare and demand a great deal of skill from the cutter.

EARRINGS
Lustrous rhodochrosite beads adorn these earrings.

DECORATIVE DUCKS
These ducks are carved from rhodochrosite and calcite.

RHODOCHROSITE CRYSTALS
This superb group of transparent, gem-quality rhodochrosite crystals is partly coated with quartz.

Quartz

Rhombohedral crystals

SPECTACULAR CRYSTAL
A group of rhodochrosite rhombohedrons perch on radiating quartz crystals.

STALACTITIC GROWTH
Particularly fine stalactitic growths, sometimes called "Inca rose," come from Catarnarca, Argentina.

TEARDROP
This rhodochrosite is faceted in a pendaloque, or teardrop, cut.

BRILLIANT
Transparent rhodochrosite is sometimes faceted into gems for collectors.

CERUSSITE

Deep striations

KNOWN SINCE ANTIQUITY and named for the Latin *cerussa*, a white lead pigment, cerussite is lead carbonate. Its crystal habits are highly varied, but include tabular, prismatic, dipyramidal, pseudohexagonal, and acicular. Thin tabular crystals are less common. It is generally colorless or white to gray, but may be blue to green with copper impurities. Cerussite is a secondary mineral, which occurs in the oxidation zone of lead veins, and is formed by the action of carbonated water on other lead minerals, particularly galena and anglesite. It is a widespread mineral, with excellent specimens coming from Tsumeb, Namibia; Broken Hill, NSW, Australia; Monteponi Mine, Sardinia; Oruro, Bolivia; Murcia, Spain; and at Phoenixville, Pennsylvania, and also from numerous mines in Arizona and California. After galena, cerussite is the most common ore of lead. It has a high refractive index, making faceted cerussite stones especially brilliant. However, they are too soft to be worn and are cut only for collectors.

TSUMEB
Excellent cerussite crystals are found at Tsumeb, Namibia.

BRILLIANT
Although very soft and fragile, transparent cerussite is occasionally faceted for collectors.

CERUSSITE CRYSTALS
This group of transparent, parallel-twinned, colorless cerussite crystals shows good tabular development.

Parallel twinning

PROPERTIES

GROUP	Carbonates
CRYSTAL SYSTEM	Orthorhombic
COMPOSITION	$PbCO_3$
COLOR	White, gray, blue to green
FORM/HABIT	Tabular, prismatic
HARDNESS	$3–3\frac{1}{2}$
CLEAVAGE	Distinct
FRACTURE	Conchoidal, brittle
LUSTER	Adamantine to vitreous
STREAK	Colorless
SPECIFIC GRAVITY	6.5
TRANSPARENCY	Transparent to translucent
R.I.	1.8–2.1

AZURITE

Azurite pigment

TAKING ITS NAME from the same Persian word as lapis lazuli—*lazhuward*, meaning "blue"—azurite is a deep blue copper carbonate hydroxide. It is azure-blue to very dark blue, and forms tabular or prismatic crystals with a wide variety of faces—over 45 may be commonly seen, as well as over 100 rarer faces. It can also be massive, stalactitic, and botryoidal. Azurite is a secondary mineral, formed in the oxidized portion of copper deposits through the action of carbonated waters on other copper minerals. It is often found with malachite. Finely crystallized specimens come from Utah, Arizona, and New Mexico, and from France, Mexico, Chile, Australia, Russia, Morocco, and especially from Tsumeb, Namibia.

It was mined in ancient Egypt, from Sinai and the eastern desert, and used as a source of metallic copper, as a pigment, and probably in the production of blue glaze. Although used primarily as an ore of copper, it was also used as a pigment in 15th to 17th century European art. Massive azurite used for ornamental purposes is sometimes called chessylite, after Chessy, France.

GLOBE, ARIZONA
The Globe Copper Mines are a great source of azurite.

DEEP BLUE
Azurite pigment was used in this 15th-century French painting in an illuminated manuscript.

Deep azure color

PROPERTIES

GROUP	Carbonates
CRYSTAL SYSTEM	Monoclinic
COMPOSITION	$Cu_3(CO_3)_2(OH)_2$
COLOR	Azure- to dark-blue
FORM/HABIT	Tabular, prismatic
HARDNESS	$3\frac{1}{2}–4$
CLEAVAGE	Perfect
FRACTURE	Conchoidal, brittle
LUSTER	Vitreous to dull to earthy
STREAK	Blue
SPECIFIC GRAVITY	3.8
TRANSPARENCY	Transparent to translucent
R.I.	1.73–1.84

CONCRETION
Spherical concretions of radiating azurite crystals, such as this, can measure more than 1 in (2.5 cm) in diameter.

CABOCHON
Azurite can be cut en cabochon. The top surface of this specimen has been faceted.

Vitreous luster

Bladed crystals

AZURITE CRYSTAL

AZURITE-MALACHITE CABOCHON

DIFFERENT AZURITE HABITS
A dark blue bladed azurite crystal (far left) contrasts with the vivid blue of an azurite and green malachite cabochon.

AZURITE CRYSTALS
This group of bladed azurite crystals comes from Chessy, near Lyon, France, a traditional source of azurite to be ground for use as a pigment, though little remains now.

ANKERITE

AUSTRIA
Erzberg, Austria, is a source of well-formed ankerite crystals.

ESSENTIALLY CALCIUM CARBONATE with varying amounts of iron, magnesium, and manganese in the structure, ankerite was named in 1825 for Austrian mineralogist M. J. Anker. It forms rhombohedral crystals similar to those of dolomite, and can also be massive or coarsely granular. Usually pale buff colored, it can also be colorless, white, gray, and brownish. Much ankerite is fluorescent. Ankerite forms as a secondary mineral from the action of magnesium-bearing fluids on limestone or dolomite. Specimens can be found in Namibia; South Africa; Austria; Japan; Canada; the western US; and elsewhere.

PROPERTIES
GROUP Carbonates
CRYSTAL SYSTEM Hexagonal/trigonal
COMPOSITION $Ca(Fe,Mg,Mn,)(CO_3)_2$
COLOR Colorless to pale buff
FORM/HABIT Rhombohedral
HARDNESS $3^1/_2$–4
CLEAVAGE Perfect
FRACTURE Subconchoidal
LUSTER Vitreous to pearly
STREAK White
SPECIFIC GRAVITY 2.9
TRANSPARENCY Translucent

Perfect cleavage
Rhombohedral crystal

ANKERITE CRYSTALS
These rhombohedral ankerite crystals have a characteristic brown color.

BARYTOCALCITE

ALSTON MOOR, ENGLAND
Barytocalcite is found in this part of Cumbria.

BARYTOCALCITE derives its name from its components: barium and calcite (calcium carbonate). It forms short to long prismatic crystals, usually striated, and can also be massive. It is colorless to white, grayish, greenish, or yellowish. Barytocalcite forms in hydrothermal veins, especially where hydrothermal solutions have invaded limestone. It is found with barite and calcite, and can be a minor ore of barium. Barytocalcite effervesces in hydrochloric acid. Crystals up to 2 in (5 cm) long are found in Cumbria, England. Other localities include Langban, Sweden, and the Krasnoyarsk region of Siberia, Russia.

PROPERTIES
GROUP Carbonates
CRYSTAL SYSTEM Monoclinic
COMPOSITION $BaCa(CO_3)_2$
COLOR White, grayish, greenish, or yellowish
FORM/HABIT Prismatic
HARDNESS 4
CLEAVAGE Perfect, imperfect
FRACTURE Uneven, brittle
LUSTER Vitreous to resinous
STREAK White
SPECIFIC GRAVITY 3.7
TRANSPARENCY Transparent to translucent

PRISMATIC CRYSTALS
These prismatic crystals are on a limestone groundmass.

Prismatic crystals
Limestone groundmass

AURICHALCITE

CHIHUAHUA, MEXICO
Copper Canyon has deposits of aurichalcite.

ITS NAME DERIVING from the Latin for "golden copper," aurichalcite is a zinc copper carbonate hydroxide. It forms acicular, sky-blue, greenish-blue, or pale green crystals, often found as radiating, tufted masses or as velvetlike encrustations. Occasionally it is massive, columnar, or lamellar. Crystals rarely exceed a fraction of an inch long. A secondary mineral, it forms in the oxidized zones of copper and zinc deposits. Localities include the western US; Nagato, Japan; Chihuahua, Mexico; Chessy, France; and Tsumeb, Namibia.

PROPERTIES
GROUP Carbonates
CRYSTAL SYSTEM Monoclinic
COMPOSITION $(Zn,Cu)_5(CO_3)_2(OH)_6$
COLOR Sky-blue, green-blue, or pale green
FORM/HABIT Acicular
HARDNESS 1–2
CLEAVAGE Perfect, brittle
FRACTURE Uneven
LUSTER Silky to pearly
STREAK Pale blue-green
SPECIFIC GRAVITY 4.2
TRANSPARENCY Transparent to translucent

Limonite groundmass

TUFTED CRYSTALS
These masses of small, tufted aurichalcite crystals are on a groundmass of limonite.

Aurichalcite

PHOSGENITE

BROKEN HILL, AUSTRALIA
This area is a source of phosgenite.

PHOSGENITE WAS NAMED in 1841 for the colorless, poisonous gas phosgen ($COCl_2$), because it contains some of the elements that are also found in phosgen. Its crystals are short prismatic, or less commonly, thick tabular. It can be massive or granular as well. Its color varies from white to yellowish, brown, or greenish. It occurs as a product of secondary alteration of other lead minerals under surface conditions. Localities include Sardinia, Italy; Tsumeb, Namibia; Dundas, Tasmania; Broken Hill, NSW, Australia; Derbyshire, England; and, in the US, Inyo County, California, and Custer County, Colorado.

PROPERTIES
GROUP Carbonates
CRYSTAL SYSTEM Tetragonal
COMPOSITION $Pb_2(CO_3)Cl_2$
COLOR White, yellow, brown, or green
FORM/HABIT Prismatic
HARDNESS $2^1/_2$–3
CLEAVAGE Perfect
FRACTURE Conchoidal, sectile
LUSTER Resinous
STREAK White
SPECIFIC GRAVITY 6.1
TRANSPARENCY Transparent to translucent

Prismatic crystals

PRISMATIC
Short, prismatic crystals are in a rock groundmass in this specimen from Sardinia, Italy.

Rock groundmass

183

MALACHITE

COPPER MINE, ZAMBIA
Malachite and chrysocolla have formed as an alteration product of copper and are visible here on the surface of the Kansanshi open-pit copper mine, Zambia.

BOHEMIAN BOTTLE
This mid-19th century Bohemian perfume bottle is made from green malachite glass and contains a gilt spherical stopper.

CARVED MALACHITE NECKLACE
This necklace includes ten panels of malachite, each carved with allegorical figures. It is part of a necklace, bracelet, earring, and pin set made by Francis Peck, Ltd., Nassau.

POSSIBLY THE EARLIEST ORE OF COPPER, having been mined in the Sinai and eastern deserts of ancient Egypt from as early as 3000 BC, malachite is a green copper carbonate hydroxide. It was used as an eye paint, a pigment for wall painting, and in glazes and the coloring of glass. Single crystals are uncommon; when found, they are short to long prismatic. Usually found as botryoidal or encrusting masses, often with a radiating fibrous structure and banded in various shades of green, malachite is also found as delicate fibrous aggregates and as concentrically banded stalactites. Its name comes from the Greek for "mallow," in reference to its leaf-green color.

Malachite occurs in the altered zones of copper deposits, where it is usually accompanied by lesser amounts of azurite (see p.182). The brilliant green of malachite is usually visible on the surface of copper deposits, and is often the first indication a prospector has of this metal's presence.

It is a minor ore of copper, but its principal use is as an ornamental material and gemstone. In ancient China, it was highly prized and called *shilu*, taking its name from its source near Shilu, Guandong Province. In the 19th century, huge deposits in the Ural Mountains of Russia supplied large amounts of malachite to Europe, with some single masses weighing up to 56 tons (see pp.186–87). It was worn in Italy as protection against the "evil eye."

The finest crystals come from Kolwezi, Democratic Republic of Congo, and can approach 4 in (10 cm) in length. The Congo also provides much of the world's supply of ornamental material. Material suitable for cutting also comes from South Australia; Morocco; Bisbee, Arizona; and Lyon in France.

ANCIENT USES

Malachite must rank as one of the most important minerals in humankind's history. It was discovered in around 4000 BC that heating malachite in a hot fire reduced it to native copper. This was probably the first smelting of metal from an ore. This led in turn to the search for other metallic ores, and to the development of metallurgy. For the first time, specialist skills and a new organization of work, in which some people devoted all their time to the mining, smelting, and forging of metal, were developed—all as a direct result of the properties of malachite. The mineral was in use in Egypt as a cosmetic and a pigment from at least 3000 BC. Its use as an eye paint may have been an attempt to ward off eye infections—it is now known that the green eye paint containing malachite had medicinal properties. In ancient Greece, it was used in amulets for children.

PROPERTIES

GROUP	Carbonates
CRYSTAL SYSTEM	Monoclinic
COMPOSITION	$Cu_2CO_3(OH)_2$
COLOR	Bright green
FORM/HABIT	Massive, botryoidal
HARDNESS	$3\frac{1}{2}$–4
CLEAVAGE	Perfect
FRACTURE	Subconchoidal to uneven, brittle
LUSTER	Adamantine to silky
STREAK	Pale green
SPECIFIC GRAVITY	3.9–4.0
TRANSPARENCY	Translucent

BOTRYOIDAL MALACHITE
This botryoidal malachite on chrysocolla is from Etoile du Congo Mine (Star of the Congo Mine), Katanga Province, Congo, known for fine crystals and massive material.

EGYPTIAN WALL PAINTING
Malachite was used as the green pigment in this Egyptian wall painting from the 18th dynasty (15th century BC). The painting is from the tomb of Nakht at Luxor and depicts Nakht and his family hunting water fowl.

MALACHITE PIGMENT

Botryoidal habit

MALACHITE HABITS

Malachite comes in a variety of habits, all of which provide beautiful and interesting patterns when cut and polished.

Radiating crystals

STALACTITIC

Growth layering

STALACTITIC CROSS SECTION

Radiating crystals

FIBROUS

Malachite encrustation

Azurite

MALACHITE WITH AZURITE

"A field of ripe cabbages with their prevailing hue of malachite green"

WALT WHITMAN, "STRAW-COLOR'D AND OTHER PSYCHES," 1892

AZTEC KNIFE

The handle of this Aztec knife from the 15th century is covered with a mosaic of malachite, turquoise, and shell. The blade is made of chalcedony.

KOREAN PAINTING

Malachite pigment is used to dramatic effect in this painting on hemp cloth of Dhratarastra, Guardian King of the East. Probably from Kyongsang Province, Korea, the painting is from the Choson Dynasty and dates from the late 18th century.

POLISHED EGG

The light and dark layers of malachite create a striking pattern in this polished egg, which has been cut to reveal the concentric banding.

PILLOW

This polished piece of malachite is cut across the botryoidal structure, to show an intricate pattern of swirls and bands.

Chrysocolla

Rock groundmass

VASE

This Chinese ritual food vessel, dating from the Sung Dynasty (10th to 12th centuries AD) is decorated with inlaid malachite and silver.

185

RUSSIAN MALACHITE

MINED IN THE URAL MOUNTAINS FROM EARLY IN THE 19TH CENTURY, RUSSIAN MALACHITE HAS BEEN USED DECORATIVELY TO FORM HUGE COLUMNS WITHIN BUILDINGS, USEFUL PIECES OF FURNITURE, AND DELICATE CARVED ARTIFACTS.

PAINTED CEILING
The ceiling of St. Isaac's Cathedral was painted by Karl Bryullov, president of the Academy of Fine Arts. The title of his work is Virgin in Glory.

THE MALACHITE ROOM
In this 1865 watercolor painting of the Malachite Room by Konstantin A. Ukhtomsky, the green malachite columns and surfaces are highlighted by the white walls. During the Russian Revolution, between June and October 1917, the Provisional Government met in this room.

Two of the world's largest gemstone deposits were found in the Ural Mountains of Russia in the early 19th century. Malachite was found in huge quantities in mines at Yekaterinburg, situated 1,025 miles (1,650 km) east of Moscow, and at the Demidoff Mine at Nizhni-Tagil (100 miles/160 km to the north of Yekaterinburg), where a single, banded mass contained more than 1,200 tons of fine material. It has been used to make objects as large as the enormous malachite pillars of St. Isaac's Cathedral in St. Petersburg, as well as intricately worked objects by Carl Fabergé. Many artifacts created using malachite from these deposits can be seen in the Hermitage Museum in Russia, and the Uffizi and St. Peter's in Italy.

St. Isaac's Cathedral, on the banks of the Neva River in St. Petersburg, is the fourth-largest domed cathedral in the world. Begun in 1818, the building took 40 years to complete, and its interior contains 16 varieties of marble, granite, malachite, and lapis lazuli. Designed by French architect Auguste de Montferrand, it incorporates eight massive malachite pillars in the mosaic-covered wall decorated with icons that separates the altar from the rest of the church.

The Malachite Room is one of the most spectacular rooms of the Winter Palace at St. Petersburg. It was rebuilt in 1837 as a drawing room for the wife of Czar Nicholas I, Alexandra Fyodorovna, to the design of architect and painter Alexander Bryullov. It features pilasters, columns, and mantelpieces in malachite mosaic set against white walls decorated with figures representing day, night, and poetry. Gilt doors and crimson hangings complete the sumptuous interior. The room is further ornamented with malachite vases and other artifacts made of malachite during the early 19th century, which were produced in the workshop of Peter Gambs from sketches by Auguste de Montferrand. In the late 19th century, small cupboards were added, decorated with mosaic panels produced by the Peterhof Lapidary Works. Virtually all the malachite from which the decoration of the room was produced was derived from the Russian deposits in the Ural Mountains.

MALACHITE JEWEL BOX
Malachite remains a favorite carving stone today. This malachite jewel box was crafted in 1989 by E. Zhiriakova and is entitled Mistress of Copper Mountain.

INTERIOR OF ST. ISAAC'S CATHEDRAL
Eight giant green columns made of Russian malachite and two of lapis lazuli grace the iconostatis of this gold-domed Russian Orthodox cathedral. They stand out dramatically against the white marble and gold leaf that cover the wall.

AUTUNITE

CORNWALL
A rich source of autunite is located in Cornwall, south-west England.

A POPULAR COLLECTORS' MINERAL, in part because it fluoresces under ultraviolet light, autunite contains uranium and is radioactive, so it must be stored away carefully and handled as little as possible to minimize exposure to radiation. Autunite forms crystals, scaly foliated aggregates, and crusts with crystals standing on edge giving a serrated appearance. As the mineral is mildly heated, water loss transforms tetragonal autunite into orthorhombic meta-autunite. Most museum specimens have at least partly converted to meta-autunite. A moist atmosphere helps to prevent dehydration. It is best stored in a well-ventilated place out of the house. If it is sealed in a container, radon builds up, so ventilation is needed upon opening.

Named for the place of its discovery, Autun, France, autunite is a secondary mineral, formed in the oxidation zone of uranium ore bodies as an alteration product of uraninite and other uranium-bearing minerals. It also occurs in hydrothermal veins and in pegmatites. It is found in England, Germany, Japan, India, Australia, Brazil, and the US.

PROPERTIES

GROUP Phosphates
CRYSTAL SYSTEM Tetragonal
COMPOSITION $Ca(UO_2)_2(PO_4)_2 \cdot 10-12H_2O$
COLOR Lemon-yellow to pale green
FORM/HABIT Tabular
HARDNESS $2-2\frac{1}{2}$
CLEAVAGE Perfect basal
FRACTURE Uneven
LUSTER Vitreous to pearly
STREAK Pale yellow
SPECIFIC GRAVITY 3.1–3.2
TRANSPARENCY Translucent to transparent

Vitreous luster

Tabular, twinned crystal aggregate

TABULAR CRYSTALS
Thin, tabular, twinned crystals characteristic of autunite are clearly visible in this lemon-yellow specimen.

Perfect basal cleavage

RADIOACTIVE DECAY

Radioactivity is the spontaneous decay of an atom's nucleus to form a new nucleus. As it decays, the atom gives off neutrons or protons, along with energy in the form of radiation. Uranium is the element that makes autunite radioactive. It has three isotopes, all of which are radioactive. The most common isotope, Uranium-238, which eventually decays to lead, has a half-life of about 4.5 billion years. This means that over 4.5 billion years, there is a 50 percent chance that any single U-238 atom will decay.

B. B. BOLTWOOD
B. B. Boltwood devised the method of dating rocks by measuring radioactive decay.

VIVIANITE

QUEBEC
Deposits of vivianite are found in Quebec and Ontario.

COLORLESS WHEN freshly exposed, vivianite becomes pale blue to greenish-blue on oxidation. It was named in 1817 for its discoverer, the English mineralogist J. G. Vivian. Vivianite occurs as elongated, prismatic, or bladed tabular crystals, or can be massive or fibrous. It is a widespread secondary mineral, forming in the weathered zones of iron ore and phosphate deposits. It can also be found as powdery concretions in clays, in recent soils and sediments, and as an alteration coating on bone. Large crystals can be found in pegmatites such as those in Maine, New Hampshire, and Georgia, and in Brazil. Other deposits occur in Japan, Germany, Bolivia, Canada, Russia, and Serbia.

PROPERTIES

GROUP Phosphates
CRYSTAL SYSTEM Monoclinic
COMPOSITION $Fe_3(PO_4)_2 \cdot 8H_2O$
COLOR Colorless to green or blue
FORM/HABIT Elongated to prismatic
HARDNESS $1\frac{1}{2}-2$
CLEAVAGE Perfect
FRACTURE Uneven
LUSTER Vitreous to earthy
STREAK Bluish-white
SPECIFIC GRAVITY 2.7
TRANSPARENCY Transparent to translucent

Clusters of elongated, prismatic crystals

Vitreous luster

A NATURAL BLUE PIGMENT

Before the development of modern synthetics, paint pigments were exclusively natural in origin. Durable blue has always been a prized color, and vivianite provides that. Vivianite pigment becomes bluer with exposure, whereas azurite becomes greener. Like most natural pigments, it has now been replaced by a synthetic version.

PRUSSIAN BLUE
Powdered vivianite was used to make Prussian blue, which can be seen in this 14th-century painting on the choir screens of Cologne cathedral.

CRYSTAL CLUSTERS
After long exposure to light, vivianite becomes bluish-black, as here.

TORBERNITE

CORNWALL
Mines in Cornwall, south-west England, yield excellent torbernite.

NAMED IN 1793 FOR Swedish mineralogist Torbern Olaf Bergmann, torbernite is one of the principal uranium-bearing minerals and a minor ore of uranium. It forms thin to thick tabular crystals, commonly square in outline, as well as foliated, micalike masses. A copper uranyl phosphate hydrate, torbernite is a secondary mineral formed as an alteration product of uraninite or other uranium-bearing minerals. It is associated with autunite, and is also radioactive, needing to be stored and handled with great care. Fine specimens occur in Cornwall, England, and the Democratic Republic of Congo.

CRYSTALS
Tabular torbernite crystals rest on an iron-rich groundmass.

Rock groundmass

PROPERTIES

GROUP	Phosphates
CRYSTAL SYSTEM	Tetragonal
COMPOSITION	$Cu(UO_2)_2(PO_4)_2 \cdot 8-12H_2O$
COLOR	Bright green
FORM/HABIT	Thin to thick tabular
HARDNESS	$2-2\frac{1}{2}$
CLEAVAGE	Perfect, basal
FRACTURE	Uneven
LUSTER	Vitreous to subadamantine
STREAK	Pale green
SPECIFIC GRAVITY	3.2
TRANSPARENCY	Transparent to translucent

Tabular torbernite crystal

ERYTHRITE

ONTARIO
Some of the best erythrite comes from Ontario, Canada.

COMMONLY CALLED COBALT BLOOM, erythrite is a cobalt arsenate hydrate that forms in the oxidized zone of cobalt and nickel deposits. Due to its bright color, it is used to indicate the presence of cobalt-nickel-silver ores. Erythrite occurs as deeply striated, prismatic to acicular crystals, commonly radiating, globular tufts of crystals, or as coatings. Fine specimens come from Ontario, Canada, and Morocco. It is also found in the southwestern US, Mexico, France, the Czech Republic, Germany, and Australia.

PROPERTIES

GROUP	Arsenates
CRYSTAL SYSTEM	Monoclinic
COMPOSITION	$CO_3(AsO_4)_2 \cdot 8H_2O$
COLOR	Purple-pink
FORM/HABIT	Prismatic to acicular
HARDNESS	$1\frac{1}{2}-2\frac{1}{2}$
CLEAVAGE	Perfect
FRACTURE	Uneven, sectile
LUSTER	Adamantine to vitreous, pearly
STREAK	Pale red
SPECIFIC GRAVITY	3.1
TRANSPARENCY	Transparent to translucent

ACICULAR CRYSTALS
These brightly colored, acicular crystals of erythrite are from Bou Azzer, Morocco.

Rock groundmass

Prismatic crystals

VARISCITE

BISBEE
Variscite occurs in this mining district in Arizona.

VARISCITE WAS NAMED FOR VARISCIA, the old name for the German district of Voightland, where it was first discovered. It rarely forms crystals, and is predominantly found as cryptocrystalline or fine-grained masses, in veins, crusts, or nodules. It forms in cavities in near-surface deposits, produced by the action of phosphate-rich waters on aluminous rocks. It commonly occurs in association with apatite and wavellite, and with chalcedony and various hydrous oxides of iron. Located in Austria, the Czech Republic, Australia, Venezuela, and in North Carolina, Utah, and Arizona, variscite is valued as a semiprecious gemstone and an ornamental material. It is porous, and, when worn next to the skin, tends to absorb body oils, which discolor it.

CONCRETIONARY VARISCITE
Variscite is often found in nodules and concretions like the sliced specimen shown here. It is sometimes mistaken for turquoise.

PENDANT
This variscite pendant on a sterling silver chain was designed by Jan McClellan. Next to the variscite are three garnets mounted in silver.

Waxy luster

CABOCHON
Variscite is sometimes polished and transformed into an inexpensive cabochon gem.

CRYSTAL FORMATION
Variscite rarely forms crystals. When it does so, they are often visible only under the electron microscope, as shown here.

Concretion

PROPERTIES

GROUP	Phosphates
CRYSTAL SYSTEM	Orthorhombic
COMPOSITION	$AlPO_4 \cdot 2H_2O$
COLOR	Pale to apple-green
FORM/HABIT	Cryptocrystalline aggregates
HARDNESS	$4\frac{1}{2}$
CLEAVAGE	Good but rarely visible
FRACTURE	Splintery in massive types
LUSTER	Vitreous to waxy
STREAK	White
SPECIFIC GRAVITY	2.6
TRANSPARENCY	Opaque
R.I.	1.6–1.7

MESOAMERICAN TURQUOISE

THE ANCIENT CIVILIZATIONS OF MESOAMERICA
(MEXICO AND CENTRAL AMERICA) TREASURED
TURQUOISE AS A MOSAIC DECORATION FOR THEIR
SOPHISTICATED ARTIFACTS, FROM MIRRORS AND KNIFE
HANDLES TO SACRED STATUES AND FUNERARY MASKS.

•

Turquoise was first used in
Mexico and Central America
during the Classic Period of
Mesoamerican civilization, between
about 200 and 900 AD. The source
of the gemstone was the Mount
Chalchihuitl Mine near Cerillos, in
what is now New Mexico. There, a
turquoise deposit was dug out with
primitive hand tools, leaving a pit
200 ft (60 m) across and up to 130 ft
(40 m) deep. It was probably mined
by native Pueblo Indians, and then
passed along trade routes to the ancient trading center of
Casas Grandes, now in Chichihuitlahua State, Mexico—
a distance of several thousand miles.

The use of turquoise spanned more than 1,000 years
of Mesoamerican history. The people of the city-state of
Teotihuacan, which dominated Mesoamerica from
around the 4th to the 7th century AD,
were among the first to use turquoise in
ancient Mesoamerica. It was still of
major importance by the time of the
Aztecs, who emerged as a civilization
in the 13th century, and ruled a large
empire in what is now central and southern
Mexico in the 15th and early 16th centuries. For
example, the Aztec fire god, the supreme solar
deity, was called *Xiuhtecuhtli*, meaning Lord of the
Turquoise, and was depicted costumed in turquoise,
with a turquoise crown and breast pendant, and a
shield covered in turquoise mosaics.

TURQUOISE MOSAICS

Turquoise was used with great technical skill in
Mesoamerican mosaics. Usually, small, irregularly
shaped pieces were highly polished and then cut to
fit tightly together to suit the design. Aztec turquoise
mosaics can consist of as many as 14,000 individual
pieces. The mosaic was typically held in place by a
vegetal pitch or gum, or by a kind of cement.

Turquoise mosaics were used to encrust shields,
helmets, knife handles, collars, medallions, ear plugs,
mirrors, animal figures, cult statues, and, most strikingly,
masks. The latter range from the trapezoid Teotihuacan
masks, many of which have been found in ancient
burial places, to Aztec funerary masks in which turquoise,
gold, and shell were overlaid on a human skull.

TEOTIHUACAN RUINS
*Built in AD 50 on the northeast
side of the Valley of Mexico, the
city of Teotihuacan was laid out
in a grid pattern with the huge
Pyramid of the Sun forming an
awe-inspiring backdrop.*

TURQUOISE SERPENT
*Shaped in the form of a
serpent, this 15th-century Aztec
pin is inlaid with turquoise.
The turquoise serpent was a
powerful symbol in Aztec
mythology. The Aztecs believed
that when the god of the Sun
awoke, he drove the Moon and
stars from the sky, armed with
his mystic weapon, the
"turquoise serpent."*

TEOTIHUACAN MASK
*Made of turquoise and shell,
this mosaic sculpture mask
is typical of the Teotihuacan
style, being trapezoid in
shape and having a straight
forehead, almond-shaped
eyes, a strong nose, and a
sensuous, half-open mouth.*

VANADINITE

THIS RELATIVELY RARE MINERAL is a lead vanadate chloride. Its crystals are usually long prisms, but can be acicular to hairlike, and, on occasion, form hollow prisms. Small amounts of calcium, zinc, and copper may substitute for lead, and arsenic can completely substitute for vanadium in the crystal structure to form the mineral mimetite (see below). Vanadinite is soluble in both hydrochloric and nitric acids. It forms as a secondary mineral in oxidized ore deposits containing lead, often associated with galena, barite, wulfenite, and limonite. It is a major source of vanadium and a minor source of lead. Superb specimens come from Minas Gerais, Brazil; Chihuahua, Mexico; Mibladen, Morocco; Leadhills, Scotland; Tsumeb, Namibia; and from many mines in the US.

BROKEN HILL
Vanadinite occurs in this part of New South Wales, Australia.

Short, prismatic crystals

VANADINITE CRYSTALS ON ROMANÈCHITE

Romanèchite groundmass

Adamantine luster

Rock groundmass

SIR HENRY ROSCOE
The English chemist Sir Henry Roscoe first isolated vanadium from vanadinite in 1867.

USES OF VANADIUM

Most of the vanadium that is extracted goes into making vanadium steels. The vanadium refines the grain of the steel, and forms carbides with the carbon present. Vanadium steel is particularly strong and hard, with considerable shock resistance. Vanadium compounds are used as catalysts in the manufacture of sulfuric acid, nylon, and in the oxidation of some organic substances.

PROPERTIES

GROUP Phosphates
CRYSTAL SYSTEM Hexagonal
COMPOSITION $Pb_5(VO_4)_3Cl$
COLOR Orange-red, yellow
FORM/HABIT Hexagonal prisms
HARDNESS 3
CLEAVAGE None
FRACTURE Uneven, brittle
LUSTER Adamantine
STREAK Whitish-yellow
SPECIFIC GRAVITY 6.9
TRANSPARENCY Transparent to translucent

RED VANADINITE
Vanadinite crystals are often brilliantly colored in shades of red and yellow. This specimen is typical, with smooth-faced, prismatic crystals.

Prismatic vanadinite crystals

MIMETITE

THIS MINERAL FORMS HEAVY, barrel-shaped crystals or rounded masses, and is also found in botryoidal, granular, tabular, and acicular aggregates. The arsenic-rich end member of a solid-solution series with pyromorphite (see opposite), mimetite is named after the Greek *mimetes*, "imitator," referring to its resemblance to pyromorphite. Its color range includes shades of yellow, orange, brown, and sometimes green; it can be colorless. Mimetite is a secondary mineral, which forms in the oxidized zone of lead deposits and other localities where lead and arsenic occur together. Excellent specimens come from Chihuahua, Mexico; Saxony, Germany; Attica, Greece; Broken Hill, Australia; and in Bisbee and Tombstone, Arizona. One single crystal from Tsumeb, Namibia, measured 2½ in (6.4 cm) by 1 in (2.5 cm).

CUMBRIA
The rocks of Cumbria in the north of England are a source of mimetite.

CAMPYLITE
This specimen, from Caldbeck Fells, Cumbria, England, contains a variety of mimetite known as campylite. It also includes baryte on nodules of manganese.

Baryte

Resinous luster

Rounded masses of mimetite

Black coronadite matrix

PROPERTIES

GROUP Arsenates
CRYSTAL SYSTEM Hexagonal
COMPOSITION $Pb_5(AsO_4)_3Cl$
COLOR Pale yellow to yellowish-brown, orange, green
FORM/HABIT Barrel-shaped crystals and rounded masses
HARDNESS 3½–4
CLEAVAGE Poor
FRACTURE Conchoidal to uneven, brittle
LUSTER Resinous
STREAK White
SPECIFIC GRAVITY 7.3
TRANSPARENCY Subtransparent

LAZULITE

BISBEE
Lazulite occurs in several localities in the US, such as Bisbee, Arizona.

LAZULITE TAKES ITS NAME from the old German *lazurstein*, "blue stone." Crystals are pyramidal, with tabular prism faces; it can also be massive and granular. It is azure-blue, sky-blue, or bluish-white to blue-green in color. It can be similar in appearance to lapis lazuli (lazurite). Lazulite occurs in aluminous metamorphic rocks, quartz veins, and granite pegmatites. Localities for fine specimens are Sweden; Austria; Switzerland; Mount Fitton, Yukon, Canada; and, in the US, the White Mountains, California; Newport, New Hampshire; Chowders Mountain, North Carolina; and Graves Mountain, Georgia.

LAZULITE IN QUARTZ
This specimen from Lincoln County, Georgia, has well-formed lazulite crystals in a groundmass of quartz.

Dipyramidal crystals

Quartz groundmass

SINGLE CRYSTAL
This single crystal of lazulite displays a dipyramidal habit.

POLISHED
Granular lazulite is cut en cabochon. *Beads and decorative items are sometimes made from it.*

PROPERTIES

GROUP	Phosphates
CRYSTAL SYSTEM	Monoclinic
COMPOSITION	$(Mg,Fe)Al_2(PO_4)_2(OH)_2$
COLOR	Various shades of blue
FORM/HABIT	Pyramidal
HARDNESS	5–6
CLEAVAGE	Indistinct
FRACTURE	Uneven to splintery
LUSTER	Vitreous
STREAK	White
SPECIFIC GRAVITY	3.1
TRANSPARENCY	Transparent to translucent
R.I.	1.61–1.64

PYROMORPHITE

DYFED, WALES
Superb examples of pyromorphite are found in this part of the UK.

PYROMORPHITE GETS ITS NAME from the Greek *pyr*, "fire," and *morphe*, "form," alluding to its property of taking up a crystalline form on cooling after it has melted to a globual. A lead phosphate chloride, pyromorphite forms a solid-solution series with mimetite (see opposite) in which phosphorus and arsenic replace one another. Crystals may be simple hexagonal prisms or rounded and barrel-shaped, spindle-shaped, or cavernous. Pyromorphite can also be globular, reniform, or granular. It is dark green to yellow-green, shades of brown, a waxy yellow, or yellow-orange. A minor ore of lead, it occurs as a secondary mineral in the oxidized zone of lead deposits with cerussite, smithsonite, vanadinite, galena, and limonite. Excellent specimens come from Dyfed, Wales; Leadhills, Scotland; Cumbria, England; Bad Ems, Germany; Broken Hill, Australia; Ussel, France; Castilla-Léon, Spain; Chihuahua, Mexico; and, in the US, Phoenixville, Pennsylvania; Leadville, Colorado; Bisbee, Arizona; and Coeur d'Alene, Idaho.

LIME-GREEN PYROMORPHITE

YELLOW-GREEN PYROMORPHITE

Prismatic crystals

Barrel-shaped crystals

PROPERTIES

GROUP	Phosphates
CRYSTAL SYSTEM	Hexagonal
COMPOSITION	$Pb_5(PO_4)_3Cl$
COLOR	Green, yellow, orange or brown
FORM/HABIT	Prismatic
HARDNESS	$3^1/2$–4
CLEAVAGE	Poor
FRACTURE	Uneven to subconchoidal, brittle
LUSTER	Resinous
STREAK	White
SPECIFIC GRAVITY	7.0
TRANSPARENCY	Subtransparent to translucent

Resinous luster

BARREL-SHAPED CRYSTALS
This mass of pyromorphite on a limonite groundmass shows typical barrel-shaped crystals.

Limonite groundmass

EUCHROITE

MISSOULA
Euchroite is found in the copper mining area of Missoula, Montana.

A RELATIVELY RARE MINERAL, euchroite was named in 1823 from the Greek for "beautiful color." It is a copper arsenate hydrate, and forms short prismatic crystals. Its color ranges from brilliant emerald-green to leek-green. It was originally found in Slovakia. It also occurs in Cramer Creek, near Missoula, Montana, where it is found lining crevices in mica schist, and there are important deposits in Bulgaria and Greece.

Vitreous luster

PROPERTIES

GROUP Arsenates
CRYSTAL SYSTEM Orthorhombic
COMPOSITION $Cu_2(AsO_4)(OH)\cdot3H_2O$
COLOR Emerald-green
FORM/HABIT Prismatic
HARDNESS $3^1/_2$–4
CLEAVAGE Imperfect
FRACTURE Uneven to subconchoidal
LUSTER Vitreous
STREAK Green
SPECIFIC GRAVITY 3–4
TRANSPARENCY Transparent to translucent

Euchroite crystals

PRISMATIC CRYSTALS
These short, prismatic crystals on a rock groundmass are from Lubietová, Slovakia.

CHILDRENITE

SAXONY
Mineral-rich Saxony in Germany has deposits of childrenite.

NAMED FOR THE English mineralogist J. G. Children in 1823, childrenite is an iron aluminum phosphate hydrate. Its crystals are pyramidal to short prismatic, thick tabular, or platy. It is sometimes found in radiating, botryoidal masses, crusts with a fibrous structure, or as massive aggregates. Prism faces are usually striated. As increasing amounts of manganese substitute for iron, it grades into eosphorite. Childrenite is found in Maine and South Dakota, England, Germany, and Brazil.

PROPERTIES

GROUP Arsenates
CRYSTAL SYSTEM Orthorhombic
COMPOSITION $FeAl(PO_4)(OH)_2\cdot H_2O$
COLOR Brown to yellowish-brown, white, or brownish-black
FORM/HABIT Pyramidal to short prismatic
HARDNESS 5
CLEAVAGE Poor
FRACTURE Subconchoidal to uneven
LUSTER Vitreous
STREAK White to yellowish
SPECIFIC GRAVITY 3.2
TRANSPARENCY Translucent

CRYSTALS
This sample is from George and Charlotte Mine, Devon, England.

Prismatic childrenite crystals

Quartz

PHARMACOSIDERITE

CORNWALL
Pharmacosiderite was first discovered in Cornwall, south-west England.

PHARMACOSIDERITE IS A POTASSIUM iron arsenate hydrate, and takes its name from the Greek *pharmakon*, meaning "poison" or "drug," an allusion to its arsenic content, and *sideros*, "iron." Its crystals are commonly diagonally striated cubes, and not many exceed a fraction of an inch. It is also rarely granular and earthy, and is quite sectile. Pharmacosiderite occurs in hydrothermal deposits, or as a secondary alteration product of arsenic-bearing minerals, such as arsenopyrite. It was first discovered in Cornwall, England; it is also found in Germany, Greece, Italy, Algeria, Namibia, Brazil, and in Utah, New Jersey, and Arizona.

PROPERTIES

GROUP Arsenates
CRYSTAL SYSTEM Cubic
COMPOSITION $KFe_4(AsO_4)_3(OH)_4\cdot6$–$7(H_2O)$
COLOR Variable greens, yellowish-brown, brown
FORM/HABIT Cubic
HARDNESS $2^1/_2$
CLEAVAGE Imperfect to good
FRACTURE Uneven
LUSTER Adamantine to greasy
STREAK Pale green to brown, pale yellow
SPECIFIC GRAVITY 2.8
TRANSPARENCY Transparent to translucent

Cubic pharmacosiderite crystals

Quartz and sulfide matrix

Adamantine luster

ARSENIC POISONING

On May 5, 1821, Napoleon died in the drawing room at Longwood on the island of St. Helena after more than four years of illness. A lock of hair examined shortly after his death was found to contain arsenic. Recently, fragments of wallpaper supposedly from the walls of the drawing room and bedroom were analyzed. Both were dyed with a green pigment that contained arsenite. In the humidity, the wallpaper would have become damp, causing the arsenite to become a poisonous vapor form of arsenic.

DEATH OF NAPOLEON
The green patterning in the wallpaper is visible in this painting by Carl von Steuben (1788–1856).

Scrap of wallpaper from Napoleon's bedroom

CUBIC CRYSTALS
This mass of green pharmacosiderite crystals was found in Wheal Gorland, Cornwall, England. Pharmacosiderite also occurs in olive or brown colors.

CHALCOPHYLLITE

TSUMEB
Fine deposits of chalcophyllite are found in Tsumeb, Namibia.

A VIVID BLUE-GREEN in color, chalcophyllite takes its name from the Greek for "copper" and for "leaf," which is a reference to its copper content and its common foliated habit. Crystals of chalcophyllite are tabular and hexagonal. Chalcophyllite is a copper aluminum arsenate sulfate hydrate. It is a widespread secondary mineral that occurs in the alteration zone of copper deposits. Although similar in appearance to other copper minerals, it is soluble in both nitric acid and ammonia. Specimens come from southwest England, France, Germany, Austria, Russia, Namibia, and Chile, and from Utah, Arizona, and Nevada.

PROPERTIES

GROUP	Arsenates
CRYSTAL SYSTEM	Hexagonal/trigonal
COMPOSITION	$Cu_{18}Al_2(AsO_4)_2(SO_4)_3(OH)_{27}\cdot33H_2O$
COLOR	Vivid blue-green
FORM/HABIT	Tabular
HARDNESS	2
CLEAVAGE	Perfect basal
FRACTURE	Uneven to subconchoidal
LUSTER	Pearly to vitreous
STREAK	Pale green
SPECIFIC GRAVITY	2.7
TRANSPARENCY	Transparent to translucent

Tabular chalcophyllite crystals

COPPER IN ART

The casting of native copper began around 4000 BC, and the smelting of copper from copper-bearing rock started sometime before 3800 BC. Although copper was first used for making weapons and implements, its ductility and malleability soon made it a material of choice for artisans. The artisans hammered the copper and cast it into statuettes and heads, which are still admired today for their artistry as well as for the skill of their craftsmen.

STATUE OF LAMMA
Dating from 1800–1600 BC, this statue of the deity was found at Ur.

HEAD OF SARGON I
This copper head of the King of Akkad was made in Mesopotamia between 2334 and 2279 BC.

BULL'S HEAD
Dating from 2500–2400 BC, this copper bull's head was crafted for Sumerian royalty.

Rock groundmass

TABULAR CRYSTALS
A mass of vivid blue, tabular chalcophyllite crystals rests on a rock groundmass.

DUFRENITE

CORNWALL
The best specimens of dufrenite are found in Cornwall, southwest England.

USUALLY FOUND IN botryoidal masses or crusts, dufrenite is a hydrous phosphate of iron. Crystals, which are relatively uncommon, are found in sheaflike aggregates with rounded ends. The mineral was named in 1833 for French mineralogist P. A. Dufrenoy. It occurs as a secondary mineral in the weathered zone of metallic veins and in iron ore deposits. It is found in Cornwall, England; Hureau, France; Bushmanland, South Africa; and New Hampshire and Alabama.

PROPERTIES

GROUP	Phosphates
CRYSTAL SYSTEM	Monoclinic
COMPOSITION	$CaFeFe_5(PO_4)_4(OH)_6\cdot2H_2O$
COLOR	Dark olive-green to black
FORM/HABIT	Massive
HARDNESS	$3^1/_2 – 4^1/_2$
CLEAVAGE	Perfect in two directions
FRACTURE	Indeterminate, brittle
LUSTER	Vitreous to silky to dull
STREAK	Yellow-green
SPECIFIC GRAVITY	3.3
TRANSPARENCY	Subtranslucent to opaque

BOTRYOIDAL MASS
This specimen of dufrenite on goethite is from Hirschberg, Germany.

Dufrenite masses

Goethite

WAVELLITE

BOHEMIA
Good wavellite specimens occur in this part of the Czech Republic.

AN ALUMINUM PHOSPHATE hydroxide hydrate, wavellite typically occurs as translucent, greenish, globular aggregates of radiating crystals, as crusts, or occasionally as stalactitic deposits. It is a secondary mineral that forms in crevices in low-grade, aluminous, metamorphic rocks, limonite and phosphate rock deposits, and, rarely, hydrothermal veins. It is found in the Czech Republic, France, Bolivia, Germany, Zaire, Australia, England, Ireland, and the US.

PROPERTIES

GROUP	Phosphates
CRYSTAL SYSTEM	Orthorhombic
COMPOSITION	$Al_3(PO_4)_2(OH,F)_3\cdot5H_2O$
COLOR	Green or white
FORM/HABIT	Radiating aggregates
HARDNESS	$3^1/_2 – 4$
CLEAVAGE	Good
FRACTURE	Subconchoidal to uneven
LUSTER	Vitreous to resinous
STREAK	White
SPECIFIC GRAVITY	2.4
TRANSPARENCY	Translucent

Radiating wavellite crystals

RADIATING CRYSTALS
Acicular crystals of wavellite form radiating aggregates on this rock groundmass.

203

BORATES AND NITRATES

BORATES

Borate minerals are compounds containing boron and oxygen. The majority of borate minerals are rare, but a few, such as borax, ulexite, colemanite, and kernite, form large, commercially mined deposits. Structurally, boron and oxygen may form a triangle (BO_3) or a tetrahedron (BO_4), each with a central boron atom.

Borates appear in two geological environments. In the first, borate–bearing solutions that result from volcanic activity flow into a closed basin, where evaporation takes place. Over time, stratified deposits of borate minerals accumulate. Basin deposits usually occur in desert regions, such as the Mojave Desert and Death Valley in California; since they are soluble in water, they are better preserved in dry environments. Borax, colemanite, and kernite are all found in evaporate deposits. In the second environment, borate minerals are formed as a result of alteration of the rocks by heat and pressure at relatively high temperatures. These borate minerals usually consist

Magnesium ion

Magnesium tetrahedron

Boron tetrahedron

CRYSTAL STRUCTURE OF BORACITE
In boracite, densely packed boron tetrahedra combine with the metal ion magnesium.

of densely packed BO_3 triangles combined with metal ions such as magnesium, manganese, aluminum, or iron. Boracite and sussexite form in this type of environment.

NITRATES

Nitrates are a small group of nitrogen– and oxygen–bearing compounds, which, because of their solubility and instability, are practically confined to arid regions and soils. The only major deposit of nitrates is in the Atacama Desert of northern Chile, where they occur under the loose soil as beds of a grayish, cemented mixture of nitrates, sulfates, halides, and sand. They contain an NO_3 group in a triangular arrangement.

BORAX

BORAX CRUST
Searles Lake, California, is the prime source of borax.

BORAX TAKES ITS NAME from the Arabic *buraq*, meaning "white." A sodium borate hydrate, its crystals are short prismatic to tabular, although in commercial deposits it is predominantly massive. Its colorless crystals dehydrate in air to become the chalky mineral tincalconite. Borax fuses easily to become a colorless glass. In mineralogy, molten beads of borax are used to test other minerals for composition: a powdered mineral sample is fused with the bead to see what color it turns and therefore what chemicals the mineral contains.

Borax is an evaporite mineral formed in dry desert lake beds, and accompanied by halite, other borates, and various evaporite sulfates and carbonates. Borax has been mined since ancient times from saline lakes in Kashmir and Tibet. Today it is the principal source of boron compounds widely used in industry. About half of the world's supply comes from the borax crusts and brine of Searles Lake in southern California. Other sources include: Boron, California; Turkey; Salar Cauchari, Salta Province, Argentina; Ladakh and Kashmir in the Indian Himalayas; and Inder, Kazakhstan.

BORAX CRYSTALS
This group of prismatic borax crystals coated with an opaque layer of tincalconite is situated on a rock groundmass.

Prismatic crystals

Coating of white tincalconite

Rock groundmass

USES OF BORON

Boron and its compounds are widely used in industry. It is an important component of glass and pottery glazes. In metallurgy, it is used as a solvent for metal oxide slags in steel-making and metal-casting, and as a flux in welding and soldering. It is also widely used as a fertilizer additive, a water softener, a disinfectant, and a soap additive.

MOUTHWASH
Boron is one of the ingredients in mouthwash.

PROPERTIES

GROUP	Borates
CRYSTAL SYSTEM	Monoclinic
COMPOSITION	$Na_2B_4O_5(OH)_4 \cdot 8H_2O$
COLOR	Colorless
FORM/HABIT	Short prismatic
HARDNESS	$2-2\frac{1}{2}$
CLEAVAGE	Perfect, imperfect
FRACTURE	Conchoidal
LUSTER	Vitreous to earthy
STREAK	White
SPECIFIC GRAVITY	1.7
TRANSPARENCY	Transparent to translucent

ULEXITE

ULEXITE, LIKE BORAX, is an important economic mineral. It was first discovered at Iquique, Tarapace, Chile, formerly part of Peru. A hydrated sodium calcium borate hydrate, ulexite is commonly found in nodular, rounded, or lenslike crystal aggregates (often resembling cotton wool balls). In these forms, it is white and has a silky or satiny luster. It less commonly forms parallel, fibrous crystals, which are colorless and have a vitreous luster; this form is known as "television stone" (see panel, right). The German chemist George Ludwig Ulex (1811–1883) determined the composition of ulexite in 1850, and it was named after him. It has also been called boronatrocalcite and natroborocalcite.

Ulexite is most commonly found in playa lakes and other evaporite basins in desert regions, where it is derived from boron-rich magmatic fluids. It occurs in the dry plains of Chile, Argentina, and Kazakhstan, and in the huge evaporate deposits of the Kramer District of Death Valley, California. It is commonly found in association with anhydrite, colemanite, and glauberite.

Ulexite's industrial uses are similar to those for borax (see panel, opposite).

DEATH VALLEY
Death Valley, California, is characterized by the playa lakes where evaporite deposits form.

GLAZED POTS
Boron compounds derived from ulexite and borax are used extensively in pottery glazes. They are also effective fluxes for melting metal and welding.

SOAP
Boron compounds derived from borax and, to a lesser extent, ulexite are important components of many soaps.

TELEVISION STONE

An unusual property of one form of ulexite is its ability to "transmit" images. This form of ulexite develops as tightly bundled, acicular crystals that effectively function like optical fibers. A piece crystallized in this way, and with each end flattened and polished perpendicular to the long direction of the crystal bundle will, when placed on print or other images, show that image on the opposite end, as in the photograph below.

TRANSMITTING PRINT
The dark line underneath this ulexite specimen appears to be on its surface. It has been "transmitted" from the back to the front.

PROPERTIES

GROUP	Borates
CRYSTAL SYSTEM	Monoclinic
COMPOSITION	$NaCaB_5O_6(OH)_6 \cdot H_2O$
COLOR	Colorless, white
FORM/HABIT	Nodular, acicular
HARDNESS	$2\frac{1}{2}$
CLEAVAGE	Perfect
FRACTURE	Uneven
LUSTER	Vitreous to silky
STREAK	White
SPECIFIC GRAVITY	2.0
TRANSPARENCY	Transparent to translucent

Parallel, acicular crystals

Surface polished, showing fiber-optic effect

Transparent specimen

ULEXITE SLICE
This ulexite specimen from the boron deposits of California has been sliced and polished to show its fiber-optic effect. This also shows its fibrous structure, composed of parallel, acicular crystals.

FERTILIZER
Borate is added to many agricultural fertilizers because boron is a vital trace element for plant growth.

HOWLITE

DEATH VALLEY
Significant howlite deposits are found in Death Valley, California.

NAMED IN 1868 for Canadian chemist Henry How, who discovered it, howlite is a calcium borosilicate hydroxide. Crystals are tabular but rare; generally, it forms nodular masses. It is usually white, often with veins of other minerals running through the nodules. When dyed, it resembles turquoise, although it is easily distinguished from turquoise by its inferior hardness (turquoise is 5–6). In addition, howlite is easily fusible. It occurs with other boron minerals, such as kernite (below right) and borax (see p.204), and is found in quantity in California, especially the Kramer district of Death Valley and San Bernardino County. It is also found in Nova Scotia and Newfoundland, Canada; Magdalena, Mexico; Saxony, Germany; the southern Urals of Russia; and Suserluk, Turkey.

STAINED HOWLITE
Tumble-polished and dyed or stained howlite looks similar to turquoise, and is sometimes sold as such.

— *Lighter color*

TURQUOISE
Turquoise can be told apart from dyed howlite by its greater hardness and depth of color.

Howlite

Greater depth of color

PROPERTIES

GROUP	Borates
CRYSTAL SYSTEM	Monoclinic
COMPOSITION	$Ca_2B_5SiO_9(OH)_5$
COLOR	White
FORM/HABIT	Nodular masses
HARDNESS	$3^{1}/_{2}$
CLEAVAGE	None
FRACTURE	Conchoidal to uneven
LUSTER	Subvitreous
STREAK	White
SPECIFIC GRAVITY	2.6
TRANSPARENCY	Translucent to opaque

NODULAR HOWLITE
This howlite nodule, from the Fraser Quarry, Hants County, Nova Scotia, Canada, still retains part of the anhydrite in which it was formed.

Subvitreous luster

Anhydrite

COLEMANITE

CALIFORNIA
The mineral-rich state of California includes deposits of colemanite.

THIS BORATE MINERAL was named in 1884 for William Coleman, the owner of the mine in California where it was discovered. Typically it occurs as crystals up to an inch or so across, and it can be massive, granular, or compact. It is pyroelectric. Colemanite is found in playas and other evaporite deposits where it replaces other borate minerals, such as borax, that were originally deposited in huge inland lakes. These deposits may be several yards thick. Colemanite in commercial deposits is usually massive, but individual crystals up to 8 in (20 cm) long have been found. The chief localities are California; Kazakhstan; Turkey; and Argentina. Colemanite is an important source of commercial borates and boric acid. It was the main source of boron (see p.207) until the 1930s.

HEAT-RESISTANT GLASS

Heat-resistant glass has been developed by the inclusion of boron compounds in place of some of the silica of normal glass. These compounds are called borosilicates. They make glass resistant to heat, chemicals, and electricity. Borosilicate glass is used in car headlights, laboratory glassware, industrial equipment, thermometers, and ovenware (including glass sold under the well-known trademark Pyrex).

FIREFIGHTER'S VISOR
Borosilicates are used in a wide range of heat-resistant items.

COMPLEX CRYSTALS
Colemanite commonly occurs as colorless, brilliant, complex crystals, as in this specimen.

Prismatic crystals

Translucent crystal

PROPERTIES

GROUP	Borates
CRYSTAL SYSTEM	Monoclinic
COMPOSITION	$CaB_3O_4(OH)_3 \cdot H_2O$
COLOR	Colorless, white
FORM/HABIT	Short prismatic
HARDNESS	$4–4^{1}/_{2}$
CLEAVAGE	Perfect, distinct
FRACTURE	Uneven to subconchoidal
LUSTER	Vitreous to adamantine
STREAK	White
SPECIFIC GRAVITY	2.4
TRANSPARENCY	Transparent to translucent

Vitreous luster

BORACITE

SAXONY, GERMANY
Boracite crystals were first found in Lüneburg, Lower Saxony.

THIS GLASSY BORATE MINERAL is, as its name suggests, a minor source of the element boron. Its crystals are pseudocubic, and also occur in massive aggregates. Generally white to gray, it shades toward light green with increasing iron content. Strongly pyroelectric and piezoelectric, it also exhibits double refraction. Boracite is found as crystals embedded in sedimentary deposits of anhydrite, gypsum, and halite. Localities include the Khorat Plateau of Thailand; Stassfurt, Hannover, and Lüneburg, Germany; Cleveland, England; Lunéville, France; Inowroclaw, Poland; and Missouri and Louisiana.

BORACITE CRYSTALS
These boracite crystals from Saxony, Germany, appear to be dodecahedrons, a classic example of pseudocubic habit.

Green color from iron

Pseudocubic habit

Vitreous luster

PROPERTIES

GROUP Borates
CRYSTAL SYSTEM Orthorhombic
COMPOSITION $(Mg,Fe)_3B_7O_{13}Cl$
COLOR White to gray, green
FORM/HABIT Pseudocubic
HARDNESS $7–7\frac{1}{2}$
CLEAVAGE None
FRACTURE Conchoidal to uneven
LUSTER Vitreous
STREAK White
SPECIFIC GRAVITY 3.0
TRANSPARENCY Subtransparent to translucent

KERNITE

BORON, CA
This area of California has extensive borate deposits, including kernite.

KERNITE IS A SODIUM BORATE HYDRATE, named for the place where it was discovered, Kern County, California. Crystals are relatively uncommon, but when found can be very large, often 2–3 ft (60–90 cm) thick. The largest discovered so far measured 8 ft by 3 ft (240 cm by 90 cm). Crystals are colorless and transparent but are usually covered by a surface film of opaque white tincalconite, a dehydration product of borate minerals. Kernite is associated with other borate minerals as veins and irregular masses formed in evaporite deposits, and crystals embedded in shale. The Boron area of Kern County produces a large portion of the boron used in the US, and kernite is one of its principal mineral sources. The deposits in Inyo, California; Catamarca and Salta Provinces, Argentina; and Kirka, Turkey, are other major world sources.

FIBROUS MASS
This specimen of kernite is from the type locality in Kern County. It shows characteristic perfect cleavage and vitreous luster.

PROPERTIES

GROUP Borates
CRYSTAL SYSTEM Monoclinic
COMPOSITION $Na_2B_4O_6(OH)_2\cdot3H_2O$
COLOR Colorless, white
FORM/HABIT Fibrous mass
HARDNESS $2\frac{1}{2}$
CLEAVAGE Perfect
FRACTURE Splintery
LUSTER Vitreous, silky, dull
STREAK White
SPECIFIC GRAVITY 1.9
TRANSPARENCY Transparent

Cleaved fibrous mass

Transparent mass

Vitreous luster

REINFORCING AGENT

Boron, derived from minerals such as kernite and colemanite, is a black, dense metal in its pure form. Boron carbide is one of the hardest synthetic substances known, being nearly as hard as diamond. It is used as an abrasive, as a reinforcing agent for military armor, and to control the rate of fission in nuclear reactors. Because of its hardness, it is also used in sandblasting nozzles and pump seals, and it is added to increase the hardness of steel. In semiconductors, small amounts of boron are also added to silicon and germanium to modify their electrical conductivity.

ARMORED TANK
Boron compounds are added to steel to harden it. Super-hardened steel is used in military armor.

SULFATES, CHROMATES, TUNGSTATES, AND MOLYBDATES

SULFATES, CHROMATES, tungstates, and molybdates are grouped together because they behave the same structurally and chemically. Around 200 sulfates are known; gypsum and baryte are very common, but most are rare. The chromates, tungstates, and molybdates are all relatively rare, but when found in concentration are important ores of the metals they contain.

CRYSTAL STRUCTURE

The sulfate minerals have a crystal structure in which four oxygen atoms are located at the corners of a tetrahedron with a sulfur atom in the center. The sulfate tetrahedron behaves chemically as a single negatively charged molecule. The chemical formulas of the sulfates all contain an SO_4 group. The basic structural unit of the chromates is also a tetrahedron formed from four oxygen atoms, each at one corner of the tetrahedron. But in the center is a chromium atom instead of a sulfur atom. The chemical formulae for chromate minerals all contain a CrO_4 group. The same type of tetrahedron forms in the molybdates and tungstates, but with an atom of molybdenum (Mo) or tungsten (W) in the center, respectively. Their chemical formulae all contain a WO_4 or a MoO_4 group.

CHROMATE — Chromium atom

MOLYBDATE — Molybdenum atom

SULFATE — Sulfur atom

TUNGSTATE — Tungsten atom

ANGLESEY
This island in Wales is the type locality for anglesite.

Rock groundmass

Prismatic crystal

ANGLESITE

ANGLESITE HAS A VARIETY of crystal habits: thin to thick tabular, prismatic, pseudorhombohedral, or pyramidal. It is also commonly massive, granular, or compact. Its crystals resemble those of barite and celestite, with which it shares a similar structure. It is colorless to white, grayish, yellow, green, or blue and often fluoresces yellow under ultraviolet light. Anglesite is lead sulfate, an alteration product of galena, and is sometimes found in concentric layers with a core of unaltered galena. It is common in the oxidation zone of lead deposits. It readily alters to cerussite, lead carbonate. Exceptionally large crystals, up to 32 in (80 cm) long, have come from Touissit, Morocco. Other fine specimens come from Tsumeb, Namibia; Broken Hill, NSW, Australia; Derbyshire, England; Siegen, Germany; Monteponi Mine, Sardinia, Italy; and Coeur d'Alene, Idaho.

PROPERTIES

GROUP Sulfates

CRYSTAL SYSTEM Orthorhombic

COMPOSITION $PbSO_4$

COLOR Colorless to white, yellow, green, or blue

FORM/HABIT Thin to thick tabular

HARDNESS $2\frac{1}{2}$–3

CLEAVAGE Good, distinct

FRACTURE Conchoidal, brittle

LUSTER Adamantine to resinous, vitreous

STREAK Colorless

SPECIFIC GRAVITY 6.4

TRANSPARENCY Transparent to opaque

ANGLESITE CRYSTALS
A large, striated prismatic crystal of anglesite is on a rock groundmass along with several smaller crystals and accessory mineral, galena.

Galena

Pyramidal crystal

Rock groundmass

ANGLESITE CRYSTAL

ROMAN LEAD MINING IN BRITAIN

The lure of metal wealth was one of the factors that prompted the Roman invasion of Britain in 43 BC. Lead was mined extensively in a number of localities, with some deposits carrying significant portions of silver. Anglesite was one of the ores the Romans sought. Lead was used extensively in the Roman world, especially for water pipes. Our modern word "plumbing" comes from the Latin for lead, *plumbum*, and lead was still used for piping until about 75 years ago.

WATER PIPE
This Roman lead water pipe still lies where it was installed nearly two millennia ago.

DISUSED LEAD MINE
This disused lead mine in Lathkill Dale, Derbyshire, was worked profitably from the 13th century until 1851.

GLAUBERITE

SEARLES LAKE
This California lake is a source of evaporites such as glauberite.

A SODIUM CALCIUM SULFATE, glauberite was named in 1802 for its similarity to another chemical, glauber's salt, which in turn was named for the German alchemist Johann Glauber. Crystals can be prismatic, tabular, and dipyramidal, all with combinations of forms. Usually gray or yellowish, it can sometimes be colorless or reddish. It has a slightly saline taste, and fuses to a white enamel. Glauberite forms under a variety of conditions, although it is primarily an evaporite, forming in both marine and salt–lake environments. It is also found in cavities in basaltic igneous rocks and in volcanic fumaroles. Glauberite was first found in crystals in the halite deposit in Villarrubia, Toledo, Spain. It also occurs in crystals in the Stassfurt potash region of Germany. Other localities include the Salt Range, Pakistan; Gypsumville, Canada; Lorraine, France; and Arizona and New Jersey.

GLAUBERITE CRYSTALS
This group of dipyramidal glauberite crystals is from Ciempozuelos, Madrid, Spain.

Dipyramidal crystals

ALCHEMY

Alchemy is the search for a method of changing base metals into gold. It was a popular if mysterious pursuit, especially in the 16th and 17th centuries, when Johann Glauber was practicing it. Alchemy was a predecessor of chemistry, and its practitioners made discoveries that laid the foundations of modern chemical knowledge.

ALCHEMIST'S WORKSHOP
This 1570 painting by Jan van der Sraet shows some of the pseudoscientific methods of alchemists.

Vitreous luster

PROPERTIES

GROUP Sulfates
CRYSTAL SYSTEM Monoclinic
COMPOSITION $Na_2Ca(SO_4)_2$
COLOR Gray, yellowish, colorless, or reddish
FORM/HABIT Prismatic, tabular
HARDNESS $2\frac{1}{2}$–3
CLEAVAGE Perfect, indistinct
FRACTURE Conchoidal
LUSTER Vitreous to waxy
STREAK White
SPECIFIC GRAVITY 2.8
TRANSPARENCY Transparent to translucent

ANHYDRITE

CHIHUAHUA
Fine anhydrite crystals are found here.

AN IMPORTANT ROCK-FORMING mineral, anhydrate, along with gypsum, is a form of calcium sulfate. Its name comes from the Greek, *anhydrous*, meaning "without water." Gypsum, which contains water in its structure, is a much more common mineral. Anhydrite alters to gypsum in humid conditions. It is usually massive, granular, or coarsely crystalline. Individual crystals are uncommon, but when found are blocky or thick tabular. It is colorless to white, but also may be brownish, reddish, or grayish, or pale shades of pink, blue, and violet. Anhydrite is one of the major minerals in evaporite deposits, and occurs most often in salt deposits associated with gypsum and halite. Massive deposits of anhydrite occur in the cap rock of the Texas–Louisiana salt domes. It is found in Nova Scotia, Canada, and in the rock salt deposits of the French Pyrénées. Fine blue crystals are found in Chihuahua, Mexico; crystals up to 4 in (10 cm) long come from Swiss deposits; and fine white crystals come from Tuscany, Italy. Anhydrite is used in fertilizers, and as a drying agent in plasters, cement, paints, and varnishes.

PROPERTIES

GROUP Sulfates
CRYSTAL SYSTEM Orthorhombic
COMPOSITION $CaSO_4$
COLOR Colorless to white, pink, blue, violet, brownish, reddish, or grayish
FORM/HABIT Massive
HARDNESS $3\frac{1}{2}$
CLEAVAGE Perfect, good,
FRACTURE Uneven to splintery
LUSTER Vitreous to pearly
STREAK White
SPECIFIC GRAVITY 3.0
TRANSPARENCY Transparent to translucent

GERMAN ANHYDRITE
This reddish specimen of anhydrite from Germany shows perfect cleavage.

Perfect cleavage

PERMIAN BASIN
This area within New Mexico and Texas holds enormous commercial deposits of anhydrite.

Translucent

Waxy luster

209

BARITE

THE NAME BARITE originates from the Greek *barys*, meaning "heavy", a reference to its high specific gravity. For the same reason, it has also been called heavy spar. It is the most common barium mineral, and the element's principal ore.

Barite crystals are sometimes tinged yellow, blue, or brown, and a rare golden barite comes from Colorado. It is frequently well crystallized, and tabular or prismatic crystals are common, as are cockscomb (or crested) aggregates. Barite can also be fibrous, massive, stalactitic, or concretionary. It also occurs as aggregate rosettes of crystals known as "desert roses." Transparent blue barite crystals can resemble aquamarine, but their softness, heaviness, and crystal shape make them easily distinguishable. Were the stone not so soft and fragile, it would make a beautiful gem, and it is cut for collectors on rare occasions.

Barite is a common accessory mineral in lead and zinc veins, where it occurs with galena, sphalerite, fluorite, and calcite. It is also found in sedimentary rocks such as limestone, in clay deposits formed by the weathering of limestone, in marine deposits, and in cavities in igneous rock. It is abundant in Spain, Germany, Canada, France, India, Romania, and localities in the US. Barite is an important economic mineral for oil and gas production, because it is used as drilling mud in oil- and gas-well drilling. It is also used as a filler in paper- and cloth-making, as an inert body in colored paints, and as a white pigment. Barium sulfate is used in medicine as a "barium meal" (see below).

STALAGMITE SECTION
Barite is sometimes found forming stalagmites. In cross section, these contain structures that look like the rings of a tree.

ALSTON MOOR, CUMBRIA
The moors of Cumbria, England, are noted for their mineral wealth, including significant deposits of barite.

OCTAGONAL MIXED
Transparent barite is sometimes faceted for collectors, although cutting it is difficult even for master cutters.

BARIUM MEAL
Barium sulfate is swallowed to highlight problems in the gastrointestinal tract on X-rays.

Tabular crystal

Vitreous luster

PROPERTIES

GROUP	Sulfates
CRYSTAL SYSTEM	Orthorhombic
COMPOSITION	$BaSO_4$
COLOR	Colorless, white, gray, bluish, greenish, beige
FORM/HABIT	Tabular to prismatic
HARDNESS	3–3½
CLEAVAGE	Perfect
FRACTURE	Uneven
LUSTER	Vitreous, resinous, pearly
STREAK	White
SPECIFIC GRAVITY	4.5
TRANSPARENCY	Transparent to translucent
R.I.	1.63–1.65

BARITE CRYSTALS
This large group of tabular barite crystals is from the Wet Grooves Mine, Yorkshire, England.

Tabular crystals

Transparent crystal

Barite

Associated calcite

Barite

Sphalerite

Prismatic crystal

Resinous luster

BARITE HABITS
Barite is an interesting collectors' mineral because it comes in a number of colors and habits. The specimens to the left are just a few examples.

CRYSTALLINE   BARITE WITH CALCITE   COCKSCOMB   PRISMATIC CRYSTALS

CELESTITE

OFTEN FORMING BEAUTIFUL transparent light to medium-blue tabular crystals, celestite can be colorless, white, light red, green, blue, or brown. It can also be massive, fibrous, granular, or nodular. It takes its name from the Latin *coelestis*, meaning "heavenly," an allusion to its color. Celestite is strontium sulfate, but barium substitutes freely for strontium in the structure, and calcium may also be present. Celestite forms in sedimentary rock such as limestones, dolomites, and sandstones. It can also be precipitated directly from sea water, and commonly occurs in evaporite deposits as a minor constituent. Occasionally it forms in hydrothermal deposits.

Collectors' specimens come from Madagascar, Mexico, Italy, Canada, and the US. Lesser amounts come from England, Slovakia, Austria, and Germany. Beds of massive celestite 10–20 ft (3–6 m) thick occur in California. Well-formed crystals commonly reach 4 in (10 cm) in length, and crystals more than 30 in (75 cm) long are known.

MADAGASCAR
The deposits of Madagascar are a prime locality for celestite crystals, including those mined and faceted for collectors.

SINGLE CRYSTAL
This is a superb example of a light blue, single prismatic crystal of celestite.

PROPERTIES

GROUP	Sulfates
CRYSTAL SYSTEM	Orthorhombic
COMPOSITION	$SrSO_4$
COLOR	Colorless, white, red, green, blue, or brown
FORM/HABIT	Tabular
HARDNESS	3–3½
CLEAVAGE	Perfect
FRACTURE	Uneven
LUSTER	Vitreous, pearly on cleavage
STREAK	White
SPECIFIC GRAVITY	4.0
TRANSPARENCY	Transparent to translucent
R.I.	1.62–1.63

FIREWORKS
Along with strontianite, celestite is the principal source of strontium, which is used to create the red color in fireworks, signal flares, and tracer bullets.

Sulfur groundmass

MIXED
Transparent celestite is sometimes cut for collectors. It is too soft and fragile to wear and is difficult to cut.

Prismatic crystals

CRYSTALS IN MATRIX
This mass of colorless, prismatic crystals of celestite is on a sulfur groundmass.

Vitreous luster

Tabular crystal

CELESTITE CRYSTALS
This specimen of superbly crystallized, blue celestite crystals is from Madagascar. The largest crystal is over 1½ in (3.5 cm) in length.

Blue coloration

Granular celestite

Small celestite crystals

GYPSUM

ONE OF NATURE'S MOST spectacular—and largest—mineral deposits lies in the desert country of south-central New Mexico. White Sands is 225 square miles (580 square km) of dazzling white gypsum sand that has been blown into dunes up to 60 ft (18 m) high. In another spectacular deposit at the Cave of Swords, Naica, Chihuahua, Mexico, numerous transparent, swordlike selenite gypsum crystals reach lengths of 6 ft (2 m) or more. Selenite, from the Greek word *selene*, meaning "the moon," is the name for transparent crystals of gypsum, but is often incorrectly used for gypsum in general. Gypsum takes its name from the Greek *gypsos*, meaning "chalk," "plaster," or "cement."

CHARACTERISTICS OF GYPSUM

Gypsum is a widespread calcium sulfate hydrate that is found in a number of forms, and is of great economic importance. It is colorless or white, but impurities tint it light brown, gray, yellow, green, or orange. It often occurs in well-developed crystals. Single crystals can be blocky with a slanted parallelogram outline, tabular, bladed, or in a long, thin shape like a ram's horn. Twinned crystals are common, and frequently form characteristic "swallowtails" or "fishtails." Gypsum is also found in a parallel, fibrous variety with a silky luster, called satin spar. The massive, fine-grained variety is called alabaster. Rosette-shaped crystals are called desert roses, and are more common and less dense than the barite "sand crystals" (see p.210) that they resemble.

Gypsum occurs in extensive beds formed by the evaporation of ocean brine, along with other minerals similarly formed—in particular, anhydrite (see p.209) and halite (see p.170). It has low solubility and so is the first mineral to separate from evaporating sea water. Once it has been deposited, it is commonly blown into dunes. Gypsum also occurs as an alteration product of sulfides in ore deposits; as disseminated crystals and rosette-shaped aggregates in sedimentary deposits, including sands and clays; and as deposits around volcanic fumaroles.

LAKE EYRE, AUSTRALIA
This great salt lake in central South Australia covers 3,600 square miles (9,300 square km), and is estimated to contain more than 4 billion tons of gypsum.

"SUN-SPANGLED" BEAD
This polished bead contains cracks that may have been caused by heat treatment and produce a "sun-spangled" effect.

PROPERTIES

GROUP Sulfates
CRYSTAL SYSTEM Monoclinic
COMPOSITION $CaSO_4 \cdot 2H_2O$
COLOR Colorless, white, light brown, yellow, pink
FORM/HABIT Prismatic to tabular
HARDNESS 2
CLEAVAGE Perfect
FRACTURE Splintery
LUSTER Subvitreous to pearly
STREAK White
SPECIFIC GRAVITY 2.3
TRANSPARENCY Transparent to translucent
R.I. 1.52–1.53

ALABASTER

Alabaster, the fine-grained, massive form of gypsum, has been used for centuries for statuary, carvings, and other ornamental purposes. Florence, Milan, and Livorno, Italy, and Berlin, Germany, are important modern centers of the alabaster trade. Alabaster is normally snow-white and translucent, but can be artificially dyed, or it may be heat-treated to make it similar in appearance to marble. In ancient times, the term was applied to other minerals of similar appearance; for example, the "alabaster" containers recovered from Tutankhamun's tomb were, in fact, made of calcite (onyx).

FISH
This fish was carved from local alabaster in Loveland, Colorado.

COUPLE
This simple modern carving was made from pale, translucent alabaster.

WHITE SANDS
The huge expanse of the deposit of gypsum sand at White Sands, New Mexico, can be seen below and from space (left).

SELENITE CRYSTAL
This single, prismatic selenite crystal comes from the Cave of Swords in Mexico.

Vertical striations

Transparent

Attachment point

Gypsum occurs widely throughout the world, but the US, Canada, Australia, Spain, France, Italy, and England are among the leading commercial producers.

USES OF GYPSUM

An important economic mineral since the time of ancient Egyptian civilization, gypsum was mined to the west of Alexandria, near Suez, in Al Fayyum, and near the Red Sea coast. It was used for mortar and plaster in the Giza necropolis, and it was used elsewhere to plaster walls, cover bodies, make statues and masks, as an adhesive, and as a filler in pigments. The Romans discovered that heating gypsum to 600°F (300°C) made a plaster that sets hard when mixed with water. This plaster was used for building, and is still widely used today.

PLASTER CAST
About 75 percent of the gypsum mined worldwide is used to make plaster of Paris.

SELENITE GYPSUM FORMS
Selenite gypsum comes in a variety of crystalline forms, including single monoclinic trapezoids, fibrous satin spar, characteristic "fishtail" twins, and in radiating clusters called desert roses.

Prism face

Termination face

SINGLE GYPSUM CRYSTAL

Prismatic crystals

Twin plane

FISHTAIL TWIN

Fibrous crystals

Silky sheen

GYPSUM SATIN SPAR

Bladed crystals

Radiating form

DESERT ROSE

CAVE OF SWORDS
The selenite crystals in the Cave of Swords, Mexico (above and right), reach more than 6 ft (2 m) in length. The cave is named for these enormous selenite crystals.

Termination face

Pearly luster

MELANTERITE

DRAWING ITS NAME from the Greek *melas*, "sulfate of iron," melanterite is a hydrous iron sulfate. It rarely forms crystals, and is generally found in stalactitic or concretionary masses. When crystals occur, they are short prisms or pseudo-octahedrons. Most samples are colorless to white, but become green to blue with increasing substitution of copper for iron. Melanterite is water soluble. It is a secondary mineral formed by the oxidation of pyrite, marcasite, and other iron sulfides, and is frequently deposited on the timbers of old mine workings. It also occurs in the altered zones of pyrite-bearing rocks, especially in arid climates, and in coal and lignite deposits, where it is an alteration product of marcasite. It is found in Russia, Italy, Germany, the Czech Republic, and the US.

PROPERTIES

GROUP Sulfates
CRYSTAL SYSTEM Monoclinic
COMPOSITION $FeSO_4 \cdot 7H_2O$
COLOR White, greenish, bluish
FORM/HABIT Stalactitic, concretionary
HARDNESS 2
CLEAVAGE Perfect
FRACTURE Conchoidal, brittle
LUSTER Vitreous
STREAK White
SPECIFIC GRAVITY 1.9
TRANSPARENCY Translucent

INDUSTRIAL USES

Melanterite, which is a sulfide of iron, has been used for hundreds of years to make ink. During the Middle Ages, oak was steeped in water with ferrous sulfate to produce a dark purplish ink. Today, iron sulfate is used in water purification as a coagulant—a substance added to water to coagulate and thus drop out minute particles that otherwise do not settle. It is also used as a fertilizer.

WATER PURIFICATION
Melanterite helps to purify water by separating out tiny particles.

MELANTERITE NODULE
This melanterite nodule shows typical massive form and some minor crystallization.

Massive habit

Blue indicates presence of copper

CHALCANTHITE

A WIDESPREAD, naturally occurring hydrated copper sulfate, chalcanthite takes its name from the Greek *khalkos*, "copper" and *anthos*, "flower." It used to be known as blue vitriol. Natural crystals are relatively rare; it usually occurs in veinlets, and as massive and stalactitic aggregates. Commonly peacock-blue, in some cases it leans toward greenish. Chalcanthite forms through the oxidation of chalcopyrite and other copper sulfates, occurring in the oxidized zone of copper deposits. It is often found forming crusts and stalactites on the timbers and walls of mine workings where it has crystallized from mine waters. In arid areas, such as Chile, it can be an important ore of copper.

PROPERTIES

GROUP Sulfates
CRYSTAL SYSTEM Triclinic
COMPOSITION $CuSO_4 \cdot 5H_2O$
COLOR Blue
FORM/HABIT Stalactitic, encrustations
HARDNESS $2\frac{1}{2}$
CLEAVAGE Not distinct
FRACTURE Conchoidal
LUSTER Vitreous
STREAK Colorless
SPECIFIC GRAVITY 2.3
TRANSPARENCY Transparent

MINING COPPER

In its earliest form, copper mining was carried out by workers using hand picks. Today, most copper mining takes place in open-pit mines. These huge craters scooped out of solid rock can be more than 1 mile (1.5 km) across. Pits such as those in Chuquicamata, Chile, are so deep that a truck loaded with ore leaving the bottom of the pit can take over an hour to drive to the surface.

CHUQUICAMATA MINE
At more than 2 miles (3 km) across, Chuquicamata, Chile, is the world's largest open-pit copper mine.

Kaolinite

Crystalline chalcanthite

Granular chalcanthite

TWO FORMS
This specimen on a rock groundmass with patches of kaolinite exhibits massive and crystalline forms.

Groundmass of rock

BROCHANTITE

THIS SECONDARY MINERAL usually forms needlelike or prismatic crystals, seldom more than a fraction of an inch long. It is also found in druse crusts and fine-grained masses. Twinning is common in crystals. A copper sulfate hydroxide, brochantite forms in the oxidation zone of copper deposits, and is usually associated with azurite, malachite, and other copper minerals. Splendid specimens come from Namibia, and Bisbee, Arizona, where prismatic crystals may exceed ½ in (10 mm). It is also found in Algeria, Morocco, Chile, Greece, Germany, Italy, England, Spain, and Australia. In Arizona and Chile it is so abundant that it is an ore of copper.

NEEDLELIKE CRYSTALS
This mass of acicular brochantite crystals rests on a groundmass of iron oxides. The specimen is from Chile.

Iron oxide groundmass

BROCHANT DE VILLIERS

Brochantite was named for the French geologist and mineralogist A. J. M. Brochant de Villiers in 1824. Born in 1772, he was the first pupil admitted to the École des Mines, and he later became its Professor of Geology and Mines. He was also Inspector-General of Mines.

EMINENT MINERALOGIST
Brochant de Villiers oversaw the construction of the geological map of France.

Mass of acicular brochantite crystals

PROPERTIES

GROUP	Sulfates
CRYSTAL SYSTEM	Monoclinic
COMPOSITION	$Cu_4SO_4(OH)_6$
COLOR	Emerald-green
FORM/HABIT	Short prismatic to acicular
HARDNESS	$3^1/2$–4
CLEAVAGE	Perfect
FRACTURE	Uneven to subconchoidal
LUSTER	Vitreous
STREAK	Pale green
SPECIFIC GRAVITY	4.0
TRANSPARENCY	Translucent

EPSOMITE

EPSOM
Epsomite was found in spring waters in the town of Epsom in Surrey, England.

FIRST FOUND AROUND mineral springs near the town of Epsom, England, epsomite is an important source of magnesium salts, which is marketed as a laxative called Epsom salts. Magnesium sulfate occurs in solution in sea water, saline lake water, and spring water. When the water evaporates, epsomite precipitates, forming lake deposits. It is also found as crusts in coal, in the weathered portions of magnesium-rich rocks, in the oxidized zones of sulfide ore deposits, and in limestone caves, such as those in Kentucky. Zinc and nickel can substitute for magnesium in the structure.

EPSOM SALTS
This widely used medication is derived from epsomite.

EPSOMITE FIBERS
The fibrous habit of this specimen is clearly visible.

Fibrous strands

Vitreous to silky luster

PROPERTIES

GROUP	Sulfates
CRYSTAL SYSTEM	Orthorhombic
COMPOSITION	$MgSO_4{\cdot}7H_2O$
COLOR	Colorless or white
FORM/HABIT	Fibrous crusts
HARDNESS	2–$2^1/2$
CLEAVAGE	Perfect
FRACTURE	Conchoidal
LUSTER	Vitreous to silky
STREAK	White
SPECIFIC GRAVITY	1.7
TRANSPARENCY	Translucent

ALUNITE

DEATH VALLEY
Deposits of alunite are found in Death Valley in California.

ALUNITE IS ALSO CALLED "alum stone." Crystals are rare; it is usually massive or granular, occurring in pockets or seams in altered volcanic rocks, such as rhyolites, trachytes, and andesites, where it forms through the rocks' chemical reaction with sulfurous vapors. Earthy masses of alunite are commonly mixed with quartz and kaolinite clay. Large deposits are found in the Ukraine, Spain, and New South Wales, Australia.

POTASH ALUM
Alunite is a source of the compound potash alum, which is used as a fixative for dyes.

PROPERTIES

GROUP	Sulfates
CRYSTAL SYSTEM	Hexagonal/trigonal
COMPOSITION	$KAl_3(SO_4)_2(OH)_6$
COLOR	White, yellowish
FORM/HABIT	Massive
HARDNESS	$3^1/2$–4
CLEAVAGE	Distinct
FRACTURE	Conchoidal to splintery
LUSTER	Dull to vitreous to pearly
STREAK	White
SPECIFIC GRAVITY	2.8
TRANSPARENCY	Translucent

MASSIVE ALUNITE
This specimen of massive alunite exhibits a compact habit.

Pearly luster

CYANOTRICHITE

URALS
These Russian mountains are a source of cyanotrichite.

THIS SULFUR MINERAL takes its name from the Greek words for "blue" and "hair." Its name well describes its usual occurrence: plushlike encrustations of tiny, acicular, radiating crystals that are pale to dark blue in color. Cyanotrichite forms in the oxidized zones of copper deposits along with other secondary copper minerals. Localities include France, Greece, Romania, Russia, and Arizona and Utah.

CYANOTRICHITE CRYSTALS
Cyanotrichite's intense blue shows clearly in this specimen from Cap Garonne, Var, France.

Rock groundmass

Radiating acicular crystals

PROPERTIES

GROUP	Sulfates
CRYSTAL SYSTEM	Orthorhombic
COMPOSITION	$Cu_4Al_2SO_4(OH)_{12} \cdot 2H_2O$
COLOR	Pale to dark blue
FORM/HABIT	Acicular, fibrous
HARDNESS	2–3
CLEAVAGE	None
FRACTURE	Uneven
LUSTER	Silky
STREAK	Pale blue
SPECIFIC GRAVITY	2.7
TRANSPARENCY	Transparent to translucent

CROCOITE

TASMANIA
Fine crocoite occurs on this Australian island.

CROCOITE IS LEAD CHROMATE, taking its name from the Greek for "saffron," after its color. Crystals are prismatic, commonly slender and elongated, and sometimes cavernous or hollow. It can also be granular or massive. Crocoite forms as a secondary mineral in the oxidized zone of lead deposits. Superb specimens come from Tasmania; other localities include Russia, Germany, and California.

ORANGE CROCOITE
This brilliant orange specimen exhibits attractive, elongated prismatic crystals.

RED CROCOITE
These well-formed prismatic crocoite crystals are from the classic locality of Dundas, Tasmania.

Adamantine luster

Prismatic crystals

PROPERTIES

GROUP	Chromates
CRYSTAL SYSTEM	Monoclinic
COMPOSITION	$PbCrO_4$
COLOR	Orange, red
FORM/HABIT	Prismatic
HARDNESS	2½–3
CLEAVAGE	Distinct in one direction
FRACTURE	Conchoidal to uneven, brittle
LUSTER	Vitreous
STREAK	Orange-yellow
SPECIFIC GRAVITY	6.0
TRANSPARENCY	Transparent to translucent

HÜBNERITE

SAN JUAN
This area of Colorado produces superb hübnerite crystals.

A MANGANESE IRON TUNGSTATE, hübnerite is found as prismatic, tabular, or flattened crystals with striated faces, and is commonly twinned. It occurs principally in granitic pegmatites and hydrothermal veins with quartz, cassiterite, topaz, and lepidolite. Good specimens come from Peru and Colorado. Formerly called wolframite, it is a major tungsten ore.

HÜBNERITE CRYSTALS
Here translucent hübnerite crystals and tarnished tetrahedrite are on quartz.

Prismatic hübnerite crystal

Adamantine luster

Quartz groundmass

PROPERTIES

GROUP	Tungstates
CRYSTAL SYSTEM	Monoclinic
COMPOSITION	$MnWO_4$
COLOR	Reddish-brown
FORM/HABIT	Prismatic, bladed
HARDNESS	4–4½
CLEAVAGE	Perfect
FRACTURE	Uneven
LUSTER	Submetallic/adamantine to resinous
STREAK	Yellow to brown
SPECIFIC GRAVITY	7.3
TRANSPARENCY	Transparent to translucent

FERBERITE

MYANMAR
Ferberite crystals can be found in Myanmar.

FERBERITE IS AN IRON TUNGSTATE which, with hübnerite (see left), constitutes the mineral formerly known as wolframite. Its black crystals are commonly elongated or flattened with a wedge-shaped appearance. Twinning is also common. It is found in granitic pegmatites and high-temperature hydrothermal veins, often with cassiterite, hematite, or arsenopyrite. Excellent specimens come from Japan, Portugal, Romania, South Korea, and Rwanda. It is an ore of tungsten.

Submetallic luster

FERBERITE CRYSTAL
This crystal is from Cínovec, Czech Republic.

PROPERTIES

GROUP	Tungstates
CRYSTAL SYSTEM	Monoclinic
COMPOSITION	$FeWO_4$
COLOR	Black
FORM/HABIT	Bladed, prismatic
HARDNESS	4–4½
CLEAVAGE	Perfect in one direction
FRACTURE	Uneven, brittle
LUSTER	Submetallic
STREAK	Black to brown
SPECIFIC GRAVITY	7.5
TRANSPARENCY	Opaque

TV TUBES
Tungsten is used in the making of television vacuum tubes.

SCHEELITE

BOHEMIA
A mineral-rich part of the Czech Republic, Bohemia is a source of scheelite.

NAMED IN 1821 for the Swedish chemist C. W. Scheele (1742–86), scheelite is calcium tungstate—a major source of tungsten. Crystals are generally bipyramidal, and twinned, but also form in granular or massive aggregates. A small amount of molybdenum is commonly present. Most scheelite fluoresces, the color ranging from blue to white. It commonly occurs in contact with metamorphic deposits, high-temperature hydrothermal veins, and less commonly in granitic pegmatites. Opaque crystals weighing up to 15 lb (7 kg) come from Arizona, and superb, often transparent crystals from Austria, Italy, Brazil, Rwanda, and Colorado.

PROPERTIES

GROUP	Tungstates
CRYSTAL SYSTEM	Tetragonal
COMPOSITION	$CaWO_4$
COLOR	White, yellow, brown, or green
FORM/HABIT	Bipyramidal
HARDNESS	$4\frac{1}{2}$–5
CLEAVAGE	Distinct
FRACTURE	Uneven to subconchoidal
LUSTER	Vitreous to greasy
STREAK	White
SPECIFIC GRAVITY	6.1
TRANSPARENCY	Transparent to translucent

Bipyramidal scheelite crystals

Magnetite groundmass

PROSPECTING
This prospector north of Abha, Saudi Arabia, uses a panning device called a "goldhound" to pan for scheelite.

USES OF TUNGSTEN

Tungsten is one of the most crucial metals used in industry. Tungsten-steel is used for rocket nozzles and other very high-temperature applications. Tungsten carbide is used in drill bits, dies, and tools for shearing metal. Pure tungsten is used in electric-light filaments. Cobalt-chromium-tungsten alloys are used for the hard-facing of wear-resistant valves, bearings, propeller shafts, and cutting tools.

ROCKET NOZZLE
The nozzle of the Saturn V rocket that launched Apollo 11 in 1969 was made of tungsten-steel.

SCHEELITE WITH MAGNETITE
This group of orange-yellow scheelite crystals with magnetite clearly shows a tetragonal bipyramidal crystal habit.

WULFENITE

TOMBSTONE
Arizona is a key locality for fine wulfenite crystals.

THE SECOND MOST COMMON molybdenum mineral after molybdenite, wulfenite "lead molybdate" is a minor source of molybdenum. It ordinarily forms as thin, square plates, or square, beveled, tabular crystals, but can also be massive or granular. Its color can be yellow, orange, red, gray, or brown. Tungsten substitutes for the molybdenum to varying degrees, although in most specimens it is present only in trace amounts. Wulfenite was named in 1845 for F. X. Wülfen (1728–1805), an Austro-Hungarian mineralogist. It is a secondary mineral, formed in the oxidized zone of lead and molybdenum deposits, and occurs with minerals such as cerussite, vanadinite, and pyromorphite. It is relatively widespread, and is often found in superb crystals, occasionally up to 4 in (10 cm) on an edge. Excellent crystals come from Mexico, Slovenia, Zambia, China, and Arizona.

PROPERTIES

GROUP	Molybdates
CRYSTAL SYSTEM	Tetragonal
COMPOSITION	$PbMoO_4$
COLOR	Yellow, orange, red
FORM/HABIT	Square tabular, prismatic
HARDNESS	$2\frac{1}{2}$–3
CLEAVAGE	Distinct
FRACTURE	Subconchoidal to uneven
LUSTER	Subadamantine to greasy
STREAK	White
SPECIFIC GRAVITY	6.5–7.0
TRANSPARENCY	Transparent to translucent

SQUARE CRYSTALS
The thin, tabular, square crystals visible in this specimen are typical of wulfenite.

Square, platy crystal

Iron oxide groundmass

Greasy luster

Tabular crystal

Greasy luster

Tabular wulfenite crystal

RED CLOUD WULFENITE
The Red Cloud Mine in southern Arizona has produced spectacular wulfenite specimens.

YELLOW WULFENITE
The wulfenite crystals on this groundmass composed principally of iron oxides show classic square, platy development.

217

SILICATES

THE MOST IMPORTANT chemical group of minerals, silicates make up about 25 percent of all known minerals and 40 percent of the most common ones. As well as being a major mineral component of Earth, they are also significant constituents of lunar samples and meteorites. Quartz, feldspar, and mica, the predominant components of granite, are silicates. All silicates contain silicon and oxygen. Silicon is a light, shiny metal that looks like pencil lead; oxygen is a colorless, odorless gas. In the silicates, these two elements combine to form structural tetrahedra, each with a silicon atom in the center and oxygen atoms at the corners. Silicate tetrahedra may exist as discrete, independent units and connect with only other silicate tetrahedra (as in quartz), or with other chemical elements such as iron, magnesium, aluminum, and so on. Tetrahedra may also share their oxygen atoms at corners, edges, or, more rarely, faces, creating variations in structure as a result. The different linkages also create voids of varying sizes, which are occupied by the ions of

QUARTZ OUTCROPPING
After silica, quartz is the most abundant mineral in Earth's crust. The bulk of quartz is massive, as in this outcropping in the Shining Rock Wilderness, North Carolina.

various metals according to the size and atomic coordination of the void. Silicates are divided into six main groups according to the structural configurations that result from the different ways in which tetrahedra and other elements are linked. The inosilicate group is subdivided into single- and double-chain inosilicates. Within these main groups there are further subdivisions, such as the feldspars and zeolites.

THE SIX SILICATE GROUPS
These illustrations show the basic arrangement of the silica tetrahedra in the six silicate groups. Both single- and double-chain inosilicates are shown.

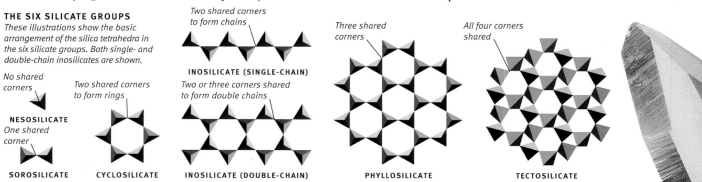

Two shared corners to form chains

No shared corners

Two shared corners to form rings

INOSILICATE (SINGLE-CHAIN)
Two or three corners shared to form double chains

NESOSILICATE
One shared corner

Three shared corners

All four corners shared

SOROSILICATE

CYCLOSILICATE

INOSILICATE (DOUBLE-CHAIN)

PHYLLOSILICATE

TECTOSILICATE

TECTOSILICATES

THE TECTOSILICATE STRUCTURE is a three-dimensional network of silica tetrahedra, with each tetrahedral unit sharing all of its four oxygen atoms. Its name comes from the Greek *tecton*, meaning "builder." Sometimes referred to as framework silicates, the tectosilicates are the largest single group of silicates, and include several rock-forming minerals. An important factor in the size of the group is the ability of aluminum to substitute for silicon in the tetrahedron. Aluminum follows only oxygen and silicon in volume in Earth's crust. Its ability to form tetrahedral groups of a similar size to silicate tetrahedra allows these aluminum groups to be easily incorporated in tectosilicate structures. Aluminum can also occupy other sites

SiO_4 tetrahedron

THREE-FOLD HELIX

SiO_4 tetrahedron

ATOMIC STRUCTURE OF QUARTZ
The silica tetrahedra that form the mineral quartz are arranged in the form of either a three-fold or a six-fold helix. This gives quartz a trigonal symmetry (see p.100).

SIX-FOLD HELIX

SiO_4 tetrahedron

TRIGONAL SYMMETRY

within the structure, where it can substitute for elements such as magnesium, ferrous iron, and titanium. The result is a large number of minerals that are produced in great abundance in the crust. They all share an SiO_4 unit in their chemical formulas.

ROCK CRYSTAL

ROCK CRYSTAL IS A COLORLESS, transparent variety of quartz. Vessels of all kinds and spheres have been carved from large crystals since ancient times, and the name rock crystal emerged in the late Middle Ages to differentiate it from the newly perfected colorless glass, to which the name crystal or crystal glass had become attached. Water-clear crystals were known to the ancient Greeks as *krystalos*—hence the name "crystal."

Quartz is silicon dioxide, the third most common mineral in Earth's crust after ice and feldspar. The name "quartz" comes from Old German and first appears in the writings of Georgius Agricola in 1530, although its origin is uncertain. Quartz comes essentially in two forms: crystalline or fully crystalline; and cryptocrystalline, formed of microscopic crystalline particles (see p.102). Crystalline quartz is usually colorless and transparent (rock crystal) or white and translucent (milky quartz, see p.220) but it can occur also in many colored varieties (see pp.220–23). Crystallized impurities occur in some crystalline quartz varieties, such as the hairlike inclusions of rutile (see p.163), needles (rutilated

DUCK BOWL
Carved in the shape of a duck, this rock crystal bowl was made in Athens c. 1200 BC.

quartz, see p.225), or green, mosslike clumps of chlorite. Quartz occurs in nearly all silica-rich metamorphic, sedimentary, and igneous rocks. The optical properties of rock crystal led to its extensive use in lenses and prisms, and as an inexpensive gemstone. Initially, oscillators for electronic components were made from natural rock crystal, but synthetic rock crystal has replaced it. Today, much rock crystal is mined for New Age crystal healing.

OSCILLATOR
Quartz is used as oscillators in electronics.

MINAS GERAIS, BRAZIL
Fine examples of rock crystals are among many minerals found in this Brazilian state.

PROPERTIES

GROUP Silicates – tectosilicates
CRYSTAL SYSTEM Hexagonal/trigonal
COMPOSITION SiO$_2$
COLOR Colorless
FORM/HABIT Prismatic
HARDNESS 7
CLEAVAGE None
FRACTURE Conchoidal
LUSTER Vitreous
STREAK White
SPECIFIC GRAVITY 2.7
TRANSPARENCY Transparent
R.I. 1.54–1.55

CRYSTAL LIP PIECE
This gold and rock crystal lip piece was awarded by the Aztec emperor Moctezuma to his bodyguard in the 16th century.

PRISMATIC CRYSTALS
This group of long prismatic crystals is from Dauphiné, France, which is a classic locality that gives its name to a type of twinned quartz crystal.

Rhombohedral termination

Agate core

Drusy coating

CRYSTALS ON AGATE

Crystal cluster

CRYSTAL CLUSTER

POLISHED BEAD
Quartz is easy to shape and, even with primitive equipment, lapidaries can produce beautiful items like this fluted bead.

CUSHION
Complex faceting techniques are often easy to use on rock crystal, producing glittering yet inexpensive results.

ROUND BRILLIANT
Rhinestones were originally cut from pebbles of quartz that were found in the Rhine River, Germany.

Twin plane

Two crystals

TWINNED CRYSTAL

Striations on prism face

FORMS OF CRYSTAL
Rock crystal is found in a number of different coatings, clusters, and twinned forms.

Prism face

ROCK CRYSTAL LORE

Rock crystal is commonly regarded in shamanistic practice as a "light-stone," an instrument of clairvoyance representing a level intermediate between the visible and the invisible. Rock crystal was traditionally used by Australian Aboriginals and the Plains Indians of North America as a talisman and to produce visions. The Navajo believed it to be rock crystal that first caused the Sun to cast its light upon the world. In ancient times it was believed that rock crystal was ice that had frozen too hard to melt.

CRYSTAL BALL
This 3-in (9-cm) rock crystal ball is used by an English medium.

CRYSTAL PENDANT
New Age practitioners use quartz for healing.

PIKE'S PEAK
This area of Colorado produces superb crystals of smoky quartz.

SMOKY QUARTZ

SMOKY QUARTZ IS THE LIGHT BROWN to nearly black variety of crystalline quartz. Black crystals are properly called morion. There is no clear color boundary between colorless and smoky quartz. It is relatively abundant, and as such it is worth less than either amethyst or citrine. In some countries, faceted smoky quartz is sold as smoky topaz quartz, in an effort to associate it with the more valuable topaz and thus increase its saleability and its price. Smoky quartz on sale is often made by irradiating rock crystal (typically that from Arkansas) to turn it dark brown.

Very dark, natural smoky quartz may be heated to give it a lighter, more attractive hue, and may turn it yellow so that it can be sold as the more valuable citrine (see opposite). Large crystals of smoky quartz are commonly found in pegmatites. Unusually fine specimens come from the Swiss Alps and, in the US, Pike's Peak, Colorado, and Alexander and Lincoln counties in North Carolina.

INTAGLIO SEAL
This portrait of an ancient Roman has been carved in smoky quartz and set in a polished oval of obsidian.

PROPERTIES

GROUP Silicates – tectosilicates	
CRYSTAL SYSTEM Hexagonal/trigonal	
COMPOSITION SiO_2	
COLOR Light brown to black	
FORM/HABIT Prismatic	
HARDNESS 7	
CLEAVAGE None	
FRACTURE Conchoidal	
LUSTER Vitreous	
STREAK White	
SPECIFIC GRAVITY 2.7	
TRANSPARENCY Translucent to nearly opaque	
R.I. 1.54–1.55	

Vitreous luster

SMOKY QUARTZ CRYSTALS
This spectacular double-terminated crystal of smoky quartz is on a groundmass of milky quartz.

Termination face

Pyramidal termination

Polished face

SINGLE CRYSTAL

CAIRNGORM COBBLE

DIFFERENT HABITS
Smoky quartz is often found as single, prismatic crystals, and in transparent, gem-quality, water-rounded cobbles.

Milky quartz groundmass

Prism face

BRILLIANT
In some countries, faceted smoky quartz is sold as smoky topaz quartz.

MIXED
Smoky quartz from the Cairngorms, Scotland, is known as cairngorm.

MILKY QUARTZ

MINAS GERAIS
Milky quartz is abundant in this part of Brazil.

THE WHITE TO GRAYISH-WHITE, translucent to nearly opaque variety of silicon dioxide, milky quartz forms hexagonal prismatic crystals that are identical to rock crystal in all respects apart from color. Both milky and transparent areas can occur within the same crystal. Crystals of milky quartz and rock crystal often occur in the same deposit. The milkiness has been attributed to the presence of minute gas bubbles trapped inside the crystal. It is by far the most common variety of quartz. White veins of massive milky quartz may be seen penetrating a wide number of rock types, and in quartz mining, milky crystals may exceed those of rock crystal in quantity.

Large quantities of milky crystals are recovered in major quartz mining areas such as Hot Springs, Arkansas, and Minas Gerais, Brazil.

PROPERTIES

GROUP Silicates – tectosilicates	
CRYSTAL SYSTEM Hexagonal/trigonal	
COMPOSITION SiO_2	
COLOR White to grayish-white	
FORM/HABIT Prismatic	
HARDNESS 7	
CLEAVAGE None	
FRACTURE Conchoidal	
LUSTER Vitreous	
STREAK White	
SPECIFIC GRAVITY 2.7	
TRANSPARENCY Translucent to nearly opaque	
R.I. 1.5	

MILKY QUARTZ
This single, prismatic crystal from Cornwall, England, rises from a group of smaller crystals.

CRUSHED QUARTZ
Milky quartz is often crushed for use as a groundcover or ornamental stone.

Vitreous luster

Vitreous luster

Termination face

DOUBLE-TERMINATED CRYSTAL

OVAL CUSHION
Milky quartz can be transparent enough to facet.

ROSE QUARTZ

MADAGASCAR
This island is one of the world's leading producers of rose quartz.

THE TRANSLUCENT or transparent pink variety of crystalline quartz, known as rose quartz, is rarely found in crystals, and when these occur they seldom exceed ½ in (1 cm) in length. It is far more commonly found as a massive aggregate. Its coloration has been attributed to traces of titanium, while its milky appearance may be due to tiny, needlelike inclusions of rutile. When rose quartz from certain localities—such as Madagascar—is cut *en cabochon* with proper orientation, it shows asterism (a star-shaped figure) like that found in sapphires, although the effect is neither as sharp nor as intense. Rose quartz is generally found in pegmatites, sometimes in masses weighing hundreds of pounds. Significant occurrences are in Madagascar, Brazil, Sweden, Namibia, Russia, Spain, Scotland, and in California and Maine.

Rose quartz has been carved since ancient times, and in modern times it has been used by "crystal healers," who attribute the properties of unconditional love and emotional healing to it if it is placed against the skin.

PROPERTIES

GROUP Silicates – tectosilicates
CRYSTAL SYSTEM Hexagonal/trigonal
COMPOSITION SiO_2
COLOR Pink, rose
FORM/HABIT Massive
HARDNESS 7
CLEAVAGE None
FRACTURE Conchoidal
LUSTER Vitreous
STREAK White
SPECIFIC GRAVITY 2.7
TRANSPARENCY Translucent to nearly opaque
R.I. 1.54–1.55

Prismatic crystal

ROSE QUARTZ CRYSTALS
This group of rare rose quartz crystals from Galiléia, Minas Gerais, Brazil, is set in massive rose quartz.

Massive rose quartz

NECKLACE
These rose quartz beads have been strung to make a delicate pink necklace.

MASSIVE ROSE QUARTZ

BRILLIANT
Rose quartz is occasionally faceted to provide gems of good brilliance.

EMERALD
This emerald cut has a cloudy appearance like most faceted rose quartz crystals.

CITRINE

ISLE OF ARRAN
Citrine is found on this island off the west of Scotland.

CITRINE IS YELLOW TO BROWNISH quartz (silicon dioxide) and resembles yellow topaz. It is colored by hydrous iron oxide, and is found in the same hexagonal crystals as the other varieties of crystalline quartz. Natural citrine is much less common than amethyst or smoky quartz, both of which can be heat-treated to turn their color into that of citrine. Most citrine that is available is in fact heat-treated amethyst, although heat-treated smoky quartz comes from some locations. As with smoky quartz, citrine is often marketed under names that confuse it with topaz, in order to inflate its price. It is easily distinguished from topaz by its inferior hardness.

Citrine occurs principally in localities that produce amethyst, and it is sometimes found as a zone of citrine in amethyst, when it is known as ametrine. Gem-quality citrine is found on the Isle of Arran, Scotland; in the Ural Mountains of Russia; near Hyderabad, India; in Dauphiné, France; in Minas Gerais, Brazil; in the Salamanca Province of Spain; and in North Carolina.

BROOCH
A faceted citrine forms the center of this gold brooch.

HEAT-TREATED AMETHYST

CITRINE CRYSTAL
This gem-quality single crystal of citrine shows some slight pitting of its faces and rounding of its edges due to erosion in a stream.

Prism face

Rhombohedral face

Vitreous luster

PROPERTIES

GROUP Silicates – tectosilicates
CRYSTAL SYSTEM Hexagonal/trigonal
COMPOSITION SiO_2
COLOR Yellow, yellow-brown
FORM/HABIT Prismatic
HARDNESS 7
CLEAVAGE None
FRACTURE Conchoidal
LUSTER Vitreous
STREAK Colorless
SPECIFIC GRAVITY 2.7
TRANSPARENCY Translucent to nearly opaque
R.I. 1.54–1.55

BRILLIANT
This faceted example of citrine shows a rich, yellow-brown color.

OVAL MIXED
Some citrine, such as this faceted example, is pale yellow in color.

COLORADO
This mineral-rich state is one of several North American localities for amethyst.

POLISHED PEBBLE
Polished and tumbled amethyst stones have an attractive mottled appearance despite their poor quality.

CRYSTAL SLICE
This slice shows how the coloring material of amethyst is attracted to certain crystal faces and not to others (known as preferential absorption).

OVAL MIXED
Faceted as an oval mixed cut, this polished amethyst stone is of a typical purplish-violet color.

RECTANGULAR STEP
This polished rectangular step cut features a band of amethyst in the center bordered on each side with clear quartz.

PRISMATIC CRYSTAL
This tall prismatic crystal from La Garita, Colorado, is typical of those worn uncut as pendants. It is shown actual size, and has a slight red tinge to its purple color due to traces of manganese.

PROPERTIES

GROUP Silicates – tectosilicates
CRYSTAL SYSTEM Hexagonal/trigonal
COMPOSITION SiO_2
COLOR Violet
FORM/HABIT Normally pyramidal terminations, sometimes prismatic
HARDNESS 7
CLEAVAGE None
FRACTURE Conchoidal
LUSTER Vitreous
STREAK White
SPECIFIC GRAVITY 2.7
TRANSPARENCY Opaque to translucent
R.I. 1.54–1.55

222

AMETHYST

A VARIETY OF VITREOUS QUARTZ with purple, violet, or red-purple coloration, amethyst derives its name from the ancient Greek *amethustos*, meaning literally "not drunk," as it was believed to guard against drunkenness (see panel, opposite). Traditionally associated with purity and piety, amethyst has also always been favored by royalty because purple is considered a regal hue.

LOCATION OF AMETHYST

Found in most countries where granitic rocks are exposed, amethyst occurs in alluvial deposits and geodes. Its coloration is principally due to traces of iron, and it is sometimes color-zoned due to twinning or preferential absorption on the rhombohedral faces. Major commercial sources of amethyst are Brazil, where it occurs in geodes that are frequently human-sized; Uruguay, Siberia, and North America. Crystals from Brazilian and Uruguayan deposits are most often found as radiating masses, with individual crystals appearing as pyramids. Lower-grade Brazilian and Uruguayan amethyst is frequently turned into citrine (see p.221) by heat treatment, which changes its color. Where both amethyst and citrine occur naturally in the same stone, the name ametrine is sometimes used.

TRADITIONAL GEMSTONE

Amethyst has a long history as a gemstone. In the ancient civilizations of Mesopotamia, amethyst was highly valued and was used to create cylinder seals, engraved with a religious design and the owner's name. The engraving was transferred to legal documents in the form of clay tablets by rolling the cylinder over the tablets. The ancient Egyptians also valued amethyst, using it in much of their jewelry. Egyptian amethyst came principally from Nubia, once a province of Egypt.

In modern times, amethyst is both faceted and cut *en cabochon*, and it has widespread use as a carving material. Its most valued shades are a deep, rich purple, and a deep purple with a reddish tinge. Uncut, prismatic crystals, such as those mined in Querétaro, Mexico, are frequently worn as jewelry.

VICTORIAN EARRINGS
This delicate pair of drop earrings features rose-cut amethyst crystals and pearls.

CONTEMPORARY NECKLACE
Fragments of polished amethyst crystals are linked together on three individual silver chains to create a pretty massed effect.

Translucent crystals

HEAT-TREATED AMETHYST
When heated, some amethyst crystals change color to yellow-brown. Many crystals sold as citrine (see p.221) are actually heat-treated amethyst.

Major rhombohedral face

CYLINDER SEAL

This Babylonian amethyst cylinder seal dates from the 18th century BC. It bears the inscription: "Ishtar Lamassi, daughter of Lushtammar, slave girl of Ninisina."

AMETHYST TIE PIN

An octagonal step-cut amethyst crystal adorns this handsome late-19th-century gold tie pin.

> "Amethyst dissipates **evil thoughts** and quickens the **intelligence.**"
>
> **LEONARDO DA VINCI**

GEMSTONE OF VIRTUE

The ancient Greeks believed that drinking wine from a cup of amethyst would make them immune to intoxication. This belief is founded upon the origin of amethyst described in Greek mythology.

According to this myth, amethyst was created by Dionysus, god of fruitfulness and wine. Angered by the purity of a young woman named Amethyst, who preferred to pay homage to the goddess Diana, he ordered two voracious tigers to devour her. Diana came to her rescue, transforming Amethyst into white quartz. Overcome with remorse, Dionysus shed tears into his goblet of red wine. Some of the wine spilled, running onto the white stone, which absorbed its color, creating the stone amethyst.

DOUBLE CUP

This hemispherical amethyst cup was cut from a 3½-lb (1.5-kg) crystal of Brazilian amethyst.

SPIRITUAL ASSOCIATIONS

In the early Christian church, amethyst was also believed to have sobering properties. The mineral was adopted as a symbol of the high spiritual state its bishops must attain, and an amethyst ring soon became part of a bishop's regalia. Even today, the highest grade of amethyst is referred to by gem-cutters as "Bishop's Grade."

In India, amethyst is associated with the crown chakra, or energy center, in the body. Meditation upon it is said to lead to mystical union with the universal consciousness. In Tibet, amethyst is considered sacred to Buddha and is often used to make rosaries.

CLERIC'S RING

This 18th-century Austrian clerical ring features a faceted step-cut amethyst surrounded by diamonds.

AARON'S BREASTPLATE

An amethyst adorns the breastplate of Aaron, high priest of the Hebrews. It represents the prophet Math, who was filled with desire to please God.

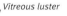

Vitreous luster

Minor rhombohedral face

SINGLE CRYSTAL

This single amethyst crystal is about 4 in (10 cm) long, but crystals exceeding 6 in (15 cm) in length are sometimes found.

Rich purple coloring

MASS OF CRYSTALS

In this mass of pyramid-shaped amethyst crystals, both minor and major rhombohedral faces can be seen. The color of pyramidal crystals darkens toward the tips.

Colorless quartz

Agate base

AVENTURINE

AVENTURINE IS THE NAME given to a variety of quartz that has a spangled appearance due to sparkling internal reflections from uniformly oriented minute inclusions of other minerals. Green aventurine is colored by green fuchsite mica; brown aventurine is colored by pyrite; and reddish-brown aventurine is due to hematite. Other inclusions can color the mineral orange, bluish-white, yellow, or bluish-green. It is always massive.

Aventurine is found in the Ural Mountains of Russia, in the state of Tamil Nadu, India; at numerous localities in Minas Gerais, Brazil; and in Rutland, Vermont. Aventurine quartz is used for jewelry, where it is cut *en cabochon*, for vases and bowls, and for other ornamental objects.

Massive form

Granular texture

PROPERTIES

GROUP Silicates – tectosilicates
CRYSTAL SYSTEM Hexagonal/trigonal
COMPOSITION SiO_2
COLOR Various
FORM/HABIT Massive
HARDNESS 7
CLEAVAGE None
FRACTURE Conchoidal
LUSTER Vitreous
STREAK White
SPECIFIC GRAVITY 2.7
TRANSPARENCY Translucent

No cleavage

Vitreous luster

GRANULAR AVENTURINE
This specimen of green aventurine shows its granular texture.

CABOCHON
A cabochon of yellow-brown aventurine shows the sparkle of its inclusions.

CABOCHON
This green cabochon has been faceted with flat faces to show off its sparkle.

CAT'S-EYE QUARTZ

THE TERM "CAT'S EYE" is applied to two different minerals: one a variety of chrysoberyl (see p.159), the other of quartz. When cut *en cabochon*, both show a single white line across the stone. Cat's-eye quartz is sometimes called Occidental cat's eye to differentiate it from the more valuable Oriental cat's eye—chrysoberyl. The two may be distinguished by their specific gravities: chrysoberyl is much denser. Cat's-eye quartz owes its chatoyancy (cat's-eye effect) and grayish-green or greenish color to parallel fibers of asbestos in the quartz; a more reddish or golden color derives from minute fibers of rutile. The main source of cat's-eye quartz is the gem gravels of Sri Lanka. It is also found in India and Australia, while inferior green stones are obtained from Bavaria, Germany.

Water-worn surface

Parallel fibers

PROPERTIES

GROUP Silicates – tectosilicates
CRYSTAL SYSTEM Hexagonal/trigonal
COMPOSITION SiO_2
COLOR Greenish
FORM/HABIT Massive
HARDNESS 7
CLEAVAGE None
FRACTURE Conchoidal
LUSTER Vitreous
STREAK White
SPECIFIC GRAVITY 2.7
TRANSPARENCY Translucent

FIBROUS CAT'S-EYE QUARTZ
In this specimen of unpolished cat's eye, no chatoyancy can be seen. The "eye" emerges only on cutting, requiring considerable expertise when selecting specimens.

Vitreous luster

GEM PANNING
In the gem fields of Sri Lanka and Myanmar, gems are usually recovered by panning stream gravels.

CABOCHON
This cabochon of grayish-green cat's-eye quartz shows a strong "eye."

CABOCHON
A fine, translucent yellow-gray cabochon also shows the "eye" effect well.

CABOCHON
This round cabochon of cat's eye has a weak "eye," but shows fibrous structure.

TIGER'S EYE

WITTENOOM GORGE
This Western Australian gorge has tiger's eye.

TIGER'S-EYE QUARTZ, ALSO SPELLED tiger-eye, is a semiprecious variety of quartz exhibiting chatoyancy, a vertical luminescent band like that of a cat's eye. Unlike cat's-eye quartz, tiger's eye is formed when parallel veins of crocidolite (blue asbestos) fibers are first altered to iron oxides and then replaced by silica. As a result, it is more opaque and has a rich yellow to brown color. When cut *en cabochon*, the gem has a fine luster. The major source of tiger's eye is Griquatown West, in South Africa. It is also found at Wittenoom Gorge, Western Australia. Hawk's eye is similar to tiger's eye except that the crocidolite is replaced by quartz without altering to iron oxide, and so it retains the gray-blue of the original asbestos.

PROPERTIES

GROUP Silicates – tectosilicates
CRYSTAL SYSTEM Hexagonal/trigonal
COMPOSITION SiO_2
COLOR Yellow-brown
FORM/HABIT Fibrous
HARDNESS 7
CLEAVAGE None
FRACTURE Conchoidal
LUSTER Vitreous
STREAK White
SPECIFIC GRAVITY 2.7
TRANSPARENCY Translucent

HAWK'S EYE
Although similar to tiger's eye, hawk's eye retains the gray-blue of the original asbestos fibers.

Crocidolite fibers

FIBROUS TIGER'S EYE
In this piece of tiger's eye, the fibers are clearly visible. The richness of its color is brought out by polishing.

Ironstone

Altered crocidolite fibers

No cleavage

NECKLACE
Beads of tiger's eye have been made into this richly colored necklace.

POLISHED SECTION
This section cut through a piece of tiger's eye has been polished to show off its fibrous structure.

SPHERE
This sphere made of tiger's eye shows off the golden sheen from the fibers.

RUTILATED QUARTZ

BAHIA, BRAZIL
The prime locality for rutilated quartz crystals is Novo Horizonte, Bahia, Brazil.

THIS VARIETY OF QUARTZ takes its name from needles of rutile (see p.163) that are enclosed within it. It is generally transparent, with any amount of needles from a few to so many that the stone may be nearly opaque. The needles can occur as sprays, or they can be randomly oriented. The rutile is generally golden in color, but it can be reddish to deep red, appearing black without intense light. The quartz can be found in well-formed crystals or in stream-rounded fragments. It is also known as Venus' hairstone. Black tourmaline, green actinolite, and green chlorite needles are also found encased in quartz in a manner similar to rutile needles.

Hexagonal quartz prisms

RUTILATED CRYSTALS
Here, two fine crystals of rutilated quartz are held in a matrix.

Reddish-brown rutile needles

RUTILE NEEDLES
The faces of this irregular piece of rutilated quartz have been polished to show the rutile needles.

Tourmaline needles

Rutile needles

SNUFF BOTTLE
This finely carved Chinese snuff bottle has been made from tourmalated quartz.

PROPERTIES

GROUP Silicates – tectosilicates
CRYSTAL SYSTEM Hexagonal/trigonal
COMPOSITION SiO_2
COLOR Colorless with gold or red needles
FORM/HABIT Prismatic
HARDNESS 7
CLEAVAGE None
FRACTURE Conchoidal
LUSTER Vitreous
STREAK White
SPECIFIC GRAVITY 2.7
TRANSPARENCY Transparent

Golden rutile

Spray of rutile

PENDANT
This cabochon of rutilated quartz, domed on top and faceted on the bottom, is set in a silver and gold pendant mount.

PHANTOM QUARTZ

WHEN GAS BUBBLES or tiny crystals of other minerals accumulate on the termination of a quartz crystal during its growth, the color of the crystal is subtly changed. This can happen at several stages, leaving a "shadow" or "phantom" of the termination at each point. Green phantoms usually result from chlorite, reddish-brown from various iron minerals, blue from riebeckite, and white from gas or liquid bubbles or as a result of etching. Phantom quartz is widespread. Blue phantoms come from São Paulo, Brazil; green phantoms from Hot Springs, Arkansas and Quartzsite, Arizona; and reddish-brown phantoms from Minas Gerais, Brazil. White phantoms are found widely throughout Brazil, and also in Arkansas.

MINAS GERAIS
This area of Brazil is one of many localities for phantom quartz.

Polished face

"Phantoms"

PHANTOM QUARTZ
This quartz crystal has the faces polished to show the "phantoms" of earlier terminations within.

PROPERTIES

GROUP	Silicates – tectosilicates
CRYSTAL SYSTEM	Hexagonal – trigonal
COMPOSITION	SiO_2
COLOR	Colorless, white, green, red-brown, or blue
FORM/HABIT	Prismatic
HARDNESS	7
CLEAVAGE	None
FRACTURE	Conchoidal
LUSTER	Vitreous
STREAK	White
SPECIFIC GRAVITY	2.7
TRANSPARENCY	Transparent

CHALCEDONY

A COMPACT VARIETY of microcrystalline quartz, chalcedony is composed of microscopic fibers. It can be mammillary, botryoidal, or stalactitic, and is found in veins, geodes, and concretions. It is white when pure, but much chalcedony contains trace elements or microscopic inclusions of other minerals, giving a range of colors. Many of these colored chalcedonies have their own variety names (see pp.227–29). Chalcedony that shows distinct banding is called agate (see pp.230–31). Occurrences of all varieties of chalcedony are extremely numerous worldwide. Its name may derive from the ancient port of Khalkedon in Asia Minor (now Turkey), where there were deposits.

Chalcedony forms in cavities, cracks, and by replacement when low-temperature, silica-rich waters percolate through pre-existing rocks, in particular volcanic rocks. Chalcedony is relatively porous, and much chalcedony (in the form of agate, for example) on the commercial market has been dyed to enhance or artificially color it.

QUARTZSITE, ARIZONA
Chalcedony is found in this area of Arizona.

CAMEO
A white layer of chalcedony has been carved away to a yellow layer of agate below to create a relief in the shape of a woman's head with intricately carved hair.

Arborescent form

Waxy luster

Botryoidal habit

UNUSUAL HABIT
This chalcedony specimen has developed in an almost arborescent form, probably as a dripstone in a hollow.

CHALCEDONY BOWL
This elegant Austrian bowl has been created from chalcedony and has intricate decorations on its rim, base, and handles.

PINK CHALCEDONY
This form of botryoidal pink chalcedony from Quartzsite, Arizona, is, along with some forms of selenite gypsum, referred to as a "desert rose."

PROPERTIES

GROUP	Silicates – tectosilicates
CRYSTAL SYSTEM	Hexagonal – trigonal
COMPOSITION	SiO_2
COLOR	White
FORM/HABIT	Microcrystalline
HARDNESS	7
CLEAVAGE	None
FRACTURE	Uneven
LUSTER	Waxy to dull
STREAK	White
SPECIFIC GRAVITY	2.7
TRANSPARENCY	Transparent to translucent

CHRYSOPRASE

CHRYSOPRASE IS A TRANSLUCENT, apple-green variety of chalcedony. Its color is derived from the presence of nickel. The color of some chrysoprase may fade in sunlight, and lighter-colored material may be confused with fine jade in cut stones. It was used by both the Greeks and Romans, and is still the most valued of the chalcedonies. Prase, a leek-green chalcedony, has a more somber hue and is much rarer. Fine chrysoprase once came from mines in Poland and former Czechoslovakia, but since 1965 the best quality material has come from Queensland, Australia. Lesser amounts are found in the Ural Mountains of Russia and in California and Brazil.

This mineral's name is derived from the Greek *chrysos* and *prase*, meaning "golden leek," and was probably applied originally to a lighter or more yellowish chrysoprase. In ancient times it was reputed to strengthen the eyesight and relieve internal pain.

QUEENSLAND
A relatively recent source of this mineral is Queensland, Australia.

Waxy luster

Massive habit

PRASE CAMEO
This subtle cameo uses the dark tones of prase in a gold setting.

MASSIVE CHRYSOPRASE
Examples such as this massive specimen of apple-green chrysoprase have been used for ornamentation since prehistoric times.

Uneven fracture

Color from chromium

PROPERTIES

GROUP Silicates – tectosilicates
CRYSTAL SYSTEM Hexagonal – trigonal
COMPOSITION SiO_2
COLOR Apple-green
FORM/HABIT Massive or microcrystalline
HARDNESS 7
CLEAVAGE None
FRACTURE Uneven
LUSTER Waxy or dull
STREAK White
SPECIFIC GRAVITY 2.7
TRANSPARENCY Translucent

CARNELIAN

A BLOOD-RED to reddish-orange translucent variety of chalcedony, carnelian is also occasionally called cornelian. Its coloration is due to the presence of iron oxide, and it can be uniformly colored or banded. Strongly banded material is known as carnelian agate. Scotland, Brazil, and Washington State are among the localities that produce finer-quality carnelian. Freshly mined carnelian, especially Indian material, is often placed in the sun to change brown tints to red. Carnelian was once thought to still the blood and calm the temper. Conversely, it was also said to give the owner courage in battle, and help timid speakers to be eloquent.

PUNE, INDIA
India produces the best examples of carnelian.

POLISHED STONE
This reddish-orange carnelian from India has been cut and polished.

EGYPTIAN RING
Carved from a single piece of carnelian, this Egyptian ring dates from 1400 BC.

BROOCH
Converted from a pendant, this Arts and Crafts brooch features a carnelian cabochon as its centerpiece.

CARNELIAN VEIN
This vivid red vein of carnelian runs through a mass of rock crystal.

Carnelian vein

Massive habit

Vitreous luster

MASSIVE CARNELIAN
This specimen of carnelian was collected from the Narmada River in northern India.

Color from iron oxide

PROPERTIES

GROUP Silicates – tectosilicates
CRYSTAL SYSTEM Hexagonal – trigonal
COMPOSITION SiO_2
COLOR Red
FORM/HABIT Massive
HARDNESS 7
CLEAVAGE None
FRACTURE Uneven
LUSTER Waxy to dull
STREAK White
SPECIFIC GRAVITY 2.7
TRANSPARENCY Translucent

ONYX

PUNE, INDIA
Fine natural onyx is found in this area of western India.

ONYX IS THE STRIPED, semiprecious variety of agate with white and black alternating bands. Relatively uncommon in nature, it can be produced artificially through dyeing pale, layered agate. The name comes from the Greek *onux*, meaning "nail" or "claw," referring to the mineral's color, and it was used by the Romans for a variety of stones including alabaster, chalcedony, and what is now called onyx marble. The name onyx is properly applied only to the agate variety. Other varieties include carnelian onyx, with white and red bands, and sardonyx (see below), with white and brown bands. As with the other chalcedonies, onyx forms from the deposition of silica at low temperatures from silica-rich waters percolating through cracks and fissures in other rocks. Natural onyx comes from India and South America. Onyx is popular for carved cameos and intaglios because its layers can be cut to show a color contrast.

PROPERTIES

GROUP Silicates – tectosilicates
CRYSTAL SYSTEM Hexagonal/trigonal
COMPOSITION SiO_2
COLOR Black and white
FORM/HABIT Cryptocrystalline
HARDNESS 7
CLEAVAGE None
FRACTURE Conchoidal
LUSTER Vitreous
STREAK White
SPECIFIC GRAVITY 2.7
TRANSPARENCY Translucent to nearly opaque

Translucent slab

ALTERNATING BANDS
This polished slab of onyx displays its characteristic alternating bands of color.

Parallel bands of black and white

ONYX SEAL
This striking Georgian copy of a Roman seal exploits the parallel layering of brown and white onyx.

ONYX CAMEO
The layers of contrasting colors in onyx make it an ideal material for carving cameos.

ONYX BROOCH
This onyx and gold mourning brooch is decorated with split pearls and has a locket back.

SARD

SRI LANKA
Ratnapura, in south-west Sri Lanka, is a famous locality for sard.

A TRANSLUCENT, light to dark brown chalcedony, sard takes its name from the Greek *Sardis*, the capital of ancient Lydia. Until the Middle Ages it shared the name "sardion" with carnelian. Bands of sard and white chalcedony are called sardonyx. Sard forms from the deposition of silica at low temperatures from silica-rich waters percolating through cracks and fissures in other rocks. One famous locality for sard is Ratnapura, Sri Lanka. Other sources are in India, Brazil, and Uruguay. It was used in Harappa, one of the oldest centers of the Indus civilization (c. 2300–1500 BC), by the Mycenaeans (1450–1100 BC), and also by the Assyrians (1400–600 BC).

POLISHED SARDONYX
White and brown-red bands are characteristic of sardonyx.

SARDONYX JEWELRY

Both sard and sardonyx have been used since ancient times for making cameos and intaglios. Wearing sard jewelry has always been considered fortunate. In the 4th century, Epiphanius, Bishop of Salamis, noted sard's medicinal value for wounds, and in the 11th century, Bishop Marbodius remarked on it as a protector against incantation and sorcery.

CAMEO
This classical cameo has been carved out of sardonyx.

Polished surface

Pitted, partly waterworn surface

PROPERTIES

GROUP Silicates – tectosilicates
CRYSTAL SYSTEM Hexagonal/trigonal
COMPOSITION SiO_2
COLOR Light to dark brown
FORM/HABIT Cryptocrystalline
HARDNESS 7
CLEAVAGE None
FRACTURE Conchoidal
LUSTER Vitreous
STREAK White
SPECIFIC GRAVITY 2.7
TRANSPARENCY Translucent to opaque
R.I. 1.5

CABOCHON
Sard that is cut as a semi-precious gem is always cut en cabochon. This translucent stone has patches of brownish-red.

PEBBLE
This smooth, oval-shaped pebble of dark brown, semi-translucent sard has a slightly pitted waterworn surface.

POLISHED INTERIOR
This piece of sard rough has been polished to show its internal brown coloration.

BAHIA
Extensive deposits of bloodstone can still be found in this part of Brazil.

BLOODSTONE

ALSO KNOWN AS HELIOTROPE, bloodstone is a dark green variety of chalcedony colored by traces of iron silicates and with patches of bright red jasper distributed throughout its mass. The name heliotrope is derived from the Greek *helio*, meaning "sun," and *trepein*, "turning." Both polished and unpolished stones show red spots on a dark green background, resembling drops of blood: hence the name bloodstone. The ancient source of bloodstone was the Kathiawar Peninsula of India, with modern sources in Brazil and Australia. Its occurrence is, as with the other chalcedonies, through deposition from low-temperature, silica-rich waters percolating through cracks and fissures in other rocks.

SNUFFBOX
This rectangular Louis XV lacquer snuffbox is inlaid with bloodstone and gold.

BLOODSTONE BOWL
This silver gilt and bloodstone bowl and setting was made by the silver engraver Paul Storr in 1824.

PROPERTIES

GROUP	Silicates – tectosilicates
CRYSTAL SYSTEM	Hexagonal/trigonal
COMPOSITION	SiO_2
COLOR	Dark green with red spots
FORM/HABIT	Cryptocrystalline
HARDNESS	7
CLEAVAGE	None
FRACTURE	Conchoidal
LUSTER	Vitreous
STREAK	White
SPECIFIC GRAVITY	2.7
TRANSPARENCY	Translucent to opaque
R.I.	1.53–1.54

ANCIENT LORE

In the first century BC, bloodstone was—according to Greek natural philosopher Damigueron—a preserver of health, and offered protection against deception. During the Middle Ages in Europe it was used in sculptures representing flagellation and martyrdom. It was believed to prevent nosebleeds, remove anger and discord, and to be a remedy for hemorrhage and inflammatory diseases. It was said to be most effective if first dipped in cold water.

BLOODSTONE RELIQUARY
This late 12th-century wooden French reliquary of St. Stephen is decorated with silver gilt and bloodstones.

Jasper spots

POLISHED SLAB
Red spots and veins of iron silicates are scattered throughout this polished slab of dark green bloodstone.

Conchoidal fracture

RED PATCHES
One face of this bloodstone has been polished to show the red spots of jasper to good effect.

ARIZONA
The Petrified Forest area of Arizona preserves some fine jasper specimens.

JASPER

AN OPAQUE, FINE-GRAINED or dense variety of cryptocrystalline quartz, jasper is related to chert (see pp.70–71). Its name is from the Greek *iaspis*, which is probably of Semitic origin. Jasper is a chalcedony incorporating various amounts of other materials that give it both its opacity and color. Brick-red to brownish-red jasper contains hematite; clay gives rise to a yellowish-white or gray, and goethite produces brown or yellow. Jasper is formed through deposition from low-temperature, silica-rich waters percolating through cracks and fissures in other rocks, incorporating a variety of materials in the process. It is found worldwide wherever crypto-crystalline quartz occurs. Beautiful examples of jasperized fossil wood are found in Arizona (see pp.334–35).

PROPERTIES

GROUP	Silicates – tectosilicates
CRYSTAL SYSTEM	Hexagonal/trigonal
COMPOSITION	SiO_2
COLOR	Red, yellow, brown, numerous others
FORM/HABIT	Cryptocrystalline
HARDNESS	7
CLEAVAGE	None
FRACTURE	Conchoidal
LUSTER	Vitreous
STREAK	White
SPECIFIC GRAVITY	2.7
TRANSPARENCY	Opaque

JASPER INTAGLIO
This early-3rd-century jasper intaglio from northern England features Silvanus-Cocidius, a Romano-Celtic hunter deity, with a hare and hound.

PHARAOH
This Egyptian pharaoh in the guise of a falcon (1555–1080 BC) is made of jasper.

ANCIENT LORE

Jasper has been used for jewelry and ornamentation since Paleolithic times. The Babylonians believed that jasper influenced women's diseases, and was a symbol of childbirth. The 11th-century Bishop of Rouen, Marbodius, stated that a jasper "placed on the belly of a woman in childbirth relieves her pangs." This comes from a time when all stones were believed to be alive and have a sex, jasper being a female stone.

Color variation from incorporated materials

COLOR VARIATION
Hematite colors this example of jasper brownish-red. Threads of white quartz veins crisscross the specimen.

White quartz vein

229

MEDFORD, OREGON
The state of Oregon is rich in agates of all kinds. The area around Medford has numerous veins of moss agate, which is seen being collected here.

AGATE

A COMMON, SEMIPRECIOUS type of chalcedony, agate is the compact, microcrystalline variety of quartz. In general, its physical properties are those of quartz. Most agates form in cavities in ancient lavas or other extrusive igneous rocks. They are characterized for the most part by color bands in a concentric form, and less often by mosslike inclusions (moss agate). The characteristic bands usually follow the outline of the cavity in which the mineral has formed. The band colors are determined by the differing impurities present, and occur in shades of white, yellow, gray, pale blue, brown, pink, red, or black. Much of the sliced agate offered on the market in particularly bright colors is dyed or stained to enhance the natural color, an easy process because of its porous nature.

TYPES OF BANDED AGATE
Other names often precede the word agate, and indicate either its visual characteristics or its place of origin. Fortification agate is a type of banded agate with angularly arranged bands that resemble an aerial view of an ancient fortress. There are several types of fortification agate. Brazilian agate is a fortification agate with banding in angled concentric circles like the fortifications of a castle. Botswana agate from Africa has beautiful dark and light banding. Mexican lace—sometimes called "crazy-lace"—is a multicolored fortification agate with highly convoluted layering. Blue lace agate from South Africa—one of the

most common kinds for sale today—is a delicate light blue with a fine interlayering of colorless agate. Fire agate has inclusions of reddish to brown hematite that give an internal iridescence to polished stones.

Banded agate is produced by a series of processes that take place in cavities in a solidified lava. As the lava cools, steam and other gases form bubbles in the liquid rock that are preserved as the lava hardens, forming cavities. Long after the rock has solidified, silica-bearing water solutions penetrate into a bubble and coagulate

AGATE DIE
This Roman die is made of agate. The dots have been carved into the surface of the die.

"Moss"

MOSS AGATE

Fortification banding

FORTIFICATION AGATE

AGATE VARIETIES
Above are examples of two agate varieties. The fortification agate is a historic specimen from the Idar-Oberstein deposit (see panel, opposite).

PROPERTIES

GROUP Silicates – tectosilicates

CRYSTAL SYSTEM Hexagonal/trigonal

COMPOSITION SiO_2

COLOR Colorless, white, yellow, gray, brown, blue, or red

FORM/HABIT Cryptocrystalline

HARDNESS 7

CLEAVAGE None

FRACTURE Conchoidal

LUSTER Vitreous to waxy

STREAK White

SPECIFIC GRAVITY 2.7

TRANSPARENCY Translucent to opaque

Yellowish color probably due to iron oxide (limonite)

Fortification banding

FORTIFICATION AGATE
This sliced specimen of fortification agate shows the parallel banding that gives it its name. The variations in color are due to different mineral inclusions picked up by the agate as the bands formed.

to form a layer of silica gel. This sequence is repeated until the hollow is filled. Some of the layers will have picked up traces of iron or other soluble material to give the bands their distinct coloring. Finally, the whole mass crystallizes, with the water being lost but the bands remaining undisturbed.

Agates have been worked since prehistoric times, and were among the world's first lapidary materials. Today, it is usually cut as thin slabs, or polished as ornaments, brooches, or pendants. When cut for jewelry, it is cut *en cabochon*.

MOSS AGATE SLICE
This beautiful moss agate, with a strong dendritic form, has been cut and polished.

OTHER TYPES OF AGATE

Moss agate does not have banding. It is white or gray with brown, black, or green moss- or treelike (dendritic) inclusions, suggestive of vegetable growth. These dendrites are not organic, but are inclusions of other minerals, most often iron or manganese oxides or chlorite. Moss agate with brown inclusions is sometimes called mocha stone. Indian moss agate often has green, mosslike dendrites. Sweetwater agate from the Sweetwater River area of Wyoming is characterized by fine, black dendrites. Moss agate forms by a variety of processes by which other minerals are included in the agate, during or after its formation. Agatized wood is fossilized wood

that has had its organic matter replaced by agate, in some cases cell by cell. The Petrified Forest in Arizona, with hundreds of acres of agatized wood in a multitude of colors, is one of nature's most spectacular sights (see pp.334–35). Bodies of agate that fill round hollows in old volcanic rocks in parallel straight bands, rather than in curved fortifications, are called "thunder eggs."

Agate is found worldwide, but Brazil, Botswana, South Africa, Mexico, Egypt, China, and Scotland are prolific sources and produce interesting varieties. Oregon, Washington, Idaho, and Montana are particularly abundant sources in the US.

MOSS AGATE PIN TRAY
A thick slice of moss agate has been carved to form a shallow bowl, or pin tray.

AGATE BRACELET
This elegant silver-mounted Scots agate bracelet was crafted in 1865.

Red color probably due to iron oxide (hematite)

POLISHED AGATE
These two examples show more variety in patterning. The geode has an agate lining and an amethyst center. The slice is Brazilian fortification agate with simple oval banding.

POLISHED GEODE

SLICE OF BRAZILIAN AGATE

IDAR-OBERSTEIN

Idar-Oberstein is a city in the Rhineland of southwest Germany, straddling the Nahe River at its confluence with the Idarbach. Agates were abundant in the area for at least 700 years, and were collected and mined there until the 20th century. An agate-working industry was well established in the then separate towns of Idar and Oberstein by 1548, using the water power of the Nahe River to drive the cutting and polishing wheels made of local sandstone. The agate workings were eventually

GEM-CUTTING SHOP
This photograph shows a cutter at work in a gem-cutting shop in the then separate town of Idar in about 1930.

extended underground in huge galleries that can be visited today. From about 1900, the local supplies were exhausted, but were replaced with agates from Brazil and Uruguay. Today Idar-Oberstein is still a gemstone- and jewelry-making center, and it has some notable museums of gems. It also hosts an annual gem and jewelry trade fair that showcases the latest trends in jewelry-making, particularly from this historic area.

VISITING THE MINE TODAY
The abandoned mines, known as Steinkaulenberg, have been cleared and divided into a researchers' area, a collectors' area, and a visitors' area.

ABANDONED OPAL MINE
These shafts of old opal test holes are part of an underground opal mine in Australia. Australia produces fine, precious and black opal.

OPAL

KNOWN SINCE ANTIQUITY, opal derives its name from the Roman word *opalus*, a Latinized version of the older Sanskrit *upala*, meaning "precious stone." Opal is hardened silica gel, and usually contains 5 to 10 percent water in submicroscopic pores. Its structure varies from essentially amorphous to partially crystalline. Precious opal is the least crystalline form of the mineral, consisting of a regular arrangement of tiny, transparent, silica spheres with water in the intervening spaces.

HOW OPAL FORMS

Opal is very widespread. In its pure form it is essentially colorless. The vast majority is common or "potch" opal in opaque, dull yellows and reds imparted by iron oxides, or black from manganese oxides and organic carbon. In potch opal, where silica spheres are present, they are of many different sizes. Opal is deposited at low temperatures from silica-bearing, circulating waters. It is found as nodules, stalactitic masses, veinlets, and encrustations in most kinds of rocks. It is especially abundant in areas of hot-spring activity and, as the siliceous skeletons of diatoms, radiolarians, and sponges, opal constitutes important parts of many sedimentary accumulations such as diatomaceous earth. It is commonly

AUSTRALIAN OPAL MINE
This miner is drilling for opals at an opal mine in Coober Pedy, South Australia. Coober Pedy is an aboriginal phrase meaning "white man in a hole."

FOSSIL BONE AND BOULDER OPAL
In the Australian opal fields, bones and shells are sometimes found replaced by precious opal (above). Boulder opal occurs when opal fills cavities in a host rock. In this specimen (right), ironstone has been split open to reveal the opal.

ZUNI EARRINGS
In these earrings made by Zuni craftspeople, opal is flanked by mother-of-pearl and inlaid with jet.

OPAL AND PEARL CROSS
This gold pendant is set with five opal cabochons and two pearls. The opals have a fine color play, showing red, green, and blue flashes.

PRECIOUS OPAL
This specimen of precious opal is from Coober Pedy, Queensland, Australia. It shows the ironstone matrix and streaks of yellowish potch opal that are characteristic of opals from this field.

VICTORIAN RING
This 19th-century ring uses a single opal in an intricate gold setting.

PROPERTIES

GROUP Silicates – tectosilicates
CRYSTAL SYSTEM Amorphous
COMPOSITION $SiO_2 \cdot nH_2O$
COLOR Colorless, white, yellow, orange, rose-red, black, or dark blue
FORM/HABIT Massive
HARDNESS 5–6
CLEAVAGE None
FRACTURE Conchoidal
LUSTER Vitreous
STREAK White
SPECIFIC GRAVITY 1.9–2.3
TRANSPARENCY Transparent to translucent
R.I. 1.37–1.47

Ironstone matrix

Potch opal

found as fossilized wood, where it preserves the wood's external appearance and cellular structure. Fossil bones and seashells have been discovered in Australia replaced by precious opal, and it also forms pseudomorphs after gypsum, calcite, feldspars, and other minerals.

Precious opals can form only in undisturbed space within another rock that is capable of holding a clean solution of silica from which water is slowly removed over a long period—perhaps thousands of years. The silica spheres slowly settle out of solution and arrange themselves into an orderly three-dimensional formation. Unless the spheres are regularly arranged and of the correct size, there is no color play, which is caused by the diffraction of light through the spheres; opal is, in effect, a diffraction grating. The larger the spheres (within the limits imposed by the wavelengths of visible light), the greater the range of color. All precious opal is probably relatively young in geological terms, since precious opal cannot withstand the heat and pressure of burial and metamorphism.

FORMS OF OPAL
These opal specimens show opal in both precious and common forms. The sil-sinter with a spherular habit is also known as fiorite, after its source: Santa Fiora, Tuscany, Italy. The black opal is from Lightning Ridge, Australia. The rose opal is potch, from France. The potch opal is from Cornwall, England.

SIL-SINTER OPAL

BLACK OPAL

ROSE OPAL

POTCH OPAL

SOURCES AND USES

Until late in the 19th century, the primary source of precious opal, including that used by the Romans, was in present-day Slovakia, where opal occurred in andesite. Today, the chief producer of precious opal is Australia, where it was discovered in 1887, with deposits in South Australia, Queensland, and New South Wales. In Australia, opal is found in sedimentary rocks such as sandstone and ironstone. The Lightning Ridge field in New South Wales, Australia, produces the rare and prized black opal, with a very dark gray or blue to black body-color and a superb color play. Until the discovery of this field in 1903, black opal was virtually unknown, and it is still the rarest form of opal. Much smaller amounts of precious opal come from India, New Zealand, Honduras, and the western United States. The other form of gem opal is called fire opal. This transparent, intensely colored opal in red, orange, or yellow also shows flashes of color. The principal sources of fire opal are Mexico and Honduras, where it is found in trachyte.

Common opal in its various forms is widely mined for use as abrasives, insulation media, fillers, and ingredients in ceramic manufacture. Precious opals are usually finished *en cabochon* because their color play shows best on smoothly rounded surfaces; fire opals are normally facet-cut. Precious opal with a variety of intense colors, including red and violet, is generally the most expensive. Unlike most other gemstones, opal may crack or lose its color if it dries. Thin slices of precious opal are often either glued to a thicker quartz base (forming a "doublet") or sandwiched between layers of quartz (forming a "triplet"), both giving the appearance of a denser, more valuable stone. Black stones, such as obsidian, are sometimes used as the backing for doublets or triplets, giving the appearance of rare black opal.

Vitreous luster

Color play

Conchoidal fracture

Blue to yellow color play

PEACOCK BROOCH
The centerpiece of this eye-catching brooch by Harry Winston, Inc. is a 32-carat black opal from Lightning Ridge, Australia. Sapphires, rubies, emeralds, and diamonds adorn the tail.

HUNGARIAN
This white opal is from an area of Slovakia, once part of Hungary. Opal from here is often called Hungarian.

SPIDERWEB OPAL
This opal gains its name from the web-like network of fine lines across its surface.

WHITE OPAL
This precious white opal cut into a cabochon shows flashes of several colors.

BLACK OPAL
Precious opal with a black body-color is rare and expensive. Here it is carved en cabochon.

FIRE OPAL
This beautiful, rich orange octagonal-cut fire opal shows an unusual degree of transparency.

FELDSPARS

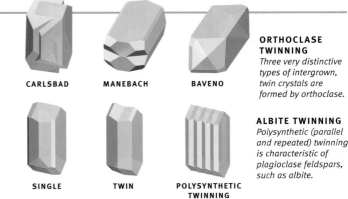

CARLSBAD **MANEBACH** **BAVENO**

SINGLE **TWIN** **POLYSYNTHETIC TWINNING**

ORTHOCLASE TWINNING
Three very distinctive types of intergrown, twin crystals are formed by orthoclase.

ALBITE TWINNING
Polysynthetic (parallel and repeated) twinning is characteristic of plagioclase feldspars, such as albite.

AMONG THE MOST IMPORTANT silicate groups is the feldspars. A group of aluminosilicate minerals that contain calcium, sodium, or potassium, they are the most common minerals in Earth's crust. Feldspars are the major component of most igneous rocks, and are found not only on Earth but also on the Moon and in meteorites. There are two groups of feldspars: the alkali feldspars and the plagioclase feldspars. The plagioclases can be differentiated from the alkali feldspars by the presence of polysynthetic twinning (see above right).

ALKALI FELDSPARS

When formed at high temperatures, a solid–solution series (see p.91) exists within the alkali feldspars between the potassium feldspar orthoclase ($KAlSi_3O_8$) and the sodium feldspar albite ($NaAlSi_3O_8$). Unlike the plagioclases, which all crystallize in the triclinic crystal system, the alkali feldspars crystallize in both the triclinic and monoclinic systems. There are also monoclinic varieties in which barium replaces some or all of the potassium. These rather rare minerals are known as barium feldspars. Albite appears as the end member of both the alkali feldspars and the plagioclases, and is considered to be both an alkali and a plagioclase feldspar.

PLAGIOCLASE FELDSPARS

The plagioclases are a major group of rock–forming feldspars that are a continuous series of solid solutions between the end members albite ($NaAlSi_3O_8$, or sodium aluminosilicate, abbreviated Ab), and anorthite ($CaAl_2Si_2O_8$, or calcium aluminosilicate, abbreviated An). Various members of intermediate composition are given names dependent on the percentages of albite or anorthite they contain. There is no other mineralogical difference between them. Selected feldspars are shown in the table below.

PINK GRANITE
The pink color of granite is due to the high percentage of alkali feldspar in its composition. The pink's intensity varies according to location. This weathered outcropping is part of the Pink Granite Coast near Ploumanac'h in northern Brittany, France.

BARIUM FELDSPARS

MONOCLINIC

CELSIAN $BaAl_2Si_2O_8$

HYALOPHANE $(K,Na,Ba)(Al,Si)_4O_8$

ALKALI FELDSPARS

MONOCLINIC

ORTHOCLASE $KAlSi_3O_8$

SANIDINE $(K,Na)AlSi_3O_8$

TRICLINIC

MICROCLINE $KAlSi_3O_8$

ANORTHOCLASE $(Na,K)AlSi_3O_8$

ALBITE (Ab) $NaAlSi_3O_8$

PLAGIOCLASE FELDSPARS

ANDESINE $NaAlSi_3O_8 - CaAl_2Si_2O_8$

BYTOWNITE $(NaSi,CaAl)AlSi_2O_8$

OLIGOCLASE $(Na,Ca)(Al,Si)AlSi_2O_8$

LABRADORITE $(Ca,Na)Al(Al,Si)Si_2O_8$

ANORTHITE (An) $CaAl_2Si_2O_8$

ORTHOCLASE

GOODSPRINGS, NEVADA
Fine orthoclase crystals are located here.

YELLOW CRYSTAL

MOONSTONE PEBBLE

MOONSTONE CRYSTALS IN ROCK

ORTHOCLASE FORMS
Colorless and yellow orthoclase crystals are the most common. Moonstone is usually white.

THE POTASSIUM-BEARING end member of the alkali feldspars (see opposite), orthoclase is a major rock-forming mineral. It is a major component of granite—its pink crystals give common granite its characteristic pink color. Orthoclase also occurs in colorless, white, cream, pale yellow, and brownish-red crystals, which are frequently twinned. It appears as well-formed, short prismatic crystals, and also in massive form. Pure orthoclase is relatively rare, as some sodium is usually present in the structure.

Orthoclase is abundant in igneous rocks rich in potassium or silica, in pegmatites, and in gneisses. It occurs worldwide. Geologists include orthoclase along with other potassium-rich feldspars under the general term K-feldspars, or K-spar for short. The name orthoclase is derived from the Greek word for "straight fracture" and alludes to the crystal's perpendicular cleavages. Adularia (see p.237) is a colorless or white variety of orthoclase, attributed to orthoclase formed in Alpine-type veins. The term valencianite was at one time used to describe adularia from the Valenciana Mine in Mexico. Moonstone is an opalescent variety of orthoclase and some other feldspars, which has a blue or white sheen known as schiller. This sheen is a result of the interlayering of orthoclase with albite (see p.239). Very thin layers yield a blue sheen, much prized in jewelry, while thicker layers give a white sheen.

SACRED STONES

Moonstone derived its name from its opalescent moonlike appearance. It was sacred in India, where it was said that if lovers placed it in their mouths during the full moon, their futures would be revealed. In 11th-century Europe, moonstone was believed to bring about the reconciliation of lovers. Sunstone—a variety of oligoclase or labradorite—is associated, like the Sun, with health, physical energy, passion, and courage. Tiny inclusions of hematite are in fact responsible for the red to orange color.

Blue sheen   **MOONSTONE**

Hematite inclusions
SUNSTONE

Orthoclase is important in ceramics, where it can be used either to make the artifact itself or as a glaze. Moonstone was used in jewelry by the Romans from AD 100, and even earlier in the Orient. Today, its best sources are Myanmar (Burma), Sri Lanka, India, Brazil, Tanzania, and the US.

MOONSTONE NECKLACE
Moonstone gems are almost always cut en cabochon to accentuate the blue sheen, as in this contemporary necklace.

PROPERTIES

GROUP	Silicates / tectosilicates
CRYSTAL SYSTEM	Monoclinic
COMPOSITION	$KAlSi_3O_8$
COLOR	Colorless, white, cream, yellow, pink, brown-red
HABIT	Short prismatic
HARDNESS	$6-6\frac{1}{2}$
CLEAVAGE	Perfect
FRACTURE	Subconchoidal to uneven, brittle
LUSTER	Vitreous
STREAK	White
SPECIFIC GRAVITY	2.5–2.6
TRANSPARENCY	Transparent to translucent
R.I.	1.51 – 1.54

ORTHOCLASE CRYSTALS
In this group of three orthoclase crystals, the crystal on the right demonstrates good prismatic habit. The largest crystal is twinned.

Crystal has unequal sides

Twinning

MOONSTONE BROOCH
This 1960s Georg Jensen leaf-design brooch features moonstones with a blue sheen.

EARRINGS
Rectangular cabochon moonstones are set in these silver earrings.

OVAL CUSHION
This orthoclase is cut in an oval cushion; the smoky, bluish sheen of schiller may be seen within it.

YELLOW STEP
A transparent yellow orthoclase from Madagascar is here faceted in a rectangular step cut.

PALE BROWN STEP
This step-cut, pale brown orthoclase is attractive, but the mineral is too brittle for regular wear.

CABOCHON
This orthoclase moonstone is cut en cabochon to highlight the ethereal beauty of its schiller.

HYALOPHANE

TOCHIGI PREFECTURE
This area in Japan, north of Tokyo, has hyalophane.

ONE OF THE LESS COMMON feldspar minerals, hyalophane is a potassium barium aluminosilicate. It takes its name from the Greek for "glass," and "to appear," a reference to its transparent, glassy crystals. Those crystals, which are frequently twinned, are prismatic and either similar in appearance to those of adularia or short prismatic like those of orthoclase. It also occurs as glassy masses. The mineral is colorless, white, pale yellow, or pale to deep pink. It is intermediate in composition between orthoclase and celsian. Hyalophane is found with manganese deposits in contact-metamorphic zones, often in association with rhodonite, spessartine, epidote, and analcime. Localities include Tochigi Prefecture, Japan; Jakobsberg, Sweden; Rhiw, Wales; Broken Hill, NSW, Australia; Binntal, Switzerland; Pahau River, New Zealand; and, in the US, Franklin, New Jersey, and the Highwood Mountains of Montana. Zorgrazski Creek, near Busovaca in Bosnia, produces large and spectacular twinned crystals.

PROPERTIES

GROUP Silicates – tectosilicates
CRYSTAL SYSTEM Monoclinic
COMPOSITION $(K,Ba)(Al,Si)_4O_8$
COLOR Colorless, white, pale yellow, or pale pink
FORM/HABIT Prismatic
HARDNESS 6–6½
CLEAVAGE Perfect, good
FRACTURE Conchoidal, brittle
LUSTER Vitreous
STREAK White
SPECIFIC GRAVITY 2.6–2.8
TRANSPARENCY Transparent to translucent

HYALOPHANE CRYSTAL
This ¼-in (6-mm) long hyalophane crystal, with pyrite in dolomite marble, is from Binntal, Valais, Switzerland.

Dolomite marble

Hyalophane crystal

Pyrite

SANIDINE

EIFEL, GERMANY
This area has several important sanidine deposits.

FORMING COLORLESS OR WHITE, glassy, transparent crystals, which can also be gray or other pale tints, sanidine is an alkali feldspar, a high-temperature form of potassium aluminosilicate. Its crystals are generally short prismatic in habit, and may reach 20 in (50 cm) in length. It is also found as granular or cleavable masses. Some sanidine falls under the general category of moonstone (see p.235), exhibiting the "schiller" effect—the internal reflections that create the "moonglow" appearance in cut stones.

Sanidine occurs in felsic volcanic rocks such as rhyolite and trachyte. It is also found in high-temperature and low-pressure metamorphic rocks. It is a very widespread mineral, with significant occurrences at Auvergne, France; the Alban Hills near Rome, Italy; La Cruz, Mexico; Mont St.-Hilaire, Canada; Eifel, Germany; and, in the US, Grant County, New Mexico, Klamath County, Oregon, and the Thomas Range of Utah. Moonstone comes from India and Sri Lanka.

Sanidine crystal

Trachyte groundmass

CERAMICS
Sanidine is one of the feldspars ground for use in ceramics.

MOONSTONE RING
This gold ring is set with a sanidine moonstone. Sanidine has white to light blue "schiller."

SANIDINE CRYSTAL
This single, well-formed prismatic crystal of sanidine rests in a groundmass of trachyte rock.

PROPERTIES

GROUP Silicates – tectosilicates
CRYSTAL SYSTEM Monoclinic
COMPOSITION $(K,Na)AlSi_3O_8$
COLOR Colorless, white
FORM/HABIT Tabular
HARDNESS 6–6½
CLEAVAGE Perfect, good
FRACTURE Conchoidal to uneven
LUSTER Vitreous
STREAK White
SPECIFIC GRAVITY 2.6
TRANSPARENCY Transparent to translucent

CELSIAN

ONE OF THE LESS COMMON of the feldspar minerals, celsian is named for Anders Celsius (1701–1744), who invented the Celsius temperature scale. A barium aluminosilicate, it has short prismatic crystals that have a habit similar to adularia crystals. Crystals are commonly twinned and can be colorless, white, or yellow, often with glassy, lustrous faces. The mineral also occurs in cleavable masses. Celsian is found in manganese- and barium-rich metamorphic rocks, often in association with diopside, witherite, and quartz. Localities include Jakobsberg, Sweden; Tochigi Prefecture, Japan; Rhiw, Wales; Broken Hill, NSW, Australia; Otjosondu, Namibia; and, in the US, Fresno and Santa Cruz counties, California.

ALASKA RANGE
These mountains in Alaska contain masses of celsian.

ANDERS CELSIUS
Celsian is named for Anders Celsius, a Swedish naturalist and astronomer.

Granular habit

Uneven fracture

Vitreous luster

PROPERTIES

GROUP Silicates – tectosilicates
CRYSTAL SYSTEM Monoclinic
COMPOSITION $BaAl_2Si_2O_8$
COLOR White, colorless, or yellow
FORM/HABIT Short prismatic
HARDNESS 6–6½
CLEAVAGE Perfect, good
FRACTURE Uneven, brittle
LUSTER Vitreous
STREAK White
SPECIFIC GRAVITY 3.1–3.5
TRANSPARENCY Transparent to translucent

GRANULAR CELSIAN
This creamy white granular specimen of celsian is from Big Creek, Fresno County, California.

ADULARIA

SWISS ALPS
The schists of the Alps provide excellent adularia crystals.

THIS FELDSPAR MINERAL is generally considered to be a more highly ordered form of orthoclase. It is found in hydrothermal veins in mountainous areas, such as the Adular Mountains of Switzerland, after which it is named. It commonly forms colorless to white, cream, pale yellow to pink, or reddish-brown, glassy, prismatic, twinned crystals. It can also be massive, granular, or cryptocrystalline. Adularia is found in low-temperature veins of felsic plutonic rocks, in hydrothermal veins, and in cavities in crystalline schists. Noteworthy localities include the Alps, where it occurs in schists, and at Betroka, Madagascar, where large, transparent crystals are found.

ADULARIA CRYSTALS
This group of glassy white adularia crystals rests on a groundmass of green actinolite.

Adularia crystal

YELLOW CRYSTAL
Internal cracks or flaws are visible in this yellow-tinged adularia crystal.

Short prismatic habit

Twinned crystals

Vitreous luster

Actinolite groundmass

PROPERTIES

GROUP Silicates – tectosilicates
CRYSTAL SYSTEM Monoclinic/triclinic
COMPOSITION $KAlSi_3O_8$
COLOR Colorless, white, yellow, pink, or reddish-brown
FORM/HABIT Short prismatic
HARDNESS 6–6½
CLEAVAGE Perfect, good
FRACTURE Conchoidal to uneven
LUSTER Vitreous
STREAK Colorless
SPECIFIC GRAVITY 2.5–2.6
TRANSPARENCY Transparent to translucent

MICROCLINE

URAL MOUNTAINS
This Russian mountain range is a prime locality for microcline.

USED IN CERAMICS and as a mild abrasive, microcline is one of the most common feldspar minerals. It is one of two forms of potassium aluminosilicate, the other being orthoclase (see p.235). Microcline forms short prismatic or tabular crystals, often of considerable size: single crystals from granite pegmatites can weigh several tons, and reach dozens of yards in length. Crystals are often multiple twinned and have two sets of fine lines (exsolution lamellae) at right angles to each other, giving a "plaid" effect that distinguishes microcline from other feldspars. It can also have a massive habit. It can be colorless, white, cream to pale yellow, salmon-pink to red, and bright green to blue-green. Its name, from the Greek for "little" and "lean," is derived from the planes of its two cleavage directions, which form a slightly oblique angle with each other.

Microcline is the most common feldspar in deep-seated, felsic rocks such as granite, granodiorite, and syenite. It is found in granite pegmatites and in metamorphic rocks such as schists and gneisses. It can be a major component of detrital sedimentary rocks. It is a very widespread mineral; exceptional specimens are found in Baveno, Italy; Irkutsk, Russia; Mont St.-Hilaire, Canada; and in South Dakota and New Mexico.

Blue-green specimens of microcline are called amazonstone or amazonite, after the Amazon River. This variety is used in jewelry, generally cut into cabochons. Gem-quality amazonite is found in the Ilmen and Ural Mountains of Russia, the Pikes Peak district of Colorado, and in Minas Gerais, Brazil.

POLISHED
Prized for its pastel blue-green color, translucent amazonstone is cut en cabochon.

PROPERTIES

GROUP	Silicates – tectosilicates
CRYSTAL SYSTEM	Triclinic
COMPOSITION	$KAlSi_3O_8$
COLOR	White, pale yellow
FORM/HABIT	Short prismatic
HARDNESS	6–6½
CLEAVAGE	Perfect, good
FRACTURE	Conchoidal to uneven, brittle
LUSTER	Vitreous, dull
STREAK	White
SPECIFIC GRAVITY	2.6
TRANSPARENCY	Transparent to translucent
R.I.	1.5

AMAZONSTONE
Also called amazonite, this blue-green variety of microcline is a semiprecious gemstone.

Fine lines on surface

Vitreous luster

AMAZONSTONE BRACELET
This broad, flexible bracelet of loop-and-ring sculptural design is set with oval amazonstones.

Amazonstone cabochon

ANORTHOCLASE

COLORADO
Gem anorthoclase is found in Colorado.

THIS MEMBER OF THE feldspar group takes its name from the Greek for "not straight fracture" (orthoclase means "straight fracture"), referring to its oblique cleavage. It is one of several feldspars that is known as moonstone when cut *en cabochon*. Crystals are prismatic or tabular, and are often multiple twinned. Like microcline, it shows two sets of fine lines (exsolution lamellae) at right angles to each other, but in anorthoclase the lamellae are much finer. It can also be massive and granular. It is colorless, white, cream, pink, pale yellow, gray, and green. Anorthoclase is a sodium potassium aluminosilicate formed in sodium-rich igneous environments. It is commonly found with augite, apatite, and ilmenite. Noteworthy specimens come from Scotland, Kenya, New Zealand, Australia, Sicily, Norway, and Antarctica.

PROPERTIES

GROUP	Silicates – tectosilicates
CRYSTAL SYSTEM	Triclinic
COMPOSITION	$(Na,K)AlSi_3O_8$
COLOR	Colorless, white
FORM/HABIT	Prismatic
HARDNESS	6–6½
CLEAVAGE	Perfect, good
FRACTURE	Conchoidal to uneven, brittle
LUSTER	Vitreous
STREAK	White
SPECIFIC GRAVITY	2.6
TRANSPARENCY	Transparent to translucent
R.I.	1.5

LARGE CRYSTAL
This specimen of a pink and gray prismatic anorthoclase crystal shows well-developed crystal faces.

MOONSTONE

Anorthoclase is one of several feldspars that show a white or silvery iridescence when cut *en cabochon*. They are classed as moonstone; other moonstones are orthoclase, sanidine, albite, and oligoclase. The iridescence, called "schiller," results from the minute interlayering of a different feldspar that develops by internal chemical separation during the process of crystallization.

SETTING STONE
This rainbow moonstone is being mounted in a silver setting.

MOONSTONE NECKLACE
This gold and silver necklace (c. 1912) is mounted with moonstones, carnelians, and labradorite.

Single prismatic crystal

Vitreous luster

ALBITE

THE PRIMARY GEOLOGICAL importance of albite is as a rock-forming mineral. Crystals are tabular or platy, often twinned, glassy, and brittle. It can also be massive and granular. Albite takes its name from the Latin *albus*, "white," a reference to its usual color, but it can also be colorless, yellowish, pink, or green. The end member of both the plagioclase and the alkali feldspars (see p.234), albite occurs widely in pegmatites and felsic igneous rocks, such as granites, syenites, and rhyolites, and is also found in low-grade metamorphic rocks. In addition, it forms through chemical processes in certain sedimentary environments. Large crystals are found in Brazil, and in South Dakota, New Mexico, and California.

PROPERTIES

GROUP Silicates – tectosilicates
CRYSTAL SYSTEM Triclinic
COMPOSITION $NaAlSi_3O_8$
COLOR White, colorless
FORM/HABIT Tabular
HARDNESS $6–6\frac{1}{2}$
CLEAVAGE Perfect, good
FRACTURE Conchoidal to uneven, brittle
LUSTER Vitreous to pearly
STREAK White
SPECIFIC GRAVITY 2.6
TRANSPARENCY Translucent
R.I. 1.4–1.5

PLAGIOCLASES IN PORCELAIN

Chinese porcelain became highly prized in Europe after its introduction around 1300. In the 1570s, attempts were made to produce porcelain as delicate-looking and tough as the Chinese by adding ground glass to the clay, but the results were unsatisfactory. It was not until 1707 in Saxony that Ehrenfried von Tschirnhaus discovered that if you mixed ground plagioclase, such as albite, with clay, you could create porcelain of similar quality.

PORCELAIN BOWL
Made in the late 14th century during the Ming dynasty, this Chinese porcelain bowl features a red design of a dragon.

THIN SECTION
This albite porphyroblast enclosing trails of graphite is in mica schist from As Sifah, Oman.

Twin lamellae

Trails of graphite

Mica

Vitreous to pearly luster

TABULAR CRYSTALS
This specimen is of a large group of tabular white albite crystals, many of which are twinned.

Twinned tabular crystals

MIXED CUT
Some albite is transparent enough to facet into brilliant gemstones, such as this mixed cut.

OLIGOCLASE

THE MOST COMMON variety of the feldspar mineral plagioclase, oligoclase is a sodium potassium aluminosilicate. Its usual habit is massive or granular, although it does form tabular crystals, commonly twinned. It can be gray, white, greenish, yellowish, brown, or colorless. Oligoclase occurs in granite, granitic pegmatites, diorite, rhyolite, and other felsic igneous rocks. In metamorphic rocks, it occurs in high-grade, regionally metamorphosed schists and gneisses. Localities include Kimito, Finland; Lisbon, Portugal; and New Hampshire and New York. Sunstone is a gemstone variety of oligoclase; when it is cut *en cabochon*, the reflections from hematite inclusions give a reddish glow and a sparkling appearance. It occurs in Kragero, Norway, and in North Carolina.

Lamellar twinning

Oligoclase

THIN SECTION
The characteristic very fine lamellar twinning is clearly visible in this section of Sierra Nevada granite.

MASSIVE OLIGOCLASE
This typical specimen of massive oligoclase is from Penland, Mitchell County, North Carolina.

PROPERTIES

GROUP Silicates – tectosilicates
CRYSTAL SYSTEM Triclinic
COMPOSITION $(Na,Ca)Al_2Si_2O_8$
COLOR Gray, white
FORM/HABIT Massive
HARDNESS 6
CLEAVAGE Perfect
FRACTURE Conchoidal to uneven, brittle
LUSTER Vitreous
STREAK White
SPECIFIC GRAVITY 2.6
TRANSPARENCY Translucent
R.I. 1.54–1.55

Perfect cleavage

Vitreous luster

SUNSTONE PIN
Sunstone has tiny plate-like inclusions of hematite or goethite oriented parallel to one another.

ANDESINE

ANDESINE OCCURS WIDELY in igneous rocks of medium silica content, especially in the rock andesite (see p.46). It is an intermediate plagioclase, a sodium calcium aluminosilicate. Andesine often forms well-defined crystals, usually exhibiting multiple twinning. Other types of twinning also commonly occur.

Andesine can be massive, or occur as rock-bound grains. Good crystals are found in Miyagi and Toyama Prefectures, Japan; Marmato, Colombia; Trentino, Italy; Cannes, France; and Bodenmais, Germany.

PROPERTIES

GROUP Silicates – tectosilicates
CRYSTAL SYSTEM Triclinic
COMPOSITION $NaAlSi_3O_8 - CaAl_2Si_2O_8$
COLOR Gray, white
FORM/HABIT Short prismatic
HARDNESS $6–6\frac{1}{2}$
CLEAVAGE Perfect
FRACTURE Conchoidal to uneven
LUSTER Subvitreous to pearly
STREAK White
SPECIFIC GRAVITY 2.7
TRANSPARENCY Transparent to translucent

Andesine phenocryst

THIN SECTION
An andesine crystal is visible here in lava of the rock andesite.

Andesite lava matrix

Andesine crystal

Triclinic crystals

Blue porphyry

ANDESINE CRYSTALS
This specimen has andesine crystals up to $\frac{3}{4}$ in (2 cm) long in blue porphyry. It was found in Estérel, Var, France.

BYTOWNITE

THE RAREST PLAGIOCLASE, bytownite is named for the locality in which it was first recognized, Bytown (now Ottawa), Canada (although the material from Bytown was later reanalyzed and found to be a mixture). Well-developed crystals are relatively uncommon, and are short prismatic to tabular, exhibiting the polysynthetic twinning characteristic of the plagioclases. Bytownite occurs in mafic and ultramafic igneous rocks, both intrusive and extrusive, and it is also found in stony meteorites. Gem-quality material is found at Nueva Casas Grandes, Chihuahua, Mexico, and Lakeview, Oregon. Other localities include: Rhum Island, Scotland; Fiskenaesset, Greenland; Chester and Lebanon counties, Pennsylvania; and Ottawa, Canada.

Perfect cleavage

Vitreous luster

MASSIVE BYTOWNITE
This specimen of bytownite is gray-brown. Bytownite is more commonly found as rock-bound grains.

PROPERTIES

GROUP Silicates – tectosilicates
CRYSTAL SYSTEM Triclinic
COMPOSITION $NaAlSi_3O_8 - CaAl_2Si_2O_8$
COLOR White, gray
FORM/HABIT Short prismatic to tabular
HARDNESS $6–6\frac{1}{2}$
CLEAVAGE Perfect
FRACTURE Uneven to conchoidal
LUSTER Vitreous to pearly
STREAK White
SPECIFIC GRAVITY 2.7
TRANSPARENCY Transparent to translucent
R.I. 1.57–1.59

RECTANGULAR
This step cut is of the yellow-orange bytownite sometimes called sunstone.

OVAL CUT
Transparent, colorless bytownite is sometimes cut in many-faceted shapes.

ANORTHITE

PURE ANORTHITE is uncommon. The calcium end member of the plagioclases, anorthite is calcium aluminosilicate and can contain up to 10 percent albite. It takes its name from the Greek *anorthos*, meaning "not straight," in reference to its triclinic form. It develops well-formed crystals, which are short prismatic, and it can also be massive and granular. Its crystals are white, grayish, or reddish, brittle, and glassy. Anorthite is a major rock-forming mineral present in many mafic igneous rocks, both intrusive and extrusive, in contact metamorphic rocks, and in some meteorites. Specimen localities include: Tunaberg, Sweden; Labrador, Canada; the Ural Mountains, Russia; Trentino, Italy; Tamil Nadu, India; and Grass Valley, California.

Anorthite crystal

Vitreous luster

PINK ANORTHITE
Here, pink anorthite crystals are associated with augite.

PROPERTIES

GROUP Silicates – tectosilicates
CRYSTAL SYSTEM Triclinic
COMPOSITION $CaAl_2Si_2O_8$
COLOR White, gray, pink
FORM/HABIT Short prismatic
HARDNESS $6–6\frac{1}{2}$
CLEAVAGE Perfect
FRACTURE Conchoidal to uneven, brittle
LUSTER Vitreous
STREAK White
SPECIFIC GRAVITY 2.7
TRANSPARENCY Transparent to translucent

LABRADORITE

LABRADOR, CANADA
Labradorite was first identified at Paul Island, Labrador, by Moravian missionaries in 1770.

THE CALCIC, MIDDLE-RANGE MEMBER of the plagioclase feldspars, labradorite seldom forms crystals, but when crystals do occur, they are tabular. It most often occurs in crystalline masses that can be microscopic or up to a yard or more across, and is commonly characterized by its "schiller" effect— a rich play of iridescent colors, principally blue, on cleavage surfaces. Crystals that display this effect are used as gemstones, cut *en cabochon*. The schiller effect is caused by the scattering of light from thin layers of a second feldspar that develops through internal chemical separation during the cooling of what was originally a single feldspar. The base color of labradorite is generally blue or dark gray, but can be colorless or white. Transparent

CAMEO
Labradorite is sometimes used as a carving material to produce unusual ornamental objects such as this cameo.

PENDANT
A labradorite cabochon forms the center of this modern silver pendant.

labradorite can be yellow, orange, red, or green. Labradorite is a major or important constituent of certain medium-silica and silica-poor igneous and metamorphic rocks, including basalt, gabbro, diorite, andesite, and amphibolite. Gemstone labradorite comes from Madagascar, Finland, and Russia. Nearly transparent material with a beautiful schiller comes from southern India, and facetable material is found in Mexico and the US. High-quality gemstone material from Finland is sometimes called spectrolite.

THIN SECTION
In this specimen, a group of labradorite crystals are in olivine gabbro.

Labradorite crystal

LAPLAND
This area produces a large quantity of highly colored labradorite, known locally as spectrolite.

PROPERTIES

GROUP Silicates – tectosilicates
CRYSTAL SYSTEM Triclinic
COMPOSITION $NaAlSi_3O_8 - CaAl_2Si_2O_8$
COLOR Blue, gray, white
FORM/HABIT Usually massive
HARDNESS $6-6\frac{1}{2}$
CLEAVAGE Perfect
FRACTURE Uneven to conchoidal
LUSTER Vitreous
STREAK White
SPECIFIC GRAVITY 2.7
TRANSPARENCY Transparent to translucent
R.I. 1.56–1.57

CHOKER
The polished oval of labradorite in this contemporary choker displays beautifully the rainbow iridescence of this gemstone.

"Schiller" effect

Polysynthetic twinning

Perfect cleavage

Vitreous luster

CABOCHON
Labradorite is usually cut en cabochon to better display the iridescent color play of the stone.

SUNSTONE
The orange feldspar found in Oregon and locally called sunstone is actually labradorite.

BLUE LABRADORITE
This beautifully colored specimen shows the polysynthetic twinning that is characteristic of the plagioclase feldspars. The twinning is apparent as a series of parallel lines on broken faces.

"SCHILLER" EFFECT
The color play is clearly visible in this specimen, in which orange, purple, and blue can be seen.

FELDSPATHOIDS

FELDSPATHOIDS ARE A GROUP of sodium- and potassium-bearing aluminosilicate minerals similar to the feldspars in chemical composition, but with physical and chemical properties that are intermediate between those of feldspars and zeolites. The feldspathoid structure consists of oxygen tetrahedra with silicon and aluminum atoms at their centers. Each oxygen atom is shared by the SiO_4 and AlO_4 tetrahedra, forming a three-dimensional framework. The open spaces in the framework can be occupied by carbonate, sulfate, or chlorine ions. Feldspathoids are mainly found in alkali-rich, silica-poor igneous and metamorphic rocks, where they occur in place of the feldspars that would have formed had there been more silica present.

Chlorine ion
Sodium ion
AlO_4 tetrahedron
SiO_4 tetrahedron
Shared oxygen atom

SODALITE CRYSTAL STRUCTURE
Sodalite has an open crystal structure. Chlorine and sodium ions exist in the large spaces between the SiO_4 and AlO_4 tetrahedra.

NEPHELINE

EIFEL, GERMANY
This is a locality for superb nepheline crystals.

THE MOST COMMON feldspathoid mineral, nepheline is an aluminosilicate of sodium and potassium. It takes its name from the Greek *nephele*, meaning "cloud," a reference to the fact that it becomes cloudy or milky when placed in strong acids. It is generally massive. When crystals are found, they are commonly hexagonal prisms, but may exhibit a variety of prism and pyramid shapes. Large crystals are often rough and pitted. Nepheline is also found as large, tabular phenocrysts. Usually white, often with a yellowish or grayish tint, it can also be gray or red-brown, depending on inclusions. It is a characteristic mineral of mafic plutonic rocks, where it may occur with spinel, perovskite, and olivine. In intermediate plutonics, such as nepheline syenites, it is often found with augite, aegirine, and low-silica amphiboles. It also occurs in some volcanics, and in some metamorphics such as nepheline gneisses. Good crystals are found at Davis Hill Mine, Bancroft, Ontario, and Mont St.-Hilaire, Canada; Eifel, Germany; Transvaal, South Africa; and in the US at Magnet Cove, Arkansas, and in the Bearpaw and Judith Mountains of Montana. It occurs in particularly beautiful crystal form with mica, garnet, and sanidine feldspar on Monte Somma, Italy. Nepheline is sometimes mined for use in the manufacture of glass and ceramics.

Rock groundmass

NEPHELINE CRYSTALS
This specimen shows well-developed crystals of nepheline filling cavities in a rock groundmass.

Hexagonal nepheline prisms

Eudialyte

THIN SECTION
Nepheline crystals with regular outlines are enclosed here in eudialyte from a nepheline syenite gneiss from Brazil.

Nepheline crystal

Massive habit

PROPERTIES

GROUP	Silicates – tectosilicates
CRYSTAL SYSTEM	Hexagonal
COMPOSITION	$(Na,K)AlSiO_4$
COLOR	White, gray, yellow, or red-brown
FORM/HABIT	Massive
HARDNESS	$5\frac{1}{2}$–6
CLEAVAGE	Poor
FRACTURE	Subconchoidal, brittle
LUSTER	Vitreous to greasy
STREAK	White
SPECIFIC GRAVITY	2.6
TRANSPARENCY	Transparent to opaque

Imperfect fracture

MASSIVE NEPHELINE
This specimen of nepheline from Arkansas shows its most typical massive habit.

LEUCITE

MOUNT KILAMANJARO
This Tanzanian mountain is an important locality for leucite.

TAKING ITS NAME from the Greek *leukos*, meaning "white," in allusion to its most common color, leucite can also be gray or colorless. It is potassium aluminosilicate, and has until recently been considered a feldspathoid, although it is now classified as a zeolite. Its crystals can be up to 3½ in (9 cm) across. Leucite is cubic at high temperatures, forming trapezohedral crystals, but at lower temperatures it is tetragonal. It also forms massive and granular aggregates, and disseminated grains. Leucite occurs only in igneous rocks, especially those that are potassium-rich and silica-poor. It is found with natrolite, alkali-feldspar, nepheline, and analcime, and occurs worldwide. Important localities are Eifel, Germany; Monte Somma, Italy; and in the US in the Leucite Hills, Wyoming, Hot Springs, Arkansas, the Bearpaw Mountains, Montana, and the Sierra Nevadas, California. Leucite is a source of alum, which is a widely used astringent.

LEUCITE CRYSTALS
In this specimen, formed at a high temperature, fine trapezohedral crystals of leucite rest in cavities in a rock groundmass. This example is from Mount Vesuvius, Italy, one of the key localities for leucite.

Trapezohedron

Rock groundmass

FERTILIZING CROPS
Because of its high potassium content, leucite is used as a fertilizer in Italy.

PROPERTIES

GROUP Silicates – tectosilicates
CRYSTAL SYSTEM Cubic/tetragonal
COMPOSITION $KAlSi_2O_6$
COLOR White, gray, or colorless
FORM/HABIT Trapezohedral
HARDNESS 5½–6
CLEAVAGE Poor
FRACTURE Conchoidal, brittle
LUSTER Vitreous
STREAK White
SPECIFIC GRAVITY 2.5
TRANSPARENCY Transparent to translucent

SODALITE

KOLA PENINSULA
This part of Russia produces massive sodalite.

NAMED IN 1811 for its high sodium content, sodalite is a feldspathoid mineral, a sodium aluminum silicate chloride. It usually forms massive aggregates or disseminated grains. Crystals are relatively rare, and are dodecahedral or octahedral. Sodalite principally occurs in silica-poor igneous rocks such as nepheline syenites and their associated pegmatites. It is sometimes found in volcanic ejecta and in contact metamorphosed limestones and dolomites. Massive sodalite is found in the Kola Peninsula, Russia; Eifel, Germany; Kishangarh, Rajasthan, India; Bancroft, Ontario, Canada; and in the US at Litchfield, Maine, Red Hill, New Hampshire, and Magnet Cove, Arkansas. Its principal use is as a gemstone. Transparent material from Mont St.-Hilaire, Canada, has been faceted for collectors, and rare crystals are found on Mount Vesuvius, Italy.

PROPERTIES

GROUP Silicates – tectosilicates
CRYSTAL SYSTEM Cubic
COMPOSITION $Na_4Al_3Si_3O_{12}Cl$
COLOR Gray, white, blue
FORM/HABIT Massive
HARDNESS 5½–6
CLEAVAGE Poor to distinct
FRACTURE Uneven to conchoidal
LUSTER Vitreous to greasy
STREAK White to light blue
SPECIFIC GRAVITY 2.1–2.3
TRANSPARENCY Transparent to translucent
R.I. 1.48

ART DECO CLOCK
Mother-of-pearl is edged by vivid blue sodalite in this Art Deco clock, which also stands on a sodalite base.

NECKLACE
This modern Egyptian necklace features beads made of sodalite (blue) and carnelian (red), as well as gold panel dividers with Egyptian motifs.

Vitreous luster

Uneven fracture

MASSIVE SODALITE
This specimen shows the intense blue exhibited by much sodalite, sometimes causing it to be mistaken for lapis lazuli.

Massive habit

PEBBLE
Cheap and plentiful, sodalite is a popular mineral for tumble-polishing.

CABOCHON
When cut and polished en cabochon, sodalite makes an attractive and inexpensive gem.

OVAL BRILLIANT
Rare, semitransparent sodalite is sometimes faceted especially for collectors.

LAZURITE

THE MINERAL LAZURITE is the main component of lapis lazuli and accounts for the stone's intense blue color, although lapis lazuli also contains pyrite and calcite, and usually some sodalite and haüyne, too. Lazurite itself, a sodium calcium aluminosilicate sulfate, forms distinct crystals; it should not be confused with the phosphate lazulite. In lapis lazuli, lazurite is well dispersed. Distinct crystals were thought to be very rare until large numbers were brought out of the mines of Badakhshan, Afghanistan, in the 1990s. The best quality lapis lazuli is intense dark blue, with minor patches of white calcite and brassy yellow pyrite. Lapis lazuli was used as a gemstone for millennia by the Egyptians: the mask of Tutankhamun, for example, has lapis

LAPIS LAZULI BEAD NECKLACE
Since ancient times, lapis lazuli has been a popular choice for beads and other forms of ornamentation.

lazuli inlays (see p.116). Other objects containing lapis lazuli, including scarabs, pendants, and beads date from much earlier, at least 3100 BC. Powdered lapis lazuli was also used as a cosmetic (the first eyeshadow), as a pigment, and as a medicine. In Sumeria, the tomb of Queen Pu-abi (2500 BC) contained numerous gold and silver jewelry pieces richly adorned with lapis. In the 4th century BC, both the Chinese and the Greeks carved various lapis lazuli artifacts. Ancient references to "sapphire," the *sapphirus* of the Romans, usually, in fact, refer to lapis lazuli. Its modern name originates in the Persian word

BADAKHSHAN
Lapis lazuli has been mined in Badakhshan, northeastern Afghanistan, since antiquity. The mines here were the source of ancient Egyptian and Sumerian material.

SCARAB RING
This ancient Egyptian gold ring contains a scarab stone carved from lapis lazuli.

EARRING
This Egyptian lapis lazuli-inlaid earring comes from the tomb of Tutankhamun, and dates from the 14th century BC.

IMITATION CABOCHON
Synthetic lapis lazuli is made in France by Pierre Gilson. It is similar in composition to lazurite, but softer.

POLISHED CABOCHON
Cabochons of natural lapis lazuli frequently display visible white veining as well as irregular flecks of pyrite.

POLISHED SLAB
This slice of lazurite has been ground with grits to give a flat surface, and polished to show its intense color to best effect.

Vitreous luster

Dodecahedral crystals

PROPERTIES

GROUP Silicates – tectosilicates
CRYSTAL SYSTEM Cubic
COMPOSITION $Na_3Ca(Al_3Si_3O_{12})S$
COLOR Various intense shades of blue
FORM/HABIT Dodecahedral when crystallized
HARDNESS $5–5\frac{1}{2}$
CLEAVAGE Indistinct
FRACTURE Uneven, brittle
LUSTER Dull to vitreous
STREAK Bright blue
SPECIFIC GRAVITY 2.4
TRANSPARENCY Translucent to opaque
R.I. 1.5 average

LAZURITE CRYSTALS
This lazurite specimen from Badakhshan, Afghanistan, shows superbly developed crystals in a matrix of calcite. The largest crystals are about $^3/_4$ in (19 mm) long.

Calcite matrix

CHINESE SNUFF BOTTLE
Chinese snuff bottles were carved from many natural materials. Lapis lazuli was a very popular material, used for bottles, bowls, and intricate figurines.

lazhuward, meaning "blue," and the Arabic word lazaward, meaning "heaven" or "sky," and came into use in Europe during the Middle Ages.

Lapis lazuli is relatively rare and commonly forms in crystalline limestones as a product of contact metamorphism. The mines in Afghanistan remain a major source. Lighter blue material comes from Chile, and some lapis is found in Italy, Argentina, the US, and Tajikistan. Diopside, amphibole, feldspar, mica, apatite, titanite (sphene), and zircon may also occur in lapis lazuli, depending on its origin. It has been synthesized by Pierre Gilson in France.

LORE OF LAPIS LAZULI

Much of the historical lore of lapis lazuli is difficult to untangle from the lore of other blue stones because of the problem of knowing exactly which blue stone was being referred to. In ancient Greece and Rome, there was a belief that *sapphirus*, probably lapis lazuli, cured eye diseases and set prisoners free. It was noted by the Greek physician Dioscorides, around AD 55, that it was an antidote for snake venom; it was an even older Assyrian cure for melancholy.

SPIRITUAL ASSOCIATIONS

Another widespread ancient belief was that it protected the wearer from the evil eye—possibly because its blue color flecked with gold pyrite resembled the night sky, the dwelling place of God. Similarly, a medieval treatise suggests that "meditation upon stone carries the soul to heavenly contemplation."

To the Buddhists of antiquity, lapis lazuli brought peace of mind and equanimity, and was good for dispelling evil thoughts.

CASKET
Containing the remains of Thomas á Becket, this English casket dates from around AD 1190 and includes gold, lapis lazuli, and semiprecious stones.

CARVED BUDDHA
Due to the association of lapis lazuli with peace, it was a popular carving material for images of the Buddha. It is still a popular choice for modern religious objects.

WILTON DIPTYCH
The intense blue of lapis lazuli pigment survives in this medieval altarpiece, now in London's National Gallery. Blue pigments made from powdered lazurite turn green with age.

Powdered lapis lazuli

PIGMENT
Powdered lapis lazuli was used for hundreds of years to make the pigment ultramarine, which has now been replaced by a synthetic alternative.

Twinned crystals

CARVED TORTOISES
This modern lapiz lazuli carving of three tortoises and a frog comes from Afghanistan.

"Strong **bull**, great of horns, perfect in form, with long, flowing beard, bright as **lapis lazuli**."

ANCIENT ASSYRIAN HYMN TO THE MOON GOD SIN

Cubic crystals

LAZURITE IN MATRIX
Lazurite dispersed in marble forms an attractive but inferior gem.

RENAISSANCE BROOCH
This brooch, created by Benvenuto Cellini (1500–71), is gold on a base of lapis lazuli surrounded by pearls. The scene depicted is from the Greek myth of Leda and the Swan.

245

THE STANDARD OF UR

THIS MYSTERIOUS OBJECT WAS FOUND IN THE ROYAL CEMETERY OF UR IN SOUTHERN IRAQ. TWO PANELS DEPICT SUMERIANS AT PEACE AND AT WAR IN A BEAUTIFUL MOSAIC OF LAPIS LAZULI, SHELL, AND RED LIMESTONE.

Dating from between 2600 and 2400 BC, the Standard of Ur was crafted in a period when incredible treasures in gold, silver, bronze, and semiprecious stones were created. During this period, Sumerian kings were buried along with their court officials, servants, and women, so that they could continue their service in the next world.

When found, lying in the corner of a chamber above the right shoulder of a man, the original wooden frame of the Standard had decayed, and the bitumen acting as glue had disintegrated. Leonard Woolley, the excavator at Ur between 1922 and 1934, believed that it was carried on a pole as a standard, but it is now thought more likely that it formed the soundbox of a musical instrument. If so, the man it was buried with may have been a court musician. The Standard was restored as a musical soundbox by the British Museum, where it currently resides. It measures 8.4 in (21.6 cm) in height and 19.3 in (49.5 cm) in length, and the two main side panels are known as "War" and "Peace," reflecting the scenes depicted on each. The lapis lazuli was probably from Afghanistan, the principal ancient source of this precious stone, the chief constituent of which is lazurite (see pp.244–45).

GRAVE NECKLACE
This necklace of gold, lapis lazuli, and carnelian was found in one of the richest tombs at Ur—the burial place of Pu-abi.

GOLD CUP
Found on the floor of the pit of the Queen's grave at Ur, this gold cup was one of four drinking vessels lying beside the Queen's sacrificial victims in the tomb. It was probably used by one of them to drink the poison that ended his life.

"STANDARD OF UR," PEACE SIDE
Animals, fish, and other goods are brought in procession to a banquet on the "Peace" panel (right). A musician plays a lyre for seated figures, who are drinking.

"STANDARD OF UR," WAR SIDE
The "War" panel (above) depicts chariots pulled by four donkeys and infantrymen carrying spears. Enemy soldiers are shown being killed with axes while others are paraded naked and presented to the King, who holds a spear.

HAÜYNE

EIFEL
This part of Germany contains substantial haüyne deposits.

NAMED FOR ONE of the pioneers of crystallography, French mineralogist René Just Haüy, haüyne is a sodium calcium aluminosilicate containing a sulfate radical. It is a feldspathoid mineral. Its crystals are dodecahedral or octahedral, and it is commonly found in rounded grains. Twinning is also common. It is blue, white, gray, yellow, green, or pink. Haüyne is one of the components of lapis lazuli, along with lazurite, calcite, pyrite, and sodalite. It is easily soluble in acids, leaving a silica gel. Haüyne is primarily found in silica-poor volcanic rocks, although it has also been found in a few metamorphic rocks. It is commonly associated with leucite, nepheline, and nosean (a sodium aluminosilicate, with which haüyne forms a partial solid-solution). The volcanic rocks of Germany, especially Niedermendig and Laacher See, Eifel, are some of its main sources. It was first identified in the volcanic rocks of Italy, and other localities include Siberia, Russia; Nanjing, China; Auvergne, France; and in the US in Cripple Creek, Colorado, Edwards, New York, Winnett, Montana, and Lawrence County, South Dakota.

BRILLIANT
Haüyne is difficult to cut, so it is rarely faceted. This small stone was faceted for a collector.

Lava groundmass

RENÉ JUST HAÜY

Haüy (1743–1822) was a priest who grew interested in crystallography in 1781 when he noticed that the fragments of a broken calcite crystal cleave along straight lines that meet at constant angles. In 1784 he showed that a crystal is built up of tiny units and that the shape of the crystal is determined by the shape of the units. In 1802 Haüy became a professor of mineralogy at the Museum of Natural History in Paris. He wrote a crystallography book at the request of Napoleon Bonaparte, as well as other key works.

RENÉ JUST HAÜY
Haüy was a French mineralogist and the founder of the study of the structure and formation of crystals.

Haüyne crystals

HAÜYNE IN LAVA
This specimen of blue haüyne crystals is from Monte Somma, Italy.

PROPERTIES

GROUP Silicates – tectosilicates
CRYSTAL SYSTEM Cubic
COMPOSITION $Na_3Ca(Al_3Si_3O_{12})(SO_4)$
COLOR Blue, white, gray, yellow, green, or pink
FORM/HABIT Dodecahedral, octahedral
HARDNESS $5^1/_2$–6
CLEAVAGE Distinct
FRACTURE Uneven to conchoidal, brittle
LUSTER Vitreous to greasy
STREAK Blue to white
SPECIFIC GRAVITY 2.5
TRANSPARENCY Transparent to translucent
R.I. 1.49–1.51

HELVITE

SAXONY
This part of Germany is a key locality for helvite crystals.

TAKING ITS NAME from the Greek *helios*, meaning "sun," due to its color, helvite forms crystals that are tetrahedral or pseudo-octahedral. It is also found in rounded aggregates. It is yellow to yellow-green, red-brown to brown, and darkens with weathering. Helvite is found in granitic and syenitic pegmatites, and in hydrothermal deposits. Crystals up to 5 in (12 cm) long come from Cosquín, Argentina. Other localities include Mont St.-Hilaire, Canada; Aquiles Serdán, Mexico; and Colorado.

Rock groundmass

PROPERTIES

GROUP Silicates – tectosilicates
CRYSTAL SYSTEM Cubic
COMPOSITION $MnBe_3(SiO_4)_3S$
COLOR Yellow, red-brown, or brown
FORM/HABIT Tetrahedral
HARDNESS 6–$6^1/_2$
CLEAVAGE Distinct
FRACTURE Conchoidal to uneven, brittle
LUSTER Vitreous to resinous
STREAK White
SPECIFIC GRAVITY 3.2–3.4
TRANSPARENCY Translucent

Helvite

CRYSTALS
These crystals of yellow helvite on a rock groundmass are from Saxony, Germany.

CANCRINITE

QUEBEC
Mont St.-Hilaire, Canada, is a cancrinite source.

CANCRINITE IS A feldspathoid mineral. Its relatively rare crystals can be a few inches across. It is usually fine-grained and massive, or in columnar masses. It is pale to dark yellow, pale orange, pale violet, or pink to purple. Cancrinite forms in syenites, in contact metamorphic zones, and in some pegmatites. Fine specimens come from the Lovozero Massif, Russia; Laacher See, Germany; and Litchfield, Maine.

PROPERTIES

GROUP Silicates – tectosilicates
CRYSTAL SYSTEM Hexagonal/trigonal
COMPOSITION $(NaCa)_8(Al_6Si_6)O_{24}(CO_3)_2 \cdot 2H_2O$
COLOR Pale to dark yellow, orange, violet, pink, or purple
FORM/HABIT Massive
HARDNESS 5–6
CLEAVAGE Perfect, poor
FRACTURE Uneven
LUSTER Vitreous
STREAK White
SPECIFIC GRAVITY 2.5
TRANSPARENCY Transparent to translucent

Cancrinite   Syenite

YELLOW CANCRINITE
This yellow cancrinite in syenite is from Litchfield, Maine.

ZEOLITES

ZEOLITES ARE A GROUP of more than 50 water-containing silicate minerals that have a particularly open type of crystal structure. They have a three-dimensional crystal framework of SiO_4 and AlO_4 tetrahedra that surrounds open cavities in which molecules of water or elements such as potassium, calcium, or sodium can fit. The cavities are interconnected by channels that run the entire length of the crystal, and are open at the crystal surface. These channels permit the relatively easy movement of ions (electrically charged atoms) between cavities, allowing zeolites to trap or exchange ions moving through them. Some zeolites are

LAUMONTITE
The calcium ions in the laumontite channels can be exchanged for sodium ions, making it useful in water softeners.

AlO_4 tetrahedron

SiO_4 tetrahedron

Calcium ion

SiO_4 tetrahedron

Cavity

NATROLITE CHANNELS
In natrolite, the tetrahedra form chains, creating linked cavities in which water and sodium molecules fit.

AlO_4 tetrahedron

extensively used in water softeners because they have the capacity to exchange their sodium ions for the calcium ions present in hard water. Some zeolites can function as molecular sieves: they allow only smaller ions to pass through the channels to be absorbed. These zeolites are particularly useful in petroleum and gas refining (see p.251).

NATROLITE

TASMANIA
Fine natrolite crystals come from Tasmania, Australia.

ALLUDING TO ITS SODIUM CONTENT, natrolite takes its name from the Greek *natrium*, which means "soda." It is a hydrated sodium aluminosilicate. Its crystals are generally long and slender, with vertical striations. They may appear pseudotetragonal, and grow up to a yard in length. Natrolite is also found in radiating masses of acicular crystals, and compact masses. It is both pyroelectric and piezoelectric. It can be pale pink, colorless, white, red, gray, yellow, or green. Some specimens fluoresce orange to yellow under ultraviolet light.

Natrolite is found in cavities or fissures in basaltic rocks, volcanic ash deposits, and veins in gneiss, granite, and other rock types. It is often associated with other zeolites, apophyllite, quartz, and heulandite. Unusually fine specimens come from Golden, British Columbia, Canada; Larne, Northern Ireland; Hegau, Germany; Mumbai, India; Canterbury, New Zealand; Cape Grim, Tasmania, Australia; and Bound Brook, New Jersey, and the Dallas Gem Mine in California.

WIDESPREAD ZEOLITE

One of the most widespread of the zeolites, natrolite was also one of the earliest studied of this mineral group. As a result, it was the first for which ion-exchange properties were discovered. It became widely used for softening water.

NATROLITE IN CAVITY
Typically, natrolite is found in cavities or vesicles in basaltic rocks.

PROPERTIES

GROUP Silicates – tectosilicates
CRYSTAL SYSTEM Orthorhombic
COMPOSITION $Na_2Al_2Si_3O_{10}\cdot2H_2O$
COLOR Pale pink, colorless, white, gray, red, yellow, or green
FORM/HABIT Acicular
HARDNESS $5–5\frac{1}{2}$
CLEAVAGE Perfect
FRACTURE Uneven, brittle
LUSTER Vitreous to pearly
STREAK White
SPECIFIC GRAVITY 2.3
TRANSPARENCY Transparent to translucent

NATROLITE CRYSTALS
This specimen comprises a radiating mass of slender, prismatic, transparent to translucent natrolite crystals.

Radiating crystals

Transparent to translucent crystals

KLAPROTH
German chemist and neurologist Martin Heinrich Klaproth named natrolite in 1803.

GMELINITE

COUNTY ANTRIM
Gmelinite is found in County Antrim, Northern Ireland.

GMELINITE IS NAMED FOR German mineralogist and chemist C. G. Gmelin. Its crystals are hexagonal plates or hexagonal prisms. It can be colorless, white, pale yellow, greenish, orange, pink, and red. It occurs in silica-poor volcanic rocks, sodium-rich pegmatites, and marine basalts. It is often intergrown with chabazite (see p.252), and associated with other zeolites, quartz, aragonite, and calcite. It is widespread but found in only small amounts. Localities include Nova Scotia, Canada; Mornington Peninsula, Australia; and New Jersey.

CANADIAN GMELINITE
This specimen is from Two Islands, Nova Scotia, Canada.

Tabular crystals

PROPERTIES

GROUP Silicates – tectosilicates
CRYSTAL SYSTEM Hexagonal
COMPOSITION $(Na, K, Ca_{0.5})_4Al_8Si_{16}O_{48}\cdot22H_2O$
COLOR Colorless to white, yellow, green, orange, or red
FORM/HABIT Platy, tabular
HARDNESS $4^{1}/_2$
CLEAVAGE Good
FRACTURE Uneven to conchoidal, brittle
LUSTER Vitreous to dull
STREAK White
SPECIFIC GRAVITY 2.1
TRANSPARENCY Transparent to opaque

HARMOTOME

SAXONY
Harmotome is found in the Harz Mountains.

COMMONLY FORMING blocky crystals, this zeolite also occurs as multiple, pseudotetragonal, pseudo-orthorhombic, or cruciform twins. All forms appear glassy, and most vary from colorless to gray. Harmotome occurs in low-temperature hydrothermal veins, in volcanic rocks, and as an alteration product of barium-containing feldspars. It is widespread, with good specimens from Idar-Oberstein, Germany; Thunder Bay, Canada; and Taimyr, Russia.

Blocky crystals

PROPERTIES

GROUP Silicates – tectosilicates
CRYSTAL SYSTEM Monoclinic
COMPOSITION $(Ba_{0.5},Ca_{0.5},K, Na)_5Al_5 Si_{11}O_{32}\cdot12H_2O$
COLOR Colorless, white, gray
FORM/HABIT Blocky, multiple twins
HARDNESS $4^{1}/_2-5$
CLEAVAGE Good, fair
FRACTURE Uneven to conchoidal, brittle
LUSTER Vitreous
STREAK White
SPECIFIC GRAVITY 2.5
TRANSPARENCY Transparent to opaque

WHITE CRYSTALS
These well-formed, blocky crystals of harmotome are set on a rocky groundmass.

LAUMONTITE

INDIA
Mumbai, India, is one of the localities that has high-quality laumontite.

LAUMONTITE is a common zeolite mineral. The French mineralogist François P. N. G. de Laumont collected the first specimen for study in 1785, and it was named for him. It occurs as simple prismatic crystals, or often as "swallowtail" twins, and also forms massive, columnar, fibrous, and radiating aggregates. Generally colorless, white, pink, or red, it can become powdery gray, pink, or yellow when partially dehydrated. Some specimens fluoresce white to yellow. Laumontite is typically found filling veins and vesicles in igneous rocks, and is also found in hydrothermal veins, pegmatites, and metamorphic rocks, and it is one of the more abundant zeolites present in sedimentary rocks. It is a widespread mineral, with excellent specimens coming from Mumbai, India; Alamos, Sonora, Mexico; and California, Oregon, and Washington. The crystal structure of laumontite makes it especially useful in water softeners.

PROPERTIES

GROUP Silicates – tectosilicates
CRYSTAL SYSTEM Monoclinic
COMPOSITION $CaAl_2Si_4O_{12}\cdot4H_2O$
COLOR Colorless, white, red
FORM/HABIT Prismatic
HARDNESS 3–4
CLEAVAGE Perfect
FRACTURE Uneven
LUSTER Vitreous, dull when dehydrated
STREAK Colorless
SPECIFIC GRAVITY 2.3
TRANSPARENCY Translucent

Prismatic crystal

Vitreous luster

USE IN WATER SOFTENERS

All zeolites have a crystal structure composed of a lattice of interlinked channels of cavities in which ions can be exchanged or trapped. This open crystal structure is known as a molecular sieve (see p.252). In laumontite, sodium ions are exchanged for calcium ions, making it ideal for softening hard water.

WATER SOFTENER

CRYSTALLINE LAUMONTITE
This specimen shows a mass of prismatic laumontite crystals.

HEULANDITE

AURANGABAD, INDIA
This part of India is a major source of heulandite crystals.

HEULANDITE IS A NAME given to a series of zeolite minerals. The group was named in 1822 for British collector and mineral dealer J. H. Heuland. It is a calcium sodium aluminosilicate hydrate. Crystals are elongated, tabular, and widest at the center, creating a characteristic coffin shape. They can be up to 5 in (12 cm) long. Heulandite is usually colorless or white, but can also be red, gray, yellow, pink, green, or brown. Heulandite is a low-temperature zeolite found in a wide range of geological environments: with other zeolite minerals filling cavities in granites, pegmatites, and basalts; in metamorphic rocks; and in weathered andesites and diabases (dolerites). It is found worldwide, with notable localities being Aurangabad, India; Gunnedah, NSW, Australia; the Faroe Islands; Berufjördhur, Fassarfell, and Randafell, Iceland; Sakha (Yakutia), Russia; Paraná, Brazil; Kilpatrick Hills, Scotland; and Oregon and New Jersey. The heulandite structure and the substitution of aluminum atoms for some of the silicon atoms give it excellent properties for use in water softeners and in petroleum refining.

Pearly luster

Coffin shape

Tabular crystals

PROPERTIES

GROUP	Silicates – tectosilicates
CRYSTAL SYSTEM	Monoclinic
COMPOSITION	$CaAl_2Si_7O_{18}\cdot6H_2O$
COLOR	Colorless, white
FORM/HABIT	Tabular
HARDNESS	$3^{1}/_2$–4
CLEAVAGE	Perfect
FRACTURE	Uneven, brittle
LUSTER	Vitreous to pearly
STREAK	Colorless
SPECIFIC GRAVITY	2.2
TRANSPARENCY	Transparent to translucent

USE IN PETROLEUM REFINING

Zeolites such as heulandite are widely used in petroleum refining as molecular sieves. The open channels of cavities in their crystal structure act as a microscopic sieve, giving them the ability to filter out particles of molecular size. This enables them to remove undesirable impurities, separate gas from liquid, and to filter various petroleum components. The chemical structure of heulandite makes it particularly useful in petroleum refining. It is used to remove paraffins to improve the combustion properties of gasoline.

PETROCHEMICAL PLANT

EXEMPLARY CRYSTALS
The classic coffin shape of heulandite crystals can be seen in this specimen from Berufjördhur, Austurland, Iceland.

PHILLIPSITE

CANADA
Phillipsite occurs at Mont St.-Hilaire, Quebec.

THE ZEOLITE PHILLIPSITE was named in 1825 for the Geological Society of London's founder, William Phillips. It is commonly found in multiple-twinned, pseudo-orthorhombic, prismatic crystals, blocky crystals, or radiating aggregates. It is usually colorless or white, but can also be pink, red, or light yellow. It is a common, low-temperature zeolite filling cavities and fissures in basalt, and in ore veins. Localities include Oregon; Giessen, Germany; Sicily, Italy; and Mont St.-Hilaire, Canada.

PROPERTIES

GROUP	Silicates – tectosilicates
CRYSTAL SYSTEM	Monoclinic
COMPOSITION	$K(Ca_{15},Na)_2(Si_5Al_3)O_{16}\cdot6H_2O$
COLOR	Colorless, white, pink, red, or yellow
FORM/HABIT	Pseudo-orthorhombic, tetragonal, cubic
HARDNESS	4–$4^{1}/_2$
CLEAVAGE	Distinct, indistinct
FRACTURE	Uneven, brittle
LUSTER	Vitreous
STREAK	Colorless
SPECIFIC GRAVITY	2.2
TRANSPARENCY	Transparent to translucent

Rock groundmass

Blocky crystals

BLOCKY PHILLIPSITE
This mass of blocky, twinned phillipsite crystals covers a rock groundmass.

SCOLECITE

HEBRIDES
Fine scolecite specimens occur in the Scottish Hebridean islands of Mull and Skye.

SCOLECITE IS A ZEOLITE. Its crystals tend to be pseudotetragonal or pseudo-orthorhombic. It is both pyroelectric and piezoelectric. Although generally white or colorless, it can be pink, salmon, red, or green. It is a common hydrothermal zeolite, found in basalts, andesites, gabbros, gneisses, amphibolites, and contact metamorphic zones, often associated with quartz, other zeolites, calcite, and prehnite. Large crystals come from Pune, India; Rio Grande do Sul, Brazil; the Isles of Mull and Skye, Scotland; and Cowlitz County, Washington.

SLENDER CRYSTALS
Scolecite crystals tend to be thin, elongated prisms, as here. They can reach 14 in (35 cm) in length.

PROPERTIES

GROUP	Silicates – tectosilicates
CRYSTAL SYSTEM	Monoclinic
COMPOSITION	$CaAl_2Si_3O_{10}\cdot3H_2O$
COLOR	Colorless, white, pink, red or green
FORM/HABIT	Thin prismatic
HARDNESS	5–$5^{1}/_2$
CLEAVAGE	Perfect
FRACTURE	Uneven, brittle
LUSTER	Vitreous
STREAK	Colorless
SPECIFIC GRAVITY	2.3
TRANSPARENCY	Transparent to opaque

Vertical striations

Prismatic crystal

QUEBEC, CANADA
Quebec is one of the localities in which large scapolite crystals are found.

SCAPOLITE

SCAPOLITE WAS ORIGINALLY believed to be a single mineral, a calcium aluminosilicate. Now it is defined as a compositional series from calcium-bearing meionite to sodium-bearing marialite. Pure end members are not found in nature, although they have been synthesized. Natural scapolites seldom approach even 80 percent of either end member. The name scapolite originated in the Greek *scapos*, meaning "rod" and *lithos*, "stone." Scapolite is still used in the gem trade to refer to any members of the scapolite group cut as gemstones.

Scapolite crystals are short to medium prismatic, often with prominent pyramidal and pinacoidal development, and can appear similar to those of vesuvianite (see p.295). They are up to 10 in (25 cm) in length. Scapolite can also be granular and massive. It can be colorless, white, gray, yellow, orange, pink, or purple, and may exhibit chatoyancy, creating a cat's-eye effect when cut *en cabochon*. Scapolites are found principally in metamorphic rocks, particularly in regionally metamorphosed rocks such as marble, calcareous gneiss,

and greenschist. The largest crystals are usually found in marble. Scapolites form less commonly around igneous intrusions, especially those of feldspathic pegmatites and gabbros. Principal occurrences for large crystals are in Quebec and Ontario, Canada, and New York State. Other important sources are in Finland, Mexico, Italy, the Czech Republic, Germany, Russia, and Norway. Gem-quality material comes from China, Myanmar, Australia, Mozambique, Ghana, Chile, and Tanzania.

Several names have been given to scapolites in the past, but have now been discarded: wernerite was the former group name, and dipyre and mizzonite were names for intermediate members of the group. Marialite was named in 1866 by the German mineralogist vom Rath for his wife Maria. Meionite was named in 1801 by French mineralogist René Just Haüy. The word is derived from the Greek word *meion*, meaning "less," alluding to its pyramidal faces, which are less steep than those of vesuvianite, with which this mineral is sometimes confused.

CABOCHON
Scapolite not quite transparent enough for faceting is cut en cabochon, as in this pale purple example.

STEP
The color of this yellow scapolite is both enhanced and displayed by faceting in a step cut. Yellow scapolite can be confused with heliodor.

MIXED
This colorless scapolite is faceted in an oval mixed cut for maximum brilliance.

Vitreous luster

Prismatic scapolite crystal

Distinct cleavage

PROPERTIES

GROUP Silicates – tectosilicates
CRYSTAL SYSTEM Tetragonal
COMPOSITION
Marialite $Na_4(Al_3Si_9O_{24})Cl$
Meionite $Ca_4(Al_6Si_6O_{24})(CO_3SO_4)$
COLOR Colorless, white, gray, yellow, orange, or pink
FORM/HABIT Prismatic
HARDNESS 5–6
CLEAVAGE Good
FRACTURE Uneven to conchoidal
LUSTER Vitreous
STREAK White
SPECIFIC GRAVITY 2.5– 2.7
TRANSPARENCY Transparent to opaque
R.I. 1.53–1.60

Rock groundmass

MARIALITE CRYSTALS
In this specimen, pink prismatic marialite crystals have formed in a cluster on a rock groundmass.

Vitreous luster

Massive habit

Massive habit

MASSIVE VARIETIES
Both of these specimens are massive in habit. The meionite variety (right) is from the Limberg Quarry, Pargas, Finland.

MEIONITE   **MASSIVE SCAPOLITE**

POLLUCITE

CONTAINING CALCIUM, SODIUM, rubidium, and lithium, pollucite is a complex hydrous aluminosilicate in the zeolite group. It is one of two minerals that were discovered in 1846 and named after the Gemini twins in Greek myth, Castor and Pollux. Pollucite was named for Pollux; castonite was named for the other twin, although it has since been renamed petalite (see p.268). Pollucite is commonly massive, or forms rounded, apparently corroded crystals. It is usually colorless or white, but can be pink, blue, or violet. Pollucite forms a solid-solution series with analcime (see p.253). It is found worldwide only in rare-earth-bearing granitic pegmatites, where it occurs with spodumene, petalite, quartz, lepidolite, eucryptite, and apatite. Crystals up to 24 in (60 cm) across have been found at Kamdeysh, Afghanistan, and it occurs at a number of other Afghan localities. The deposit at Bernic Lake, Manitoba, Canada, has an estimated 350,000 tons of mostly massive material, although crystals up to 1 in (2.5 cm) across are also found there. Gem material is found at Elba, Italy, and in the US in Maine, Connecticut, South Dakota, and California.

GEMINI TWINS
Pollucite was named for one of the two Gemini twins, Pollux, seen in this relief by Agostino di Duccio (1418–1481).

Massive habit

PROPERTIES

GROUP	Silicates – tectosilicates
CRYSTAL SYSTEM	Cubic
COMPOSITION	$(Cs,Na)(AlSi_2)O_6H_2O$
COLOR	Colorless, white, pink, blue or violet
FORM/HABIT	Massive
HARDNESS	$6\frac{1}{2}$–7
CLEAVAGE	None
FRACTURE	Conchoidal to uneven
LUSTER	Vitreous to greasy
STREAK	White
SPECIFIC GRAVITY	2.7–3.0
TRANSPARENCY	Transparent to translucent
R.I.	1.51

MASSIVE POLLUCITE
This massive pollucite specimen is from Buckfield, Maine. Crystals with sharp faces are uncommon.

STEP
Colorless pollucite is faceted for collectors in a variety of shapes. The step cut emphasizes its transparency.

CUSHION
Colorless pollucite can be cut in cushion or brilliant cuts for maximum sparkle. It is faceted mainly for collectors.

Greasy luster

CESIUM ATOMIC CLOCK
Pollucite is a source of cesium, used in atomic clocks for ultra-precise time measurement.

NOSEAN

IN THE SAME FAMILY as sodalite, nosean is a sodium aluminum silicate sulfate hydrate. It was named in 1815 for German mineralogist Karl Wilhelm Nose. It is generally massive or granular. When crystals occur, they are dodecahedral, but rarely exceed $\frac{1}{4}$ in (6 mm) in length. Its color varies from colorless and white to gray, brown, and blue. Nosean is found in low-silica volcanics such as phonolites (see p.47), where it often occurs as crystals in cavities in the rock groundmass. It has also been found in lava bombs. Nosean was first discovered near the Laacher See district of Germany, and has also been found in Cornwall, England; the Alban Hills, south of Rome, Italy; Cantal, France; the Cape Verde Islands; and in the US at Cripple Creek, Colorado, and the La Sal Mountains of Utah.

PROPERTIES

GROUP	Silicates – tectosilicates
CRYSTAL SYSTEM	Cubic
COMPOSITION	$Na_8Al_6Si_6O_{24}(SO_4)\cdot H_2O$
COLOR	Colorless, white, gray, brown, or blue
FORM/HABIT	Massive, granular
HARDNESS	$5\frac{1}{2}$
CLEAVAGE	Poor
FRACTURE	Uneven to conchoidal
LUSTER	Vitreous
STREAK	Colorless
SPECIFIC GRAVITY	2.3
TRANSPARENCY	Transparent to translucent

LAVA BOMBS
Globules of molten rock containing nosean can be hurled hundreds of yards from a volcano and solidify before landing.

Sanidine, an associated mineral

Well-formed nosean crystals

NOSEAN CRYSTALS
Here, small, dodecahedral nosean crystals have formed within a rock groundmass of sanidine. The vitreous luster appears on fresh crystal surfaces.

CHRYSOTILE

THE MOST IMPORTANT asbestos mineral, chrysotile is the fibrous variety of the magnesium silicate mineral serpentine (see p.257) and accounts for about 95 percent of all asbestos in commercial use. Chrysotile is in fact three distinct minerals: clinochrysotile, orthochrysotile, and parachrysotile. They are chemically identical, but orthochrysotile and parachrysotile have orthorhombic rather than monoclinic crystals. They are indistinguishable in hand specimens, and clinochrysotile and orthochrysotile may even occur within the same fiber. Individual chrysotile fibers are white and silky, but aggregate fibers in veins are usually green or yellowish. The mineral can even take on a golden appearance; its name is derived from the Greek for "hair of gold." Chrysotile fibers are actually tubes in which the structural layers of the mineral are rolled in the form of a spiral.

Chrysotile principally occurs as veins in altered peridotite, along with other serpentine minerals. Fibers are generally oriented across the vein and are less than ½ in (1.3 cm) long. Large deposits occur in Quebec, Canada, and in the Ural Mountains of Russia. It is also found in England, Scotland, Switzerland, Serbia, Australia, Mexico, South Africa, Zimbabwe, Swaziland, and in various locations in the US.

URAL MOUNTAINS
Russia's Ural Mountains are a treasure-house of mineral deposits, including large amounts of chrysotile.

PROPERTIES

GROUP Silicates – phyllosilicates
CRYSTAL SYSTEM Monoclinic
COMPOSITION $Mg_3Si_2O_5(OH)_4$
COLOR White, green, yellowish, golden
FORM/HABIT Fibrous
HARDNESS 2–3
CLEAVAGE Perfect
FRACTURE None
LUSTER Subresinous to greasy
STREAK White
SPECIFIC GRAVITY 2.6
TRANSPARENCY Translucent to opaque

CHRYSOTILE FIBERS
The fibrous nature of chrysotile is apparent in this specimen, in which a mass of flexible chrysotile crystals rests on a rock groundmass.

Mass of thin fibers

Bent and broken fibers

Broken fiber

Greasy luster

Chrysotile fiber

THIN SECTION
This false-color scanning electron micrograph of chrysotile shows masses of intertwining tubes of fibers lying roughly parallel to one another.

ASBESTOS FIBERS

Asbestos is not a mineral name, but a general term applied to any of several minerals that readily separate into long, flexible fibers. Aside from chrysotile, the other asbestos minerals are amphiboles, and include the fibrous forms of actinolite, tremolite, anthophyllite, and riebeckite. Asbestos fiber is freed by crushing its surrounding rock, and the fibers are then further separated, usually by a blowing process. At one time, the longest fibers were spun into yarn, and the shorter fibers used in paper, millboard, and asbestos-cement building material. Asbestos was also widely used in brake linings, gaskets, and insulation; and in roofing shingles and floor and ceiling tiles. Spun asbestos fabrics were used for safety apparel and for theater curtains. It was discovered in the 1970s that inhalation of some forms of asbestos fibers could result in a fatal form of lung cancer. Most countries now ban asbestos products.

ASBESTOS WORKERS
Protective clothing is worn for the safe removal of asbestos from buildings, ships, and other structures.

ASBESTOS TAILINGS
Asbestos tailings (waste products) are an environmental hazard in some locations.

KAOLINITE

CLAY MINERALS ARE FAR removed, at least in their outward appearance, from more attractive and glamorous minerals, such as gold and diamonds. Yet, by providing the raw material for clay, pottery, and tiles, they have played a vital part in the progress of human civilization. Important among these vital minerals is kaolinite. Its name originates from the hill in China (Kao–ling) where it was mined for centuries.

Kaolinite is an aluminum silicate hydrate that forms microscopic pseudohexagonal plates in compact or granular masses and in micalike piles. Crystals range in size from about 0.1 micrometer to 10 micrometers long. Three other minerals, dickite, nacrite, and halloysite, are chemically identical to kaolinite but crystallize in the monoclinic system. All four have been found together, and are often visually indistinguishable.

Kaolinite is a natural product of the alteration of mica and plagioclase and alkali feldspars under the influence of water, dissolved carbon dioxide, and organic acids. It often occurs with other clay minerals, quartz, mica, sillimanite, tourmaline, and rutile. The ore of kaolinite is kaolin, millions of tons of which are used annually. Kaolin is used in both raw and refined form in agriculture; as a filler in some food (such as chocolate); mixed with pectin as an antidiarrheal; as a binder in talcum and other powders; as a filler and strengthener in rubber; as a paint extender; and as a dusting agent in foundry operations.

KAOLINITE MINE
This kaolinite mine at Gunheath, St. Austell, is at the heart of the china clay industry in Cornwall, England. Kaolinite is also mined in China, Chile, Germany, Russia, the Czech Republic, France, and Brazil.

CHINA CLAY

Kaolinite is the principal component of china clay, the soft white clay that is an essential ingredient in the manufacture of china and porcelain. When mixed with 20 to 35 percent water, it can be molded under pressure, and the shape is retained after the pressure is removed. Thus, intricate ceramic products such as tableware and statuary can be formed or sculpted from it. It was the essential ingredient of Chinese porcelain. It began to be manufactured in Europe in the 17th century, creating a huge china-clay mining industry. Large deposits are thought to have formed when feldspar was eroded from rocks such as granite and deposited in lake beds, where it weathered into kaolin.

CHINESE PORCELAIN
These two porcelain bowls, painted with delicate blue designs, were made during the Ming Dynasty (1368–1644).

CHINA CLAY MINE, CORNWALL
The discovery of china clay in Cornwall in 1746 made possible the English porcelain industry.

NIGERIAN MASK
This late 19th- or early 20th-century helmet mask of a maiden spirit is mainly wood and kaolin.

ROLLS OF PAPER
Kaolin is used in the making of paper. Glossy paper has a high kaolin content.

IMPURE KAOLINITE
Kaolinite can be found mixed with other oxides, such as the iron oxide that imparts an orange color to this specimen.

Earthy luster

Quartz

Crystal shape of feldspar

PROPERTIES

GROUP	Silicates – phyllosilicates
CRYSTAL SYSTEM	Triclinic
COMPOSITION	$Al_2Si_2O_5(OH)_4$
COLOR	White when pure
FORM/HABIT	Massive
HARDNESS	2–2½
CLEAVAGE	Perfect
FRACTURE	Unobservable
LUSTER	Earthy
STREAK	White
SPECIFIC GRAVITY	2.6
TRANSPARENCY	Opaque

CORNISH KAOLINITE
The kaolinite in this specimen from Goonbarrow Pit, Cornwall, England, is derived from weathered potassium feldspar.

TALC

URAL MOUNTAINS
The Ural Mountains in Russia are one of the many localities for deposits of talc.

TALC IS A COMMON MINERAL, easily distinguishable by its extreme softness. Crystals are rare; talc is most commonly found in foliated, fibrous, or massive aggregates. It can be white, colorless, pale to dark green, and yellowish to brown, and is often found mixed with other minerals, such as serpentine and calcite. Dense, high-purity talc is called steatite. Talc is a metamorphic mineral found in veins and in magnesium-rich rocks. It is often associated with serpentine, tremolite, and forsterite and occurs as an alteration product of ultramafic igneous rocks. It is widespread, and found in most areas of the world where low-grade metamorphism occurs. Talc is used in lubricants and leather dressings, as well as in ceramics, such as toilets, paint, paper, roofing materials, plastic, and rubber.

Greasy luster

Translucent

METAMORPHIC MINERAL
The lines in this specimen were produced by stress during metamorphism.

PROPERTIES

GROUP Silicates – phyllosilicates
CRYSTAL SYSTEM Triclinic or monoclinic
COMPOSITION $Mg_3Si_4O_{10}(OH)_2$
COLOR White, colorless, green, yellow to brown
FORM/HABIT Foliated and fibrous masses
HARDNESS 1
CLEAVAGE Perfect
FRACTURE Uneven to subconchoidal
LUSTER Pearly to greasy
STREAK White
SPECIFIC GRAVITY 2.8
TRANSPARENCY Translucent

TOILETRIES
Finely ground talc is the principal component of talcum powder and other toiletries.

RELIQUARY
This Buddhist reliquary, with its narrow base and neck, and featherlike design on the sides, is made of steatite.

SOAPSTONE

The name soapstone is given to compact masses of talc and other minerals due to their soapy or greasy feel. Soapstone has been used since ancient times for carvings, ornaments, and utensils. In more recent times, the Inuit people of Canada have become known for their soapstone carvings of birds and animals.

LION–DOG
This Chinese lion–dog forms part of a soapstone seal, or "chop."

PYROPHYLLITE

BISBEE
One of several locations in the US for pyrophyllite is Bisbee, Arizona.

PYROPHYLLITE, an aluminum silicate hydroxide, rarely forms distinct crystals. It is usually found in granular masses of flattened lamellae, but is often so fine grained as to appear textureless. It is sometimes found in coarse laths and radiating aggregates. It can be colorless, white, cream, brownish–green, pale blue, or gray. Its name is from the Greek for "fire" and "leaf," referring to its tendency to exfoliate when heated. Pyrophyllite forms by the low-grade metamorphism of aluminum–rich sedimentary rock, such as bauxite. It was carved by the ancient Chinese into small images and ornaments. It is widespread, with commercial deposits in California and North Carolina,; Canada; and South Africa. Coarse, radiating, lathlike clusters are found in Brazil and the state of Georgia.

COMMERCIAL USES

Pyrophyllite is mined commercially for use as a filler in paints and rubber, in cosmetics, and in dusting powders. Some "talcum" powder may, in fact, be pyrophyllite. It has good insulating properties because of its high melting point and low electrical conductivity, and is more useful than talc in heat resistors. The main world suppliers for industrial pyrophyllite are China, Korea, and the US.

FIRE BRICKS
The very good insulating properties of pyrophyllite mean that it is widely used in heat resistors.

COSMETIC USES
Finely powdered pyrophyllite gives a sheen to lipsticks.

PROPERTIES

GROUP Silicates – phyllosilicates
CRYSTAL SYSTEM Triclinic or monoclinic
COMPOSITION $Al_2Si_4O_{10}(OH)_2$
COLOR White, colorless, brown-green, pale blue, gray
FORM/HABIT Compact masses
HARDNESS 1–2
CLEAVAGE Perfect
FRACTURE Uneven
LUSTER Pearly to dull
STREAK White
SPECIFIC GRAVITY 2.7–2.9
TRANSPARENCY Transparent to translucent

PYROPHYLLITE STARS
This aggregate of pyrophyllite displays radiating groups of laths, with associated quartz.

Radiating mass of pyrophyllite crystals

Quartz crystals

MUSCOVITE

SOUTH DAKOTA
The Black Hills of South Dakota are one of many localities where muscovite occurs.

MUSCOVITE, ALSO CALLED common mica, potash mica, or isinglass (the latter name from its use in Russia for window panes), is the most common member of the mica group. Typically tabular with a hexagonal or pseudohexagonal outline, crystals also commonly occur as lamellar masses and fine-grained aggregates. It is usually colorless or silvery-white, but it can also be brown, light gray, pale green, or rose-red. It is an extremely common rock-forming mineral, and occurs in metamorphic rocks, in granites, and in veins and pegmatites. A single crystal mined in India was 10 ft (3 m) in diameter and 16 ft (5 m) long.

MICA WINDOW
Thin, transparent sheets of mica make good windows that are hard to break.

HOPEWELL MICA
This bird's foot was cut from mica in 500 BC– AD 500 in Iowa.

THE MICA GROUP

The micas are among the principal rock-forming minerals. They are classic phyllosilicates: sheets of tightly bonded tetrahedra that are poorly bonded to each other. Minerals of the mica group have perfect cleavage, allowing them to be split into thin, flexible leaves. Micas are potassium aluminosilicate hydrates with sodium, lithium, magnesium, or iron also present in certain varieties.

Strong bond between tetrahedra and octahedra

Weak bond between K^+ ions and tetrahedra

CRYSTAL STRUCTURE OF MUSCOVITE

FLAT CRYSTALS
This specimen includes a group of tabular muscovite crystals and green crystals of apatite.

Tabular, pseudohexagonal crystal

Apatite

Leaves of mica visible

PROPERTIES

GROUP	Silicates – phyllosilicates
CRYSTAL SYSTEM	Monoclinic
COMPOSITION	$KAl_2(Si_3Al)O_{10}(OH,F)_2$
COLOR	Colorless, silvery-white, pale green, rose, brown
FORM/HABIT	Tabular
HARDNESS	$2\frac{1}{2}$
CLEAVAGE	Perfect basal
FRACTURE	Uneven
LUSTER	Vitreous
STREAK	Colorless
SPECIFIC GRAVITY	2.8
TRANSPARENCY	Transparent to translucent

GLAUCONITE

ANTRIM
Glauconite occurs in this county of Northern Ireland.

GLAUCONITE IS A MEMBER of the mica group, named in 1828 from the Greek *glaukos*, meaning "blue-green," an allusion to its color. Widespread, it usually occurs as rounded aggregates and pellets of fine-grained, scaly particles. It forms in shallow marine environments. The sedimentary rock greensand is so called because of the green color imparted by glauconite.

FINE GRAINS
This typical massive aggregate includes glauconite grains.

Aggregate of small grains

PROPERTIES

GROUP	Silicates – phyllosilicates
CRYSTAL SYSTEM	Monoclinic
COMPOSITION	$(K,Na)(Mg,Al,Fe)_2(Si,Al)_4O_{10}(OH)_2$
COLOR	Yellow-green, green, blue-green
FORM/HABIT	Rounded aggregates
HARDNESS	2
CLEAVAGE	Perfect basal
FRACTURE	Uneven
LUSTER	Dull to earthy
STREAK	N/D
SPECIFIC GRAVITY	2.4– 2.9
TRANSPARENCY	Translucent to opaque

Dull luster

PHLOGOPITE

STERLING HILL
Phlogopite occurs at this mine in New Jersey.

PHLOGOPITE BELONGS to the mica group. Its name derives from the Greek *phlogos*, "firelike," alluding to the red-brown color of some varieties. Its crystals are tabular to pseudohexagonal, and it usually occurs as platy aggregates. It can be colorless, pale yellow, and reddish to dark brown, often with a coppery look. Some specimens exhibit asterism (see p.152). Widespread, phlogopite is found in metamorphosed limestones and in igneous rocks.

PROPERTIES

GROUP	Silicates – phyllosilicates
CRYSTAL SYSTEM	Monoclinic
COMPOSITION	$KMg_3AlSi_3O_{10}(OH)_2$
COLOR	Colorless, pale yellow to brown
FORM/HABIT	Tabular or pseudohexagonal
HARDNESS	$2\frac{1}{2}$–3
CLEAVAGE	Perfect basal
FRACTURE	Uneven
LUSTER	Pearly to submetallic
STREAK	Brownish-white
SPECIFIC GRAVITY	2.9
TRANSPARENCY	Transparent to translucent

Prismatic, twinned phlogopite crystals

PHLOGOPITE CRYSTALS
These pseudohexagonal phlogopite crystals are in a rock groundmass.

261

BIOTITE

PIKE'S PEAK
This Colorado locality yields good biotite specimens.

BIOTITE, ALSO CALLED black mica, is very widespread and is common in both igneous and metamorphic rocks. It forms large crystals in granites and granite pegmatites, and forms tabular to short prismatic crystals, often pseudohexagonal in cross section. It is usually black or brown in color, but can be pale yellow to tan, or bronze. It readily cleaves into thin, flexible sheets. Notable localities include Mull, Scotland; Bancroft, Ontario, Canada; and, in the US, Pike's Peak, Colorado, Adirondack Mountains, New York, and King's Mountain, North Carolina.

JEAN BIOT (1774–1862)
Biotite was named in 1847 for the French physicist Jean Biot, who studied the optical properties of the micas.

Vitreous luster

Tabular crystal

PROPERTIES

GROUP Silicates – phyllosilicates
CRYSTAL SYSTEM Monoclinic
COMPOSITION $K(Mg,Fe)_3(AlSi_3)O_{10}(OH,F)_2$
COLOR Black, brown, pale yellow, tan, or bronze
FORM/HABIT Tabular
HARDNESS $2\frac{1}{2}$–3
CLEAVAGE Perfect basal
FRACTURE Uneven
LUSTER Vitreous to submetallic
STREAK White to pale
SPECIFIC GRAVITY 2.7–3.4
TRANSPARENCY Transparent to translucent

DARK MICA
The pseudohexagonal outline of many crystals can be seen clearly in this specimen of biotite in calcite from Frontenac County, Canada.

LEPIDOLITE

DIXON, NEW MEXICO
Deposits of lepidolite can be found in New Mexico.

THIS LIGHT MICA CONTAINS a substantial portion of lithium and is Earth's most common lithium-bearing mineral. Its name is from the Greek *lepidos*, meaning "scale," and *lithos*, "stone." Crystals may appear pseudohexagonal. Lepidolite is also found as botryoidal or reniform masses, and as fine- to coarse-grained interlocking plates. Its perfect cleavage yields thin, flexible sheets. Although typically pale lilac, it can be colorless, pale yellow, or gray. It is one of the few minerals containing significant quantities of rubidium, which is used to determine the age of rocks more than 10 million years old. It occurs almost exclusively in granitic pegmatites, where it is associated with other lithium minerals, beryl, topaz, quartz, tourmaline, and spodumene. Major occurrences are in the Ural Mountains, Russia; Skuleboda, Sweden; Coolgardie, Western Australia; Penig, Saxony, Germany; the Czech Republic; Bernic Lake, Canada; Itinga, Brazil; Honshu, Japan; and at various US localities. It is economically important as a major source of lithium, and is used to make glass and enamels.

HIGH-TECH USES OF LITHIUM

Lithium, a soft, white, lustrous metal, is the lightest of the solid elements. One of the latest uses of lithium is in electro-optical ceramics—materials that are optically transparent and with optical properties that vary with applied voltage. Lithium niobate ($LiNbO_3$) and lithium tantalate ($LiTaO_3$) are used in switches, modulators, and demodulators for high-speed optical communications.

WEATHER BALLOON
Lithium hydride is used to generate hydrogen to fill weather balloons.

Vitreous luster

PROPERTIES

GROUP Silicates – phyllosilicates
CRYSTAL SYSTEM Monoclinic
COMPOSITION $K(Li,Al_3)(AlSi_3)O_{10}(OH,F)_2$
COLOR Pale lilac, colorless, yellow, or gray
FORM/HABIT Tabular to short prismatic
HARDNESS $2\frac{1}{2}$–$3\frac{1}{2}$
CLEAVAGE Perfect basal
FRACTURE Uneven
LUSTER Vitreous to pearly
STREAK Colorless
SPECIFIC GRAVITY 3.0
TRANSPARENCY Transparent to translucent

Tabular lepidolite crystal

DISTINCTIVE COLOR
Numerous violet lepidolite crystals protrude from this pegmatite specimen. The pseudohexagonal outline of many crystals is clearly visible.

VERMICULITE

THE NAME VERMICULITE is applied to a group of silicate minerals in which various chemical substitutions occur in the molecular structure. The term is also used to refer to a type of clay. Vermiculite may be completely interlayered with other micas and claylike minerals. It usually forms tabular, pseudohexagonal crystals, or platy aggregates. When heated to nearly 572°F (300°C), vermiculite can expand quickly and strongly to 20 times its original thickness. It occurs as large pseudomorphs replacing biotite; as small particles in soils and ancient sediments; at the interface between felsic, intrusive rocks and mafic rocks; and by hydrothermal alteration of iron-bearing micas. Large deposits occur in Mount Strangways, Australia; Transvaal, South Africa; Fazzan, Libya; Coahuila, Mexico; Prayssac, France; Nova Ves, the Czech Republic; and in the US at Bare Hills, Maryland; Macon County, North Carolina; and Pinal County, Arizona.

Pseudo-hexagonal outline

Foliated habit

VERMICULITE LAYERS
This specimen of vermiculite was mined in Pennsylvania.

PROPERTIES

GROUP	Silicates – phyllosilicates
CRYSTAL SYSTEM	Monoclinic
COMPOSITION	$(Mg,Fe,Al)_3(Al,Si)_4O_{10}(OH)\cdot 4H_2O$
COLOR	Gray-white, golden-brown
FORM/HABIT	Foliated, expanded crystals
HARDNESS	1–2
CLEAVAGE	Perfect
FRACTURE	Uneven
LUSTER	Oily to earthy
SPECIFIC GRAVITY	2.6
TRANSPARENCY	Translucent

USES OF VERMICULITE

Expanded vermiculite is very light. It is widely used in concrete and plaster, for thermal and acoustic insulation, as a packing medium, a filler/extender in paper, paint, or plastics, for growing seeds, and as a soil conditioner.

GROWING MEDIUM
Vermiculite is used in horticulture as it retains water and offers good aeration.

INSULATION
Vermiculite is widely used in the attics of houses for thermal insulation.

FUCHSITE

THE CHROMIUM-BEARING VARIETY of muscovite mica, fuchsite is generally found in concentric, curved aggregates and as flakes. Its perfect cleavage yields thin, flexible plates. The intensity of its color depends on chromium concentration, which may be up to 25 percent. Fuchsite is found where hydrothermal solutions have replaced carbonates in gold deposits, and in metamorphic rocks in corundum and staurolite schists. It is found in New Hampshire and in Manitoba, Canada.

MEXICAN FUCHSITE
This specimen shows characteristic curved aggregates.

Curved aggregate

PROPERTIES

GROUP	Silicates – phyllosilicates
CRYSTAL SYSTEM	Monoclinic
COMPOSITION	$K(Cr,Al)_2(AlSi_3)O_{10}(OH,F)_2$
COLOR	Light to medium green
FORM/HABIT	Curved aggregates
HARDNESS	$2\frac{1}{2}$
CLEAVAGE	Perfect basal
FRACTURE	Uneven
LUSTER	Vitreous to pearly
STREAK	White
SPECIFIC GRAVITY	2.8–2.9
TRANSPARENCY	Transparent to opaque

ZINNWALDITE

ZINNWALDITE BELONGS TO the mica group. Its crystals are tabular to short prismatic, often pseudohexagonal in shape. It is found in hydrothermal veins and granitic pegmatites. Specimens come from Altenburg, Germany; Zinnwald, the Czech Republic; Baveno, Italy; many localities in Japan; Virgem de Lapa, Brazil; and, in the US, at Pike's Peak, Colorado, and Amelia Court House, Virginia.

CZECH ZINNWALDITE
This specimen is from a classic locality at Cinovec, Severocesk, the Czech Republic.

Vitreous luster

PROPERTIES

GROUP	Silicates – phyllosilicates
CRYSTAL SYSTEM	Monoclinic
COMPOSITION	$K(LiFeAl)_3(AlSi_3)O_{10}(F,OH)_2$
COLOR	Gray-brown
FORM/HABIT	Tabular to short prismatic
HARDNESS	$2\frac{1}{2}$–4
CLEAVAGE	Perfect
FRACTURE	Uneven
LUSTER	Vitreous to pearly
STREAK	White
SPECIFIC GRAVITY	2.9–3.0
TRANSPARENCY	Transparent to translucent

CLAY MINERALS

IT IS VITAL TO MAKE A DISTINCTION between the common use of the word "clay," to describe a very fine-grained, rather plastic rock, and clay minerals. The potter working with "clay" may be working with a material made up of several clay minerals, as well as with particles of other minerals that are "clay-sized"—less than 0.005 mm long. Clay rocks and clay minerals share some properties, such as their ability to swell.

STRUCTURE OF CLAY MINERALS

The clay minerals are a group of sheet silicate minerals that crystallize primarily in the monoclinic system. They are generally white, buff, or yellowish when pure, and only rarely form visible crystals. The various clay minerals are hard to tell apart in hand specimens. Seen under a microscope, most crystals of clay minerals are pseudohexagonal plates. Clay minerals generally consist of two structural units: a layer of silicon-oxygen tetrahedra arranged in a hexagonal network in two dimensions; and two layers of close-packed oxygen or hydroxyl ions. This second component creates sites in which metals, usually sodium, calcium, aluminum, magnesium, or iron, are located.

Most clays are the result of the weathering of feldspars or other aluminum-rich minerals. Different clay minerals can result from the same parent rock depending

GREEN RIVER CANYON
Cracked, drying, sedimentary clay lines the banks of the Green River in Utah.

BENTONITE

HALLOYSITE

ILLITE

BROWN NONTRONITE

GREEN NONTRONITE

CLAY VARIETIES
Above is a selection of clay minerals. Although these specimens appear different from each other, in practice clay minerals are often hard to tell apart as hand specimens.

EXTRACTING CLAY IN PERU
A man extracts clay to be used in the manufacture of tiles in Chinipampa, Peru. Tile and mud-brick are major building materials in much of the world.

MAYAN TERRA-COTTA SCULPTURE
The ancient Mesopotamian world used clay extensively for terra-cotta sculpture as well as for pottery.

THIN SECTION
The platy, pseudohexagonal nature of clay minerals is clearly visible here. The platy characteristic gives clay its rather plastic qualities.

Thin plates

on the climate and the amount, chemistry, and flow of water involved in the weathering process. Clay minerals are widespread in sedimentary rocks, such as mudstones and shales, in marine sediments, and in soils.

TYPES AND USES

There are more than a dozen clay minerals, and different sources include different minerals. Those usually defined as clay minerals are montmorillonite, nontronite, kaolinite (see p.259), dickite, nacrite, illite, glauconite, and celadonite. Sometimes chlorites, vermiculite (see p.263), polygorskite, and pyrophyllite are also included. Clay rocks usually contain a mixture of clay minerals. Sedimentary clay, a clastic sediment formed at the bottom of rivers, lakes, and seas, is composed mainly of illite and kaolinite, but can contain many other minerals, including other clay minerals. It is used for

Quartz

brick-making. The clay rock bentonite, derived mainly from volcanic ash, has a large component of the clay mineral montmorillonite, and is used in the petroleum industry as drilling mud—a heavy suspension consisting of clays, chemical additives, and weighting materials, employed in rotary drilling. China clay, formed by the deep weathering of granites, is composed mainly of kaolinite, but may also contain significant portions of other clay minerals. It is used in the manufacture of porcelain, paint fillers, and pharmaceuticals, among other things. Ball clay is an impure china clay that also contains a substantial amount of illite and other minerals. It is used in high-quality ceramics.

TERRA-COTTA DISH
As terra cotta (literally "baked earth"), clay has been used for millennia in a variety of ceramics.

RED ROOFS
Clay is widely used for tiles, here on the steep roofs of houses in Lübeck, Germany. It has been a popular choice for centuries wherever it is locally abundant.

PROPERTIES OF MONTMORILLONITE

GROUP Silicates – phyllosilicates
CRYSTAL SYSTEM Monoclinic
COMPOSITION $(Na,Ca)(Al,Mg)_2Si_4O_{10}(OH)_2 \cdot nH_2O$
COLOR White to buff, pale yellow, pink
FORM/HABIT Platy
HARDNESS 1–2
CLEAVAGE Perfect
FRACTURE Uneven
LUSTER Earthy
STREAK White
SPECIFIC GRAVITY 2.1
TRANSPARENCY Translucent to opaque

Clusters of pseudohexagonal montmorillonite crystals

MONTMORILLONITE
Montmorillonite is a clay mineral that is most commonly found in deposits of bentonite. This specimen includes visible crystals— these are rare among clay minerals.

MINGUN PAYA
The uncompleted pagoda of Mingun Paya in Myanmar was begun in the 18th century by King Bodawpaya, and would have been 500 ft (150 m) tall. It is still the world's largest all-brick structure.

THE USES OF BRICK

After flint, clay was the next most important mineral in the early history of humanity. The use of clay in pottery-making long predates recorded human history. Gigantic buildings, such as the ziggurats of Mesopotamia (including the Tower of Babel), were built from mud-brick, and the evidence suggests that the builders of the first stone pyramid took inspiration from the earlier mud-brick examples. But the use of mud-brick was far from limited to dramatic buildings. Entire cities such as Ur, Babylon, Nineveh, and virtually all the houses scattered across the ancient Mesopotamian countryside were built from mud-brick.

MODERN MUD-BRICK

Unfired mud-brick is far from an antiquated building material. In the same areas of the world where ancient mud-brick buildings were erected, mud-brick is still the cheapest and most readily available building material. In dry climates in North and South America, mud-brick, called adobe, is still a material of choice for even the most modern dwellings.

The properties that make clay ideal for brick-making—plasticity when wet and coherence when dry—make it ideal for other purposes such as the lining and sealing of dams, canals, and reservoirs, and it is also an important component of Portland cement.

FIRED BRICK

The everyday mud-bricks in the ancient world were sun-dried, but those used for more important buildings were fired. By the 1st century BC, the Romans were making massive use of fired bricks to create structures that stand to this day, such as the massive Baths of Caracalla in Rome. The Byzantines inherited Roman techniques of brickwork, and from them knowledge was passed on to the Ottoman Turks. The Italians were the next to adopt fired-brick architecture, which became common in Italy in the 11th century. Over the next two centuries the knowledge spread to the rest of Europe and finally to the Americas.

DJENNE MOSQUE
The great mosque in this ancient trading city in southern Mali is made from mud-brick.

BRICKMAKERS
Workers in Dhaka, Bangladesh, stack raw bricks made from river-bottom mud to be fired before use.

CHAMOSITE

CHAMOSON
Chamoson was discovered in Chamoson in the Swiss Alps.

CHAMOSITE IS USUALLY MASSIVE, often occurring in earthy aggregates. Its crystals can be tabular, pseudohexagonal, or pseudorhombohedral. It is found mainly in sedimentary ironstones such as chamosite oolites, in marine clays, and in some low-grade metamorphosed ironstones. Localities include France, Poland, the Czech Republic, Germany, Western Australia, Japan, England, South Africa, and, in the US, Pennsylvania, Arkansas, Colorado, Michigan, and Maine.

PROPERTIES

GROUP Silicates – phyllosilicates
CRYSTAL SYSTEM Monoclinic
COMPOSITION
$Fe_3(Fe_2Al)(Si_3AlO_{10})(OH)_8$
COLOR Green to greenish-black
FORM/HABIT Massive
HARDNESS $2^1/_2$–3
CLEAVAGE Perfect
FRACTURE Uneven
LUSTER Oily to vitreous
STREAK White green to gray
SPECIFIC GRAVITY 3.0–3.3
TRANSPARENCY Translucent

Massive habit

Earthy luster

MASSIVE CHAMOSITE
This is a specimen of massive chamosite. Crystals are rarely seen.

CAVANSITE

PUNE, INDIA
Pune has the best specimens of cavansite.

CAVANSITE AND ITS POLYMORPH pentagonite are both hydrous calcium vanadium silicates. This mineral was named after some of the elements it contains: calcium (Ca), vanadium (V), and silicon (Si). Cavansite forms aggregates of prismatic crystals, and also occurs as platelets and in rosettes. It is blue to greenish-blue in color, and is found in basalts in association with zeolites, and in tuffs. The finest specimens of cavansite come from Pune, India; cavansite also occurs at Lake Owyhee State Park, Oregon, where it was discovered, and near Globe, also in Oregon.

PROPERTIES

GROUP Silicates – phyllosilicates
CRYSTAL SYSTEM Orthorhombic
COMPOSITION
$Ca(VO)Si_4O_{10}·4H_2O$
COLOR Blue to greenish-blue
FORM/HABIT Prismatic
HARDNESS 3–4
CLEAVAGE Good
FRACTURE Conchoidal
LUSTER Vitreous
STREAK White
SPECIFIC GRAVITY 2.2–2.3
TRANSPARENCY Transparent to translucent

Heulandite

Cavansite rosette

CAVANSITE ROSETTE
This cavansite rosette on heulandite is from Wagholi Quarry, Pune, India.

Rock groundmass

CHRYSOCOLLA

CORNWALL
Chrysocolla is found with copper in this part of England.

THE TERM CHRYSOCOLLA originates in ancient times, and was applied by the Greek philosopher Theophrastus in 315 BC to various materials used in soldering gold. The name is derived from the Greek *chrysos*, meaning "gold," and *kolla*, meaning "glue." Chrysocolla is commonly very fine grained and massive. Crystals are very rarely seen, but can form botryoidal, radiating aggregates. It is frequently intergrown with other minerals such as quartz, chalcedony, or opal to yield a harder, more resilient gemstone variety. Chrysocolla intergrown with turquoise and malachite from Israel is called Eilat stone. Chrysocolla forms as a decomposition product of copper minerals, especially in arid regions. It is found worldwide. Localities include Cornwall, England, Israel, Mexico, the Czech Republic, Australia, the Congo, and New Mexico, Arizona, and Utah. Gemstone pieces sometimes exceed 5 lb (2.3 kg) in weight.

GREEN CHRYSOCOLLA
Chrysocolla is intergrown here with turquoise and malachite.

PROPERTIES

GROUP Silicates – phyllosilicates
CRYSTAL SYSTEM Orthorhombic
COMPOSITION
$Cu_2H_2(Si_2O_5)(OH)_4·nH_2O$
COLOR Blue, blue-green
FORM/HABIT Massive
HARDNESS 2–4
CLEAVAGE None
FRACTURE Uneven to conchoidal
LUSTER Vitreous to earthy
STREAK Pale blue, tan, gray
SPECIFIC GRAVITY 2.0–2.4
TRANSPARENCY Translucent to nearly opaque

CHRYSOCOLLA WITH AZURITE
Chrysocolla is copper silicate hydroxide. It is commonly associated with malachite and azurite.

Chrysocolla

Rock groundmass

PEBBLE
This tumble-polished pebble is bright blue chrysocolla.

CABOCHON
Green chrysocolla is seen here within a reddish iron oxide.

CABOCHON
Blue and green chrysocolla are intermixed here.

ANTIQUE BRACELET
This antique silver bracelet is set with a chrysocolla cabochon.

Associated azurite

CLINOCHLORE

BAHIA, BRAZIL
Fine clinochlore crystals come from Bahia.

KÄMMERERITE
This variety is also known as chromian clinochlore.

REFERRING TO ITS OPTICAL SYMMETRY and color, clinochlore takes its name from the Greek *klinen*, meaning "to incline," and *chloros*, "green." Crystals are tabular to blocky, with a tabular pseudohexagonal or pseudo-orthorhombic habit. Clinochlore forms a solid-solution series with chamosite. It forms as a product of low-grade regional and contact metamorphism, as a hydrothermal alteration product, in marine clays and soils, in amygdales in volcanic rocks, and in fissure veins. Localities include Pajsberg, Sweden; Quebec, Canada; Banff, Scotland; Valais, Switzerland; Bahia, Brazil; Marienberg, Germany; Russia's Ural Mountains; and, in the US, in Brewster, New York, Lancaster County, Pennsylvania, and Lowell, Vermont.

Tabular crystals

Rock groundmass

PROPERTIES

GROUP Silicates – phyllosilicates
CRYSTAL SYSTEM Monoclinic
COMPOSITION $Mg_3(Mg_2Al)(Si_3AlO_{10})(OH)_8$
COLOR Green
FORM/HABIT Tabular
HARDNESS $2\frac{1}{2}$
CLEAVAGE Perfect
FRACTURE Uneven
LUSTER Vitreous to dull
STREAK Pale yellow
SPECIFIC GRAVITY 2.6–2.9
TRANSPARENCY Translucent

CLINOCHLORE CRYSTALS
These tabular clinochlore crystals rest on a rock groundmass.

APOPHYLLITE

ISLE OF SKYE
This Scottish island has apophyllite crystals.

ONCE CONSIDERED TO BE a single mineral, apophyllite is now divided into two distinct species—fluorapophyllite and hydroxyapophyllite. They form a solid-solution series in which fluorine can predominate over oxygen and hydrogen, and vice versa. Specimens whose precise chemical composition has not been established are still called apophyllite. It is commonly found as glassy prismatic, blocky, or tabular white to grayish crystals. Colorless and green material from India is sometimes faceted as a collector's gem. Its name comes from the Greek *apo*, meaning "to get," and *phyllazein*, meaning "leaf," a reference to the way in which the mineral separates into flakes or layers when it is heated.

Apophyllite frequently occurs with zeolite minerals in basalt, and less commonly in cavities in granites. It is also found in metamorphic rocks, and in hydrothermal deposits. Apophyllite is a widespread mineral. Crystals up to 8 in (20 cm) in length are found at Bento Gonsalves, Brazil. Other localities include Mont St.-Hilaire, Canada; St. Andreasberg, Germany; the Isle of Skye, Scotland; Guanajuato, Mexico; India, and, in the US, Paterson, New Jersey, Ashe County, North Carolina, Lebanon, Pennsylvania, and Centreville, Virginia.

Prismatic habit

PINK CRYSTAL
This superb example of a pink apophyllite crystal is $2\frac{1}{2}$ in (6 cm) long.

APOPHYLLITE CRYSTALS
In this specimen from Rahuri, India, blocky green crystals of apophyllite rest on a groundmass of stilbite.

Stilbite

Blocky crystals

PROPERTIES

GROUP Silicates – phyllosilicates
CRYSTAL SYSTEM Tetragonal
COMPOSITION $KCa_4Si_8O_{20}(F,OH)\cdot8H_2O$ (fluorapophyllite)
COLOR Colorless, pink, green, or yellow
FORM/HABIT Tabular, prismatic
HARDNESS $4\frac{1}{2}$–5
CLEAVAGE Perfect
FRACTURE Uneven, brittle
LUSTER Vitreous
STREAK Colorless
SPECIFIC GRAVITY 2.3–2.4
TRANSPARENCY Transparent to translucent

Apophyllite *Rock groundmass*

PINK APOPHYLLITE

Apophyllite *Basalt*

GREEN APOPHYLLITE

Stilbite

Basalt groundmass *Apophyllite*

REDDISH-PINK APOPHYLLITE

MINES IN INDIA
Pune and Mumbai in India are prolific producers of apophyllite. Vendors sell trays of specimens on street corners.

COLORS OF APOPHYLLITE
As well as being pink and green, apophyllite can be cream, pale yellow, or reddish. Most commonly it is colorless.

267

PETALITE

MINAS GERAIS
Petalite is among the many minerals found in this area of Brazil.

A LITHIUM ALUMINUM SILICATE, petalite was named in 1800 for the Greek word for "leaf," a reference to its perfect cleavage, which allows it to peel off in thin, leaflike layers. Lithium was first recognized as a new chemical element in 1817 by Johan August Arfvedson from its occurrence in this mineral. Petalite is rarely found as individual crystals and most commonly occurs as aggregates. It is colorless to grayish–white, and occasionally light pink or green. It forms in granitic pegmatites along with albite, quartz, and lepidolite. It is widespread, with notable occurrences in Canada, Sweden, Italy, Russia, Australia, Zimbabwe, and California and Maine. Facet-grade petalite is found in Brazil, yielding collectors' stones of up to 50 carats. Petalite is generally cut only for collectors, since it is too fragile to wear as jewelry.

Perfect cleavage

Vitreous luster

LEAFLIKE LAYERS
This translucent, pinkish specimen shows the perfect cleavage and vitreous luster typical of petalite.

PROPERTIES

GROUP	Silicates – phyllosilicates
CRYSTAL SYSTEM	Monoclinic
COMPOSITION	$LiAlSi_4O_{10}$
COLOR	Colorless to grayish-white, pink, or green
FORM/HABIT	Usually as aggregates
HARDNESS	$6^{1}/_{2}$
CLEAVAGE	Perfect basal
FRACTURE	Subconchoidal
LUSTER	Vitreous
STREAK	White
SPECIFIC GRAVITY	2.4
TRANSPARENCY	Transparent to translucent
R.I.	1.50–1.51

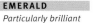

EMERALD
Particularly brilliant pieces of gem petalite can be faceted into striking emerald cuts.

MIXED
This petalite gem has a triangular mixed cut, which is ideal for bringing out its brilliance.

CUSHION
This fine specimen of gem petalite has a cushion mixed cut. Petalite is generally cut only for collectors.

LITHIUM BATTERIES

Along with spodumene and lepidolite, petalite is an important source of lithium. Its high chemical activity makes possible the tiny batteries used in personal pagers, heart pacemakers, and cameras. Lithium batteries are also used in military equipment and for aerospace applications. Experimentation with lithium compounds such as lithium-titanium disulfide promises a new generation of high-efficiency batteries.

LITHIUM BATTERIES

ALLOPHANE

HOKKAIDO
This locality in Japan is one of many for allophane.

A WEATHERING PRODUCT of volcanic ash or a hydrothermal alteration product of feldspars, allophane is almost invariably mixed with other minerals such as opal, limonite, and gibbsite. An amorphous aluminosilicate hydrate mineral, allophane has a variable chemical composition, in part due to impurities. It is white to tan, but can also be bright blue, green, or yellow. It is fairly widespread.

WHITE ALLOPHANE
Originating from London, England, this specimen shows typical white allophane.

Rock groundmass

PROPERTIES

GROUP	Silicates – phyllosilicates
CRYSTAL SYSTEM	Amorphous
COMPOSITION	$Al_2Si_2O_7 \cdot 3H_2O$ to $Al_2SiO_5 \cdot 2H_2O$
COLOR	White to tan or green, green, blue or yellow
FORM/HABIT	Crusts and masses
HARDNESS	3
CLEAVAGE	None
FRACTURE	Conchoidal
LUSTER	Waxy to earthy
STREAK	White
SPECIFIC GRAVITY	2.8
TRANSPARENCY	Translucent

Allophane

OKENITE

BOHEMIA
Okenite occurs in Bohemia in the Czech Republic, among other localities.

NAMED FOR THE GERMAN NATURALIST Lorenz Oken in 1828, Okenite is a calcium silicate hydrate. Its crystals are fibrous or bladed, and lathlike. It is sometimes found in spherical masses of radiating fibers. Okenite is often found associated with zeolites, apophyllite, quartz, prehnite, and calcite in basalts. It is found in many localities, including Mumbai, India, where there are fine, white, furlike aggregates.

ACICULAR OKENITE
This spherical mass of acicular okenite with laumontite is from Mumbai, Maharashtra, India.

Laumontite

PROPERTIES

GROUP	Silicates – inosilicates
CRYSTAL SYSTEM	Triclinic
COMPOSITION	$Ca_5Si_9O_{23} \cdot 9H_2O$
COLOR	Colorless, white, pale yellow, or blue
FORM/HABIT	Fibrous, bladed
HARDNESS	$4^{1}/_{2}$–5
CLEAVAGE	Perfect
FRACTURE	Splintery
LUSTER	Pearly to vitreous
STREAK	White
SPECIFIC GRAVITY	2.3
TRANSPARENCY	Transparent to translucent

Spherical mass of okenite crystals

PREHNITE

HARZ MOUNTAINS
Prehnite occurs in these mineral-packed German mountains.

NAMED IN 1789 for its discoverer, Hendrik von Prehn, a Dutch military officer, prehnite commonly occurs as globular, spherical, or stalactitic aggregates of fine to coarse crystals. Rare individual crystals are short prismatic to tabular, many with curved faces. It can be pale to mid-green, tan, pale yellow, gray, or white. Prehnite is often found lining cavities in volcanic rocks, associated with zeolites and calcite, and in mineral veins in granite. Crystals measuring over an inch come from Canada. It is also found in many other localities worldwide. Transparent material from Australia and Scotland is faceted for collectors. Some fibrous material is cut *en cabochon* to show a cat's-eye effect. Other cut prehnite has been marketed under the name Cape emerald.

RADIATING MASSES
A group of radiating crystal masses of prehnite resting on a rock groundmass gives a botryoidal form to this specimen.

Curved prehnite crystal

Vitreous luster

PROPERTIES
- **GROUP** Silicates – phyllosilicates
- **CRYSTAL SYSTEM** Orthorhombic
- **COMPOSITION** $Ca_2Al_2Si_3O_{10}(OH)_2$
- **COLOR** Green, yellow, tan, or white
- **FORM/HABIT** Tabular, botryoidal masses
- **HARDNESS** 6–6½
- **CLEAVAGE** Distinct basal
- **FRACTURE** Uneven, brittle
- **LUSTER** Vitreous
- **STREAK** White
- **SPECIFIC GRAVITY** 2.9
- **TRANSPARENCY** Transparent to translucent
- **R.I.** 1.61–1.64

CABOCHON
Translucent prehnite is often polished en cabochon. Some show a cat's eye.

STEP
This semitransparent prehnite has been faceted in a step cut to good effect.

MIXED
This yellowish faceted prehnite is not fully transparent, but it is still a beautiful gem.

BRILLIANT
This faceted oval prehnite shows good color and transparency.

GREEN PREHNITE
Prehnite occurs in several colors. Here green, spherical masses can be seen on a rock groundmass.

SEPIOLITE

ONTARIO
Deposits of sepiolite are found in this part of Canada.

A COMPACT, EARTHY, claylike, often porous, mineral, sepiolite is a magnesium silicate hydrate. It takes its name from its resemblance to the light and porous bone of the cuttlefish *Sepia*. It is perhaps better known by its popular name of meerschaum, from the German for "sea-foam." Porous aggregates appear to be softer than its crystals, and many are light enough to float on water. It is usually found in nodular masses of interlocking fibers, which give it a toughness that belies its mineralogical softness. It is usually white or gray, and may be tinted yellow, brown, or green. Sepiolite is an alteration product of rocks such as serpentinite and magnesite. It is found as irregular nodules in alluvial deposits near Eskisehir, Turkey, the most important commercial deposit.

SEPIOLITE BEADS
These intricately fashioned beads have been carved out of sepiolite.

PROPERTIES
- **GROUP** Silicates – phyllosilicates
- **CRYSTAL SYSTEM** Orthorhombic
- **COMPOSITION** $Mg_4Si_6O_{15}(OH)_2 \cdot 6H_2O$
- **COLOR** White, gray, pinkish
- **FORM/HABIT** Massive
- **HARDNESS** 2–2½
- **CLEAVAGE** Good but rarely seen
- **FRACTURE** Uneven
- **LUSTER** Dull to earthy
- **STREAK** White
- **SPECIFIC GRAVITY** 2.1–2.3
- **TRANSPARENCY** Opaque

TOBACCO PIPES
Meerschaum sepiolite is soft when first extracted, but it hardens on drying. Its chief use is for tobacco pipes, which are often intricately carved. As they are smoked, meerschaum pipes develop a lovely golden-brown patina.

Dull luster

MASSIVE SEPIOLITE
This specimen of massive sepiolite shows a characteristic dull, earthy luster.

269

SINGLE-CHAIN INOSILICATES

INOSILICATES TAKE THEIR NAME from the Greek word for "thread." They are sometimes referred to as chain silicates. Single–chain inosilicates are composed of chains of silica tetrahedra, and contain the Si_2O_6 silica group in their chemical formulae. Many of these silicates are fibrous in nature. The pyroxenes are a major mineral group within the single–chain inosilicates, and all share structural and chemical similarities. There are over 20 pyroxenes, and they are important rock–forming minerals. They are distinguished from the amphiboles by their two perfect cleavages at about 87 and 93 degrees to each other, those of the amphiboles being at about 124 and 56 degrees.

Magnesium octahedron

Magnesium octahedron

SiO_4 tetrahedron

Calcium atom within polyhedron

SiO_4 tetrahedron

Oxygen atom

DIOPSIDE CRYSTAL STRUCTURE
This pyroxene mineral consists of simple chains of SiO_4 tetrahedra, linked at two corners, strongly bonded to magnesium octahedra and weakly bonded to calcium polyhedra.

SiO_4 tetrahedron

CaO_6 octahedron

SiO_4 tetrahedron

Calcium octahedron

Oxygen atom

WOLLASTONITE CRYSTAL STRUCTURE
This pyroxene mineral consists of chains of SiO_4 tetrahedra cross-linked by irregular CaO_6 octahedra, creating highly compressed single chains.

PIGEONITE

MULL, SCOTLAND
This island off the west of Scotland has deposits of pigeonite.

A MEMBER OF THE pyroxene group of minerals, pigeonite is generally found as rock-bound grains, with well-formed crystals being relatively rare. It is brown, purplish-brown, or greenish-brown to black in color. An iron-rich variety is sometimes called ferropigeonite.

Pigeonite is found in many lavas and smaller intrusive rock bodies, where it is the dominant pyroxene, and it is an important component of andesites and diabases. It is a widespread mineral, with notable localities at Skaergaard, Greenland; Mull, Scotland; Labrador, Canada; Mount Wellington, Tasmania; and in the US at Pigeon Point, Minnesota, Goose Creek, Virginia, and Lambertville, New Jersey. It is also found in meteorites, and in the mare basalts on the Moon. These are areas of basalt that were once thought to have been seas. *Mare* is Latin for "sea."

THIN SECTION
As the pigeonite in this gabbro cooled, it exsolved its calcium content in two generations of calcium-rich augite to create the branches and needles of a pine tree.

PIGEON POINT
Pigeonite is named after the place where it was discovered: Pigeon Point, Minnesota.

Perfect cleavage

MARE IMBRIUM
Maria, the large, dark, relatively flat areas of the Moon once believed to be seas, are basalts containing pigeonite.

PURPLE-BROWN PIGEONITE
This specimen of pigeonite comes from the Kovdor Pit, Kola Peninsula, Russia.

Cleavage mass

PROPERTIES

GROUP Silicates – inosilicates

CRYSTAL SYSTEM Monoclinic

COMPOSITION $(Mg,Fe,Ca)_2(Si_2O_6)$

COLOR Brown to black

FORM/HABIT Granular

HARDNESS 6

CLEAVAGE Good

FRACTURE Uneven to conchoidal, brittle

LUSTER Vitreous

STREAK White to pale brown

SPECIFIC GRAVITY 3.2–3.5

TRANSPARENCY Semi-transparent

ENSTATITE

HARZ MOUNTAINS
Iridescent enstatite comes from Germany's Harz Mountains.

A COMMON MINERAL in the pyroxene family, enstatite is magnesium silicate. Its name comes from the Greek *enstates*, meaning "opponent"—it is used as a refractory to line ovens and kilns, thus it is an "opponent" of heat. Enstatite forms a solid-solution series with ferrosilite—$(Fe,Mg)_2(Si_2O_6)$—in which iron substitutes for magnesium. Bronzite is an intermediate variety of enstatite, and is brown with a metallic luster. Enstatite generally occurs as rock-bound grains, or in massive aggregates. When it develops well-formed crystals, they tend to be short prismatic, often with complex terminations. It is found less often as fibrous masses of parallel, acicular crystals. It is colorless, pale yellow, or pale green, and becomes darker with increasing iron content, turning greenish-brown to black. Enstatite is a very widespread mineral, commonly occurring in mafic and ultramafic igneous rocks, and in meteorites. While it is an important rock-forming mineral, its only commercial use is as a gemstone. Localities producing gem-quality enstatite are Mysore, India (for star-enstatite); Canada (iridescent enstatite); the gem gravels of Myanmar and Sri Lanka (facet-grade material); and Arizona.

Uneven fracture

FIBROUS ENSTATITE
Enstatite is sometimes found as fibrous masses of parallel, acicular crystals, as are many of the single-chain inosilicates.

CABOCHON
Enstatite is one of the gems that produces a cat's-eye effect when cut en cabochon.

MIXED
Facet-grade enstatite, here in an oval mixed cut, is recovered from the gravels of Myanmar and Sri Lanka.

PROPERTIES

GROUP Silicates – inosilicates
CRYSTAL SYSTEM Orthorhombic
COMPOSITION $Mg_2Si_2O_6$
COLOR Colorless, yellow, green, brown, or black
FORM/HABIT Massive
HARDNESS 5–6
CLEAVAGE Good to perfect
FRACTURE Uneven
LUSTER Vitreous
STREAK Gray to white
SPECIFIC GRAVITY 3.1–3.9
TRANSPARENCY Translucent to opaque
R.I. 1.65–1.68

MASSIVE ENSTATITE
This massive, gray-brown specimen of enstatite comes from Bamle, Telemark, Norway. Its dark color indicates it is from the ferrosilite end of the solid-solution series.

Prism face

AEGIRINE

KOLA PENINSULA
Aegirine occurs on this Russian peninsula.

AEGIRINE WAS NAMED in 1835 for Aegir, the Scandinavian god of the sea, a consequence of its being first discovered in Norway. A member of the pyroxene mineral group, aegirine is a sodium iron silicate. Its crystal habit tends to be prismatic and acicular. The prism faces are often lustrous and striated, while the faces of terminations are often etched and dull. Its color is dark green, reddish-brown, or black. It forms a solid-solution series with hedenbergite and diopside (see p.272).

Aegirine is found worldwide in mafic igneous rocks, especially in syenites and syenitic pegmatites. It is also found in metamorphosed iron-rich sediments, and in schists and fluid-enhanced metamorphic rocks. Notable localities include Kongsberg, Buskerud, Norway; Mont St.-Hilaire, Canada; Westland, New Zealand; and in the US at Magnet Cove, Arkansas, and in the Cuyuna Range of Minnesota.

PROPERTIES

GROUP Silicates – inosilicates
CRYSTAL SYSTEM Monoclinic
COMPOSITION $NaFe(Si_2O_6)$
COLOR Dark green, red-brown, or black
FORM/HABIT Prismatic
HARDNESS 6
CLEAVAGE Good to perfect
FRACTURE Uneven
LUSTER Vitreous
STREAK Yellow-green to pale green
SPECIFIC GRAVITY 3.5–3.6
TRANSPARENCY Translucent to opaque

Vertical striations

Groundmass

Vitreous luster

AEGIRINE CRYSTAL
This specimen is a long prismatic crystal in a rocky groundmass. Its characteristic vertical striations can easily be seen.

271

MYANMAR
Myanmar has been a source and exporter of jadeite for hundreds of years; ancient jadeite implements are found there.

IMPERIAL JADE
This cabochon shows the color and translucency characteristic of the finest imperial jade.

JADEITE SPHERE
Jadeite is worked into many shapes and forms, including this sphere of mottled green.

JADEITE

THERE ARE TWO DIFFERENT minerals that are commonly called "jade": jadeite and nephrite. Jadeite is a mineral in its own right, a pyroxene; nephrite, an amphibole (see pp.280–81), is a variety of tremolite or actinolite. Jadeite is made of interlocking, blocky, granular crystals, whereas nephrite crystals are fibrous. These two differing textures can sometimes help distinguish between them: nephrite often appears fibrous or silky; jadeite commonly has a more sugary or granular texture. Crystals of jadeite do occur, but they are rare. They are usually found in hollows within massive material, and are short prismatic in habit. Jadeite appears in a number of colors, whereas nephrite has a much more limited color range. Pure jadeite is white. Its other colors include green, colored by iron; lilac, colored by manganese and iron; and pink, brown, red, blue, black, orange, and yellow, colored by inclusions of other minerals. Emerald-green jadeite, colored by chromium, is called imperial jade.

Jadeite generally occurs in metamorphic rocks with a higher-pressure origin than nephrite, although some has been found in lower pressure metamorphic rocks.

JADEITE BEADS
Darkly iridescent gray-green jadeite stones have been cut into beads of various sizes, and strung together to make this appealing necklace.

Although generally recovered as alluvial pebbles and boulders, it is also found in the rocks in which it originally formed. It is widespread in metamorphic rocks formed at subduction zones. Weathered jadeite typically develops a brown skin, which is often incorporated into carvings. It frequently has a dimpled "orange-peel" surface when polished.

Myanmar is a major source of jadeite, and in particular imperial jade. Other sources are in Japan and California. Ancient tools and weapons of jadeite are found in Myanmar, in the same way that nephrite objects have been discovered in China. A very small amount of jadeite found its way into China over the centuries, and from the 18th century it was imported in large quantities from Myanmar and soon displaced nephrite as a favored carving material. Because of its value, other green stones are often misnamed "jade."

MESOAMERICAN JADE

For the Indians of Mexico, Central, and South America, jadeite had a cultural value similar to nephrite in China. It was a symbol of water and the burgeoning of plant life. Known as *chalchihuitil*, it was more precious than gold. The Olmecs were the first Mesoamericans to discover and carve jade—perhaps 3,000 years ago. Across Mexico and Central America it was used in the most precious objects: masks, depictions of the gods, and ritual items.

POWERFUL AND SACRED STONE
Jadeite was cast into sacred wells as a offering to the gods. It was sometimes inlaid in the heart in sacred sculptures, and a piece of jadeite placed in the mouth of a deceased nobleman was believed to serve as his or her heart in the afterlife. Jade grave goods were essential for members of the nobility in most Mesoamerican cultures. They were often "killed"—ritually broken—so they could accompany their owner into the afterlife. When powdered and mixed with herbs, jadeite was used to treat fractured skulls and fevers, and to resurrect the dying. Mesoamerican jadeite principally came from sources in Guatemala and Costa Rica.

JAGUAR MASK
The jaguar god represented power, night, war, and sacrifice to the Mayans, who created this terrifying jadeite mask.

Greasy luster

"Orange-peel" surface

MAYAN MASK
This Pre-Columbian feline mask of a man from Oaxaca is made from red jadeite.

MEXICAN MASK
This Olmec mask of blue jadeite dates from 800–400 BC.

MEXICAN MASK
This 18th-century jadeite mask has the smooth surface achieved by modern abrasives.

DRAGON VASE

This exquisite carving (right) makes use of a pale green to lavender color variation to highlight the dragon motif.

SNUFF BOTTLE

Snuff bottles, such as this one (above), were produced in China in the 18th and 19th centuries; particularly prized were those carved from jadeite.

JADEITE REACHES EUROPE

Until the late 16th century, virtually all European jade was nephrite. When the Spanish reached Mexico, they discovered that the Aztecs prized a green stone that was similar in appearance to, and believed to be the same stone as, European jade. They were told by the Aztecs that this stone cured internal ailments, especially those of the liver, spleen, and kidneys. This stone was brought back to Europe, along with the belief in its healing powers. The Spanish called the stone *piedra de ijada* ("loin stone"), which was mistranslated into French as *pierre de jade*, from which the word "jade" is derived. The jade from South America was believed to be the same as the Old World jade until 1863, when a Chinese carving was analyzed and discovered to be a different stone. The new stone was given the name jadeite, meaning derived from "jade."

MOCTEZUMA AND CORTÉS

In this 16th-century painting, Moctezuma kneels before the Spanish conquistador Hernando Cortés. Moctezuma offered him gifts made of jadeite and turquoise, but Cortés refused them, considering them worthless.

Polished surface

Brown rind

"Thank God they're only after the **gold** and **silver**—they don't know about **jade**."

AZTEC EMPEROR MOCTEZUMA, AFTER ENCOUNTERING CORTÉS

WEATHERED JADEITE

The lavender coloring of this massive jadeite specimen is caused by manganese and iron impurities. The mineral is partly polished to show its color and is covered with the brown "rind" characteristic of weathered jadeite.

JADEITE COBBLE

LILAC JADEITE

PROPERTIES

GROUP Silicates – inosilicates

CRYSTAL SYSTEM Monoclinic

COMPOSITION $Na(Al,Fe)Si_2O_6$

COLOR White, green, lilac, pink, brown, orange, yellow, red, blue, or black

FORM/HABIT Massive, crystals rare

HARDNESS 6–7

CLEAVAGE Good

FRACTURE Splintery

LUSTER Vitreous to greasy

STREAK White

SPECIFIC GRAVITY 3.2–3.4

TRANSPARENCY Transparent to translucent

R.I. 1.66–1.68

IMPERIAL JADE

JADEITE COLORS

The cobble (top) has a "window" cut in it to show the green of the jadeite beneath the "rind." The imperial jade (above) has been polished to bring out its color.

275

ASTROPHYLLITE

USUALLY OCCURRING as bladed crystals radiating from a common center (a form known as stellated), astrophyllite is a hydrous sodium potassium iron manganese titanium silicate. It derives its name from the Greek *astron*, meaning "star," and *phyllon*, "leaf." When it cleaves, it forms very brittle, thin leaves. Astrophyllite is golden-yellow to dark brown. It forms in cavities in igneous rocks, such as alkali granites, and especially in syenites and syenite pegmatites. It is also found in gneisses. Astrophyllite is usually associated with albite, aegirine, arfvedsonite, zircon, nepheline, titanite, and other minerals. Specimens come from its place of discovery in Norway, as well as localities in Spain, Russia, Tajikistan, Egypt, Guinea, Canada, South Africa, and Arkansas, Colorado, and Washington.

PIKE'S PEAK
This mineral-rich area of Colorado contains deposits of astrophyllite.

Submetallic luster

Radiating groups of crystals

BLADED CRYSTALS
This mass of radiating, bladed astrophyllite crystals shows a typical, leaflike cleavage.

PROPERTIES

GROUP Silicates – inosilicates
CRYSTAL SYSTEM Triclinic
COMPOSITION $(K,Na)_3$ $(Fe,Mn)_7Ti_2(Si_8O_{24})(O,OH)_7$
COLOR Golden-yellow to dark brown
FORM/HABIT Bladed, stellated
HARDNESS 3
CLEAVAGE Perfect
FRACTURE Uneven, brittle
LUSTER Submetallic to pearly
STREAK Yellow
SPECIFIC GRAVITY 3.4
TRANSPARENCY Translucent in thin laminae

WOLLASTONITE

A CALCIUM SILICATE, wollastonite occurs as rare tabular crystals or massive, coarse-bladed, foliated, or fibrous masses. Its colors are white, gray, or pale green. It has six known structural variations, one of which is monoclinic. The variations are indistinguishable in hand specimens. Wollastonite occurs as a result of the contact metamorphism of limestones, and is formed in igneous rocks from their contamination by carbonaceous inclusions. It also appears in regionally metamorphosed rocks in slates, phyllites, and schists. It is often accompanied by other calcium-containing silicates such as diopside, tremolite, grossular garnet, and epidote. Deposits are found in Italy, Romania, Mexico, Canada, Northern Ireland, Japan, Australia, and in Utah, Michigan, California, New York, and Arizona.

VESUVIUS
Mount Vesuvius, Italy, is one of several localities in Italy for wollastonite.

PROPERTIES

GROUP Silicates – inosilicates
CRYSTAL SYSTEM Triclinic
COMPOSITION $CaSiO_3$
COLOR White, gray, green
FORM/HABIT Tabular, massive
HARDNESS $4\frac{1}{2}$–5
CLEAVAGE Perfect
FRACTURE Uneven to splintery
LUSTER Vitreous to silky
STREAK White
SPECIFIC GRAVITY 2.9
TRANSPARENCY Translucent in thin laminae

INDUSTRIAL USES

Wollastonite is used in ceramic products, including floor and wall tiles, ceramic electrical insulators, and porcelain fixtures. It is also used in welding-rod coatings and in paints, and as a replacement for asbestos.

Wollastonite fuses at fairly low temperatures, making it an excellent flux. It is electrically nonconductive, and it has virtually no volatile materials within it to interfere with its various applications. As a result, most automotive and aviation spark plugs have insulators made from wollastonite.

ELECTRICAL INSULATOR
Ceramic electrical insulators use wollastonite due to its low conductivity.

CERAMIC TILES
Wollastonite is a raw material for many tiles.

W. H. WOLLASTON
Wollastonite was named for this English mineralogist and noted scientist in 1818. Wollaston discovered palladium and rhodium.

Splintery fracture

Fibrous mass

SILKY LUSTER
This mass of coarse-bladed, parallel crystals of wollastonite reveals a splintery fracture and silky luster.

RHODONITE

URALS
Rhodonite is found in the Ural Mountains in Russia.

TAKING ITS NAME from the Greek *rhodon*, meaning "rose," which is this mineral's typical color, rhodonite is a manganese silicate. It occurs as rounded crystals, masses, or grains, and is often coated or veined black with manganese oxides. Rhodonite is found in various manganese ores, often with rhodochrosite, or as a metamorphic product of rhodochrosite. It has been used as a manganese ore in India, but it is more often mined as a gem and ornamental stone. Sources are Brazil, Canada, Sweden, Russia, England, and the US. Crystals are found in Peru, New Jersey, and Australia.

RHODONITE IN MATRIX
These aggregates of tabular rhodonite crystals rest on a groundmass of manganese oxides.

PROPERTIES

GROUP Silicates – inosilicates
CRYSTAL SYSTEM Triclinic
COMPOSITION $(Mn,Ca)_5(Si_5O_{15})$
COLOR Pink to rose-red
FORM/HABIT Tabular
HARDNESS 6
CLEAVAGE Perfect
FRACTURE Conchoidal to uneven
LUSTER Vitreous
STREAK White
SPECIFIC GRAVITY 3.5–3.7
TRANSPARENCY Translucent
R.I. 1.71–1.73

Vitreous luster
Tabular crystals
Groundmass of manganese oxide
Uneven fracture

USE IN JEWELRY

Rhodonite is primarily cut *en cabochon*, as beads, and is used as a carving material. Massive rhodonite is relatively tough, and is particularly good as a carving medium. Some rhodonite is streaked with black veins, and many carvers and cutters prefer this to the plain pink. Very rarely, rhodonite is found as transparent material, which is sometimes faceted for collectors. It is extremely fragile, and great care must be taken during faceting.

RHODONITE EARRINGS AND BOX
The rhodonite box makes a feature of the black streaking in the mineral. The earrings use cabochon beads of rhodonite.

MASSIVE RHODONITE
This specimen of rough rhodonite shows the intense coloration and fine texture of the best gem-quality material.

POLISHED PEBBLE
Medium-grade rhodonite is a popular material for tumble-polishing, and is widely sold.

PECTOLITE

MONT ST.-HILAIRE
This Canadian mountain is one of the localities for pectolite.

PECTOLITE'S COMPACT STRUCTURE is responsible for its name, which is derived from the Greek *pektos*, meaning "congealed" or "well put together." Its crystals are elongated and flattened, but it more often occurs as acicular sprays or radially fibrous masses. It may be white, pale tan, or pale blue. Some specimens are triboluminescent—that is, they give off light with friction. Fibrous varieties yield dangerously sharp splinters. Pectolite is a hydrothermal mineral found in cavities in basaltic and andesitic igneous rocks, in basalt cavities associated with zeolites, and in mica peridotites. Pectolite occurs widely in Canada, England, and the US. Other specimen localities include Italy, the Dominican Republic, Greenland, Russia, and Japan.

Radiating aggregates of crystals
Acicular habit

PROPERTIES

GROUP Silicates – inosilicates
CRYSTAL SYSTEM Triclinic
COMPOSITION $NaCa_2(Si_3O_8)(OH)$
COLOR White, tan, blue
FORM/HABIT Acicular
HARDNESS 4½–5
CLEAVAGE Perfect
FRACTURE Uneven, brittle
LUSTER Vitreous to silky
STREAK White
SPECIFIC GRAVITY 2.8–2.9
TRANSPARENCY Translucent

ACICULAR CRYSTALS
This mass of radiating groups of acicular pectolite crystals shows clearly the mineral's tendency to break into sharp splinters.

LARIMAR
Some pectolite from the Dominican Republic and Bahamas is sky-blue; it has the trade name Larimar.

277

DOUBLE–CHAIN INOSILICATES

SiO₄ tetrahedron

Hydrogen atom

Magnesium octahedron

TREMOLITE DOUBLE CHAIN

THIS GROUP OF SILICATES includes two of the most common types of silicate minerals—the amphiboles and the pyroxenes. The basic structural unit of double–chain inosilicates consists of two interconnected chains of silica tetrahedra. The amphiboles are distinguished from the similar–looking pyroxenes by their two perfect cleavages at approximately 124 and 56 degrees to each other; those of the pyroxenes being approximately 87 and 93 degrees. In general, amphibole minerals tend to be long and slender, whereas the pyroxenes are short and sturdy.

Magnesium octahedron

SiO₄ tetrahedron

Calcium polyhedron

Hydrogen ion

TREMOLITE STRUCTURE
In tremolite crystals, double chains of SiO₄ tetrahedra are linked by magnesium octahedra and irregular calcium polyhedra.

HORNBLENDE

NORWEGIAN FJORD
Well-formed hornblende crystals are found in Norway.

THE NAME HORNBLENDE is applied to what are now recognized as a group of minerals, but only detailed chemical analysis makes it possible to tell them apart. The two end-member hornblendes are both calcium-rich and monoclinic in crystal structure. They are ferrohornblende and magnesiohornblende, in which magnesium substitutes for iron in the chemical composition. To the collector or the geologist in the field, they are both simply known as hornblende. Other elements can also appear in the crystal structure of the group as a whole,

SINGLE CRYSTAL
This single, short prismatic, double-terminated crystal is from Lukov, Severocesky Kraj, Czech Republic.

Prism face

Termination

especially chromium, titanium, and nickel, the concentrations of which are one indicator of metamorphic grade. Crystals of hornblende are most commonly bladed and unterminated, and often show a pseudohexagonal cross section. Well-formed crystals are short to long prismatic. The mineral also occurs as cleavable masses, and as radiating groups. Its colors are green, dark green, and brownish–green to black. Hornblende occurs widely in metamorphic rocks, especially in amphibolites, hornblende schists, gneisses, and mafic igneous rocks. A few localities for well-formed crystals are Oslo, Norway; Renfrew, Ontario, Canada; and throughout the Piedmont metamorphic province of Pennsylvania and Delaware. It also occurs with ruby in the Harts Range, Northern Territory, Australia.

Vitreous luster

Prismatic hornblende crystal

Plagioclase

Twinned hornblende crystal

Quartz

THIN SECTION
Here a lozenge-shaped hornblende crystal, with twinning, is visible in granodiorite.

Vertical striations

HORNBLENDE CRYSTALS
This specimen comprises a particularly fine group of prismatic hornblende crystals embedded in a rock groundmass.

PROPERTIES

GROUP	Silicates – inosilicates
CRYSTAL SYSTEM	Monoclinic
COMPOSITION	e.g.: $Ca_2(Fe^2,Mg)_4(Al,Fe^3)(Si_7Al)O_{22}(OH,F)_2$
COLOR	Green, black
FORM/HABIT	Prismatic
HARDNESS	5–6
CLEAVAGE	Perfect
FRACTURE	Uneven, brittle
LUSTER	Vitreous
STREAK	White to gray
SPECIFIC GRAVITY	3.1–3.3
TRANSPARENCY	Translucent to opaque

TREMOLITE

TREMOLITE IS AN ABUNDANT and widespread amphibole that forms a solid-solution series (see p.91) with ferro-actinolite. Iron can substitute in increasing amounts for magnesium. The name actinolite is used for intermediate compositions. Both minerals have the same structure, and their colors vary with increasing iron content from colorless to white, gray, gray-green (tremolite), green, dark green and nearly black. Their crystals are short to long prismatic when well-formed, but are more commonly found in unterminated bladed crystals, in parallel aggregates of bladed crystals, or in radiating groups. Tremolite and actinolite form thin, parallel, flexible fibers up to 10 in (25 cm) in length, which have found commercial use as asbestos. These amphiboles are the product of both thermal and regional metamorphism. Good crystals come from Kantiwa, Afghanistan, and Edwards, New York. Actinolite occurs in Monte Redondo, Portugal, and Washington State.

THIN SECTION
This tremolite, with an acicular habit, is in quartz from a siliceous dolomitic limestone.

Thin, prismatic crystals

Quartz

Tremolite

Tremolite

ACTINOLITE
This specimen is formed of a group of thin, prismatic crystals of actinolite. Its dark color is due to its high iron content.

PROPERTIES

GROUP	Silicates – inosilicates
CRYSTAL SYSTEM	Monoclinic
COMPOSITION	$Ca_2(Mg,Fe^2)_5Si_8O_{22}(OH)_2$
COLOR	Colorless, white, gray green to green-black
FORM/HABIT	Bladed
HARDNESS	5–6
CLEAVAGE	Perfect
FRACTURE	Splintery, brittle
LUSTER	Vitreous to silky
STREAK	White
SPECIFIC GRAVITY	2.9–3.4
TRANSPARENCY	Transparent to translucent

Featherlike aggregate of tremolite crystals

Vitreous to silky luster

TREMOLITE CRYSTALS
This specimen has plumose aggregates of white, bladed tremolite crystals.

ANTHOPHYLLITE

THE AMPHIBOLE anthophyllite was named from the Latin *anthophyllum*, meaning "clove," in reference to its color. The iron and magnesium content is variable in its structure. Iron-rich anthophyllite is called ferroanthophyllite; when sodium is present, it becomes sodium-anthophyllite. Anthophyllites are clove-brown to dark brown, pale green, gray, or white. They are usually found in columnar to fibrous masses. Crystals are uncommon, and are prismatic and usually unterminated. Anthophyllite is commonly produced by regional metamorphism of ultramafic rocks. It is an important component of some crystalline schists and gneisses, and is found worldwide. Some important localities are Glen Urquhart, Scotland; Miass, Russia; and Macon County, North Carolina, and Kamiah, Idaho. Anthophyllite is a minor asbestos mineral.

RADIATING CRYSTALS
This specimen is a mass of fibrous, radiating crystals of anthophyllite.

THIN SECTION
Here, large, bladed prisms of anthophyllite can be seen in a gneiss.

Cordierite

Anthophyllite

PROPERTIES

GROUP	Silicates – inosilicates
CRYSTAL SYSTEM	Orthorhombic
COMPOSITION	$(Mg,Fe)_7Si_8O_{22}(OH)_2$
COLOR	Clove- to dark brown, pale green, gray, or white
FORM/HABIT	Massive, fibrous
HARDNESS	5½–6
CLEAVAGE	Perfect, imperfect
FRACTURE	Uneven
LUSTER	Vitreous
STREAK	Colorless to gray
SPECIFIC GRAVITY	2.8–3.6
TRANSPARENCY	Transparent to nearly opaque

Mass of fibrous radiating crystals

Vitreous luster

NEPHRITE

Waxy luster

NEPHRITE IS ONE OF TWO different minerals commonly known as jade. The other is jadeite (see pp.274–75), a pyroxene. Nephrite is more common and widespread than jadeite. Technically, "nephrite" is not a mineral name, but the name applied to the tough, compact form of either the amphibole tremolite (see p.279) or actinolite. Both are calcium magnesium silicate hydroxides, and structurally identical, except that in actinolite some of the magnesium is replaced by iron. Nephrite is composed of a mat of tightly interlocking fibers, creating a stone tougher than steel. Where nephrite is found, especially in China and New Zealand, this toughness brought it into use very early on for tools and weapons. Its color varies with its composition: dark green when iron-rich; cream-colored when magnesium-rich. White nephrite is essentially pure tremolite, and is sometimes called "mutton-fat jade."

The geologist A. G. Werner gave it the mineral name nephrite in 1780, from the Latin *nephrus*, meaning "kidney," alluding to the use of this form of "jade" in Europe to treat kidney disease. The term "jade" evolved from the Spanish *piedra de ijada*, meaning "loin stone," a stone of similar appearance to nephrite brought from the New World by the Spanish, which was, in fact, jadeite. Nephrite is formed in metamorphic environments, especially in metamorphosed ultramafic rocks where it is associated with talc and serpentine, and in regionally metamorphosed areas where dolomites have been intruded by mafic rocks.

Large deposits of nephrite are found on the Kobuk River in Alaska; in British Columbia, Canada; in Xinjing Autonomous Region, probably the original Chinese source; and near Lake Wakatipu, Otago, New Zealand, the Maori source. It is also found near Lander, Wyoming, and in Mariposa and Siskiyou counties, and in Monterey and Morro

KOBUK RIVER, ALASKA
This US locality is a major source of nephrite, with large deposits of good-quality material.

GREEN DROPLET
This mid-green nephrite gem is homogeneous in color. It has been cut en cabochon in the form of a droplet, and polished.

BLACK DROPLET
This polished cabochon droplet is made of iron-rich black nephrite from Wyoming.

DAGGER HANDLE
This subtly carved antique dagger handle is made from fine, light-colored nephrite.

JADE TIKI
Hei tikis are worn by the Maori of New Zealand and are passed down through generations.

> "Better to be shattered jade than unbroken pottery."
>
> **CHINESE PROVERB**

Massive habit

ANCIENT CHINESE JADE CARVING

RITUAL PRISM
This Chinese ritual prism was created during the 3rd millennium BC.

In ancient China, jade was called *yu*, and was believed to embody *yang*, or cosmic energy. As a result, jade was attributed life-giving qualities. In the social order, jade became the very embodiment of sovereignty and power. Taoists believed that it guaranteed immortality, and Confucius regarded jade as an important ritual material. From Confucian belief evolved a unique system of ritual jade to validate the hierarchical structure of Chinese feudal society: the king was entitled to the *gui* jades named *zhen*, and the five classes of the nobility were assigned the stones called *huan*, *xin*, *gong*, *gu*, and *pu*. The wearing of jade came to virtually dominate court ritual by the first centuries AD. Burial customs, especially those of the nobility, included the use of jade. Gold and jade were placed in all nine body openings, and other objects of jade frequently accompanied the deceased. The most extravagant use of jade was the construction of a burial suit of gold and jade (see pp.282–83) in the hope of preserving the body from decay. For the living, jade was taken internally in the belief that it regenerated the body.

PI DISC
This decorative disc from AD 25–220 includes a grain pattern and dragon-shaped knob. Pi discs usually accompanied burials.

DRAGON
Intricately carved, this jade dragon pendant was made in about 500 BC.

Bays, California; in the Lake Baikal area of Siberia; and in Ch'unch'on, South Korea. In addition, it is found in Australia, Mexico, Brazil, Taiwan, Zimbabwe, Italy, Poland, Germany, and Switzerland.

NEPHRITE HIPPO
This hippopotamus carved from nephrite has hooves cast in gold. It was made by the Fabergé workshop, St. Petersburg, in 1908–17.

IDEAL CARVING STONE
Nephrite's tough structure makes it ideal for carving, and virtually no distinction was made until relatively recently between nephrite and jadeite when referring to "jade." Nephrite has been carved by the Chinese for more than 3,000 years, and it was only about 200 years ago that a preference developed there for Burmese jadeite. Other stones are similar to jade in appearance, though they are usually of inferior hardness, and some incorporate "jade" in their name: "soft jade," "Korean jade," and "Transvaal jade." None of these are jade—neither nephrite nor jadeite. Serpentine is widely carved in China today, and is the stone most often mistaken for (and sold as) jade.

CARVING JADE
This woman is one of many highly skilled people in China who carve designs in nephrite and similar stones.

WEAVING TOOLS
These three weaving implements from New Zealand make use of the durability of nephrite. The two larger tools were probably used to make fishing nets.

PROPERTIES

GROUP Silicates – inosilicates
CRYSTAL SYSTEM Monoclinic
COMPOSITION
$Ca_2(Mg,Fe)_5(Si_8O_{22})(OH)_2$
COLOR Cream, light to dark green
FORM/HABIT Massive
HARDNESS 6½
CLEAVAGE Perfect
FRACTURE Splintery, brittle
LUSTER Dull to waxy
STREAK White
SPECIFIC GRAVITY 2.9–3.4
TRANSPARENCY Translucent to nearly opaque
R.I. 1.61–1.63

NEPHRITE AXHEAD
This axhead of New Zealand nephrite makes full use of the stone's toughness. Tools such as this were among the first uses of nephrite. It was even called "ax stone" in some cultures.

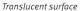

Splintery fracture

Translucent surface

Waxy luster

NEPHRITE BOULDER
This small boulder of nephrite has been sliced through and polished to reveal its quality.

Splintery fracture

CHINESE BURIAL SUITS

IN ANCIENT CHINA, JADE WAS BELIEVED TO PRESERVE THE DECEASED
BODY FROM DECAY. THIS LED TO THE CREATION OF SOME OF THE MOST
UNUSUAL STONE ARTIFACTS CREATED BY MAN: JADE BURIAL SUITS.

MISSING PRINCESS
*Princess Tou Wan's suit was
found in a disarticulated state.
Nothing but a pinch of dust
remained of her body.*

Jade burial suits were made for the most part during
the Han Dynasty (206 BC–AD 220), and consisted of
several thousand small jade plaques sewn together
with metal wires. The nature and value of the metal
used was determined by the deceased's social rank. Only
royalty could wear suits sewn with gold thread; nobles
were allowed suits sewn with silver thread; and lesser
nobles were permitted bronze thread. The most
elaborate suit ever made was that of Prince Nanyue
(died c. 122 BC); found in Guangzhou, it consisted of
4,000 jade plaques sewn together with gold wire.

In 1955, two tombs were discovered in separate caves
dug into cliffs at Mancheng in the province of Hebei,
90 miles (145 km) southwest of Beijing. Surrounded by
over 10,000 objects of art, they contained the coffins of
Prince Liu Shen and his wife, Princess Tou Wan. Their
bodies, laid there almost 2,000 years ago, were encased

LABOUR OF DEVOTION
*The restored suit of Princess Tou Wan consists of 2,156 jade
plaques sewn together with about 24 oz (700 g) of gold thread.
It is estimated that, using the technology of the Han period, such
a suit would have taken 10 years to construct.*

in suits of jade. The stone was thought to contain properties that went far beyond the physical preservation of the body. The prince and princess were entombed in jade suits to ensure their immortality, and to protect their bodies from marauding demons.

The construction of jade suits may have evolved from the practice of attaching pieces of jade to cloth and draping the cloth over the deceased. Jade plugs were also fashioned and placed in each of the body's nine orifices. The jade used was exclusively nephrite, mined in the regions of Khotan (Ho-t'ien) and Yarkand in central Asia. Each plaque was individually made by sawing a slice of nephrite from a boulder, probably with a mud saw. This tool is a smooth-edged, thin metal strip, either of bronze or iron. The blade is drawn back and forth across the line to be cut, while mud or fine sand is fed into the cut. Eventually the saw abrades its

RESTORING THE SUIT
Chinese conservators spent many hours meticulously piecing together the disassembled jade plaques of Princess Tou Wan's suit.

way through the stone. Jade is very tough, and each cut would have taken a number of days. Each slice was then shaped into a plaque, ground flat, and polished. Holes for sewing the plaques together were drilled in the four corners, using an equally time-consuming sand drill. The plaques were then sewn together, totally encasing the body.

COMPLETED RESTORATION
The finished restoration of Princess Tou Wan's suit (below and right) shows how her entire body was encased by closely attached jade plaques. Her head lay supported by a gilded bronze headrest, itself ornamented with jade plaques.

RICHTERITE

MONT ST.-HILAIRE
Transparent green crystals occur in this region of Quebec, Canada.

NAMED IN 1865 FOR THE German mineralogist Theodore Richter, the amphibole mineral richterite is a sodium calcium magnesium silicate. Where iron replaces the magnesium in the structure, the mineral is called ferrorichterite; if fluorine replaces the hydroxyl, it is fluororichterite. Richterite crystals are long and prismatic, or prismatic to fibrous aggregates, or rock-bound crystals. Richterite is brown, grayish-brown, yellow, brownish- to rose-red, or pale to dark green. Richterite occurs in thermally metamorphosed limestones, and in contact metamorphic zones. It also occurs as a hydrothermal product in mafic igneous rocks, and in manganese-rich ore deposits. Localities include Mont St.-Hilaire, Quebec, and Wilberforce and Tory Hill, Ontario, Canada; Långban and Pajsberg, Sweden; West Kimberley, Western Australia; Sanka, Myanmar; and, in the US, at Iron Hill, Colorado; Leucite Hills, Wyoming; and Libby, Montana.

PROPERTIES

GROUP Silicates – inosilicates
CRYSTAL SYSTEM Monoclinic
COMPOSITION $Na(Ca,Na)Mg_5Si_8O_{22}(OH)_2$
COLOR Brown, yellow, red, or green
FORM/HABIT Prismatic
HARDNESS 5–6
CLEAVAGE Perfect
FRACTURE Uneven, brittle
LUSTER Vitreous
STREAK Pale yellow
SPECIFIC GRAVITY 3.0–3.5
TRANSPARENCY Transparent to translucent

RICHTERITE PRISMS
Prismatic richterite crystals are scattered throughout a groundmass of quartz.

Richterite crystals

Quartz groundmass

GLAUCOPHANE

ZERMATT
This area of Switzerland is a source of glaucophane.

GLAUCOPHANE AND ITS associated minerals are known as the glaucophane facies, and their presence indicates that metamorphism has occurred under particular temperature and pressure conditions. Glaucophane is a common amphibole mineral, a sodium magnesium aluminum silicate, which falls under the general term asbestos. Where iron replaces the magnesium it is known as ferroglaucophane. Its crystals are slender and prismatic, and it can also be massive, fibrous, and granular. It is gray, lavender-blue, or bluish-black, and fuses readily to form a green glass. Its name is derived from the Greek *glaukos*, meaning "bluish-green," and *phainesthai*, "to appear." Glaucophane occurs in schists formed by the low-temperature, high-pressure metamorphism of sodium-rich sediments, or by the introduction of sodium into the metamorphic process. It is often accompanied by epidote, almandine, chlorite, and jadeite. It is widespread, with Switzerland, Wales, Scotland, Greece, Italy, Japan, and Colorado among its localities.

PROPERTIES

GROUP Silicates – inosilicates
CRYSTAL SYSTEM Monoclinic
COMPOSITION $Na_2(Mg_3Al_2)Si_8O_{22}(OH)_2$
COLOR Bluish-gray to black
FORM/HABIT Slender prismatic
HARDNESS 6
CLEAVAGE Distinct
FRACTURE Uneven to conchoidal
LUSTER Vitreous to pearly
STREAK Gray-blue
SPECIFIC GRAVITY 3.2
TRANSPARENCY Transparent to translucent

ANGLESEY
Just off the northwest coast of Wales, Anglesey has fine examples of glaucophane.

ITALIAN GLAUCOPHANE
This specimen from Polloni, Piedmont, Italy, shows glaucophane with fuchsite, rutile, and pyrite.

Dark blue-green glaucophane

Pyrite

RIEBECKITE

RIEBECKITE IS A SODIUM IRON SILICATE in the amphibole family. It forms prismatic, striated crystals, their color depending on the concentration of iron in the structure. An asbestiform variety of riebeckite is named crocidolite, and is commonly called blue asbestos. Riebeckite is found in felsic igneous rocks, such as granites and syenites, and in felsic volcanics, especially sodium-rich rhyolites.

Crocidolite is of metamorphic origin and is formed under moderate temperature and pressure from ironstones. Crocidolite occurs in Robertstown, South Australia; Henan Province in China; Cochabamba, Bolivia; and South Africa. Silica-replaced crocidolite occurs in several colors, and is the golden-brown gem tiger-eye and the blue hawk's eye. Its principal source is the South African asbestos deposit..

WESTERN AUSTRALIA
These asbestos tailings show the presence of crocidolite.

PROPERTIES

GROUP Silicates – inosilicates
CRYSTAL SYSTEM Monoclinic
COMPOSITION $Na_2(Fe^{2+}_3 Fe^{3+}_2)Si_8O_{22}(OH)_2$
COLOR Dark blue, black
FORM/HABIT Prismatic
HARDNESS 6
CLEAVAGE Perfect
FRACTURE Uneven
LUSTER Vitreous, silky
STREAK Blue-gray
SPECIFIC GRAVITY 3.3–3.4
TRANSPARENCY Transparent to translucent
R.I. 1.54–1.55

Rock groundmass

Fibrous crystals

BLUE ASBESTOS

TIGER-EYE
Silica-saturated crocidolite forms the gemstone tiger-eye.

HAWK'S EYE
Silica-saturated blue crocidolite becomes the gemstone hawk's eye.

RIEBECKITE CRYSTALS
The long, striated crystals characteristic of riebeckite are clearly visible in this specimen.

ASBESTOS

Asbestos is the name given to the thin, flexible fibers of some minerals, such as riebeckite and tremolite (see p.279). Its silky fibers have been spun into cloth and mixed with other minerals to form wallboard, roofing, and weatherproofing for houses. Originally valued for its fireproof qualities and its ability to withstand electricity and strong acid, it was later discovered that its minute fibers can cause cancer when inhaled. Mining has now ceased globally for blue asbestos. (See also p.258.)

ASBESTOS FIREPROOF GEAR
Asbestos cloth was once made into fireproof clothing for firefighters.

Group of prismatic crystals

Vertical parallel striations

ARFVEDSONITE

ARFVEDSONITE IS A MEMBER of the amphibole group. When lithium and magnesium replace iron in the structure, it forms the mineral eckermannite. Arfvedsonite forms well-developed crystals less often than the other amphiboles; it is generally found as massive aggregates. When crystals do occur, they are short to long prismatic or tabular, and often twinned. Arfvedsonite fuses readily, leaving a magnetic glass globule. It occurs in felsic igneous rocks and their associated pegmatites, often with other amphiboles and pyroxenes, such as aegirine and augite. It is also found in regional metamorphics. Arfvedsonite is relatively widespread; crystals occur in Colorado and New Hampshire; the Kola Peninsula, Russia; around Oslo, Norway; and at Mont St.-Hilaire, Canada.

COLORADO
This mineral-rich state has deposits of arfvedsonite.

PROPERTIES

GROUP Silicates – inosilicates
CRYSTAL SYSTEM Monoclinic
COMPOSITION $Na_3(Fe^{2+}_4 Fe^{3+})Si_8O_{22}(OH)_2$
COLOR Blue-black to black
FORM/HABIT Massive aggregates
HARDNESS 5½–6
CLEAVAGE Perfect
FRACTURE Uneven
LUSTER Dull to vitreous
STREAK Pale to dark blue-gray
SPECIFIC GRAVITY 3.4
TRANSPARENCY Translucent

Rock groundmass

Vitreous luster

DISCOVERY

Arfvedsonite was discovered near Ilimaussaq, Greenland, and recognized as a new mineral in 1923. It was named for the Swedish chemist Johan Arfvedson (1792–1841), who discovered the element lithium in 1817. It is still found in Greenland, at Ilimaussaq and Narssarssuk.

GREENLAND

ARFVEDSONITE FRAGMENTS
This specimen shows a mass of arfvedsonite crystal fragments set in a rock groundmass.

CYCLOSILICATES

CYCLOSILICATES TAKE THEIR name from cyclo, meaning "circle," and are so named because their crystals consist of closed, ringlike circles of tetrahedra that share corners. They are sometimes also referred to as ring silicates. Each tetrahedron shares two of its oxygen atoms with other tetrahedra, and the rings thus formed may have three members (such as benitoite), four members (such as axinite), or six members (such as beryl). Their chemical formulae will each have some multiple of $SinO3n$, where "n" reflects the number of rings.

BERYL

TOURMALINE

RING CRYSTAL STRUCTURES
Both beryl and tourmaline contain sixfold rings of SiO_4 tetrahedra.

Oxygen atom

BeO_4 tetrahedron

AlO_6 octahedron

Stacked SiO_4 tetrahedra

BERYL CRYSTAL STRUCTURE
In beryl, the six-fold rings of SiO_4 tetrahedra are stacked to form channels. They are linked by BeO_4 tetrahedra and AlO_6 octahedra.

DIOPTASE

KAZAKHSTAN
Superb dioptase specimens come from Kazakhstan.

DIOPTASE CAN SUPERFICIALLY resemble emerald—sufficiently so that crystals mined from the rich deposit in Kazakhstan were wrongly identified as such when sent to Czar Paul in 1797. History does not record his reaction. Were it not for its softness and good cleavage, dioptase would make a superb gemstone to rival emerald in color. Its prismatic crystals, often with rhombohedral terminations, can be highly transparent, and it is from this that its name is derived: *dia*, from the Greek for "through," and *optazein*, meaning "visible," or "to see." Transparent examples can be weakly pleochroic, and intensely colored specimens can be translucent. Dioptase also occurs in crystalline and massive aggregates. It forms where copper veins have been altered by oxidation. Superb specimens still come from Kazakhstan; and also from Iran, Namibia, the Congo, Argentina, Chile, and the US.

PROPERTIES

GROUP	Silicates – cyclosilicates
CRYSTAL SYSTEM	Hexagonal/trigonal
COMPOSITION	$CuSiO_2(OH_2)$
COLOR	Emerald- to blue-green
FORM/HABIT	Prismatic
HARDNESS	5
CLEAVAGE	Perfect
FRACTURE	Uneven to conchoidal
LUSTER	Vitreous to greasy
STREAK	Pale greenish-blue
SPECIFIC GRAVITY	3.3
TRANSPARENCY	Transparent to translucent

DIOPTASE CRYSTALS
These fine, prismatic dioptase crystals are on quartz, on chrysocolla. The specimen comes from Kaokoveld, Namibia.

Dioptase crystals

Vitreous luster

Chrysocolla groundmass

SUGILITE

INDIA
Sugilite deposits are found in the Madhya Pradesh region of India.

DISCOVERED IN 1944, sugilite was recognized as a mineral only in 1976. It is named for Japanese petrologist Ken-ici Sugi, its co-discoverer. A sodium potassium lithium silicate hydrate, it contains variable amounts of iron, manganese, and aluminum. It is usually massive or granular, but when crystals do occur, they are small (less than $3/4$ in/2 cm) across and prismatic. It is pale to deep pink, brownish-yellow, or purple. The pink to purple coloration is caused by manganese; the pink material is aluminum-rich, and the purple is iron-rich. Sugilite forms in metamorphosed manganese deposits, and as xenoliths in marble. It is found at Mont St.-Hilaire, Canada; Iwagi Island, Japan; Kuruman, South Africa; and Faggiona, Italy.

Purple coloration

MASSIVE SUGILITE
Purple sugilite, such as this specimen from Kuruman, Northern Cape Province, South Africa, is used for gemstones.

Massive habit

PROPERTIES

GROUP	Silicates – cyclosilicates
CRYSTAL SYSTEM	Hexagonal
COMPOSITION	$KNa_2(Fe,Mn,Al)_2Li_3Si_{12}O_{30} \cdot H_2O$
COLOR	Pink, brown-yellow, or purple
FORM/HABIT	Massive
HARDNESS	$5^{1}/_{2}$–$6^{1}/_{2}$
CLEAVAGE	Poor
FRACTURE	Subconchoidal
LUSTER	Vitreous
STREAK	White
SPECIFIC GRAVITY	2.7–2.8
TRANSPARENCY	Translucent to opaque
R.I.	1.60–1.61

CABOCHON

Sugilite is always cut en cabochon when used as a gemstone. It is relatively new to the gemstone market.

PEBBLE

Valued for their vivid purple color, sugilite pebbles are sometimes polished in rock tumblers.

CORDIERITE

CORDIERITE WAS NAMED for French geologist Pierre L. A. Cordier, who first described it in 1813. It can be blue, violet-blue, gray, or blue-green. Gem-quality blue cordierite is known as iolite, and because of its color is also called "water sapphire." Cordierite is pleochroic, exhibiting three colors. Crystals are prismatic, and the best blue color is seen down their length; their pleochroism is so pronounced that they may appear colorless when viewed across the crystal. It occurs in high-grade, thermally metamorphosed rocks. It is also found in schists and gneisses, and more rarely in pegmatites and quartz veins. In addition to Sri Lanka and Myanmar, there is a major source of iolite near Madras, India. Flawless crystals up to 2 in (5 cm) are found on Garnet Island, Northwest Territories, Canada. Gem material also comes from Madagascar, Tanzania, and South Africa.

MYANMAR
Iolite is found in the gem gravels of Myanmar and Sri Lanka.

PROPERTIES

GROUP Silicates – cyclosilicates
CRYSTAL SYSTEM Orthorhombic
COMPOSITION $(Mg,Fe)_2Al_4Si_5O_{18}$
COLOR Blue, blue-green, gray-violet
FORM/HABIT Short prismatic, granular
HARDNESS $7–7\frac{1}{2}$
CLEAVAGE Moderate to poor
FRACTURE Conchoidal to uneven
LUSTER Vitreous to greasy
STREAK White
SPECIFIC GRAVITY 2.6
TRANSPARENCY Transparent to translucent
R.I. 1.53–1.55

PANNING FOR GEMSTONES
Among the gem gravels of northern Myanmar, gemstones such as iolite are found by traditional panning.

CORDIERITE CRYSTALS
This group of short prismatic cordierite crystals occurs in a rock groundmass. Common cordierite is used as a heat-resistant material.

Cordierite crystal

Rock groundmass

Cordierite crystal

Cordierite crystal

CRYSTAL IN MATRIX

IOLITE
Iolite is sometimes faceted into cubes to demonstrate its strong pleochroism.

STEP
Some dark gemstones can be faceted in various ways to best display their color.

MIXED
Iolite shows good color and brilliance with small facets.

BENITOITE

DISCOVERED IN 1907 by a prospector who mistook it for sapphire, benitoite is barium titanium silicate. It is generally blue to dark blue, although it can be colorless, white, or, rarely, pink. It is strongly dichroic, with blue, cut stones appearing blue or colorless when seen from different angles. It has strong color dispersion, making it nearly as brilliant as diamond. It is found in hydrothermally altered serpentine and in veins in schist. Gem-quality crystals are generally small, with cut stones seldom exceeding 5 carats. Its principal gem source is San Benito Mine, California, where it was first discovered; pink crystals have been found at a nearby mine. It is also found at Esneux, Belgium; Niigata Prefecture, Japan; and Magnet Cove, Arkansas.

SAN BENITO COUNTY, CA
Benitoite was named after its place of discovery.

PROPERTIES

GROUP Silicates – cyclosilicates
CRYSTAL SYSTEM Hexagonal
COMPOSITION $BaTiSi_3O_9$
COLOR Blue, colorless, pink
FORM/HABIT Platy
HARDNESS $6\frac{1}{2}$
CLEAVAGE Imperfect
FRACTURE Conchoidal to uneven
LUSTER Vitreous
STREAK White
SPECIFIC GRAVITY 3.7
TRANSPARENCY Transparent to translucent
R.I. 1.76–1.80

Benitoite crystals

Benitoite

Natrolite

CRYSTALS IN MATRIX

BENITOITE CRYSTALS
These specimens from the San Benito Mine show good crystal form and color intensity.

Pyramidal crystal

CRYSTAL

SAN BENITO MINE
In San Benito, California, this mine is both the discovery locality and the main source for gem benitoite.

BENITOITE IN A MATRIX
This group of intense blue dipyramidal benitoite crystals rests on a rock matrix, along with natrolite.

Natrolite

Pyramidal benitoite crystals

BRILLIANT
This brilliant cut benitoite shows good blue color looking straight into the stone.

MIXED
Seen side-on, the blue color has nearly disappeared, demonstrating the dichroism of benitoite.

287

TOURMALINE

PALA, CALIFORNIA
Some of the world's most beautiful tourmaline specimens come from the Pala district, San Diego, California.

TOURMALINE STAMP

PLASTER IMPRESSION

ALEXANDER THE GREAT, STAMP AND PLASTER IMPRESSION
This is a superb intaglio in zoned purple-yellow tourmaline depicting the head of Alexander the Great, dating to the 3rd or 2nd century BC.

TOURMALINE IS THE NAME GIVEN to a family of borosilicate minerals of complex and variable composition, but all members have the same basic crystal structure. There are 11 species in the tourmaline group, including elbaite, dravite, schorl, and liddicoatite. Numerous varieties are also recognized, including indicolite (blue), achroite (colorless), rubellite (pink or red), and verdelite (green), and these variety names can apply to more than one tourmaline species. Only the major ones are discussed here. Elbaite forms a solid-solution series with dravite, and dravite forms a solid-solution series with elbaite and with schorl.

ABUNDANT GEMSTONE

Crystals of tourmaline are generally prismatic. Colored crystals are very strongly dichroic, and frequently display color zoning. Tourmaline is abundant, and its best-formed crystals are usually found in pegmatites and in metamorphosed limestones in contact with granitic magmas. Tourmaline minerals are resistant to weathering, so they accumulate in gravel deposits—the origin of its name is the Singhalese word turamali, meaning "gem pebbles." For the same reason, tourmaline is an accessory mineral in some sedimentary rocks. Gem-quality tourmaline occurs in numerous localities. Tourmaline's piezoelectric properties mean that it is also an important industrial mineral. It is employed in pressure devices such as depth-sounding equipment and other apparatus that detect and measure variations in pressure. It is also used in optical devices for polarizing light.

Although many of its transparent varieties are valued as gems, most tourmaline is dark, opaque, and not particularly attractive except as well-formed mineral specimens. Probably the most common tourmaline is schorl, a black, opaque, iron-rich mineral. Its prismatic crystals may reach several yards long. Dravite is a very dark-colored (usually brown) tourmaline, rich in magnesium. It is sometimes cut as a gem, and its color can be lightened by heat-treatment. It is found in the gem gravels of Sri Lanka, and in the US, Canada,

BUDDHA PENDANT
Tourmaline is a favorite material of gem carvers, who make pieces such as this rubellite pendant.

Quartz crystal

MOUNT MICA MINES

Although tourmaline is a relatively common mineral, gem-quality tourmaline is almost exclusively limited to pegmatites (see p.36). In 1820, elbaite of exceptional clarity was discovered and mined at Mount Mica in eastern Maine. Although the mine never produced the same quantities as the Pala, California, mines (the Pala mines produced 130 tons between 1902 and 1911), Maine tourmaline was more highly prized by cutters and carvers. The Mount Mica mines were revitalized in 1972 when another rich pocket of tourmaline was found. Although the deposits are depleted, mining continues, and tourmaline is still the state gem of Maine.

TOURMALINE MINER
In this photograph from the end of the 19th century, Loren Merrill, a mining entrepreneur, poses in one of the largest pockets of tourmaline ever found at Mount Mica.

Albite

WATERMELON

INDICOLITE

**WATERMELON IN
CROSS SECTION**

TOURMALINE COLORS
*The specimens shown here
are a sample of the great
variety that exists in the
tourmaline family.
Coloration can vary
lengthwise in a crystal as
in the black and green
crystal, which also contains
pink at one end, or in
cross section, as in the
watermelon crystals. It can
also be constant, as in the
blue indicolite.*

**BLACK, GREEN,
AND PINK**

*Elbaite
crystal*

*zoned
green at
base*

Mexico, Brazil, and Australia. Liddicoatite provides a
small amount of gem material, principally from the
Czech Republic, Russia, and Madagascar. A pink
tourmaline cabochon has been discovered set in a
gold ring of Nordic origin dating from AD 1000.

VARIETY OF COLORS

Elbaite provides the most gemstone material. Usually
green, it can have many different colors, including
pink or red, blue, and green; it can also be colorless.
Yellow-green is the most common of all gem
tourmaline color varieties. Emerald-green is much
rarer and more valuable, and, until the 18th century,
it was often confused with emerald. Most emerald-
green stones come from Brazil, Tanzania, and Namibia.

The most dramatic of the color-zoned gems is the
"watermelon" tourmaline, which, when sliced across
the crystal, shows a red or pink center
surrounded by a rim of green. Some crystals
are pink at one end and green at the other.

The superb red and green crystals from
the Pala district, San Diego, the
color-zoned watermelon crystals
from Brazil, and the magnificent red
prismatic crystals from Madagascar
and Mozambique are among the most
stunningly beautiful gem materials. Other significant
gem deposits are found in Maine; Russia; Afghanistan;
Pakistan; Nigeria; and Namibia.

PROPERTIES

GROUP	Silicates – cyclosilicates
CRYSTAL SYSTEM	Hexagonal/trigonal
COMPOSITION	$Na(Mg,Fe,Li,Mn,Al)_3Al_6(BO_3)_3Si_6$ $\cdot O_{18}(OH,F)_4$
COLOR	Black, green, brown, red, blue, yellow, or pink
FORM/HABIT	Prismatic, acicular
HARDNESS	$7–7\frac{1}{2}$
CLEAVAGE	Indistinct
FRACTURE	Uneven to conchoidal
LUSTER	Vitreous
STREAK	Colorless
SPECIFIC GRAVITY	3.0–3.2
TRANSPARENCY	Transparent to translucent
R.I.	1.61–1.64

INDICOLITE STEP
*This emerald-cut, greenish-
blue tourmaline gemstone
is an example of indicolite.
It comes from a deposit in
Paraiba, Brazil.*

RUBELLITE STEP
*The rich red color of some
rubellite is well illustrated
by this superb translucent
stone faceted in an
emerald cut.*

WATERMELON STEP
*This stone is faceted from
watermelon tourmaline to
show both colors of this
type of gem.*

MIXED CUSHION
*Orange coloration in
tourmaline is uncommon.
This orange-brown gem,
faceted in a mixed cushion
cut, is dravite.*

ROUND BRILLIANT
*This brilliant-cut colorless
tourmaline stone is a rare
variety of elbaite, known
as achroite.*

*Pink
tourmaline*

**SPIDER
BROOCH**
*This attractive
spider has two
tourmaline
cabochons set
into gold.*

*Broken crystal
of elbaite*

Schorl

SCHORL
*In this specimen, short
prismatic crystals of schorl
are on a rock groundmass
with scalenohedra of
calcite.*

Calcite

*Rock
groundmass*

ELBAITE CRYSTALS
*In this specimen from the type
locality of the island of Elba, Italy,
elbaite rests on a groundmass of
quartz and albite.*

SLICE NECKLACE
*This modern design
uses slices of tourmaline,
cut to reveal the watermelon
effect, on an intricate gold chain.*

*Tourmaline
slice*

*Watermelon
effect*

289

URAL MOUNTAINS
The Ural Mountains of Russia have rich deposits of gemstones, including aquamarine.

PROPERTIES

GROUP	Silicates – cyclosilicates
CRYSTAL SYSTEM	Hexagonal
COMPOSITION	$Be_3Al_2Si_6O_{18}$
COLOR	Green, blue, yellowish
FORM/HABIT	Prismatic
HARDNESS	$7\frac{1}{2}$–8
CLEAVAGE	Indistinct
FRACTURE	Uneven to conchoidal
LUSTER	Vitreous
STREAK	White
SPECIFIC GRAVITY	2.6–2.8
TRANSPARENCY	Transparent to translucent
R.I.	1.57–1.58

CABOCHON
When cut en cabochon, some aquamarines—like this gemstone—show a cat's-eye effect.

RECTANGULAR STEP
Step cuts are frequently used for aquamarine to show off the deep blue color.

SQUARE CUSHION
Prismatic crystals like those of aquamarine are usually cut in squares or rectangles to preserve the gemstone material.

OVAL MIXED
This aquamarine has been faceted in a mixed cut. The effect—as with all gemstones—is to deepen the color of the stone.

BERYL: AQUAMARINE

FEW PEOPLE HAVE EVER heard of the mineral beryl, but almost everyone has heard of its principal gemstone varieties—emerald (see pp.292–93) and aquamarine, the most common variety. Before 1925, its solitary use was as a gemstone, but since then many important uses have been found for beryllium. Common beryl—a beryllium aluminum silicate—is now widely sought as the ore of this rare element. Other gemstone varieties (see opposite) are heliodor (golden yellow), morganite (pink), and goshenite (colorless). Common beryl ranges in color from tan to pale green, pale or sky blue, or yellowish. It is a minor constituent of many granitic rocks and their associated pegmatite dikes, of mica schists, and of gneisses. The name "beryl" is derived from the Greek *beryllos*, applied to many green stones.

Much beryl production is a byproduct of the mining of feldspar and mica, and no large deposits have been found. However, beryl crystals, which normally occur as columnar, hexagonal prisms, are found from time to time: a 220-ton crystal was found in Brazil, and a crystal 19 ft (5.8 m) long and 5 ft (1.5 m) in diameter was discovered in South Dakota.

Aquamarine, meaning "sea water," is almost universally found in cavities in pegmatites or in alluvial deposits, and forms larger and clearer crystals than emerald. One transparent crystal from Brazil weighed 245 lb (110 kg). In the 19th century, sea-green aquamarine was highly valued; today, sky-blue crystals imparted by traces of iron are preferred. In ancient times, aquamarine amulets engraved with Poseidon were thought to protect sailors.

AQUAMARINE CRYSTAL
This shows the often complex termination seen on beryl crystals.

GREENISH AQUAMARINE

Complex termination

Prism face

BERYL CRYSTALS
These crystals are prismatic. The greenish aquamarine can be heat-treated to turn it blue.

Prism face

BERYL CRYSTAL

NUCLEAR FUEL ELEMENT
Beryllium is used to regulate the flow of neutrons in beryllium moderated reactors.

MOUNT ANTERO

At just over 14,000 ft (4,250 m), Mount Antero, in the Rocky Mountains of Colorado, is the highest gemstone locality in North America. Although the site is famous for its aquamarine, lesser amounts of phenakite and other pegmatite minerals are also found here. Because of its high altitude, it is accessible to collectors for only two to three months of the year.

ANTERO CRYSTAL
This crystal was discovered at Mount Antero.

AQUAMARINE CRYSTALS
This mass of prismatic aquamarine crystals is from Dusso, Karakoram Range, northern Pakistan.

Prismatic crystal

Vitreous luster

Rock groundmass

MORGANITE

MINAS GERAIS, BRAZIL
This is a prime locality for morganite.

MORGANITE IS GEM-QUALITY beryl that is colored pink, rose-lilac, peach, orange, or pinkish yellow, by the presence of cesium or manganese. Morganite crystals often show color banding, with a sequence from blue near the base to nearly colorless in the center, to peach or pink at the termination. Morganite is also dichroic, and tends to form squat, tabular crystals. It is commonly found in lithium-rich pegmatites with lepidolite and tourmaline. It comes from a number of localities in Minas Gerais, Brazil, with some crystals reaching 55 lb (25 kg) in weight. Other important localities include Pala, California; Muiane, Mozambique; Elba, Italy; and several localities in Madagascar. Morganite is almost always faceted, and stones with a yellow or orange tinge are sometimes heat-treated to improve the pink color.

J. PIERPONT MORGAN
Morganite is named for the American banker and gem enthusiast J. Pierpont Morgan.

PROPERTIES

GROUP Silicates – cyclosilicates
CRYSTAL SYSTEM Hexagonal
COMPOSITION $Be_3Al_2Si_6O_{18}$
COLOR Pink, rose-lilac, peach, orange, or pinkish-yellow
FORM/HABIT Tabular
HARDNESS $7\frac{1}{2}$–8
CLEAVAGE Indistinct
FRACTURE Uneven to conchoidal
LUSTER Vitreous
STREAK White
SPECIFIC GRAVITY 2.6–2.8
TRANSPARENCY Transparent to translucent
R.I. 1.57–1.58

MORGANITE ROUGH
This piece of gem morganite has been broken from a larger crystal. Its pink color comes from manganese.

Morganite band / Heliodor band
COLOR-BANDED CRYSTAL
Tourmaline inclusions

TABULAR CRYSTAL

MORGANITE CRYSTALS
Morganite tends to form squat, tabular crystals that are often color-banded.

ROUND BRILLIANT
This is a richly colored morganite brilliant cut. Brazil produces pink morganite crystals such as this.

OVAL MIXED
An oval mixed cut highlights the lighter shade of morganite. Some pale morganite is from California.

MIXED DROPLET
This droplet-shaped morganite has been faceted in what is known as a mixed pendaloque.

GOSHENITE

PAKISTAN
Northern Pakistan has deposits of goshenite.

THE COLORLESS VARIETY of beryl, goshenite is named after Goshen, Massachusetts, where it was first found. It is the least common of the gem beryls. As with most of the other beryls, goshenite is principally found in pegmatites. Current sources are the Ural Mountains of Russia; Minas Gerais, Brazil; Dassu, Pakistan; and Ampangabe, Madagascar. The German word for spectacles, *brille*, may derive from the word "beryl," given that colorless beryl was once used for eyeglass lenses.

PROPERTIES

GROUP Silicates – cyclosilicates
CRYSTAL SYSTEM Hexagonal
COMPOSITION $Be_3Al_2Si_6O_{18}$
COLOR Colorless
FORM/HABIT Prismatic
HARDNESS $7\frac{1}{2}$–8
CLEAVAGE Indistinct
FRACTURE Uneven to conchoidal
LUSTER Vitreous
STREAK White
SPECIFIC GRAVITY 2.6–2.8
TRANSPARENCY Transparent to opaque
R.I. 1.57–1.58

FANCY CUT
Gem cuts with many facets bring out the sparkle in colorless material such as goshenite.

Pinacoid face / *Pyramid face*

CRYSTAL
This goshenite crystal shows a hexagonal outline and a flat termination.

HELIODOR

NORTH CAROLINA
This state is rich in heliodor.

HELIODOR HAS CRYSTALS that are generally columnar hexagonal prisms. It is found in granitic pegmatites, and its name derives from the Greek *helios*, meaning "sun." The Ural Mountains of Russia produce the best-quality stones. Heliodor is also found in Nigeria, Namibia, Brazil, and the Ukraine. Localities in the US are Connecticut, Maine, North Carolina, and Pennsylvania.

PROPERTIES

GROUP Silicates – cyclosilicates
CRYSTAL SYSTEM Hexagonal
COMPOSITION $Be_3Al_2Si_6O_{18}$
COLOR Yellow or golden yellow
FORM/HABIT Prismatic
HARDNESS $7\frac{1}{2}$–8
CLEAVAGE Indistinct
FRACTURE Uneven to conchoidal
LUSTER Vitreous
STREAK White
SPECIFIC GRAVITY 2.6–2.8
TRANSPARENCY Transparent to translucent
R.I. 1.57–1.58

RECTANGULAR STEP
This rectangular step-cut heliodor shows a fine, golden-yellow color. Iron is the coloring agent.

Prismatic crystal with complex termination

PRISMATIC CRYSTAL
This prismatic crystal of heliodor is on a rock groundmass.

Rock groundmass

291

BERYL: EMERALD

EMERALD IS THE GRASS-GREEN variety of the mineral beryl; other colors of beryl are aquamarine, morganite, goshenite, and heliodor (see pp.290–91). Its name originates in the Greek word *smaragdos*, which seems to have been given to a number of green stones besides emerald. The "emerald" of the Scriptures probably meant carbuncle, a garnet, and *smaragdus*, referred to by Pliny, almost certainly included several species. Thus, historical references to "emerald" cannot be assumed to indicate the modern mineral.

SOURCES OF EMERALDS

Several rich deposits of emeralds in Colombia were discovered and exploited after the Spanish conquest of South America. The deposits at Muzo and Coscuez are still being worked. The emeralds occur within thin veins of white calcite or quartz, in dark shale, and in a black bituminous limestone. After the discovery of the Colombian deposits, emeralds were shipped from South America in huge quantities. A glut of emeralds in Europe ensued, triggering a brisk trade of the gemstones to the Middle East and India, where they were especially favored by the Mogul rulers. In about 1830, emeralds were discovered in the Ural Mountains of Russia, where they occur in mica or chlorite schist. They have also been found in mica schist in Austria, in granite in Norway, and in a pegmatite vein in New

URAL MOUNTAINS, RUSSIA
These mineral-rich mountains have been mined for emeralds for nearly two centuries.

CRYSTAL IN QUARTZ

CRYSTAL IN MICA SCHIST

CRYSTALS IN PEGMATITE

PRISMATIC CRYSTAL

EMERALD CRYSTALS
These specimens illustrate several modes of occurrence for emerald, with associated minerals, and an unusually long, prismatic emerald crystal.

EMERALD CRYSTAL
This unusually large, walnut-sized crystal is in the Oxford University [England] mineral collection. It is from Santa Fé de Bogotá, Colombia.

Prism face

TRAPICHE EMERALD
The starlike pattern in this emerald cabochon is carbonaceous material trapped during its crystallization.

CHIMU FUNERARY MASK
This South American gold mask has emerald beads for eyes.

South Wales, Australia. Other sources include Brazil, South Africa, Zimbabwe, Pakistan, Zambia, and North Carolina.

Emerald's green color results from trace chromium. Trace vanadium may also be present, and beryls colored by vanadium alone

MUZO EMERALD MINE
The emerald mine near Muzo, Colombia, is in a region of rugged mountains.

PROPERTIES

GROUP Silicates – cyclosilicates
CRYSTAL SYSTEM Hexagonal
COMPOSITION $Be_3Al_2Si_6O_{18}$
COLOR Green
FORM/HABIT Prismatic
HARDNESS $7\frac{1}{2}$–8
CLEAVAGE Imperfect
FRACTURE Uneven to conchoidal
LUSTER Vitreous
STREAK White
SPECIFIC GRAVITY 2.6–3.0
TRANSPARENCY Transparent to translucent
R.I. 1.57–1.60

can be emerald-green, but there are differences in opinion as to whether or not they should be called emerald. Flawless emeralds are rare, so various treatments have been devised to hide or disguise flaws. Cameos, intaglios, and beads can make the best of a flawed stone, and inferior stones are sometimes oiled to fill and disguise cracks and enhance color. In faceted stones, the "emerald-cut" was devised to minimize loss of valuable material. Basically rectangular, to fit the shape of the normally prismatic emerald crystals, the stone is cut in parallel steps with truncated corners to best display and enhance the color.

After considerable effort, emerald was finally synthesized in 1937. Synthetic emeralds are currently manufactured in the United States, and appear very similar to natural crystals, rivaling them in color and beauty. The world's greatest collection of natural emeralds is held in the Republic of Bogotá Bank in Columbia. The largest crystal in the collection weighs 1,795 carats (12³/4 oz/360 g).

THE LORE OF EMERALD

To the Egyptians, emeralds were a symbol of fertility and life. The Aztecs called emerald *quetzalitzli* and associated it with the *quetzal*, a bird with long green plumage—a symbol of seasonal renewal. In Europe, alchemists regarded emerald as the stone of Mercury (Hermes)—messenger of the gods and conductor of the souls of the dead.

When held in the mouth, emerald was believed to be a cure for dysentery and was worn as a preventive for epilepsy. It was also said to assist women in childbirth, drive away evil spirits, and protect the chastity of the wearer. It was held to have great medicinal value if administered internally, and in particular it was said to be good for the eyesight. In the 17th century, Anselmus de Boot, physician to the Holy Roman Emperor, recommended an amulet of emerald to prevent panic, cure fever, and stop bleeding. Unfortunately, emerald was also considered to be an enemy of sexual passion. Albertus Magnus, writing in the 13th century, noted that when King Bela of Hungary embraced his wife, his magnificent emerald broke into three pieces!

SPANISH INQUISITION NECKLACE
The rich, velvety color and exceptional clarity make the central, barrel-shaped emerald in this necklace (which weighs about 45 carats) among the world's finest.

ANCIENT EMERALD MINES

As early as 1300 BC, emeralds were being mined in Upper Egypt at Jabal Sukayt and Jabal Zabgrah near the Red Sea coast, east of Aswan. Most emeralds used in historical jewelry would have been from these mines, which, after the conquest of Egypt by Alexander the Great, became known as "Cleopatra's Mines." These workings were rediscovered around 1817, but now yield only poor-quality emeralds. These emeralds occur in mica schist and talc schist (see p.83). Only one other source was known in antiquity: Habachtal, near Salzburg, Austria.

CLEOPATRA'S MINES
This 19th-century photograph was taken when Cleopatra's Mines were still being worked.

THE HYLLE JEWEL
This Lombardic, late-14th-century initial M with annunciation figures is set with cabochon emeralds, rubies, pearls, and diamonds.

"A livelier emerald twinkles in the grass, A purer sapphire melts into the sea."

TENNYSON, MAUD

EMERALD RING
This classic emerald-cut emerald mounted in platinum is flanked by two brilliant-cut diamonds in this elegant 1940s-style ring.

MOGUL PENDANT
In this 17th-century Indian pendant, the hexagonal emerald has been carved and set in a gold mount.

ART DECO BRACELET
Carved 25-carat emeralds are set in platinum and interspersed with 20-carat mixed-cut diamonds in this French Art Deco bracelet.

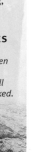

SYNTHETIC
This synthetic Gilson emerald pendeloque has a good green color with characteristic veil-like inclusions.

EMERALD CUT
The emerald cut was specifically designed for emeralds to minimize loss of material in cutting.

MIXED CUT
This mixed-cut emerald shows the cloudier material that is sometimes faceted.

CABOCHON
This emerald has an unusual octagonal cut—a cabochon top half and a faceted bottom half.

POLISHED PEBBLE
Emerald too cloudy to facet or too light in color for cabochons is sometimes tumble-polished.

SOROSILICATES

THERE ARE MORE THAN 70 sorosilicate minerals, although only the crystalline epidote–group minerals and vesuvianite are common. Sorosilicates consist of double-tetrahedral groups in which one oxygen atom is shared by two tetrahedra. This sharing gives the group its name: *soro*, which is derived from the Latin for "sister."

AlO$_6$ octahedron

SiO$_4$ tetrahedron

Iron octahedron

Calcium ion

EPIDOTE CRYSTAL STRUCTURE
In epidote, paired and isolated SiO$_4$ tetrahedra are linked by AlO$_6$ tetrahedra to form chains. Calcium and iron fill the cavities in the framework.

HEMIMORPHITE

DERBYSHIRE
This English county is a classic locality for hemimorphite.

HEMIMORPHITE IS ONE of two minerals formerly called calamine in the US. Its name is derived from the Greek *hemi*, meaning "half," and *morphe*, "form," a reference to its crystal form. Hemimorphite crystals are double-terminated prisms with a differently shaped termination at each end, a property shown by very few other minerals. Hemimorphite can also be botryoidal, massive, granular, fibrous, or form encrustations. Usually colorless or white, it can also be pale yellow, pale green, or sky–blue. It is a secondary mineral formed in the alteration zone of zinc deposits. Well-crystallized specimens come from Algeria, Namibia, Germany, Mexico, Spain, and many localities in the US.

GREEN HEMIMORPHITE
This group of green hemimorphite crystals forms rounded aggregates on a rock groundmass.

PROPERTIES

GROUP Silicates – sorosilicates
CRYSTAL SYSTEM Orthorhombic
COMPOSITION Zn$_4$Si$_2$O$_7$(OH)$_2$·H$_2$O
COLOR Colorless, white, yellow, blue, or green
FORM/HABIT Asymmetric, prismatic, tabular, botryoidal
HARDNESS 4^1/$_2$–5
CLEAVAGE Perfect, good, poor
FRACTURE Uneven, brittle
LUSTER Vitreous
STREAK White
SPECIFIC GRAVITY 3.4–3.5
TRANSPARENCY Transparent to translucent

WHITE HEMIMORPHITE
Clusters of radiating, tabular hemimorphite crystals encrust a rock groundmass in this specimen.

Crystal clusters

Rounded masses

Rock groundmass

Rock groundmass

DANBURITE

DANBURY
Danburite was discovered in 1839 in Danbury, Connecticut.

DANBURITE IS CALCIUM BOROSILICATE. Its crystals are glassy and prismatic, resembling topaz, but it is easily distinguished from topaz by its poor cleavage. It can also be granular. It is colorless, amber, yellow, gray, pink, or yellow-brown. Some specimens fluoresce blue to blue-green. Generally a moderate to low-temperature contact-metamorphic mineral, danburite is also found in ore deposits formed at relatively high temperatures. It is sometimes found in pegmatites and in evaporites. It occurs associated with cassiterite, chalcopyrite, smoky quartz, anhydrite, axinite, fluorite, and corundum. Localities include Uri, Switzerland; Presov, Slovakia; and Russell and DeKalb, New York, and Ramona, California. Danburite is cut as a gemstone, both faceted and *en cabochon*. Gem danburite comes from Dalnegorsk, Russia, in crystals 12 in (30 cm) long and 4 in (10 cm) in diameter; Mogok, Myanmar; Charcas, Mexico; and Imalo, Madagascar. A 108-carat faceted stone is in the collection of the Geological Museum in London.

BRILLIANT
Transparent danburite is faceted into gems for collectors. This gemstone is from Myanmar.

Vitreous luster

PROPERTIES

GROUP Silicates – sorosilicates
CRYSTAL SYSTEM Orthorhombic
COMPOSITION CaB$_2$Si$_2$O$_8$
COLOR Colorless, yellow
FORM/HABIT Prismatic
HARDNESS 7–7^1/$_2$
CLEAVAGE Indistinct
FRACTURE Subconchoidal to uneven
LUSTER Vitreous to greasy
STREAK White
SPECIFIC GRAVITY 3.0
TRANSPARENCY Transparent to translucent
R.I. 1.63–1.64

Transparent crystal

DANBURITE CRYSTAL
This specimen is a transparent single crystal. Although danburite has crystals that are like those of topaz, they lack the brilliance of topaz.

AXINITE

CORNWALL
Fine axinite is found in this part of southwest England.

THIS GROUP OF MINERALS takes its name from the ax-head shape of its crystals. There are four minerals in the group: ferro-axinite, the most common (described by the formula in the Properties box); magnesio-axinite, where magnesium replaces the iron in ferro-axinite; manganaxinite, where manganese replaces the iron in ferro-axinite; and tinzenite, intermediate in composition between ferro-axinite and manganaxinite. Axinite occurs not only as ax-head-shaped crystals but also as rosettes, and in massive and granular forms. The most familiar color of axinite is clove-brown; varieties can also be gray to bluish-gray, honey-, gray-, or golden-brown; pink, violet-blue, yellow, orange, or red. Color is not reliable for identification, and crystals of the four are essentially indistinguishable in hand specimens. Axinite is most commonly found in low-temperature and contact metamorphic rocks, and also in mafic igneous rocks. It is found worldwide; gem axinite comes from the US, Russia, and Australia.

PROPERTIES

GROUP Silicates – sorosilicates
CRYSTAL SYSTEM Triclinic
COMPOSITION $Ca_2FeAl_2(BSi_4O_{15})(OH)$
COLOR Clove-brown, gray to bluish-gray, pink, violet, yellow, orange, or red
FORM/HABIT Ax-shaped crystals
HARDNESS 6½–7
CLEAVAGE Good, poor
FRACTURE Uneven to conchoidal, brittle
LUSTER Vitreous
STREAK Colorless to light brown
SPECIFIC GRAVITY 3.2–3.3
TRANSPARENCY Transparent to translucent
R.I. 1.67–1.70

CRYSTALS
In this unusual specimen, a smaller, wedge-shaped axinite crystal has grown onto a larger axinite crystal.

STEP
Axinite is faceted as a gem, although fine-cut stones are small, seldom exceeding 5 carats.

BRILLIANT
This fine, brilliant-cut axinite is in an unusual and delicate shade of violet.

Tabular, wedge-shaped crystals

Vitreous luster

AXINITE CRYSTALS
This mass of well-formed, transparent, tabular, wedge-shaped axinite crystals has formed on a rock groundmass.

ILVAITE

TYROL
The Italian Tyrol is a source of ilvaite.

NAMED FOR THE LOCATION of its discovery, the Italian island of Elba—*Ilva* in Latin—ilvaite frequently occurs in short to long prismatic crystals, commonly striated vertically. It is also coarsely crystalline, massive, or granular in habit. It fuses to a magnetic bead, and is soluble in hydrochloric acid. Ilvaite is generally found in contact metamorphic zones with zinc, copper, and iron ores. It is occasionally found in syenites. Large crystals come from Elba, and from Dalnegorsk, Russia. It is also found at St.. Andreasberg, Lower Saxony, Germany; Saitama and Niigata prefectures, Japan; and many localities in the US.

PROPERTIES

GROUP Silicates – sorosilicates
CRYSTAL SYSTEM Monoclinic or orthorhombic
COMPOSITION $CaFe_3OSi_2O_7(OH)$
COLOR Black to grayish-black
FORM/HABIT Short to long prismatic
HARDNESS 5½–6
CLEAVAGE Distinct, indistinct
FRACTURE Uneven, brittle
LUSTER Submetallic to dull
STREAK Greenish to brownish-black
SPECIFIC GRAVITY 4.0
TRANSPARENCY Opaque

Striations along crystal

Prismatic crystal

ILVAITE CRYSTALS
This specimen consists of parallel, prismatic ilvaite crystals.

VESUVIANITE

MOUNT VESUVIUS
Vesuvianite is named for its place of discovery in Italy.

FORMERLY CALLED IDOCRASE, vesuvianite has crystals that are prismatic and glassy, and are usually colored green or chartreuse, but can be yellow to brown, yellow–green, red, black, blue, or purple. Numerous elements may substitute in the structure, including tin, lead, manganese, chromium, zinc, and sulfur. Vesuvianite is formed by the contact metamorphism of impure limestones, and it is found in marbles and granulites, frequently accompanied by grossular, wollastonite, diopside, and calcite. Gemstone localities include Sakha, Siberia; and, in the US, Sanford and Auburn, Maine, Olmsteadville, New York, Franklin, New Jersey, and San Benito County, California.

PROPERTIES

GROUP Silicates – sorosilicates
CRYSTAL SYSTEM Tetragonal or monoclinic
COMPOSITION $Ca_{10}(Mg,Fe)_2Al_4(SiO_4)_5(Si_2O_7)_2(OH,F)_4$
COLOR Green, yellow
FORM/HABIT Prismatic
HARDNESS 6½
CLEAVAGE Poor
FRACTURE Subconchoidal to uneven, brittle
LUSTER Vitreous to resinous
STREAK White to pale greenish-brown
SPECIFIC GRAVITY 3.4
TRANSPARENCY Transparent to translucent
R.I. 1.70–1.75

Vertical striations

VESUVIANITE CRYSTALS
This superb specimen consists of prismatic vesuvianite crystals.

CABOCHON
Vesuvianite is both faceted and cut en cabochon for collectors.

CUSHION
Transparent vesuvianite is faceted for collectors but is too soft to wear.

NESOSILICATES

NESOSILICATES HAVE ISOLATED groups of silica tetrahedra. *Nesos* is Greek for "island," a reference to the fact that the silica tetrahedra are not attached to each other. Another name for this group is orthosilicates. The sides of the crystals are typically equal in length, and they have relatively poor cleavage. Molecules within the structure tend to be densely packed, resulting in a relatively high specific gravity and hardness. Nesosilicates have an SiO_4 chemical unit in their formulae. Olivine and the garnets all belong to this group of silicates.

Oxygen atom

Cross-linking SiO_4 tetrahedron

Aluminum atom

ANDALUSITE CRYSTAL STRUCTURE
Andalusite consists of chains of edge-linked AlO_6 octahedra, cross-linked by SiO_4 tetrahedra. A second set of aluminum atoms occurs in five-fold coordination, between the octahedral chains.

Edge-linked AlO_6 octahedra

OLIVINE

ZEBIRGET, RED SEA
Olivine was introduced into Europe from this island in the Red Sea by the Crusaders in the Middle Ages.

WHILE THE NAME OLIVINE may be unfamiliar, most people will have heard of its gemstone variety: peridot, which has been mined for over 3,500 years on the former John's Island in the Red Sea, now called Zebirget. "Olivine" is applied o any mineral belonging to the forsterite-fayalite solid-solution series, in which iron and magnesium substitute freely in the structure. Fayalite (Fe_2SiO_4) is the iron end member, and forsterite (Mg_2SiO_4) is the magnesium end member. The most common intermediate olivines have compositions near the forsterite end of the series, and most peridot is about 90 percent forsterite. The olivine group also includes the rare mineral liebenbergite (Ni, $Mg)_2SiO_4$) and the less rare tephroite ($Mn^{2+}_2SiO_4$).

OLIVINE PROPERTIES
Crystals are tabular, often with wedge-shaped terminations—although well-formed crystals are rare. Olivine can also be massive or granular. Forsterite-fayalite olivines are usually yellowish-green but can be yellow, brown, or gray. In addition to the usual green color of common olivine—a result of the small amounts of iron that are almost invariably present—its color can vary from white for pure forsterite to black for fayalite, but both are very unusual.

OLIVINE IN THE CRUST
Olivine is inferred to be a major component of Earth's upper mantle, and as such is probably one of the most abundant mineral constituents of the planet. Olivine has also been found in some lunar rocks and in stony and stony-iron meteorites. It is generally the first mineral to crystallize from rocks with relatively low silica content; thus, its composition reflects to some extent that of its parent magma. Thick accumulations can occur as a result of olivine

VOLCANIC BOMB
Volcanoes emitting mafic lavas sometimes explosively hurl peridot-rich "bombs."

PERIDOT CRYSTAL
This beautiful peridot crystal originates from Sapat, near Naran, Pakistan. Pakistan is the principal source for gem-quality olivine. Peridot is generally found where there has been little opportunity for alteration, such as in dry climates or in recently formed rocks such as ultramafic lavas.

Secondary clay minerals

Natural fracture

MONTICELLITE

MOUNT VESUVIUS
Monticellite is found on this Italian volcano.

MONTICELLITE WAS NAMED in 1831 for the Italian mineralogist Teodoro Monticelli. Crystals are rare, but when found they are short prismatic and often rounded. It is more often found as grains. Monticellite forms in contact metamorphic zones in limestone, and is sometimes found in mafic igneous rocks. It is associated with forsterite, magnetite, apatite, biotite, vesuvianite, and wollastonite. Localities include Bancroft, Ontario, Canada; Nassau, Germany; Siberia, Russia; Kushiro, Hokkaido Prefecture, Japan; Hobart, Tasmania, Australia; and several sources in the US.

Monticellite   Calcite

BROWN MONTICELLITE
Brown monticellite occurs with green apatite and calcite in this specimen from Arkansas.

Apatite

PROPERTIES

GROUP	Silicates – nesosilicates
CRYSTAL SYSTEM	Orthorhombic
COMPOSITION	$CaMgSiO_4$
FORM/HABIT	Granular
HARDNESS	5½
CLEAVAGE	Poor
FRACTURE	Conchoidal
COLOR	Colorless, white, brown
STREAK	White
LUSTER	Vitreous to oily
SPECIFIC GRAVITY	3.0
TRANSPARENCY	Transparent to translucent

NECKLACE AND BROOCH
Orange citrine and pale yellow peridot are set in this necklace designed by Sybil Dunlop.

TIFFANY BROOCH
A central oval-cut green peridot is surrounded by a band of topaz and an outer border of green enamel in this elegant brooch.

crystals settling through a body of magma that is still partly magnetic. Olivine occurs most commonly in mafic and ultramafic igneous rocks such as basalt and peridotite. In general, the forsterite (magnesium–rich) end of the olivine series forms in low- and very low-silica environments, including metamorphosed limestones and dolomite, while the fayalite (iron–rich) olivines form in more silica–rich conditions. Common olivine is very widespread; peridot comes from China, Myanmar, Brazil, Australia, South Africa, Norway, and from Hawaii and Arizona.

In the presence of water at low temperatures, olivine readily undergoes hydrothermal alteration, forming serpentine, talc, chlorite, or magnetite. Common olivine has a high melting point, and is used in the manufacture of heat-resistant bricks.

Transparent olivine crystal

THE LORE OF PERIDOT

Peridot beads were made by the Egyptians as early as 1580–1350 BC. Peridot was considered a symbol of the Sun from ancient times to the Middle Ages, and an early Greek manuscript informs us that it confers royal dignity on its bearer. To be protected from evil spirits, the owner of a peridot should have it pierced, strung on the hair of a donkey, and tied around the left arm—according to the 11th-century French bishop Marbodius, at least. Strangely for such an ancient gem, there is relatively little other esoteric lore associated with it. In all likelihood, this is because it was grouped with other green stones as Pliny's *smaragdus* stone (see p.292).

TOPKAPI THRONE
This gold throne in Istanbul's Topkapi Palace is decorated with 955 peridot cabochons.

SOLID-SOLUTION SERIES
The olivine group includes a solid-solution series with iron-rich fayalite and magnesium-rich forsterite as its end members.

Light color from magnesium

FORSTERITE

Crystal face

Dark color from iron

FAYALITE

PROPERTIES

GROUP	Silicates – nesosilicates
CRYSTAL SYSTEM	Orthorhombic
COMPOSITION	$(Mg,Fe)_2SiO_4$
COLOR	Green, yellow, brown, white, or black
FORM/HABIT	Tabular, massive, granular
HARDNESS	6½–7
CLEAVAGE	Imperfect
FRACTURE	Conchoidal
LUSTER	Vitreous
STREAK	White
SPECIFIC GRAVITY	3.3–4.3
TRANSPARENCY	Transparent to translucent
R.I.	1.64–1.69

POLISHED PEBBLE
Small pieces of peridot are tumble-polished for use in Baroque-style jewelry.

STEP
Dark green peridot is faceted in step cuts to reveal and display its color.

MIXED
Peridot that is a lighter green is cut with a multitude of facets to deepen its color.

ANDRADITE

GERMANY
Andradite is found in the Eifel district of Germany.

ANDRADITE, A TYPE OF GARNET, is a calcium iron silicate, which has several variety names, each related to its color. The yellowish variety is called topazolite, because of its resemblance to topaz; yellowish-green or emerald-green forms are called demantoid or, commercially, Uralian emerald; black andradite is called melanite. Other colors are brownish-red, brownish-yellow, and grayish-green. The green of demantoid is caused by the presence of chromium; yellow to black is due to titanium. Andradites make spectacular gems, with greater color dispersion (separation of light into colors) than diamonds. Andradite is commonly found with grossular in contact-metamorphosed limestone, and in mafic igneous rocks. Gem demantoid comes from the Ural and Chutosky Mountains of Russia, and Valmalenco, Italy; topazolite from Saxony, Germany, and California.

DEMANTOID GARNET RING
Cut with many triangular facets, andradite has eye-catching sparkle and brilliance.

MELANITE
This andradite specimen, from Arendal, Aust-Agder, Norway, is the variety called melanite.

Vitreous luster

Black coloring

BRILLIANT MELANITE
This melanite gem, faceted in a brilliant cut, is a typical black, opaque stone. Melanite rarely shows any transparency.

MIXED
The high color dispersion of andradite results in brilliant faceted stones, as can be seen in this mixed cut.

PROPERTIES

GROUP	Silicates – nesosilicates
CRYSTAL SYSTEM	Cubic
COMPOSITION	$Ca_3Fe_2(SiO_4)_3$
COLOR	See text
FORM/HABIT	Dodecahedral, trapezohedral
HARDNESS	6½–7
CLEAVAGE	None
FRACTURE	Conchoidal, brittle
LUSTER	Vitreous
STREAK	White
SPECIFIC GRAVITY	3.8
TRANSPARENCY	Transparent to translucent
R.I.	1.85–1.89

GROSSULAR

TANZANIA
Gem-quality green grossular comes from Tanzania.

IN REFERENCE TO its gooseberry-green color, the calcium aluminum silicate grossular is named for the Latin *grossularia*, "gooseberry." Its predominantly dodecahedral crystals can also be white, colorless, pink, cream, orange, red, honey, brown, or black. Crystals up to 5 in (13 cm) are known. When reddish-brown, it is called hessonite (see opposite). Grossular is ordinarily found in both regional and thermal calcium-rich metamorphic rocks, and occasionally in meteorites. Massive greenish grossular is sometimes marketed under the name South African, or Transvaal, jade. Most grossular is opaque to translucent, but transparent, pale to emerald-green faceting material (marketed as tsavorite in the US and tsavolite in Europe) comes from Kenya and Tanzania.

FROG BROOCH
This sparkling, delicate brooch combines diamonds with a line of green grossular gems along the frog's back.

Grossular crystal

GROSSULAR ON DIOPSIDE
These grossular crystals, from Piedmont, Italy, are on a groundmass of diopside.

Diopside

PROPERTIES

GROUP	Silicates – nesosilicates
CRYSTAL SYSTEM	Cubic
COMPOSITION	$Ca_3Al_2(SiO_4)_3$
COLOR	See text
FORM/HABIT	Dodecahedral
HARDNESS	6½–7
CLEAVAGE	None
FRACTURE	Conchoidal
LUSTER	Vitreous
STREAK	White
SPECIFIC GRAVITY	3.6
TRANSPARENCY	Transparent to translucent
R.I.	1.69–1.73

PINK POLISHED SLAB
This slab cut through a large grossular crystal shows color-zoning within the crystal.

HORSE STATUE
This stylized mythical horse with an elaborate saddle and head is carved out of mottled grossular.

COLOR RANGE
Grossular comes in a wide range of colors, as these gems demonstrate.

HESSONITE

THE REDDISH-BROWN variety of grossular (see opposite), hessonite is a calcium aluminum silicate. Mostly found in dodecahedral crystals, its color is due to manganese and iron inclusions. Its popular name is "cinnamon stone." Hessonite is found principally in calcareous metamorphosed rocks. The most important source of gem-quality hessonite is in the gem gravels or metamorphic rocks of Sri Lanka, but other localities also produce superb material: Lowell, Vermont; the Jeffrey Mine, Quebec, Canada; Coahuila and Zacatecas, Mexico; the Isle of Mull, Scotland; and the Ala Valley, Piedmont, Italy. The Romans and ancient Greeks carved cameos and intaglios, and cut cabochons from hessonite.

ART DECO BROOCH
This brooch is designed as a microphone with a cushion-shaped hessonite garnet surrounded with diamonds, on a diamond "stand."

Vitreous luster

HESSONITE CLUSTER
The dodecahedral crystals of cinnamon stone, or hessonite, cluster in this superb specimen.

Striated crystal

Twinned crystals

PROPERTIES

GROUP	Silicates – nesosilicates
CRYSTAL SYSTEM	Cubic
COMPOSITION	$Ca_3Al_2(SiO_4)_3$
COLOR	Reddish-brown
FORM/HABIT	Dodecahedral
HARDNESS	7
CLEAVAGE	None
FRACTURE	Conchoidal
LUSTER	Vitreous
STREAK	White
SPECIFIC GRAVITY	3.7
TRANSPARENCY	Transparent to translucent
R.I.	1.73–1.75

LALIQUE PLAQUE
In this 1905 design, circular-cut hessonite, peridot, and garnet gems accent the main motif of a maiden's head in profile with cascading, plum-colored, enameled hair.

ROUND MIX
The color of lighter hessonite is enhanced by a multitude of small facets.

OVAL MIX
Deeper-colored hessonites show their color most effectively through broader facets.

UVAROVITE

THE RAREST OF ALL the gem garnets is uvarovite, the calcium chromium silicate. It was named in 1832 for the Russian nobleman Count Uvarov. Its predominantly dodecahedral crystals are almost always too small to be cut. Uvarovite's brilliant green color comes from chromium – the same coloring agent that is in ruby and emerald, which is known to have an inhibiting effect on crystal growth. It is probable that uvarovite's small crystals are a result of this. Uvarovite is found in chromium–bearing igneous and metamorphic rocks. Some of the largest crystals come from Outokumpu, Finland. It is also found in Russia's Ural Mountains, the Bushveld Complex, South Africa, California, and Silesia, Poland.

UVAROVITE CRYSTAL
This dodecahedral uvarovite crystal is in a skarn matrix.

Dodecahedral crystal

Skarn matrix

Crust of uvarovite crystals

Rock groundmass

PROPERTIES

GROUP	Silicates – nesosilicates
CRYSTAL SYSTEM	Cubic
COMPOSITION	$Ca_3Cr_2(SiO_4)_3$
COLOR	Bright green
FORM/HABIT	Dodecahedral, trapezohedral
HARDNESS	$6\frac{1}{2}$–7
CLEAVAGE	None
FRACTURE	Uneven to conchoidal, brittle
LUSTER	Vitreous
STREAK	White
SPECIFIC GRAVITY	3.8
TRANSPARENCY	Transparent to translucent
R.I.	1.86–1.87

TINY CRYSTALS
A crust of tiny uvarovite dodecahedrons covers a rock groundmass. This specimen is from Zalostoc, Mexico.

MYANMAR
Much of the world's supply of gem zircon comes from the gem gravels of Myanmar, formerly Burma.

ZIRCON

ONE OF THE FEW STONES to approach diamond in fire and brilliancy, zircon is such a superb gem due to its high refractive index and color dispersion. Its colorless stones can closely resemble diamonds, and they have been intentionally and mistakenly substituted for them. Zircon exhibits double refraction, and bottom facets seen through the top of a cut stone will appear double. Diamond does not share this property, and so this is a useful test for distinguishing between the two gemstones; zircon is also significantly softer than diamond, and cut stones will show wear on the edges of the facets.

Zircon has been known since antiquity, and takes its name from the Arabic *zargun*, derived in turn from the Persian *zar*, meaning "gold," and *gun*, "color." It has been mined for over 2,000 years from the gem gravels of Sri Lanka, and was used as a gemstone in Greece and Italy as far back as the 6th century AD. It forms prismatic to dipyramidal crystals, which can be colorless, yellow, gray,

ZIRCON BRACELET
Colorless faceted zircon gems alternate with orange gems in this modern gold-plated bracelet.

ZIRCON RINGS
In the ring above, the yellow zircon in the center is flanked by pale blue zircons. The ring to the left sparkles with a deep blue zircon.

RECTANGULAR STEP
This colorless zircon cut in a rectangular step cut was produced by heat treating reddish-brown material.

OVAL BRILLIANT
Green zircons, such as this oval brilliant, are often stones in which the trace elements have undergone partial decay.

CUSHION BRILLIANT
Golden-yellow zircons such as this cushion brilliant are produced when blue zircon is reheated in the presence of oxygen.

ROUND BRILLIANT
Blue zircon is produced by heat-treating brown gem zircon. Virtually all commercial blue zircon is heat-treated.

PROPERTIES

GROUP Silicates – nesosilicates
CRYSTAL SYSTEM Tetragonal
COMPOSITION $ZrSiO_4$
COLOR Colorless, brown, red, yellow, orange, blue, green
FORM/HABIT Prismatic to dipyramidal
HARDNESS $7\frac{1}{2}$
CLEAVAGE Imperfect
FRACTURE Uneven to conchoidal
LUSTER Adamantine to oily
STREAK White
SPECIFIC GRAVITY 4.6–4.7
TRANSPARENCY Transparent to opaque
R.I. 1.93–1.98

AFGHAN ZIRCON
This specimen of zircon crystals, up to $1\frac{1}{4}$ in (3 cm) long, in a feldspar and biotite matrix is from Afghanistan.

Twinned zircon crystal

Feldspar and biotite groundmass

Small zircons

Biotite

USING ZIRCON TO DATE ROCKS

Zircon crystals are extremely hard, allowing them to survive in many types of rock. They are also resistant to chemical and physical change. These characteristics make them ideal for dating very old rocks radiometrically. Radioactive isotopes, such as uranium, decay at a known rate over time, forming what are known as daughter isotopes. This means that by measuring the number of daughter isotopes in a zircon crystal within a rock, and comparing that number with the original number of atoms, it is possible to determine how much decay has taken place and estimate the age of the crystal and therefore the rock.

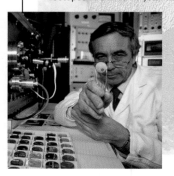

DATING CRYSTALS
Here, a scientist uses an ion probe generator to date zircon crystals.

green, brown, blue, and red. Single crystals can reach a considerable size: examples weighing up to 5 lb (2 kg) and 10 lb (4 kg) have been found in Australia and Russia, respectively. Its colored varieties have been given other names in the past, although these are now obsolete: the transparent red variety has been called hyacinth (jacinth); clear and colorless zircon from Sri Lanka has been called Matura diamond; and the name "jargon" or "jargoon," derived from the Arabic *zargun*, has been applied to all other gem colors.

Green zircon represents the green foliage of the kalpa tree, a gemstone tree that is a symbolic Hindu offering to the gods. Elsewhere in the East, wearing zircon was believed to endow the wearer with wisdom, honor, and riches. It was also an amulet for travelers.

INDUSTRIAL USES OF ZIRCON

Zircon is a silicate mineral, zirconium silicate, and is the principal source of the rare metal zirconium, a highly corrosion-resistant metal used to coat the interiors of nuclear reactors. Zircon crystals almost always contain traces of the radioactive elements hafnium, uranium, and thorium. These eventually destroy the crystal structure, which can often be restored by heating (see panel, above right). Zircon is also useful because it has a high melting point and is therefore used to

make foundry sand, heat-resistant materials, and ceramics. Because of its hardness, zircon is also used to make industrial abrasives.

Zircon is widespread as a minor constituent in silica-rich igneous rocks; it also occurs in metamorphic rocks. It is resistant to weathering, and because of its relatively high specific gravity it concentrates in stream and river gravels, and in beach deposits. Gem varieties are mostly recovered from stream gravels in Sri Lanka, Thailand, Myanmar, Australia, and New Zealand. Beach sands are a major source of commercial production, particularly in India, Australia, Brazil, and Florida. Other key localities are Canada, Mexico, Norway, France, and Pakistan.

HEAT-TREATING ZIRCONS

Heat-treating minerals to change their color or improve their clarity has been a widespread practice for centuries. It may well have begun with zircon. Brown stones from Thailand and Sri Lanka turn blue or colorless when heated; in blue stones that have lost their color, reheating will reestablish the blue color. The process itself does not require expensive apparatus. The zircons to be treated are placed in a clay pot, intermixed with fine sand; the pot is then heated in the coals of a campfire for a period determined by long experience. After slow cooling, the newly colored stones are separated from the sand, and cut. Blue zircon reheated in the presence of oxygen changes to golden-yellow, the source of the name *zargun*. Because the word is of ancient origin, so, too, must be the practice of heat-treating.

HEAT-TREATED CUT GEM

UNTREATED CRYSTALS

HEAT-TREATED CRYSTALS

FLORAL BROOCH
This floral brooch, in an Indian-style silver setting, contains colorless, blue, yellow and brown faceted zircons.

Syenite groundmass

Zircon crystal

ZIRCON IN SYENITE

Pyramidal terminations

Prism face

SINGLE CRYSTAL

Prismatic crystals

Feldspar

PRISMATIC CRYSTALS

ZIRCON CRYSTALS
Zircon crystals are most commonly found in igneous rocks, especially syenite, and in association with feldspar, garnet or monazite. They conform to the tetragonal system of symmetry and are usually prismatic.

Biotite

PANNING
This woman is panning for zircon gems in river gravels in the ex-Khmer Rouge heartland of Pailin in western Cambodia.

TOPAZ

THE LEGENDARY ISLAND of Topazios, just off the coast of Egypt in the Red Sea and now called Zebirget, is one source of the name "topaz." It is also thought to derive from *tapaz*, the Sanskrit word for "fire." Many authorities believe that the stone called topaz today was unknown to the ancients and that the name *topazos* referred to olivine (peridot, see p.298–99) as Topazios was a well-known locality for that gem. It follows that the "topaz" in the Old Testament may also have been peridot. The gem was used in ancient Egypt, Greece, and Rome, the Roman source being faraway Sri Lanka.

URAL MOUNTAINS
The finest display specimens are from Russia's Urals, where sky-blue crystals may reach 12 in (30 cm) or more in length.

NECKLACE
This 1950s gold-plated necklace combines rectangular-cut, prong-set sherry topaz gems with circular cuts of amber.

COLORS OF TOPAZ
In addition to the well-known sherry color, topaz is also found in yellow, orange, pink, brown, shades of blue, and occasionally green.

YELLOW TOPAZ

BROWN TOPAZ CRYSTAL

WIDE VARIETY OF COLORS

Topaz is aluminum silicate fluoride hydroxide. Its well-formed crystals have a characteristic lozenge-shaped cross section, and striations parallel to their length. They are found in a wide range of colors, with the sherry-yellow stones from Brazil being particularly valuable. Pink topaz is even more valuable, but natural pink stones are rare. In 1750 a Parisian jeweler discovered that yellow Brazilian topaz becomes pink on exposure to a moderate heat, and most pink topaz today is heat-treated yellow material. Some blue topaz is almost indistinguishable from aquamarine with the naked eye. However, much of the deep blue topaz on the market is derived from irradiated and heat-treated colorless topaz. The natural color in many cases is unstable: for example, brown topaz from Siberia and Utah is prone to bleaching by sunlight.

Colorless topaz is sufficiently refractive that when brilliant-cut, it has been mistaken for diamond. The Braganza diamond (1,640 carats) in the Portuguese crown during the 17th century was thought then to be the largest diamond ever found but is now thought to have been a colorless topaz.

NATURAL BLUE CRYSTAL

BLUE TOPAZ

PROPERTIES

GROUP Silicates – nesosilicates
CRYSTAL SYSTEM Orthorhombic
COMPOSITION $Al_2SiO_4(F,OH)_2$
COLOR Colorless, blue, yellow, pink, brown, green
FORM/HABIT Prismatic
HARDNESS 8
CLEAVAGE Perfect basal
FRACTURE Subconchoidal to uneven
LUSTER Vitreous
STREAK Colorless
SPECIFIC GRAVITY 3.4–3.6
TRANSPARENCY Transparent to translucent
R.I. 1.62–1.63

ZEBIRGET
Zebirget (also spelled Zabargad) in the Red Sea is on the site of the ancient Topazios, said to be the earliest source of topaz.

Albite

OCTAGONAL STEP
The color of this octagonal step-cut gem is a natural topaz blue.

OVAL STEP
The blue color of this oval step cut has probably been enhanced.

OVAL STEP
Topaz occasionally comes in pink, as in this superb oval step cut.

TEARDROP MIXED
The golden-yellow of this teardrop mixed cut is that most often associated with topaz.

BRILLIANT
The brilliance of this nearly colorless topaz has been enhanced by many extra facets.

Topaz is formed by fluorine-bearing vapors given off during the last stages of the crystallization of various igneous rocks, typically occurring in cavities in rhyolites, granites, pegmatite dikes, and hydrothermal veins. It is also found in alluvial deposits as water-worn pebbles. Perfect cleavage causes crystals to break easily, with the result that part of a crystal often remains in the matrix.

Aside from Russia, Brazil and Nigeria are major producers of topaz. Beautiful crystals come from Japan, and the first modern use of the term "topaz" occurred in 1737 when applied to the abundant yellow crystals from Saxony, Germany. Gem topaz is also found in Colorado, Texas, and California; the Cairngorm Mountains of Scotland; Sri Lanka; Myanmar; Australia; Tasmania; Pakistan; and Mexico. Common topaz is found in a number of localities worldwide.

Yellow andradite garnet is known as "topazolite" due to its resemblance to topaz. The name "topaz" is also applied to other stones—often to increase the market appeal of much cheaper material. Citrine—yellow quartz—has been called "false topaz," "quartz topaz," and "Madeira topaz"; yellow sapphire was long referred to as "Oriental topaz"; and smoky quartz has been marketed as "smoky topaz" or "smoky topaz quartz."

BRAZILIAN TOPAZ

Brazil is a famous locality for topaz, as well as other gems. The Brazilian state of Minas Gerais is the world's largest producer of topaz, and the world's largest preserved crystal, weighing 596 lb (271 kg), is from there. The well-known sherry-yellow crystals come from Ouro Preto, Minas Gerais, where they occur in a kaolinitic matrix. The Ouro Preto deposit was discovered in 1735, and literally tons of topaz have been recovered from it. A 385-ton topaz crystal was reported in 1944 from Mugui, Espirito Santo, also in Brazil.

ORIGINAL ROUGH GEM
The Brazilian Princess was faceted from this 75-lb (34-kg) crystal.

SHERRY TOPAZ
The Ouro Preto deposit is the world's largest commercial source of sherry topaz.

BRAZILIAN PRINCESS
The faceted Brazilian Princess is nearly 6 in (14.5 cm) across and weighs 21,005 carats.

BROOCH
Two sherry-colored topaz gems have been used to form the thistles in this brooch based on the famous Scottish emblem.

Prismatic crystal

Small albite crystals

Single crystal of microcline

Termination face

Stream-rounded surface

TOPAZ CRYSTAL
This superb prismatic, pinkish-brown-colored topaz from Afghanistan is over 3 in (8 cm) tall, and weighs nearly 1 lb (0.5 kg). It rests, along with albite, on a microcline crystal.

TOPAZ PEBBLES
Like other dense gemstones, stream-rounded topaz accumulates in placer deposits. Placer topaz is mined in Nigeria and Brazil.

AUSTRIA
Excellent titanite specimens come from the Tyrol area of Austria.

TITANITE

FORMERLY CALLED SPHENE, titanite is one of the few stones with a color dispersion higher than that of diamond, making faceted stones cut from its transparent crystals fiery and brilliant. Unfortunately, these are almost exclusively cut as gemstones for collectors, as the mineral is generally too brittle and soft to be used in jewelry.

Titanite is a calcium titanium silicate mineral that may also contain significant amounts of iron, and minor amounts of thorium or uranium. The name sphene originates from the Greek *sphen*, meaning "wedge," a reference to the typical wedge shape of its crystals. It is also found in prismatic crystals, and can be massive, lamellar, or compact. Gem-quality crystals occur in yellow, green, or brown, and it can also be black, pink, red, blue, or colorless. This wide color range is a result of the number of other elements that can substitute in its structure in addition to iron, thorium, and uranium. Tin and aluminum are but two

TITANITE RING
Faceted titanites, such as the brilliant cut set in this gold ring, have superb fire and intense colors.

CROSS
This cross features heart-shaped titanite gems, set within diamonds.

that can make up as much as 10 percent of the mineral's composition. Titanite is strongly pleochroic and is also double refractive; this is seen as doubling of the back facets, adding to the brilliance of faceted stones. Titanite is widely distributed as a minor component of silica-rich igneous rocks and associated pegmatites, gneisses, and schists. Notable occurrences of the mineral are in Austria, Italy, Norway, Switzerland, Madagascar, Canada, Mexico, Brazil, Sweden, Germany, Russia, Pakistan, and New Jersey and New York.

RECTANGULAR STEP
This is a faceted, yellow-green, rectangular step-cut titanite. Although it has high fire, titanite is cut mainly for collectors.

OVAL STEP
This brownish-yellow titanite has been faceted in an oval step cut. Although beautiful, titanite is too soft to wear.

CUSHION MIXED
The top of this orange-yellow stone is cut with triangular facets, and the bottom in rectangular steps.

TRIANGULAR
This triangular yellow titanite shows the brilliance for which the stone is noted.

PROPERTIES

GROUP Silicates – nesosilicates

CRYSTAL SYSTEM Monoclinic

COMPOSITION $CaTiSiO_5$

COLOR Yellow, green, brown, black, pink, red, or blue

FORM/HABIT Wedge-shaped or prismatic

HARDNESS 5–5½

CLEAVAGE Imperfect

FRACTURE Conchoidal

LUSTER Vitreous to greasy

STREAK White

SPECIFIC GRAVITY 3.5–3.6

TRANSPARENCY Transparent to translucent

R.I. 1.84–2.03

TITANITE CRYSTALS
These interpenetrating, wedge-shaped titanite crystals, 1½ in (3.5 cm) long, are from Russia.

Wedge-shaped crystal

Wedge-shaped crystal

Vitreous luster

Imperfect cleavage

Wedge-shaped crystal

Twinned crystals

CRYSTALS IN MATRIX

Wedge-shaped crystal

TRANSPARENT CRYSTALS

CRYSTAL GROUPS
On the far left is a mass of wedge-shaped titanite crystals in a matrix. The specimen on the left is a group of large transparent crystals, which are also wedge-shaped.

Rock groundmass

ANDALUSITE

ANDALUSITE CRYSTALS are commonly prismatic with a square cross section. The mineral can also be massive, or have elongated or tapered crystals. It is pink to reddish-brown, white, gray, violet, yellow, green, or blue. Gem-quality andalusite is strongly pleochroic with yellow, green, and red within the same stone depending on the color of the stone and the direction of viewing. A yellowish-gray variety called chiastolite occurs as long prisms enclosing symmetrical wedges of carbonaceous material. These, in cross section, make a cross. Chiastolite takes its name from the Greek *chiastos*, meaning "cross." Andalusite is found locally in low-grade metamorphic rocks, and in regional metamorphic rocks,

where it is associated with corundum, kyanite, cordierite, and sillimanite. It is also found rarely in granites and granitic pegmatites. Crystal localities include Belgium, South Australia, Russia, Germany, and the US. Gem-quality andalusite is found in Minas Gerais, Brazil, and the gem gravels of Sri Lanka.

Prismatic crystal

BROWN CRYSTALS
This fine group of prismatic andalusite crystals on a rock groundmass has a vitreous luster.

ANDALUSITE CRYSTALS
This group of prismatic andalusite crystals from the Austrian Tyrol is in a groundmass of quartz.

Prismatic crystal

Quartz groundmass

RECTANGULAR STEP
Transparent andalusite is relatively uncommon. It is faceted into gems for collectors.

CHIASTOLITE CROSS SECTION
Twinned crystals of andalusite, called chiastolite, are sometimes worn as charms.

PROPERTIES

GROUP Silicates – nesosilicates
CRYSTAL SYSTEM Orthorhombic
COMPOSITION Al_2OSiO_5
COLOR Pink, brown, white, gray, violet, yellow, green, or blue
FORM/HABIT Prismatic
HARDNESS $6^1/_2–7^1/_2$
CLEAVAGE Good to perfect, poor
FRACTURE Conchoidal
LUSTER Vitreous
STREAK White
SPECIFIC GRAVITY 3.2
TRANSPARENCY Transparent to nearly opaque
R.I. 1.63–1.64

SILLIMANITE

OCCURRING IN LONG, SLENDER, glassy crystals, or in blocky, poorly terminated prisms, sillimanite is an aluminum silicate. Commonly colorless to white, it can also be pale yellow to brown, pale blue, green, or violet. It is distinctly pleochroic with yellowish-green, dark green, and blue within the same stone when seen from different angles. Sillimanite is characteristic of high-temperature, regionally and thermally metamorphosed, clay-rich rocks, and is one of three polymorphs of Al_2SiO_5 (see kyanite, p.310). A common metamorphic mineral, it is often found with corundum, kyanite, and cordierite. Crystals come from Mull, Scotland; Vltava, the Czech Republic; Assam, India; La Romaine, Quebec, Canada; and, in the US, Macon County, North Carolina, and Chester, Connecticut. Common sillimanite is used in heat-resistant ceramics and car spark plugs.

PROPERTIES

GROUP Silicates – nesosilicates
CRYSTAL SYSTEM Orthorhombic
COMPOSITION Al_2OSiO_5
COLOR Colorless, white, pale yellow, blue, green, or violet
FORM/HABIT Prismatic to acicular
HARDNESS 7
CLEAVAGE Perfect
FRACTURE Uneven
LUSTER Silky
STREAK White
SPECIFIC GRAVITY 3.2–3.3
TRANSPARENCY Transparent to translucent
R.I. 1.66–1.68

SILLIMAN
Sillimanite was named for Professor Benjamin Silliman, a geologist and chemist who founded the American Journal of Science.

Fibrous structure

Perfect cleavage

FIBROUS SILLIMANITE
This mass of parallel, fibrous crystals of sillimanite is from West Chester, Pennsylvania.

Silky luster

FIBROLITE
The columnar, fibrous form of sillimanite is called fibrolite. It is sometimes cut en cabochon, as here.

CUSHION MIXED
Facet-grade sillimanite occurs in the gem gravels of Sri Lanka and Myanmar, and in Brazil.

KYANITE

NAMED FROM THE GREEK *kyanos*, "dark blue," for its color, kyanite occurs principally as elongated, flattened blades, and less commonly as radiating, columnar aggregates. It is usually blue and blue-gray, but can also be green or colorless. Kyanite's former name, disthene (meaning "two strengths"), refers to its characteristic variable hardness. It is about 4½ when scratched parallel to the C (long) axis, but 6 when scratched perpendicular to this. Kyanite is formed during the regional metamorphism of clay-rich sediments. It is one of three polymorphs of Al_2SiO_5. The other two are sillimanite and andalusite. Each polymorph indicates metamorphism within particular temperature and pressure ranges. Gem occurrences include Bahia, Brazil; the St.. Gotthard region of Switzerland; and Yancy County, North Carolina.

SPARK PLUGS
Kyanite is a major raw material for the aluminum silicate mullite, which is used in spark plugs and heat-resistant porcelains.

KYANITE BLADES
This specimen of kyanite with quartz, from northern Brazil, shows the characteristic elongated, bladed habit of kyanite crystals.

KYANITE CRYSTALS
These single crystals of kyanite show prismatic development.

PROPERTIES

GROUP	Silicates – nesosilicates
CRYSTAL SYSTEM	Triclinic
COMPOSITION	Al_2SiO_5
COLOR	Blue, green
FORM/HABIT	Bladed
HARDNESS	4½; 6 (see text)
CLEAVAGE	Perfect
FRACTURE	Splintery
LUSTER	Vitreous
STREAK	Colorless
SPECIFIC GRAVITY	3.6
TRANSPARENCY	Transparent to translucent
R.I.	1.71–1.73

THIN SECTION
Kyanite crystals can be seen in this section in different orientations, revealing different cleavage patterns.

Vitreous luster

Quartz

Kyanite

Kyanite showing twinning and cleavage

Rock groundmass

Long, bladed crystal

WILLEMITE

WILLEMITE, NAMED FOR KING WILLEM I of the Netherlands, is a zinc silicate. Usually massive, it sometimes forms short, prismatic crystals or fibrous aggregates. Its is light to yellow-green, yellow-brown, red-brown, or colorless, and fluoresces bright green under ultraviolet light. Willemite is found in the oxidized zones of zinc deposits, and in metamorphosed limestones. It is often found with hemimorphite, smithsonite, franklinite, and zincite. Localities include Mont St.-Hilaire, Canada; Långban, Sweden; Attica, Greece; Mumbwa, Zambia; Tsumeb, Namibia; the Flinders Ranges, South Australia; and Pima, Arizona. The most important site for willemite is the Franklin Mine, New Jersey (see p.158). Willemite is locally an important zinc ore.

TROOSTITE
This variety of willemite, known as troostite, is from the Franklin Mine in New Jersey. Specimens from Franklin show particularly strong green fluorescence.

EARLY TV TUBE
Because of its green fluorescence, willemite was used as a phosphor in early color television tubes.

Prismatic willemite crystal

Vitreous to resinous luster

PROPERTIES

GROUP	Silicates – nesosilicates
CRYSTAL SYSTEM	Hexagonal/trigonal
COMPOSITION	Zn_2SiO_4
COLOR	Green, red-brown
FORM/HABIT	Massive
HARDNESS	5–5½
CLEAVAGE	Good
FRACTURE	Conchoidal to uneven
LUSTER	Vitreous to resinous
STREAK	Colorless
SPECIFIC GRAVITY	4.0
TRANSPARENCY	Transparent to translucent

STAUROLITE

TAOS, NM
Cruciform twins of staurolite are found in this part of New Mexico.

NAMED FROM THE GREEK *stauros*, "cross," for its characteristic crosslike twinned form, staurolite is a widespread mineral. It occurs with garnet, tourmaline, and kyanite or sillimanite in mica schists and gneisses and other regionally metamorphosed aluminum-rich rocks. It forms only under a specific range of temperatures and pressures and is thus very useful in determining the conditions under which the metamorphic rock formed. Staurolite's cruciform twins, known as "fairy crosses," are made into ornaments and amulets. They are found in Fannin, Georgia, and Taos, New Mexico; Brittany, France; and Rubelita, Brazil.

Prismatic staurolite crystal
Twinned staurolite crystals

STAUROLITE IN MICA SCHIST

Kyanite

STAUROLITE CRYSTALS
These staurolite crystals from Taos, New Mexico show several forms of twinning.

Schist

Staurolite

KYANITE-STAUROLITE SCHIST
In this specimen staurolite occurs with kyanite in regionally metamorphosed schist.

PROPERTIES

GROUP	Silicates – nesosilicates
CRYSTAL SYSTEM	Monoclinic
COMPOSITION	$(Fe,Mg)_4Al_{17}(Si,Al)_8O_{45}(OH)_3$
COLOR	Brown
FORM/HABIT	Pseudo-orthorhombic prismatic
HARDNESS	$7-7^1/_2$
CLEAVAGE	Distinct
FRACTURE	Conchoidal
LUSTER	Vitreous to resinous
STREAK	Colorless to gray
SPECIFIC GRAVITY	3.7
TRANSPARENCY	Transparent to opaque
R.I.	1.74–1.75

TRAPEZE
Staurolite can be transparent enough to facet, as in this trapeze-cut stone.

PHENAKITE

PIKE'S PEAK
This area of Colorado is a principal locality for crystals of phenakite.

A RARE BERYLLIUM MINERAL, phenakite was named in 1833 from the Greek for "deceiver," alluding to its being mistaken for quartz. Its crystals are predominantly rhombohedral, and less commonly short and prismatic. Phenakite occurs in pegmatites, granites, and mica schists. Large crystals are found near Yekaterinburg in the Ural Mountains of Russia, and in Colorado. Transparent crystals are faceted for collectors. Its indices of refraction are higher than topaz and its brilliance approaches that of diamond. A stream-pebble of phenakite weighing 1,470 carats was found in Sri Lanka, and faceted to a 569-carat oval.

PROPERTIES

GROUP	Silicates – nesosilicates
CRYSTAL SYSTEM	Hexagonal/trigonal
COMPOSITION	Be_2SiO_4
COLOR	Colorless, white
FORM/HABIT	Rhombohedral
HARDNESS	$7^1/_2-8$
CLEAVAGE	Indistinct
FRACTURE	Conchoidal
LUSTER	Vitreous
STREAK	Colorless
SPECIFIC GRAVITY	3
TRANSPARENCY	Transparent or translucent
R.I.	1.65–1.67

Vitreous luster
Twinned crystal

RHOMBOHEDRAL PHENAKITE
This phenakite crystal from the Ural Mountains of Russia shows multiple parallel twinning.

EUCLASE

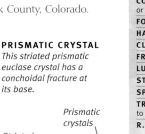

URAL MOUNTAINS
Russia's southern Ural mountains contain gem-quality euclase.

EUCLASE TAKES ITS NAME from the Greek *eu*, "good," and *klasis*, "fracture," in reference to its perfect cleavage. It forms striated prisms, often with complex terminations. Generally white or colorless, it can also be pale green or pale to deep blue. It occurs in low-temperature hydrothermal veins, granitic pegmatites, and in some metamorphic schists and phyllites. Transparent euclase is faceted for collectors. Gem euclase comes from Minas Gerais and several other localities in Brazil; and Park County, Colorado.

PRISMATIC CRYSTAL
This striated prismatic euclase crystal has a conchoidal fracture at its base.

PROPERTIES

GROUP	Silicates – nesosilicates
CRYSTAL SYSTEM	Monoclinic
COMPOSITION	$BeAlSiO_4(OH)$
COLOR	Colorless, white, blue, or green
FORM/HABIT	Prismatic
HARDNESS	$7^1/_2$
CLEAVAGE	Perfect
FRACTURE	Conchoidal, brittle
LUSTER	Vitreous
STREAK	White
SPECIFIC GRAVITY	3.0
TRANSPARENCY	Transparent to translucent
R.I.	1.65–1.67

Prismatic crystals
Striated crystal
Rock groundmass

BLUE MASS
This mass of well-developed, blue prismatic crystals is on a rocky groundmass.

HUMITE

STERLING HILL
This famous New Jersey mine is a key locality for humite.

NAMED IN 1813 for the English mineral and art collector Sir Abraham Hume (1749–1838), humite is a silicate of magnesium and iron. It is generally found in granular masses, with well-formed crystals being rare. Humite is yellow to dark orange or reddish-orange in color. Manganese substitutes for iron in the structure to form a complete solid-solution with manganhumite.

Humite occurs in contact- and regionally metamorphosed limestones and dolomites, where it is often found with cassiterite, hematite, mica, tourmaline, quartz, and pyrite. Humite occurs worldwide, but a few noteworthy locations are Persberg, Sweden; Isle of Skye, Scotland; Mount Vesuvius, Italy; Valais, Switzerland; and in the US at Brewster, New York, Franklin, New Jersey, and Sterling Hill, New Jersey (manganhumite).

Yellowish-brown humite crystals

Rock groundmass

HUMITE CRUST
In this specimen, a crust of yellowish-brown humite crystals with accessory mica covers a rock groundmass.

PROPERTIES

GROUP	Silicates – nesosilicates
CRYSTAL SYSTEM	Orthorhombic
COMPOSITION	$(Mg,Fe)_7(SiO_4)_3(F,OH)_2$
COLOR	Yellow to dark orange
FORM/HABIT	Granular
HARDNESS	6–6½
CLEAVAGE	Poor
FRACTURE	Subconchoidal to uneven
LUSTER	Vitreous
STREAK	Yellow to orange
SPECIFIC GRAVITY	3.2–3.3
TRANSPARENCY	Transparent to translucent

NORBERGITE

MOUNT VESUVIUS
This Italian volcano is a locality for norbergite.

DISCOVERED IN and named after Norberg, Sweden, norbergite is hydrous magnesium silicate. It is a member of the humite group of minerals. It rarely forms crystals, and is usually granular in habit. It is light yellowish-brown, white, or rose in color, fluorescing yellow under shortwave ultraviolet light. Norbergite occurs in contact-metamorphic and regionally metamorphosed rocks where there is contact between magnesium-rich sedimentary rocks and granites. It is often found with forsterite, diopside, phlogopite, and brucite. Localities include Franklin, New Jersey, and Edenville, New York; Bihar, India; Pitkyaranta, Russia; Mount Vesuvius, Italy; and Lyangar, Tajikistan.

Norbergite encrustation

NORBERGITE CRUST
Yellow norbergite encrusts this specimen from Canada.

PROPERTIES

GROUP	Silicates – nesosilicates
CRYSTAL SYSTEM	Orthorhombic
COMPOSITION	$Mg_3SiO_4(F,OH)_2$
COLOR	Light yellowish-brown, white, or rose
FORM/HABIT	Granular
HARDNESS	6–6½
CLEAVAGE	Distinct
FRACTURE	Uneven to subconchoidal, brittle
LUSTER	Vitreous
STREAK	Yellowish
SPECIFIC GRAVITY	3.1–3.2
TRANSPARENCY	Transparent to translucent

CHONDRODITE

SKYE
This Scottish island is a good source of chondrodite.

A MEMBER of the humite group, chondrodite takes its name from the Greek for "granule," a reference to its usual occurrence as isolated grains. Crystals are blocky and 1 in (2.5 cm) or more long. Chondrodite is yellow, orange, brownish-red, or greenish-brown in color. It forms in contact-metamorphosed limestones and dolomites, kimberlites, ultramafic rocks, and marbles. It occurs worldwide, but a few noteworthy localities are Skye, Scotland; Cardiff, Canada; Passau, Germany; Kamioka, Japan; Nordmark, Sweden; Slyudanka, Russia; and various locations in the US. Chondrodite should not be confused with chondrite, which is a type of meteorite.

Rock groundmass

Twinned chondrodite crystals

CHONDRODITE CRYSTALS
Reddish chondrodite crystals are with gray magnetite on a groundmass.

PROPERTIES

GROUP	Silicates – nesosilicates
CRYSTAL SYSTEM	Monoclinic
COMPOSITION	$(Mg,Fe,Ti)_5(SiO_4)_2(F,OH,O)_4$
COLOR	Yellow, orange, brown-red, or green-brown
FORM/HABIT	Granular
HARDNESS	6–6½
CLEAVAGE	Indistinct
FRACTURE	Conchoidal to uneven, brittle
LUSTER	Vitreous to greasy
STREAK	Yellow
SPECIFIC GRAVITY	3.1–3.2
TRANSPARENCY	Translucent to transparent

DATOLITE

TASMANIA
Good datolite crystals are found here.

A RELATIVELY UNCOMMON mineral, datolite is occasionally cut as a collectors' gemstone. Its name comes from the Greek word for "to divide," a reference to the granular occurrence of some of its varieties. Its crystals are generally platy to short prismatic, but may also be blocky or in spherical aggregates. Other habits are massive, compact, and cryptocrystalline. It can be colorless, white, gray, yellowish, pale pink, greenish-white, or green. Datolite occurs as veins and cavity linings in mafic igneous rocks and in metallic-ore veins. It is also found in gneisses and dolerites (diabases). Some notable deposits exist in Charcas, Mexico; Miyazaki Prefecture, Japan; Dalnegorsk, Russia; St. Andreasberg, Germany; Moravia, the Czech Republic; and in the US in New Jersey, Virginia, Massachusetts, and Connecticut.

PROPERTIES

GROUP	Silicates – nesosilicates
CRYSTAL SYSTEM	Monoclinic
COMPOSITION	$CaBSiO_4(OH)$
COLOR	Colorless, white, yellowish, pale pink, or green
FORM/HABIT	Platy to short prismatic
HARDNESS	$5–5\frac{1}{2}$
CLEAVAGE	Imperfect
FRACTURE	Uneven to subconchoidal, brittle
LUSTER	Vitreous to greasy
STREAK	White
SPECIFIC GRAVITY	2.9–3.0
TRANSPARENCY	Transparent to translucent

Pyramid face

Prism face

DATOLITE CRYSTAL
This semitransparent, colorless single crystal of datolite shows prism and pyramid faces.

DUMORTIERITE

BAHIA, BRAZIL
Gem-quality dumortierite occurs here and in Mexico, South Africa, and Japan.

DUMORTIERITE IS generally found as fibrous aggregates of radiating crystals, or it can be massive. Individual crystals are acicular prismatic. Its usual colors are pinkish-red or violet to blue, but it can be brown or greenish. Dumortierite occurs in pegmatites, in aluminum-rich metamorphic rocks, and in rocks that are metamorphosed by boron-bearing vapor derived from hot, intruding bodies of granite. Localities include Kutná Hora, the Czech Republic; Tvedestrand, Norway; the Kounrad Mine, Kazakhstan; and Fremont County, Colorado, Petaca, New Mexico, and Dillon, Montana.

PROPERTIES

GROUP	Silicates – nesosilicates
CRYSTAL SYSTEM	Orthorhombic
COMPOSITION	$(Al,Fe)_7(BO_3)(SiO_4)_3O_3$
COLOR	Pinkish-red, bluish-violet, brown, or greenish
FORM/HABIT	Fibrous aggregates
HARDNESS	7–8
CLEAVAGE	Distinct, imperfect
FRACTURE:	Uneven, brittle
LUSTER	Vitreous
STREAK	White or bluish-white
SPECIFIC GRAVITY	3.2–3.4
TRANSPARENCY	Transparent to translucent
R.I.	1.66–1.72

BLUE DUMORTIERITE
Bluer shades result from titanium substitution for iron.

CABOCHON
Dumortierite is frequently cut en cabochon, as here, or polished to make decorative stones.

Massive form

CHLORITOID

SHETLAND ISLES
Chloritoid is found in this Scottish island group.

NAMED FOR ITS RESEMBLANCE to chlorite, chloritoid is usually massive or foliated, often with curved plates. Its crystals are pseudohexagonal or tabular. Chloritoid occurs in low- to medium-grade, metamorphosed, fine-grained sediments, and is a useful mineral in the interpretation of the metamorphic environment. It is also found in lavas, tuffs, and rhyolites. It is a widespread mineral: localities include Ottre, Belgium; Hualien, Taiwan; and Pennsylvania and North Carolina.

PROPERTIES

GROUP	Silicates – neosilicates
CRYSTAL SYSTEM	Monoclinic or triclinic
COMPOSITION	$(Fe,Mg,Mn)_2Al_4Si_2O_{10}(OH)_4$
COLOR	Dark to grayish-green
FORM/HABIT	Foliated, massive
HARDNESS	$6\frac{1}{2}$
CLEAVAGE	Perfect
FRACTURE	Uneven
LUSTER	Vitreous to subadamantine
STREAK	White
SPECIFIC GRAVITY	3.5–3.8
TRANSPARENCY	Translucent

CHLORITOID CRYSTALS
This specimen is from Ile de Groix, Morbihan, France.

Chloritoid

Rock groundmass

GADOLINITE

RUSSIA
Gadolinite deposits are found on the Kola Peninsula, Russia.

GADOLINITE EXISTS IN TWO FORMS: yttrian gadolinite, the most common; and cerian gadolinite. Lanthanum, scandium, dysprosium, and neodymium can be present, and gadolinite is an important source of all of these. It is generally found in compact masses, but when crystals occur, they are prismatic. It is green, blue-green, or rarely pale green when fresh; brown or black when altered. Gadolinite is relatively widespread in granite and granitic pegmatites. Large crystals are found at Ytterby, Sweden and Iveland, Norway. Other localities include Japan, Germany, and the US.

PROPERTIES

GROUP	Silicates – nesosilicates
CRYSTAL SYSTEM	Monoclinic
COMPOSITION	$Y_2FeBe_2Si_2O_{10}$
COLOR	Green, blue-green
FORM/HABIT	Compact masses
HARDNESS	$6\frac{1}{2}–7$
CLEAVAGE	None
FRACTURE	Conchoidal, brittle
LUSTER	Vitreous to greasy
STREAK	Greenish-gray
SPECIFIC GRAVITY	4.4–4.8
TRANSPARENCY	Opaque to nearly transparent

GADOLINITE CRYSTAL
This single, prismatic crystal is from Texas.

Prismatic crystal

Greasy luster

ORGANIC GEMS

GENERATED by organic (biological) processes, organic gems may or may not be crystalline, and in some cases contain the same mineral matter, such as calcite or aragonite, as that generated through inorganic processes. Organic gems are judged by the same criteria as gemstones of mineral origin: beauty and durability. They were popular in ancient times because they are softer than minerals and easily worked by primitive methods.

The first discovered use of bone and ivory in carvings was during the Upper Paleolithic Period, from 40,000 to 10,000 years ago. These were probably not for decoration, but give a good indication of the first awareness of the working properties of these organic materials. The first items for adornment appear during the Mesolithic Period (8000 to 2700 BC) and were produced from shell, bone, and ivory. Organic gem materials were popular trade items: Baltic amber artifacts and salt-water shells are found over 600 miles from their places of origin; and freshwater pearls were widely valued and traded.

PENDANT
Seashells have long been valued objects for decoration.

SHELL BEACH
This profusion of conch shells covers a pebble beach on the island of Grand Bahama in the Caribbean.

BALTIC COAST
The Baltic coast has been a source of amber for at least three millennia. It still produces 90 percent of the world's amber.

CAUGHT IN RESIN
As resin from trees dried 40–60 million years ago, insects and spiders sometimes became trapped in the sticky substance and were fossilized with it.

AMBER

AMBER IS FOSSILIZED RESIN, principally from extinct coniferous trees, although amberlike substances from earlier trees are known. It is generally found in association with lignite coal, itself the fossilized remains of trees and other plant material. Amber and partially fossilized resins are sometimes given mineral-like names depending on where they are found, their degree of fossilization or the presence of other chemical components. For example, resin from the London clay and resembling copal resin is called copalite. At least 12 other names are applied to minor variants. The word "electricity" is derived from the Greek name for amber, *electrum*. This is because amber can acquire an electric change when rubbed, a property that was described in about 600 BC by Thales, and is one of the most useful for identifying amber. For several thousand years, the largest source of amber has been the extensive deposits along the Baltic coast, extending intermittently

PROPERTIES

GROUP Organics – hydrocarbons
CRYSTAL SYSTEM None
COMPOSITION Hydrocarbon (C,H,O)
FORM/HABIT Amorphous
HARDNESS 2–2½
CLEAVAGE None
FRACTURE Conchoidal
COLOR Yellow, sometimes brownish or reddish
STREAK White
LUSTER Resinous
SPECIFIC GRAVITY 1.1
TRANSPARENCY Transparent to translucent
R.I. 1.54–1.55

FLY IN FRESH RESIN
Resin oozing from trees, such as in this modern example, often traps insects, other small arthropods, and plant remains, which over time may became fossilized.

Polished amber

GEORGIAN NECKLACE
Amber has long been valued for jewelry, partly due to its light weight and warmth to the touch.

from Gdánsk around to the coastlines of Denmark and Sweden. It is both mined and recovered from Baltic shores after heavy storms. It has been widely traded since ancient times, and a cup carved from amber was discovered in a British Bronze Age burial. Perhaps the largest single use of amber was the creation of the "Amber Room" in Catherine the Great's palace in Russia, a huge room totally lined and decorated with cut amber. The amber from this room was pillaged by the Nazis in World War II, and was probably destroyed in a fire; however, the room has now been completely restored using newly cut amber (see pp.316–17).

THE LORE OF AMBER

Amber is said to represent the dividing line between individual and cosmic energy, the individual's soul and the universal soul. It has been used to symbolize divinity, and a face the color of amber is often seen on representations of saints and heroes. The Greek god Apollo wept tears of amber when he was banished from Olympus. The electrical properties of amber led to claims that amber rosaries and amulets act as condensers of current, discharging excessive energy in those who wear the amulet or handle the beads. It is also said that if a man keeps a piece of amber on him, he will never be betrayed by sexual impotence.

CHINESE EAR ORNAMENT
This Chinese ear ornament is carved in the shape of a panda bear. Dehydration of the amber over the years has caused the surface to crack.

POLISHED AMBER
A characteristic golden orange color, this amber bead is transparent with a resinous luster.

"SUN-SPANGLED" BEAD
This polished bead contains cracks that may have been caused by trapped and flattened drops of water or by heat treatment.

Translucent crystal

Resinous luster

Conchoidal fracture

BROOCH
This embossed silver brooch of naturalistic form is set with a yellow Baltic amber cabochon and three suspended amber drops.

AMBER NODULE
Transparent to translucent, most amber is golden yellow to golden orange, and usually occurs as nodules or small, irregularly shaped masses. When first found, it can have a dull and pitted surface.

NECKLACE AND EARRINGS
Small pieces of amber can be tumble-polished to create attractive baroque stones for necklaces and earrings.

TEARS OF THE HELIADES

According to Greek mythology, the god Phaethon lost control of his father Zeus's Sun chariot and drove it too close to Earth, setting it ablaze. In fury, Zeus struck Phaethon dead with a lightning bolt. His body fell into the Eridanus River and was buried on its shores by the nymphs of the stream. Later, Phaethon's three sisters, the Heliades, found his grave and wept day and night. Their wasting bodies took root, becoming transformed into trees, and their tears hardened into drops of amber.

THE GRIEVING HELIADES
Entitled The Sisters of Phaethon, *this dramatic oil on slate was painted by Santi di Tito in 1572.*

THE AMBER ROOM

DESCRIBED AS THE EIGHTH WONDER OF THE WORLD
AFTER ITS INSTALLATION IN THE CATHERINE PALACE IN
1765, THE AMBER ROOM SURVIVED THE 1917 RUSSIAN
REVOLUTION, BUT ITS INTRICATELY CARVED PANELS
MYSTERIOUSLY DISAPPEARED DURING WORLD WAR II.

KING FREDERICK I
*The original Amber Room
was the inspiration of King
Frederick I of Prussia, who died
two years after it was installed
at his Berlin palace in 1711.*

The Amber Room began its extraordinary history in Prussia. A Danish craftsman, Gottfried Wolffrani, was commissioned by King Frederick I of Prussia to carve an amber chamber for the royal palace at Charlottenburg. Wolffrani was replaced by the Danzig craftsmen Ernst Schacht and Gottfried Turow, who finished the amber panels in 1711. They were installed not at Charlottenburg Palace, but in the smoking room of the royal palace in Berlin.

In 1716, Czar Peter I went to Berlin to forge an alliance with Frederick's son and successor, Frederick William I, against the Swedish king, Charles XIII. To mark their successful agreement, the Prussian king gave the czar the Amber Room. Packed into 18 crates, the panels were carried by horse and wagon to St. Petersburg in April 1717. There they remained until, in 1755, Empress Elisabeth I had them moved to the beautiful Catherine Palace at Tsarskoye Selo.

The room intended for the amber panels was larger than their original chamber in Berlin, so the carving of ten more panels was commissioned in the same style. By 1763 the enlarged Amber Room was complete.

The ornate panels alternated with 24 Venetian-mirrored rectangular columns, which rested on amber bases. A mirror mounted in amber, a gift to Empress Elisabeth from King Frederick II, was also incorporated in the design. To unite the baroque and rococo features, the floor was inlaid with mother-of-pearl; gilded rocaille adorned the white doors; and four Florentine mosaics embellished the rich amber walls.

The Amber Room survived the 1917 Russian Revolution untouched, but in 1941 it was stripped by the invading German army and the amber panels shipped to Königsberg Castle in eastern Prussia. In the spring of 1945, the crates containing the Amber Room were almost certainly consumed by a fire that destroyed much of the castle, although many believed that the missing treasure was moved from the castle and hidden elsewhere by the Nazis. However, after many failed searches, finally, in 1979, the Russian government commissioned the rebuilding of the Amber Room in the Catherine Palace. It was completed in 2003,

PRUSSIAN EAGLE
*Seen on a panel of the Amber
Room, this eagle is an emblem
of the Prussian king, a
reminder that the room was
originally commissioned to
grace a Prussian palace.*

FAITHFUL REPRODUCTION
*The recreation of the historic Amber Room began in 1982 and
required the services of a team of specialist amber carvers. In the
mid-1990s, the work was threatened by a lack of funds, but the
project was saved by a large donation from a German sponsor.*

PEARL

MUSSELS WITH PEARLS
Pearls occur in a variety of mollusk species, and in a wide range of localities in both fresh and sea water.

PEARL IS A CONCRETION formed by a mollusk and consisting of the same material as the mollusk's shell, which is principally the mineral aragonite (see p.180). In addition to aragonite, the shell contains small amounts of conchiolin, a hornlike organic substance; together these are called nacre, or mother-of-pearl. The finest pearls are those produced by mollusks whose shells are lined with mother-of-pearl; such mollusks are limited to certain species of salt-water oysters and freshwater clams. The shell-secreting cells are located in a layer of the mollusk's body tissue called the mantle. When a foreign particle enters the mantle, the cells build up more or less concentric layers of pearl around it to protect the mantle. Baroque pearls are irregularly shaped pearls that have grown in muscular tissue; blister pearls are those that grow adjacent to the shell and are flat on one side.

Pearls are valued by their translucence, luster, play of surface color, and shape. The most valuable are spherical or droplike, with a deep luster and good color play. In the jewelry industry, salt-water pearls are commonly referred to as Oriental pearls; those produced by freshwater mollusks are called freshwater pearls.

Cultured pearls are those that have been grown on a pearl farm. A tiny sphere of mother-of-pearl is implanted in the mantle of the nacre-producing mollusk,

CANNING MERMAN
This late-16th-century jewel uses four baroque pearls, including one to form the body.

BOMBAY BUNCH
Mumbai (formerly Bombay), India, has been an important center of the pearl trade for centuries. Pearls are sorted by size and strung together to sell.

which is then placed in the waters of the farm. The oyster forms a pearl around the tiny sphere, which is then harvested up to two years later (see pp.324–25).

The color of pearls varies with the mollusk and its environment. A pearl can be any delicate shade from black to white, cream, gray, blue, yellow, green, lavender, and mauve. Rose-tinted Indian pearls are particularly prized. Pearls vary from the size of tiny seeds—called seed pearls—to one large baroque pearl that weighed 3 oz (90 g). Some of the finest pearls are found in the

Mother-of-pearl-coated metal castings

PEARL BUDDHAS
Metal castings of Buddha were placed into this living shell, which then formed a mother-of-pearl layer over them.

MARINE-CULTURED PEARLS
Marine-cultured pearls can be grown to uniform sizes and colors, depending on the chemistry of the local sea water.

Pearly luster

Uniform color

Conchiolin covering

Iridescent mother-of-pearl layer

Tahitian black pearl

Black mother-of-pearl

Black blister pearl

MARINE-CULTURED PEARL NECKLACE
The pearls in this exquisite contemporary necklace of marine-cultured pearls show uniformity of color and size.

MARINE BLACK-LIPPED OYSTER AND BLACK PEARL
The black-lip shell, a mollusk that produces black mother-of-pearl, also produces black cultured pearls.

Persian Gulf from Oman to Qatar, the waters between India and Sri Lanka, and the islands of the South Pacific. The Gulf of California, the Gulf of Mexico, and the waters of the Pacific coast of Mexico produce dark-hued pearls with a metallic sheen, as well as good-quality white pearls. Freshwater pearling has been known in China since before 1000 BC, and there is a pearl industry in the streams of Bavaria. Freshwater pearls have also been recovered from the Mississippi River in and several rivers in England and Ireland.

PROPERTIES

GROUP	Organic gems
CRYSTAL SYSTEM	Orthorhombic
COMPOSITION	Principally $CaCO_3$
COLOR	White, cream, black, blue, yellow, green, or pink
FORM/HABIT	Reniform
HARDNESS	3
CLEAVAGE	None
FRACTURE	Uneven, brittle
LUSTER	Pearly
STREAK	White
SPECIFIC GRAVITY	2.7
TRANSPARENCY	Opaque
R.I.	1.55–1.68

FARMED OYSTER PEARLS
Virtually all oyster pearls on today's market are cultured pearls grown on oyster farms in fresh or salt water.

FRESHWATER PEARLS
Freshwater pearls have the same luster and vitality as marine pearls. They were more accessible to early civilizations than marine pearls.

Natural pink color

Growth layers

FRESHWATER PEARL NECKLACE
This necklace created from a set of baroque (irregularly shaped) freshwater pearls loses nothing in beauty when compared to its marine counterparts.

Baroque pearls

PEARL CROSS SECTIONS
These sections cut through three pearls show the concentric rings of accumulated aragonite the mollusk has secreted over time to coat the implanted irritant, which is at the center.

EARRINGS
These American Indian earrings include mother-of-pearl, jet, and spondyllus.

MOTHER-OF-PEARL

The pearl industry began not to harvest pearls but to extract mother-of-pearl, also known as nacre. This hard layer of mostly calcium carbonate is secreted by some mollusks, such as oysters, and lines the inside of their shells. A beautifully iridescent and durable substance, mother-of-pearl has been used for millennia for utensils, and for ornamentation such as buttons and inlays.
Oysters harvested for mother-of-pearl are cleaned, split open, and dried, and their meat is sold for human consumption. Around one in 10,000 oysters collected for mother-of-pearl contains a natural pearl. Overall, mother-of-pearl is more valuable than pearl.

FRESHWATER MUSSEL WITH BLISTER PEARLS
This mussel contains a number of blister pearls; these are attached to the shell and so are flat on one side when they are removed.

Blister pearls

COYOTE
This American Indian coyote totem is fashioned from hundreds of pieces of intricately carved mother-of-pearl.

CULTIVATING PEARLS

NATURALLY HIGHLY VARIABLE AND SCARCE, PEARLS WERE TRADITIONALLY RECOVERED BY DIVING. TODAY, THE WIDESPREAD CULTIVATION OF OYSTER PEARLS HAS BROUGHT MORE PERFECTLY ROUND, OFTEN LARGER GEMS TO THE JEWELRY MARKET.

The cultivation of pearls in freshwater mussels is thought to have begun in 13th-century China. These pearls were "blister" pearls—hemispherical pearls formed between the mussel and its shell. The production of whole cultured pearls, and its subsequent industry, was started in the 1890s by Mikimoto Kokichi of Japan. After long experimentation, he discovered that a very small mother-of-pearl bead introduced into the tissue of a mollusk that produced mother-of-pearl—a process known as "seeding"— stimulated it to produce a perfect, round pearl.

Today, pearl farms can be found in sea water and freshwater. When immature pearl oysters raised in containers are two to three years old, they are implanted with a tiny sphere of mother-of-pearl. Taken to coastal waters or to deeper freshwater, the oysters are then suspended in wire nets or contained in some other way so that growth takes place in natural conditions. Divers tend the growing oysters, ensuring that they have enough plankton to feed on and are not overcrowded, until they are ready for harvesting from 13 months to two years later and their pearls are extracted. Japan, northern Australia, and to a lesser extent Fiji are major producers of marine cultured pearls. The Mississippi River is a major site of freshwater pearl production.

A pearl's color—and hence its value—depends upon the waters from which it comes. Pearls from Japan are cream or white with greenish tones; Persian Gulf pearls are usually cream; black or reddish-brown pearls come from Mexico; pink pearls are from Sri Lanka; Australian pearls are white with greenish or bluish shades; and pearls from the Gulf of Panama are golden-brown. Cultured pearls from Japanese and Australian waters are the most popular.

EARLY PEARL FISHING
This miniature by Flemish artist Jehan de Grise shows pearl fishing in the gulf around Malabar, India. It is taken from the manuscript Travels of Marco Polo *(dated c. AD 1400).*

OYSTER BEDS
In modern cultured pearl farming, seeded oysters or other pearl-bearing mollusks are suspended in baskets, and tended by divers using the latest diving technology.

A HANDFUL OF PEARLS
Perfectly spherical pearls can be produced by a pearl oyster if the seed implanted is also a perfect sphere. The size depends on the size of the seed and the length of time the oyster is allowed to grow on the farm.

FOSSILS

PLANTS | INVERTEBRATES | VERTEBRATES

HOW FOSSILS ARE FORMED

BURGESS SHALE
Soft-bodied Middle Cambrian fauna are preserved in this shale in the Canadian Rockies.

A FOSSIL IS A REMNANT, IMPRESSION, OR TRACE of an organism that has lived in a past geologic age. Some have been preserved in fine–grained sedimentary rock, such as limestone or shale. The most common fossils found are of plants and animals that once lived in a sea or lake. Typically, after an organism dies, the soft parts decompose, leaving only hard parts—the shell, teeth, bones, or wood. Buried in layers of sediment, they gradually turn to stone.

STAGES OF FOSSILIZATION

Fossilization is a hit-or-miss process, since normally the body of a dead creature decays, leaving no trace. The main factor is whether or not the plant or animal dies in a location where fossilization can take place. On a sea bed, where sediments are accumulating rapidly, the chances are good; in an environment where there is little or no sediment accumulation before the plant or animal completely decomposes, the chances are poor. Consequently, the fossil record is highly biased toward marine organisms with hard parts, such as shells. Where fossilization does occur, it goes through the same stages each time, but how long it takes can vary greatly.

Decomposing body
Silt of sea bed

Remains are trapped in sediment

Additional layers
Skeleton replaced by minerals

Excavation frees fossil
Erosion partly reveals fossil

1 SILT ACCUMULATION
A dead animal's body must be rapidly covered by silt. If it remains exposed, it will simply disintegrate on the surface.

2 MINERALIZATION
Enveloped by sediment, the soft tissue dissolves but minerals are absorbed by the pores of the skeleton.

3 CONSOLIDATION
The pressure of successive layers of silt hardens both the fossilized skeleton and the surrounding silt into rock.

4 EXPOSURE
Massive land upheaval lifts the rock layer to the surface. Wind and rain reveal the fossil.

UNALTERED PRESERVATION

Under exceptional conditions, organisms can be fossilized in an unaltered state. Minute creatures called diatoms belonging to the kingdom Protista have skeletons of silicon dioxide, which often remain unaltered. Marine- and lake-dwelling invertebrate animals, such as corals, mollusks, brachiopods, and bryozoans, have a calcareous skeleton or shell, which may be found fundamentally unaltered, even in rocks of great age. Under even rarer circumstances, organic matter that was rapidly sealed from the air or the attack of other organisms can remain virtually intact for millions of years. Insects, small animals, and plant remains sealed in amber are the classic example. It has even been suggested that DNA might be recovered from some of them.

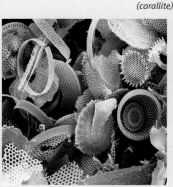

FOSSILIZED DIATOMS
Diatoms are tiny single-celled animals. Their skeletons of silicon dioxide undergo fossilization with little or no structural alteration.

Individual plant (corallite)

FOSSIL CORAL CABOCHON
Some coral skeletons remain essentially unchanged during fossilization.

FOSSILIZED AND MODERN SHELLS
A number of modern mollusks evolved sufficiently long ago to have fossilized equivalents. The fossils vary in character, depending on the materials in which they were originally buried. Their coloration is very rarely preserved (see mussel fossil, right).

Chalk preservation

TRITON FOSSIL AND SHELL

Limestone preservation

BRACHIOPOD FOSSIL AND SHELL

Retained coloration

MUSSEL FOSSIL AND SHELL

MINERAL PRESERVATION

Most organisms are subjected to changes during fossilization. In a process known as permineralization, water seeping through the rock deposits calcium carbonate or other mineral salts in the pores of the shell or bone, fossilizing the remains. In some cases, the organic matter is completely replaced by minerals as it decays. This process is known as mineralization, or replacement, and can be seen in petrified wood. The bones of vertebrates, and some shells, are made of calcium phosphate, and may undergo the same processes. In other cases, circulating acid solutions dissolve the original shell or bone, leaving a cavity of identical shape. Circulating calcareous or siliceous solutions may then deposit new material in the cavity, creating a cast of the original shell. The original impression, the "negative" of the cast, is called the mold.

Pyrite replacement

Fossilized bark

FOSSILIZED WOOD
Also known as petrified wood, fossilized wood can be subjected to such a high degree of mineral replacement, literally cell by cell, that the detail of its original cell structure is preserved exactly.

PYRITIZED AMMONITE
Sediments containing iron and sulfur occasionally form pyrite during lithification. If animal remains are present, pyrite may replace them.

TRACE FOSSILS

Organisms leave behind them traces in the form of tracks, trails, or even borings. Fossilized footprints of dinosaurs preserved in Glen Rose, Texas, and Lark Quarry, Winton, Queensland, Australia, reveal much about the weight and speed of the dinosaurs. Tracks of feeding and burrowing worms reveal how those animals lived.

FOSSILIZED WORM TRACKS
Fossils of soft-bodied animals such as worms are not found, but their fossilized tracks in rocks provide evidence of their existence.

DINOSAUR TRACKS
Tracks have yielded information about dinosaur species—what they weighed, their mobility and length of stride, and how many traveled in a herd.

FOSSIL IMPRESSIONS

Many fossils are simply the impression of a plant or animal left in the rock. These are created when an object, such as a leaf, is buried in sediment. During or after the hardening of the sediment, the leaf decays and disappears, leaving its imprint. Occasionally, the imprint of soft tissue—such as dinosaur skin—is discovered. In very rare instances, even imprints of internal organs have been preserved in rock.

FOSSILIZED LEAVES
The intricately fossilized impressions left in rock by leaves provide paleobotanists with a wealth of information about the structures of extinct plant species.

PRESERVING SOFT TISSUE

The soft parts of animals or plants are very rarely fossilized. Insects trapped in amber before they could decompose, and mammoths frozen intact in ice, are rare instances in which soft tissue is preserved. In 1997, in Jarkov, Siberia, Russia, a 23,000-year-old mammoth was found frozen in permafrost—the most perfectly preserved mammoth found to date. The excavated permafrost block was airlifted to an ice cave for study.

INSECT IN AMBER
Amber perfectly preserves insects from decomposition. Mosquitoes can still have the blood of their victims inside them.

MAMMOTH TUSKS
These enormous tusks from the Jarkov mammoth are being prepared for transportation on a sledge.

THE FOSSIL RECORD

ROCK-DATING TOOL
This fossil ammonite provides an accurate age-date for the rock in which it is found.

THE COMPLEX HISTORY OF LIFE ON EARTH, preserved in fossils worldwide, is known as the fossil record. By studying fossils, geologists can identify patterns of progressive changes over time that represent the evolution of a particular group or species. Geologists have been able to assign relative ages to the strata of rocks in which specific fossils occur, and consequently divide the history of Earth into a sequence of periods, collectively known as geologic time. Fossils provided some of the earliest clues to the existence of plate tectonics, confirming that the continents once comprised a continuous landmass.

GEOLOGIC TIME

The vast interval of time occupied by Earth's geologic history is known as geologic time. It extends from the age of the oldest known rocks—about 3.9 billion years ago—to the present day. Geologic time is Earth's history represented by and recorded in rock strata. The units of geologic time were originally established largely through the study of the fossil record and stratigraphy—the correlation and classification of rock strata. Due to evolutionary changes over geologic time, with the appearance of new species and the disappearance of old, certain types of organisms are characteristic of particular parts of the geologic record. Their fossils provide the means by which divisions in the record are made. The

geologic history of various geographic areas, and finally of Earth as a whole, has been reconstructed through correlating the strata in which specific types of fossils occur. Recent advances in radiometric dating methods (see below) have permitted the relative geologic time scale derived from the fossil record to be assigned absolute dates.

The fossil record also provides evidence that Earth's surface consists of immense, moving plates, and that the continents once fitted together in a single, huge landmass. The correlation of rock strata and their fossils on different continents suggested that the strata may once have been continuous, and also dated their times of separation.

DIVISIONS OF GEOLOGIC TIME
The divisions of geologic time provide a calendar against which to set events in Earth's history. The divisions also provide a universal frame of reference for geologists, climatologists, biologists, and paleontologists. In descending order of duration, these divisions are the eon, era, period, and epoch. These units of time, and the point of appearance of some of the organisms from the fossil record that characterizes them, are shown below.

	First land plants	First land vertebrates				First dinosaurs	First birds		First primates		Early human ancestors	Homo sapiens
EON	Phanerozoic—age of abundant and evident life											
ERA	Paleozoic—age of ancient life					Mesozoic—age of dominant reptiles			Cenozoic—age of dominant mammals			
PERIOD	Cambrian	Ordovician	Silurian	Devonian	Carboniferous	Permian	Triassic	Jurassic	Cretaceous	Paleogene			Quaternary
EPOCH					Mississippian Pennsylvanian				Lower Upper	Paleocene Eocene Oligocene Miocene Pilocene		Pleistocene Holocene	
	543	490	443	418	354 323	290	252	199.5	142 99	65 54.8 33.5 24	5	1.8 0.01	0

INDEX FOSSILS

Some fossils occur within limited time spans and yet are widespread enough to identify geological relationships over large areas. Even if the type of rock differs, or the strata are at different levels, if certain specific combinations of fossils are present in two distinct locations (see below), then geologists know that both strata are of similar age. Such fossils are known as index fossils. The order of strata and the fossil record reveal the relative age of different rock strata, but not in absolute terms how old they are.

INDEX TRILOBITE
Paradoxides is a useful trilobite for dating Middle Cambrian Rocks.

RADIOMETRIC DATING

Radiometric dating is a method of providing an absolute date for some minerals, rocks, and fossils. Radioisotopes of some elements, such as lead, carbon, and zircon, decay at a known rate. So, by measuring the amount of decayed isotopes of one of these elements within a particular mineral, rock, or fossil, and comparing it with the amount yet to decay, an absolute date of formation of the material can be established.

RADIOCARBON DATING
This dating technique is used for most fossils. However, it is useful only for very recent life forms in which bone or tissue remains unfossilized.

Stratum 1
Stratum 2
Same age
Same age
Stratum 1
Stratum 2

PALEOECOLOGY

As well as recording the biological history of life on Earth, the fossil record preserves the climatic history of the planet. The climatic conditions experienced by an area are reflected both in the rocks themselves and in the fossils preserved in them. For example, certain species of coral require warm, shallow water, and certain types of flowering plants will grow only in colder, drier environments. However, climatic conditions cannot be inferred by the presence of only one type of fossil. All of the fossils present (the assemblage) are taken into account in the assessment.

RADIOLARIA
Microscopic fossils of radiolarian skeletons are good indicators of ocean environments.

FOSSILIZED CORAL
Corals are relatively delicate life forms. Because of their sensitivity, they act as barometers of changes to climates and marine habitats.

FOSSIL FUELS

All fossil fuels contain carbon, and were formed from the remains of organic matter as a result of geologic processes. They include coal, petroleum, natural gas, shale oil, and bitumen. Around 90 percent of all the energy used in the industrially developed nations is produced from fossil fuels. Our reliance on them creates two major problems: depletion and pollution. Both of these have potentially serious consequences for our future on Earth and for all other life on our planet.

WILLIAM SMITH
This Englishman's 1815 geologic map of England and Wales was the predecessor of all geologic maps.

DEPLETION

The term depletion does not simply mean the exhaustion of existing deposits. There are strict limits, derived from the current state of technology, that determine how much of each deposit is economically recoverable. For example, a seam of coal 10 ft (3 m) thick cannot be economically recovered if it is buried under 300 ft (100 m) of other sediments that have to be removed before it can be mined.

POLLUTION

The principal concern regarding the burning of fossil fuels is its effect on the climate. All fossil fuels release carbon dioxide into the atmosphere when they are burned. Carbon dioxide makes up only about 0.03 percent of the air, but by absorbing infrared radiation, it has a huge effect on the heat balance of the atmosphere. With increased carbon dioxide in the atmosphere from burning fossil fuels, some of Earth's heat, which normally escapes back into space, is trapped, creating the possibility of potentially deadly climate change.

OIL FIELD
The search for oil relies heavily upon stratigraphy determined by the fossil record. Microfossils in drill cores and cuttings aid the search.

COAL SEAMS
Coal is the fossilized remains of plants accumulated over millions of years. Here, coal seams form in Portuguese cliffs.

BANDED JURASSIC LIMESTONE
This coastal cliff in Glamorgan, Wales, consists of exposed beds of Jurassic limestone; the stratification is useful for age-dating.

PLANTS

MAGNOLIA
Fossilized magnolia leaves 20 million years old have been found in Idaho.

THE FIRST FOSSIL EVIDENCE of land plants dates from the Ordovician Period (490 to 443 million years ago). It is believed that land plants evolved from marine algae that moved onto the land. The first plant fossils of a visible size were the psilophytes, which date from the Silurian Period (443 to 418 million years ago). Consisting of slender, forking tubes only an inch or so in length, they were little more than creeping root systems with no leaves.

The key evolutionary step during the Silurian was the development of vascular plants—those with an inner structure permitting the flow of water and nutrients through the entire plant. During the Early Devonian Period (418 to 354 million years ago), plants developed small clusters of light–capturing cells on their surfaces that eventually evolved into leaves. By the end of the Devonian, tree–sized plants called lycopods had evolved.

ALGAE

ALGAE WERE some of the earliest organisms to appear on Earth. Their fossil remains date back to the Precambrian, although the fossil record is far from complete. Those that fossilized had structures impregnated with silica, calcite, or aragonite, or had thick-walled cysts (body cavities). Fossils range from more or less complete individuals to carbonized impressions. The two genera shown here belong to different phyla in the kingdom Protista.

Bythotrephis gracilis

Impression

BYTHOTREPHIS SPECIMEN

BRANCHING
Bythotrephis *had a simple branching structure and little or no calcification. This brown alga is mainly found as impressions. It can be mistaken for worm burrows.*

Mastopora favus

Honeycomb pattern

GLOBULAR
Mastopora *was a green alga with a globular structure covered by a calcified coating. A reef dweller, it lived from the Ordovician to the Silurian.*

MASTOPORA SPECIMEN

HORSETAILS

THERE ARE LIVING SPECIES of horsetails, more properly referred to as sphenopsids. Their stems are conspicuously jointed, and the leaves form whorls around the stem. They grew in moist, rich soils; their tubers are found fossilized in fossil soils. Fossil sphenopsids are found as far back as the Late Devonian.

Asterophyllites equisetiformis

Jointed stem

GIANT HORSETAIL
Asterophyllites *was a giant horsetail, reaching 33 ft (10 m) in height. It lived from the Late Carboniferous to the Early Permian, in wetlands and swamps. Other horsetail species were closer to the size of the modern equivalents, reaching 20 in (50 cm) in height.*

ASTEROPHYLLITES SPECIMEN

MODERN SPHENOPSID

FERNS

FERNS, OR PETROPHYTA, enter the fossil record in the Middle Devonian. They vary in size from tiny, gauzy plants to large tree ferns several yards tall. Although their fossils can be confused with those of sphenopsids, fossil fern leaves are flat and arranged on fronds.

MODERN FERN

TREE FERN
Pecopteris *was a large tree fern that lived from the Early Carboniferous to the Early Permian. It reached 13 ft (3 m) in height. It usually broke up before fossilization.*

Pecopteris unita

MAZON CREEK
This site in Illinois is a rich area for fossilized ferns.

PECOPTERIS SPECIMEN

Impression

LYCOPODS

LYCOPODS ARE called club mosses today. They first appeared in the Late Silurian, and were most abundant during the Late Carboniferous. Modern lycopods are small, herbaceous plants, but during the Carboniferous they were the size of large trees, with dense foliage and their spores contained in cones. Fossils of lycopod logs that measure up to 3 ft (1 m) in diameter have been found.

MODERN CLUB MOSS

Bark

Scalelike surface

LEPIDODENDRON SPECIMEN

CLUB MOSS
Lepidodendron is the most prolific fossilized club moss, being found worldwide. It thrived during the Carboniferous, growing in hot, humid swampland. It reached 100 ft (30 m) in height.

Lepidodendron aculeatum

SEED FERNS

THESE PLANTS ORIGINATED in the late Devonian and were widespread toward the end of the Paleozoic Era. Known more properly as pteridosperms, they persisted into the Mesozoic, when they became extinct. They were small trees with fernlike leaves, some of which reached heights of up to 25 ft (8 m). Their foliage is not easily distinguished from that of other ferns of the period, but evidence of seeds puts the pteridosperms in their own group.

Paripteris gigantea

PARIPTERIS SPECIMEN

POLLEN ORGAN
Preserved in this fossil is the seedlike, pollen-bearing organ, or potoniea, of the Carboniferous Paripteris; it formed at the base of each leaf frond. The fern grew to a height of 16 ft (5 m) and lived in higher-altitude regions of hot swampland. Its fossils are found worldwide.

FORKED LEAVES
This shrublike fern reached a height of 13 ft (4 m) and is noted for its unusual "Y"-forked leaf. It is a Triassic fossil commonly found in the Southern Hemisphere, where it inhabited tropical forests of tree ferns.

DICROIDIUM SPECIMEN

Dicroidium species

Alethopteris serlii

ALETHOPTERIS SPECIMEN

FERN FROND
This fossilized frond segment is from Alethopteris, which grew to 16 ft (5 m). A Lower Carboniferous to Early Permian seed fern, it has thick, strong-veined leaflets. It flourished in hot swamps worldwide.

WEGENER'S THEORY OF CONTINENTAL DRIFT

Born in Berlin in 1880, Alfred Wegener taught meteorology at Hamburg and geophysics at the University of Graz. In about 1910, noting the apparent close fit between the coastlines of Africa and South America, he developed the idea that in the Late Paleozoic Era (about 250 million years ago) all the present-day continents had formed a single large mass that subsequently broke apart. He discovered that many closely related fossil organisms occurred in similar rock strata on widely separated continents, particularly those found both in the Americas and in Africa. The moving apart of the continents he termed "continental drift." However, he was unable to explain satisfactorily the driving forces behind the continents' movement, and by 1930 his theory had been rejected by most geologists and had fallen into obscurity. It was not until the 1960s that sea-floor spreading was discovered, and his theory was resurrected as an important part of the now well-accepted theory of plate tectonics.

WEGENER
Fifty years passed before evidence appeared to support Wegener's theories. He died in 1930.

Glossopteris species

KEY TO THEORY
Glossopteris fossils found on different continents played an important part in Wegener's concept of continental drift.

GLOSSOPTERIS SPECIMEN

A SINGLE LANDMASS
Alfred Wegener theorized that all of the continents were once connected in a single landmass that he named Pangea, which subsequently broke apart.

EUROPE · ASIA
NORTH AMERICA
AFRICA
SOUTH AMERICA
AUSTRALIA

170 MYA

NORTH AMERICA
EUROPE · ASIA
AFRICA
SOUTH AMERICA

95 MYA

Leaf

THE ARIZONA PETRIFIED FOREST

COVERING A VAST AREA OF ARIZONA, THE FOSSILIZED WOOD OF THE PETRIFIED FOREST PRESERVES AN ENTIRE TRIASSIC ECOSYSTEM.

ARGENTINIAN FOREST
There are a number of petrified forests worldwide. The Petrified Forest National Park (above) is in Santa Cruz province, southern Argentina.

The Arizona Petrified Forest National Park occupies an area of 146 sq miles (378 sq km) approximately 20 miles (30 km) east of Holbrook, Arizona. The area is high desert, and extends into the Painted Desert (see p.66). Erosion has exposed extensive areas of petrified, or fossil, wood, including whole logs and entire trees.

Formed by the invasion of minerals into cavities between and within the cells of natural wood, this fossil wood is preserved from the Triassic Period (200–250 million years ago), when the Petrified Forest area of Arizona was a large basin on the edge of the huge landmass known as "Pangea" (see p.333). Lush forests covered the landscape, with towering coniferous trees up to 9 ft (3 m) in diameter and almost 200 ft (60 m) tall. Ferns, cycads, and giant horsetails lined the waterways.

THE PROCESS OF PETRIFICATION

As trees died or fell, some were deposited directly in river beds or on floodplains, while others were washed into the current area of the forest by flood water. Most of the trees decomposed, but others were buried in the accumulating sediments, which included a considerable amount of volcanic ash. Silica from the ash was dissolved by ground water, and as it percolated downward, it filled or replaced cell walls, crystallizing as chalcedony—cryptocrystalline quartz. The ground water was also iron-rich, which combined with quartz during petrification, creating the rainbow of colors seen in the fossil wood of Arizona today. Eventually the forest area was buried by further accumulation of sediments. Many millions of years later, all of north-central Arizona, including the solidified sediments containing the fossilized logs, was uplifted, creating the Colorado Plateau. Erosion removed the overlying rock layers and exposed the petrified logs.

CROSS SECTION
The cell-by-cell replacement of original plant tissue by silica was so precise that in many instances the internal structure—sometimes even the cell structure—was faithfully reproduced, as well as the log's external shape.

Preserved growth rings

Original cell structure replaced by chalcedony

PETRIFIED FOREST LANDSCAPE
Brilliant reds and yellows predominate in the Forest today. Most of the fossilized logs are from three extinct trees: Araucarioxylon arizonicum, Woodworthia, *and* Schilderia.

CONIFERS

PLANTS THAT REPRODUCE by means of an exposed seed, including all conifers, are known as gymnosperms. Conifers are usually shrubs or trees that produce woody cones of various shapes and sizes. The leaves are often needle-shaped but can be flat and broad. Their woody trunks are often rich in resin. They made up a large part of Jurassic forests, although they appeared earlier, in the Late Carboniferous. Coniferous fossils can be needles or leaves, cones, or the wood itself. Most fossil wood, commonly called petrified wood, is from conifers. Large deposits of fossil conifer wood are referred to as petrified forests (see The Arizona Petrified Forest, pp.334–35).

Conifer species

IDENTIFYING SIGNS
Fossil coniferous wood often shows immaculately preserved cell structure and growth rings. It is possible in some instances to determine individual species, but to do so usually requires close microscopic examination and detailed knowledge.

Wide growth ring

CONIFEROUS WOOD SPECIMEN

Shale

Branch imprint

SEQUOIADENDRON SPECIMEN

Sequoiadendron affinis

GIANT REDWOOD
Sequoiadendron *trees were giant redwoods like the modern* Sequoia *but even larger. Some reached a height of 260 ft (80 m). They lived from the Jurassic to the Recent.*

DESERT FOREST
The Petrified Forest National Park in Santa Cruz Province of Argentina has an area of 39 square miles (100 square km). Once a forest of Araucaria trees (see far right), it was buried by a rapid fall of volcanic ash during the Early Cretaceous.

ARAUCARIA SPECIMEN

MONKEY PUZZLE
Araucaria *trees appeared in the Jurassic and are found worldwide—living species include the monkey puzzle tree and the Norfolk Island pine. Minutely silicified fossils, such as the* Araucaria *cone shown above, were created in the Petrified Forest of Argentina (see left).*

Araucaria miribilis

MODERN ARAUCARIA

ANGIOSPERMS

FLOWERS CHARACTERIZE angiosperm plants, of which there are over 250,000 living species. They first appeared in the Early Cretaceous, although the oldest fossil remains from that time are limited to pollen grains. The earliest angiosperm plant fossils are most similar to small bushes or small herbaceous plants. At the beginning of the Late Cretaceous, woody angiosperms began to evolve, including several modern groups, such as the magnolia, laurel, sycamore, and rose families. In general, the woody angiosperms have broad leaves that are often fossilized, but fossil angiosperm wood is difficult to distinguish from fossil conifer wood. Fossil palm wood is the one exception (see *Palmoxylon*, right).

ANCESTRAL OAK
Quercus, *the genus name for oak trees, appeared during the Eocene. Found worldwide, its fossilized wood exhibits the same characteristics as living oak.*

Quercus species

QUERCUS SPECIMEN

Palmoxylon species

Vascular pores

PALMOXYLON SPECIMEN

EARLY PALM
Palmoxylon *is a typical fossil palm wood. It has no growth rings and has many dark, round spots—the vascular tissues through which water and other fluids were conducted in the tree. It lived from the Paleocene to the Pliocene, and is found worldwide.*

MODERN PALM

INVERTEBRATES

EARLY FOSSIL EVIDENCE of invertebrates, the first multicellular animals, comes from the Pound Quartzite of the Ediacara Hills, north of Adelaide, South Australia. These fossils date from about 700 to 670 million years ago, during the Precambrian Period (which began about 3.8 billion years ago). The fossils include soft corals, sponges, jellyfish, various kinds of worms, and as-yet unexplained forms. It was not until around the beginning of the Cambrian Period, 543 million years ago, that animals first began to develop hard shells. Because these are preserved more readily as fossils, we have a much clearer picture of the evolution of invertebrate life beyond that time. The rapid diversification of life during the Cambrian Period is referred to as the Cambrian Explosion, although some paleontologists think it may just represent an explosion of easily fossilized life. Evidence of land invertebrates—arthropod tracks—appears in the Ordovician.

EDIACARAN FOSSIL
This Late Precambrian specimen from Australia is one of the earliest fossils of a complex animal life form.

FORAMINIFERA

FORAMINIFERA ARE MINUTE, sometimes microscopic, single-celled organisms, some of which secrete a shell made of calcite. They belong to the kingdom Protista. They have lived since the Cambrian in a wide range of ocean environments. There are many species of them, and they have existed in such large numbers that their shells can constitute an entire rock unit. Limestone principally made of these shells is called foraminiferal limestone, and may appear to be made from grains of rice.

Shell · **ALVEOLINA SPECIMEN**

SHELLS OF THE PYRAMIDS
Nummulites is a relatively large foraminiferan with a shell made up of small internal chambers, rather like those of a nautilus. The pyramids of Egypt were built from nummulitic limestone, which is found in Europe, Asia, and the Middle East.

Nummulites ghinensis

NUMMULITES SPECIMEN

GRAINS OF RICE
Alveolina *has the grain-of-rice shape typical of a number of foraminiferan species. It is a common species in foraminiferal limestones. Identification of individual foraminiferan species is difficult for the nonprofessional.*

Alveolina elliptica

ALVEOLINA ELLIPTICA

WORMS

MANY SOFT-BODIED invertebrate groups are loosely called worms, but fossils of worms rarely occur. What are preserved are their burrows and the tubes of calcite, secreted by some of them as dwellings, which in some areas were numerous enough to be reef-forming. Body details of some worms are preserved in the Middle Cambrian Burgess Shale of Canada, and the even earlier Ediacaran rocks of Australia.

Rotularia bognoriensis

Glomerula plexus

Coiled tube

SEA SPIRAL
Rotularia *was a ridged living tube coiled into a flat spiral. This worm was free-living on the sandy floors of shallow oceans. It lived during the Eocene, and is found mainly in Europe.*

MODERN SEA WORM

ROTULARIA SPECIMEN

GLOMERULA SPECIMEN

TANGLED TUBES
The living tubes of Glomerula *grew irregularly and twisted, with the tubes of a number of individuals intertwining. It was probably a filter-feeder, and the convoluted masses of worms lived unattached on the sea bed.* Glomerula *is found worldwide, and survived from the Early Jurassic to the Paleocene.*

SPONGES

FOSSIL SPONGES APPEAR from the Cambrian onward, and reached their peak during the Cretaceous. Sponges are animals that feed by filtering nutrients from water. Several classes of sponges have become extinct, but living sponges have evolved little from their earliest ancestors. As fossils, they can be mistaken for corals, but the surfaces of sponges only show the coarsest ornamentation, and their walls tend to be thicker than those of corals.

ACTINOSTROMA SPECIMEN

Irregular shape

GLASS SPONGE
Hydnoceras *represents the class of sponges sometimes called glass sponges. Their skeletons are composed of tiny, needlelike splinters of silica in a meshlike network. Living examples are confined to deep water, but they were once found at all depths.*

Hydnoceras tuberosum

MODERN SPONGE \ *Main opening*

HYDNOCERAS SPECIMEN

Concentric growth layers

REEF-BUILDER
Actinostroma *is an example of a stromatoporoid sponge. The skeleton was composed of calcareous splinters. They lived in large colonies and were major reef-builders. In the Silurian and Devonian they were concentrated in such numbers that their skeletons became important rock-formers.*

Actinostroma clathratum

BRYOZOANS

BRYOZOANS FIRST APPEARED in the Ordovician, and more than 4,000 species are living today. These creatures appeared in the Ordovician and resemble miniature corals, and are easily confused with them. Like corals, they are colony animals, but they are more closely related to brachiopods. They secrete calcareous skeletons, and each individual forms connections with its neighbors. They form freestanding colonies, or sheetlike encrustations on stones or other shells.

Schizoretepora notopachys

COMPLEX FRONDS
This Schizoretepora *bryozoan is a colony of complex folded fronds. It is one of several similar-appearing species, and is found worldwide.*

SCHIZORETEPORA SPECIMEN

SEA MAT
Constelleria, *a sea mat, lived from the Ordovician to the Silurian, and is typical of a freestanding bryozoan, living on the sea bed. It is found in North America, Europe, and Asia.*

Fenestella plebeia

FENESTELLA SPECIMEN

LACE CORAL
Fenestella, *a lace coral, is found both as a freestanding bryozoan and as a flat encrustation. It lived from the Silurian to the Permian and is found worldwide.*

Constellaria antheloidea

CONSTELLARIA SPECIMEN

GRAPTOLITES

A GROUP OF SMALL, floating, aquatic, colonial animals that first appeared during the Cambrian Period, graptolites became extinct during the Carboniferous Period. They had a fingernail-like outer covering and no mineralized hard parts. They are most frequently preserved as carbonaceous impressions on black shales, although they are sometimes found in limestones. They had one or more branches, and are easily mistaken for fossil plants rather than animals. They underwent distinct evolutionary changes over time, making them very useful for age-dating rocks.

Orthograptus intermedius

STRAIGHT BRANCH
Orthograptus *is a typical branchlike graptolite, exhibiting a single branch that is actually two branches back to back. It is found worldwide in rocks of the Lower to Middle Ordovician.*

Triangular section

ORTHOGRAPTUS SPECIMEN

Coiled form

MONOGRAPTUS SPECIMEN

Monograptus convolutus

COILED BRANCH
Monograptus *is one of a group of single-branch graptolites with distinctive theca (the tubular structure that housed each individual). They evolved rapidly, were distributed worldwide, and are useful for dating and correlating Silurian rocks.*

CORALS

FIRST APPEARING in the Ordovician, corals are found mainly as treelike or tube-like fossils. Corals are anemone-like organisms that secrete calcareous skeletons. Each individual in the colony forms its own living space called a calice. Calices of corals that live in colonies can be circular (as in *Favosites*), polygonal (as in *Actinocyathus*), or elongate (as in *Trachyphylla*). Through geologic time, corals have formed extensive limestone deposits and reefs. Corals can be mistaken for bryozoans, algae, or sponges. Two coral groups are extinct (Rugosa and Tabulata).

CAPITAN REEF
The fossil-rich Capitan Reef in southeastern New Mexico is the home of the huge Carlsbad Caverns.

Septastraea marylandica

TABULATE CORAL
Halysites is an example of the extinct group Tabulata. Its calices are arranged in chains, rather than in clumps, which curve, divide, and rejoin. Halysites lived during the Jurassic in warm, shallow water and in reefs.

HALYSITES SPECIMEN

Halysites catenularius

Calice

RUGOSA CORAL
An extinct Rugosa coral from the Early Carboniferous, Actinocyathus developed polygonal calices in a honeycomb-like pattern. It lived in shallow water.

ACTINOCYATHUS SPECIMEN

Actinocyathus crassiconus

SEPTASTRAEA SPECIMEN

HORN CORAL
Septastraea colonies have a varied form: some are branching, like the specimen above; others form nodular masses. The coral lived in warm water, in shallow reefs, from the Miocene to the Pliocene.

Colpophyllia stellata

COLPOPHYLLIA SPECIMEN

CORAL REEFS AND ATOLLS
Found in many shallow, warm-water seas, coral reefs and atolls provide evidence of highly diverse fossil fauna and flora. The bulk of a reef is a mass of cemented skeletons and shell fragments of animals that once inhabited the reef. The Solnhofen Limestone in Germany—which during the Jurassic was an extensive coral reef with lagoons—has provided geologists with evidence of more than 450 species of Jurassic animals.

BRAIN CORAL
Colpophyllia, an example of the Scleractinia group, has living relatives. These are commonly called brain corals, and live in warm, shallow seas and in reefs.

TRACHYPHYLLIA SPECIMEN

MODERN CORAL
When the corals living today die, their hard parts remain as part of the reef structure, helping it grow over time.

MODERN CORAL

SOLITARY CORAL
Trachyphyllia, one of the Scleractinia group, appeared in the Miocene and still has living relatives. It grows on the sea floor in areas of flat sand, and around reefs. These solitary corals can appear similar to extinct Rugosa corals.

Trachyphyllia chipolana

CRUSTACEANS | TRILOBITES

CRUSTACEANS ARE carnivorous creatures belonging to the phylum Arthropoda (see panel, right). Crabs, lobsters, shrimp, and woodlice are modern crustaceans and are mainly aquatic, like their fossil ancestors. They differ from trilobites and other arthropods in that they have two pairs of appendages in front of the mouth, and three pairs of limbs near the mouth that function as jaws. The last abdominal appendage may be flattened to form a tail fan.

MODERN CRAB

Large claw

Abdomen

PALEOCARPILIUS SPECIMEN

MUD CRAB
Paleocarpilius *is one of several species of crabs that are found as fossils. It lived in Europe and Africa, but various other crab species are found across the world. Separated claws, legs, and shells are also common.*

Paleocarpilius aquilinus

BARNACLE
Appearing in the Eocene Period, Balanus *still inhabits the world's oceans. Fossil barnacles are found worldwide and look much like their modern counterparts.*

Calcareous plate

Balanus concavus

BALANUS SPECIMEN

ALTHOUGH NOW EXTINCT, trilobites were arthropods, a large and successful group of living organisms. Trilobites first appeared at the beginning of the Cambrian, and a few species persisted into the Permian. They had an external skeleton composed of material similar to that of the shells of modern beetles. Most trilobites had a pair of compound eyes, although some of them were eyeless. Their sizes range from only a fraction of an inch to the huge *Paradoxides harlani*, which grew to more than 18 in (45 cm) in length. Trilobites are easily recognized by their distinctive three-segment form, consisting of a head, tail, and segmented thorax. Trilobites could roll themselves up for protection like the modern woodlouse (which is actually a crustacean), and *Phacops* is often found in a rolled-up position.

DEFENSE POSITION
Phacops *had large eyes and lived in shallow, warm seas. This specimen was found in the defensive rolled-up position. This species is distributed worldwide.*

MODERN WOODLOUSE

Phacops africanus

Rolled-up position

PHACOPS SPECIMEN

Thorax

ACADAGNOSTUS SPECIMEN

Acadagnostus exaratus

TINY TRILOBITE
This trilobite was $\frac{1}{36}$ in (8 mm) long, blind, with two thoracic segments. It was found in North America, Europe, and Australia, and lived in deep water.

STRAWBERRY HEAD
The head shield of this trilobite earned it the name of the "strawberry-headed" trilobite. It lived worldwide in shallow seas during the Lower Ordovician to Silurian.

TRILOBITE BROOCH
This superbly fossilized trilobite has been mounted in a gold brooch.

ARTHROPODS

The bodies of all arthropods are covered by a shell, and it is this suit of armor that has allowed the group to become so successful. In addition, the shell fossilizes easily, providing a good fossil record. There are four subphyla of arthropods: *Trilobita*, *Uniramia* (including the class *Insecta*), *Crustacea*, and *Chelicerata*.

BURGESS SHALE
This shale in the Canadian Rockies is a rich source of trilobites and many other kinds of fauna.

Curved shell

Head tubercules

Encrinurus variolaris

ENCRINURUS SPECIMEN

CHELICERATES

LIKE OTHER ARTHROPODS (see panel, opposite), chelicerates have an external skeleton made of a material composed of chitin (a complex sugar) and protein. The body is segmented into a head and thorax shield, and an abdomen. The segments bear six pairs of jointed appendages—the first pair, the chelicerae, are claws for catching food; the second pair has various functions; and the remaining pairs are dedicated to movement. They lack the antennae of other arthropods. Chelicerates include eurypterids, horseshoe crabs, scorpions, and spiders. The latter two groups may have evolved from their sea–dwelling ancestors. All chelicerates are relatively uncommon in fossil form.

HORSESHOE CRAB

Mesolimulus *lived from the Jurassic to the Cretaceous, and is an ancestor of modern horseshoe crabs. It was tolerant of changes in salinity, and laid its eggs in shallow mud-flats. This particular species is found in Europe and the Middle East.*

MESOLIMULUS SPECIMEN

Mesolimulus walchii

SEA SCORPION

Paracarcinosoma *is a eurypterid, a scorpion-like sea creature from the Silurian, and a contemporary of trilobites. It has been suggested that the decline in trilobite species was due to the eurypterids. They are found in Europe, North America, and Asia, and lived in the sea and in fresh to brackish water.*

Paired appendages

Abdomen

Paracarcinosoma obesa

PARACARCINOSOMA SPECIMEN

Graeophonus analicus

EARLY SPIDER

Graeophonus *is a close relative of modern spiders. Its eyes were raised from its head on distinct knobs. It is found in North America and Europe, where it flourished in shallow-water habitats such as swamps and lagoons.*

GRAEOPHONUS SPECIMEN

INSECTS

INSECTS LIVE BOTH ON land and in fresh water, and are distinguished from other arthropods (see panel, opposite) by having three pairs of legs. The earliest insects appeared in the Devonian, and were followed in the Permian by giant insects such as the dragonflies of the order Protodonata, some of which had a wingspan of more than 20 in (50 cm). Damselflies and mayflies evolved around this time, and still exist today. The first insects were wingless, but by the Upper Carboniferous wings had evolved, providing the first powered flight. Most insect fossils are identifiable if well preserved.

Wing imprint

DRAGONFLY

Petalura *is a typical dragonfly, found in Europe and Australasia. It is a carnivorous insect—nymphs and adults feed on small aquatic and flying animals. Petalura is found in rocks from the Jurassic to the Recent.*

Petalura species

PETALURA SPECIMEN

Abdomen

MODERN DRAGONFLY

WATER BEETLE

Hydrophilius *is a type of insect, commonly called a water beetle, that survives today. It evolved in the Pleistocene. The beetle feeds on plant and animal matter, and its larvae are carnivorous. This specimen is preserved in tar sand.*

COCKROACH

Cockroaches *have been around for a very long time. This specimen is from the Lower Carboniferous and was found in the UK.*

Embedded beetle

Tar sand

Hydrophilius species

HYDROPHILIUS SPECIMEN

Archimylacris eggintoni

Ironstone nodule

ARCHIMYLACRIS SPECIMEN

341

BRACHIOPODS

ABUNDANT AS FOSSILS, brachiopods appeared at the beginning of the Cambrian Period, and a few species are still living today. More than 35,000 species are known, with more being discovered each year. In some Paleozoic rocks they are the most abundant fauna. Brachiopods are bottom-feeding marine animals composed of two shells, or valves. Viewed from above, the shells are symmetrical. Most fossil brachiopods have a small hole at the central tip of the bottom valve. Here there emerged a fleshy stalk, called a pedicle, with which the brachiopod attached itself to the sea floor. There are two main groups within the phylum Brachiopoda: the Articulata, the shells of which are hinged, and the hingeless Inarticulata.

SMOOTH SHELL
Pentamerus *inhabited shallow water, often in huge numbers. It is from the Silurian, and is found worldwide.*

Convex shell

Opening for pedicle

PENTAMERUS SPECIMEN

Pentamerus oblongus

LAMP SHELL
Digonella *and brachiopods of similar appearance are sometimes referred to as lamp shells. Found worldwide, the animal is from the Middle Jurassic. It lived in shallow waters, where it attached itself to soft mud or fragments of other shells.*

Digonella digona

DIGONELLA SPECIMEN

RIBBED SHELL
Platystrophia *is an Ordovician brachiopod found worldwide. It lived on lime mud and sandy sea floors.*

Platystrophia biforata

PLATYSTROPHIA SPECIMEN

Sharp rib

LAMP SHELLS EMBEDDED IN ROCK
Digonella *and other lamp shells are often found fossilized in clusters, half-buried in fine-grained, muddy limestones.*

BUTTERFLY SHELL
Perhaps the most recognizable of all brachiopods, the spirifers are sometimes called butterfly shells. Mucrospirifer *is from the Devonian, lived on soft mud, and is found worldwide.*

Deep fold

Overlapping growth layers

MUCROSPIRIFER SPECIMEN

Mucrospirifer mucronata

Chonetes species

Short spines

LITTLE RELATIVE
Chonetes *is a comparatively small brachiopod, with a thin shell. It lived from the Carboniferous to the Permian, and is distributed worldwide. It lived on soft lime mud.*

CHONETES SPECIMEN

LEPTAENA SPECIMEN

WRINKLED SHELL
An Ordovician brachiopod, Leptaena *is usually found in fine-grained, limey shales. Its wrinkles helped to anchor it in sand. It is found worldwide.*

Leptaena species

FARO BEACH, GOTLAND
Gotland, a Swedish island in the Baltic Sea, is a rich source of brachiopod fossils.

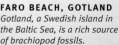

SCAPHOPODS AND CHITONS

Helminthochiton turnacianus

SCAPHOPODS AND CHITONS are two classes of mollusks (see panel, p.344). Scaphopods had tapering, tubelike shells, which were open at both ends. The head and foot of the animal occupied the larger end, which was buried in sea-floor sediment. Chitons had a shell of eight overlapping segments, similar to trilobites. Underneath they had a foot that exerted a powerful grip on hard surfaces.

Dentalium sexangulum

DENTALIUM SPECIMEN

HELMINTHOCHITON SPECIMEN

TOOTHLIKE SHELL
Dentalium is a typical scaphopod. It appeared in the Middle Triassic, but still has living relatives. It lived in a fairly wide range of ocean-floor environments.

COAT-OF-MAIL SHELL
Helminthochiton is an Ordovician to Carboniferous chiton that lived in warm seas on algae-covered debris. It is usually found as segments in Europe and North America.

BIVALVES

THESE MOLLUSKS (see panel, p.344) are composed of two valves connected by a hinge of organic material. The valves generally have interlocking teeth along the line of the hinge. They differ from brachiopods in that the valves are not symmetrical, and they lack a pedicle hole. There are many different kinds of bivalves, and they are classified by their hinges. Most bivalves were filter-feeders, and many burrowed into sediment, stone, or wood. Others attached themselves by means of their foot to other submerged objects.

Pinna hartmannii

FIMBRIA SPECIMEN

Net ornament

PEN SHELL
Also known as the pen shell or fan mussel, Pinna appeared in the Early Carboniferous and is still present. It lives in groups, with its pointed end buried in the sea-floor sediment.

BASKET SHELL
Found worldwide, examples of Fimbria still live today. This bivalve appeared in the Middle Jurassic, living in warm, shallow seas. Its ornamentation gives its surface a netlike appearance.

PINNA SPECIMEN

Fimbria subpectunculus

PIERRE SHALE
The Cretaceous Pierre Shale of the western US contains countless numbers of bivalve fossils.

Ligament pit

PECTEN SPECIMEN

GRYPHEA SPECIMEN

Gryphea arcuata

GLYCYMERIS SPECIMEN

Glycymeris brevirostris

BITTERSWEET CLAM
Glycymeris developed a thick shell, with weak growth ribs and ornamentation. The area of the hinge is grooved and triangular. It lived in shallow waters, burrowing in sand and mud.

DEVIL'S TOENAIL
Gryphea is popularly called the devil's toenail. It is a thick, curled shell, in which the smaller valve fits like a lid into the larger valve. It lived from the Lower Triassic to the Lower Jurassic, on muddy sea beds.

SCALLOP FOREBEAR
The strong radiating ribs and fan shape are the most noticeable features of Oxytoma. It lived from the Lower Triassic to the Lower Cretaceous, dwelled in a variety of marine environments, and is found worldwide.

OXYTOMA SPECIMEN

Pecten beudanti

Oxytoma

SCALLOP
Pecten appeared in the Eocene, and today's scallop species are living relatives. It has a large, circular shell, with broad, radiating ribs. Its right valve is convex, while its left valve is concave. Scallops prefer moderately shallow waters, and a clean, sandy sea bed.

GASTROPODS

FIRST APPEARING IN the Cambrian Period, gastropods have developed into the most successful of all mollusks (see panel, below). There are over 60,000 living species, inhabiting marine, freshwater, and terrestrial environments. The living animal has a head with eyes and a mouth, and a large foot for crawling. All of these disappear during fossilization, so classification is based on shell characteristics. In general, gastropods have a single, spiral, asymmetric shell principally composed of aragonite, although some have calcite interlayering. A few species show no spiraling. Most gastropods are easily recognizable as such, although a few, such as *Platyceras*, can somewhat resemble certain bivalves.

MODERN CONUS

Conus sauridens

CONICAL CARNIVORES
Cone shells, represented here by Conus, first appeared in the Lower Cretaceous and are still living. They are carnivores, eating worms, other mollusks, and even fish. They live in a variety of ocean environments and are found worldwide.

CONUS SPECIMEN

SEA SNAIL
Platyceras, which lived worldwide from the Silurian to the Early Carboniferous, existed in close cooperation with crinoids, and has been found fossilized connected to them. Its shell is tightly wound for the first few coils, then rapidly spreads outward.

Platyceras haliotis

PLATYCERAS SPECIMEN

TURRITELLA
Commonly known as turritella, this gastropod first appeared in the Lower Eocene and has modern relatives. A large deposit of silicified Archimediella occurs in Wyoming, where it is called Turritella Agate.

Archimediella pontoni

Flattened whorl

Square opening

ARCHIMEDIELLA SPECIMEN

CALLISTOMA SPECIMEN

TOP SHELL
Cone-shaped Callistoma first appeared in the Early Cretaceous. It is informally called a top shell. It is extensively ornamented with granulated spiral cords. Callistoma remains an inhabitant of rocky shorelines worldwide.

Callistoma nodulosum

Granulated whorl

Sharp-edged whorl

EUOMPHALUS SPECIMEN

RIDGED DISC
Euomphalus lived from the Silurian to the Middle Permian. It has a disc-shaped, coiled shell with a slightly raised spire. The whorls are stepped, creating a sharp ridge between them. This sea snail lived on marine vegetation, and is found worldwide.

Euomphalus pentangulus

ROUNDED SPIRE
Bourguetia lived from the Middle Triassic to the Lower Jurassic. Although similar in appearance to land snails, it lived among coral reefs in shallow, warm seas. Fossils of this sea snail are found principally in Europe and New Zealand.

Bourguetia semanni

Whorls regularly increasing in size.

BOURGUETIA SPECIMEN

Long spire

MOLLUSKS

The phylum Mollusca comprises a large and varied group of animals that, for the most part, have lived in salt water. A few moved into fresh water, and an even smaller group, the snails, moved onto the land. Most mollusks have calcium carbonate shells. There are six main groups, or classes, of mollusks: monoplacophorans, chitons, scaphopods, bivalves, gastropods, and cephalopods. All mollusk groups appeared during the Cambrian,

apart from the scaphopods, which appeared during the Ordovician. By the end of the Cambrian, mollusks were to be found everywhere and in great variety. There are currently about 75,000 living species of mollusks, thriving in a great range of salt-water and freshwater habitats.

MUSSELS
For centuries people have collected mussels and consumed the soft-bodied animals inside them.

NAUTILOIDS AND AMMONOIDS

THESE TWO GROUPS OF CEPHALOPODS are among the most advanced mollusks (see panel, opposite). Ammonoids evolved from nautiloids, which appeared during the Ordovician. Only a single genus of nautiloid survives today, the pearly nautilus. Nautiloids and ammonoids are both characterized by a series of internal chambers that permitted the animal to control its own buoyancy. All the chambers were connected by a central stem called a siphuncle. Most were good swimmers, and were scavengers, carnivores, or both. In general, nautiloids can be distinguished from ammonoids by the pattern formed by their sutures, the seams between their chambers. In nautiloids, the line of the sutures is straight or gently curving. In ammonoids it is highly complex, often appearing fernlike. The ammonoids emerged in the Devonian, and became extinct at the end of the Cretaceous. They evolved rapidly, and are good fossils for dating Late Paleozoic and Mesozoic rocks.

CENOCERAS SPECIMEN

Cenoceras species

MODERN CHAMBERED NAUTILUS

NAUTILOID SIMPLICITY
Cenoceras is a nautiloid, and exhibits the straight or gently curving lines of its sutures. A marine animal that lived from the Lower Triassic to the Middle Jurassic, it was a bottom-feeder.

Rounded shell

Mantelliceras species

PATTERN OF JOINS
The ammonoid Phylloceras illustrates the elaborate suture patterns developed by the ammonoids. Its external ornamentation was simple, but the polished internal mold (right) shows the complex suturing of its chambers. It lived from the Early Jurassic to the Lower Cretaceous, and its streamlined shape suggests it was a good swimmer.

PHYLLOCERAS SPECIMEN

MANTELLICERAS SPECIMEN

Phylloceras species

PROMINENT RIBS
Mantelliceras shows the heavier ribbing developed by many ammonoids. A European species is shown above, but others of similar appearance, some with heavier and more elaborate ribbing, evolved in other parts of the world during the Cretaceous.

Goniatites crenistria

EVOLVED SUTURING
Goniatites shows the increasing elaboration of suturing present in intermediates between nautiloids and ammonoids. It is distributed worldwide, and lived during the Early Carboniferous. It was a denizen of shallow, shelving seas and reefs.

POPULAR COLLECTION SITE
The beaches at Lyme Regis, England, are littered with rocks bearing thousands of ammonite specimens.

GONIATITES SPECIMEN

BACCULITES SPECIMEN

Bacculites species

STRAIGHT AMMONOID
In effect, Bacculites was an uncoiled ammonoid, since only the first portion of its shell was coiled. It occurred in huge numbers in some localities, almost to the exclusion of any other ammonoid species. Some individuals grew to more than 3 ft (1 m) in length. Bacculites lived during the Lower Cretaceous.

345

BELEMNOIDS AND SQUID

BELEMNOIDS AND SQUID are members of the cephalopod group of mollusks (see panel, p.344) that includes today's cuttlefish, octopus, and squid. Belemnoids are found particularly frequently as fossils because they had a hard internal shell made from calcite, known as the guard. While on rare occasions soft parts are found fossilized, the guard is usually all that remains. Belemnoids first appeared during the Early Carboniferous Period and became extinct during the Eocene.

achyteuthis abbreviata

U-shaped chamber

Guard

PACHYTEUTHIS SPECIMENS

Pyrite replacement

GUARDED PREDATOR
Pachyteuthis *is a typical belemnite, and its guard is found fossilized worldwide. It lived from the Middle to Late Jurassic, and was a scavenger or predator. The U-shaped hole at the bottom of the guard housed the chambered internal shell that helped to regulate buoyancy.*

SLIM SCAVENGER
Belemnitella *is a Late Cretaceous belemnite that inhabited shallow waters. Its guard tapers gently and has a pointed tip. It is often found grouped in large numbers.*

MODERN SQUID
A close living relative of the belemnites, the squid has an internal support, the pen, made of chitin, a hornlike substance.

Impression of veins on guard surface

Belemnitella mucronata

BELEMNITELLA SPECIMEN

ECHINOIDS

COMMONLY CALLED SEA URCHINS and sand dollars, echinoids are a group of echinoderms (see panel, right) with a rigid, globular skeleton made of thin calcite plates. Many possessed spines, also made of calcite, attached to the body by a ball-and-socket arrangement. The spines were used for defense and, in some cases, walking. Some echinoids were bottom-feeders, foraging on the sea bed; others tended to burrow into soft silt layers. Spines are often found fossilized separately.

ECHINODERMS

Characterized by their hard, spiny covering or skin and their five-fold radial symmetry, the phylum Echinodermata appeared as fossils in the Lower Cambrian. They evolved rapidly into many species in eight different classes, including the echinoids, asteroids, crinoids, ophiuroids, blastoids, and cystoids. They are well represented in the fossil record, with approximately 13,000 fossil species so far described.

MODERN ECHINOID
Today's spiny sea urchin is a living relative of species now known only from fossils.

STARFISH
Modern starfish species belong to one class of living echinoderms.

Tubercle

Temnocidaris sceptrifera

Detached spine

LAKE TEXOMA
Many Lower Cretaceous echinoids are found around this lake on the Texas–Oklahoma state line.

SPINY SEA URCHIN
Temnocidaris *is a Lower Cretaceous spiny echinoid found mainly in Europe. It has five radially arranged plates with large tubercles (the tubercles are the attachment points for the spines).*

SEA URCHINS FOSSILIZED IN CHALK
These superb examples of the Cretaceous sea urchin Tylocidaris *retain many of their clublike spines.*

TEMNOCIDARIS SPECIMEN

Attached spine

Encope micropora

SAND DOLLAR
Encope *appeared in the Miocene and is still a living species. Commonly called a sand dollar, it lives in tropical waters and shows the bilateral symmetry common in burrowing echinoids.*

ENCOPE SPECIMEN

HEMIASTER SPECIMEN

Hemiaster batnensis

HEART URCHIN
Hemiaster *is representative of a group of echinoids commonly called heart urchins. It appeared in the Cretaceous, is found worldwide, and has living relatives. It buried itself in mud and lived by filter-feeding organic material from the mud.*

ASTEROIDS

POPULARLY CALLED STARFISH, asteroids are a group of echinoderms (see panel, opposite), recorded as far back as the Ordivician. They usually have five arms, although a few species have more. The body has relatively little calcified material in its makeup, so entire examples preserved as fossils are very rarely found.

Pentasteria cotteswoldiae

BURROWER
Pentasteria, *an asteroid of the Jurassic to Middle Cretaceous, is found principally in Europe. It probably burrowed into shallow sand.*

PENTASTERIA SPECIMEN

CRINOIDS

ALSO KNOWN AS SEA LILIES, crinoids are a group of echinoderms (see panel, opposite) that usually possess a cup-shaped body and five or more feathery arms. They are attached to the sea bed by a flexible stem made up of disclike plates that are either circular or pentagonal in cross-section. The cup is also made of a number of loosely connected plates. The cup and the stem tend to fall apart after death, so crinoid fossils are most often found as segments of stems and arms, and as disarticulated cup-plates. Crinoid skeletal components are made of calcite and fossilize well. Complete crinoids are rare and beautiful fossils. Crinoids evolved rapidly into a large number of now-extinct species, and thus are good index fossils for dating rocks, particularly those of the Paleozoic Era.

MODERN SEA LILY ON A SPONGE

SAGENOCRINITES SPECIMEN

SEA LILY
Sagenocrinites *is found in Europe and North America. This Middle Silurian crinoid shows all the basic components of crinoid skeletons: the cup-shaped body, arms, and stem.*

Sagenocrinites expansus

OPHIUROIDS

ALTHOUGH THEY ARE starfishlike in appearance, ophiuroids are more closely related to the echinoids. Commonly called brittle stars, they have flat, disclike bodies, with five flexible arms different in structure to those of the asteroids. Living ophiuroids are found in huge masses on the sea floor, and fossil remains suggest that the same was true of earlier species. In areas with a strong current, they use some of their arms to link to each other, and other arms to capture food. Since their arms are long and fragile, it is rare to find complete fossilized specimens.

BRITTLE STAR
Geocoma *is a Jurassic ophiuroid found worldwide. Its habitat was lime mud. The arms are unusually long and covered by fine spines.*

Geocoma carinata

Long arms

Small central disc

GEOCOMA SPECIMEN

BLASTOIDS

AN EXTINCT CLASS of echinoderm (see panel, opposite), the blastoids existed from the Middle Ordovician to the Late Permian. They were sedentary animals that, rather like the crinoids, remained anchored to the sea floor by a stem consisting of a column of linked, circular plates. Blastoids had a highly regular structure; their body region consisted of three circles of five plates, made of calcium carbonate and shaped like a rosebud. Many blastoid species are useful as index fossils. While they can be mistaken for crinoids, blastoids lack attachments for arms, and their bodies are often found intact.

SEDENTARY ANIMAL
Pentremites *is one of the most common, widespread, and easily recognizable blastoids. It is abundant in Carboniferous marine sediments in the US. It lived attached to hard layers on the sea-bed.*

Openings

PENTREMITES SPECIMEN

Pentremites pyriformis

Broad, biconical form

CYSTOIDS

LIVING FROM the Ordovician to the Devonian, the cystoids are an extinct group of echinoderms (see panel, opposite). They bear a superficial resemblance to crinoids but lack the crinoids' true arms. They fed by filtering water through short limbs called brachioles. Anchorage to the sea floor was achieved by wrapping their short, tapering stems around any convenient fixed object. Useful index fossils for the Ordovician, cystoids are relatively uncommon fossils.

Body interior

Pleurocystes rugeri

PLEUROCYSTES SPECIMEN

Brachiole

TUBE-FEEDER
This specimen of Pleurocystes *clearly shows the typical components of a cystoid: the short, tapered stem, the two brachioles (feeding tubes), and the large plates that make up the theca (body).*

347

VERTEBRATES

GEORGES CUVIER
This French naturalist (1769–1832) first identified vertebrates as a distinct group.

THE EARLIEST FOSSILS of vertebrates (a sub-phylum of the phylum *Chordata*) are microscopic scale-bones belonging to the jawless fish (agnathans), which proliferated in the Silurian and Devonian. Bone, cartilage, and the enamel-like substance that forms teeth first occurred in fish. The modification of these substances in later fish contributed to the evolution of the first amphibians, able to live on dry land. Amphibians appeared in the Devonian, followed by the first full-time land dwellers, the reptiles, early in the Carboniferous. In the Triassic, one major branch of reptiles gave rise to mammals, while another brought giant reptiles, flying and aquatic reptiles, lizards, and snakes. Mammals were therefore present concurrently with dinosaurs in the Cretaceous, but only became prominent after their demise at the end of that period. Fossils of land animals are less common than those of marine vertebrates because natural opportunities for fossilization, which depends on burial soon after death, occur much less often.

FISH

THE FIRST SKELETAL REMAINS of fish occur in the Devonian. Fish fossils can range from entire skeletons to scale-bones or teeth. In some localities, such as the vast Eocene lakes of western North America, literally millions of fish were killed on different occasions as a result of volcanic ash falls. In some former lake-bottom sediments, a dozen or more complete sardine-sized fish skeletons can be recovered from a single square yard of shale. Fish teeth of various species are commonly found as fossils, such as the examples from *Ceratodus* illustrated below. As with other animal groups, the fossil record for fish is still incomplete.

GALEOCERDO SPECIMEN

GALEOCERDO
Galeocerdo has survived since the Eocene, and is known to us as the tiger shark. It inhabits coastal waters worldwide.

Galeocerdo cuvier

Enamel covering

SCALES
Lepidotus lived from the Triassic to the Cretaceous. This fragment of flank displays the fossilization of fish scales—often the only part of the fish to fossilize.

LEPIDOTUS SPECIMEN

Lepidotus species

Immature teeth

Mature teeth

SPIRAL OF TEETH
Helicoprion, a member of the shark family, had front teeth set in a spiral containing as many as 180 teeth. It lived in the Early Permian, is found worldwide, and was probably a marine predator hunting in the mid-depths.

HELICOPRION SPECIMEN

Helicoprion bessonowi

GREEN RIVER, WYOMING
The Green River Formation of Wyoming was once the bottom of one of an extensive series of Eocene lakes. It is particularly rich in fish fossils.

LUNGFISH
Ceratodus was a lungfish that lived from the Early Triassic to the Paleocene. It was a freshwater fish, and a bottom-feeder. Its teeth, which are actually tooth-plates, are frequently found as fossils.

Ceratodus tiguidensis

CERATODUS SPECIMENS

Ridged margin

PRESERVED BY ASH
This complete Priscacara skeleton was recovered from the Eocene lake bed that covered much of western Wyoming. Fine volcanic ash fell into the lake and smothered the fish, then buried and preserved their skeletons.

Dorsal fin   *Spine*

Priscacara liops

PRISCACARA SPECIMEN

AMPHIBIANS AND REPTILES

MODERN FROG
Frogs first appeared in the Mesozoic; modern frogs were to evolve during the Eocene.

IN THE UPPER Devonian, amphibians became the first vertebrates to adapt to living on the land. Resembling today's salamanders in appearance, these amphibians still relied on water for laying and hatching their eggs. The next evolutionary step occurred in the Carboniferous, with the emergence of reptiles. Having developed waterproof eggs, in addition to body scales that prevented dehydration, many reptiles were freed from the need to remain in a wet environment. Amphibian and reptile fossils are most likely to be fragmentary, consisting of solid bones or individual teeth, but in rare instances fairly complete skeletons or eggs are discovered.

FROG FOREBEAR
This Rana *fossil is a rare, complete amphibian skeleton.* Rana *appeared in the Eocene, and is still living. It is found worldwide, except in Australasia.*

RANA SPECIMEN

Rana pueyoi

TRICERATOPS SPECIMEN

Triceratops prorosus

THREE HORNS
One of the best known of all dinosaurs, the Lower Cretaceous three-horned Triceratops *was the most advanced of the horned dinosaurs.*

TURTLE SHELL
Well-preserved fossil shells of turtles and tortoises are often found. The marine turtle Cimochelys *lived during the Lower Cretaceous, and fossils are found principally in Europe.*

Cimochelys benstedi

CIMOCHELYS SPECIMEN

BIRDS

IT IS NOW GENERALLY agreed that birds evolved from one of the families of carnivorous dinosaurs, although exactly which is still unclear. The first identifiable bird remains are found in the Late Jurassic, although the main explosion in bird species did not occur until the Cretaceous, when many reptiles became extinct. Today there are more than 8,600 bird species. As bird bones are hollow, thin-walled, and fragile, fossils are relatively rare.

DAWN BIRD
Hesperornis, *a flightless, diving dawn bird, lived during the Late Cretaceous. It ate fish, and lived around warm seas.*

HESPERORNIS SPECIMEN

Hesperornis regalis

Nostril

DODO
Raphus, *commonly called the dodo, became extinct in the 17th century.*

RAPHUS SPECIMEN

Raphus cucullatus

MAMMALS

THE FIRST MAMMALS appeared during the Cretaceous Period, having evolved from therapsid reptiles. The explosion in mammalian species did not take place until after the extinction of the dinosaurs and other reptiles at the end of the Cretaceous. Fossilized mammal bones are hollow and generally thick-walled. Mammal teeth are multifaceted, enamel-covered, and have bony roots. Many fossil mammals can be identified from teeth alone.

Ursus speleus

URSUS SPECIMEN

BEAR BONES
The name Ursus *refers to a group that includes cave, brown, and grizzly bears. It evolved during the Pliocene and is still around today. Caves in Europe, in particular, are very rich in fossilized cave bear remains.*

Homo habilis

HOMO HABILIS SPECIMEN

EARLY MAN
Homo habilis *represents a middle stage in the evolution of* Homo sapiens, *the modern human.* Homo habilis *appeared during the Lower Pliocene and disappeared during the Lower Pleistocene. Remains of this hominid are found in Africa.*

OLDUVAI GORGE, TANZANIA
Paleontologists have found the fossilized remains of more than 50 hominids in rocks of the Olduvai Gorge in northern Tanzania.

THE DINOSAUR QUARRY

FIRST DISCOVERED IN 1909 AND DECLARED A NATIONAL MONUMENT IN 1915, THE DINOSAUR QUARRY IN THE WESTERN U.S. IS ONE OF THE RICHEST SOURCES OF DINOSAUR BONES IN THE WORLD, CONTAINING 1,600 BONES FROM 11 DIFFERENT DINOSAUR SPECIES.

AERIAL VIEW OF THE QUARRY
The Quarry is located in the high desert country straddling the state line between north-eastern Utah and northwestern Colorado. Part of the Morrison Formation, it was once a river channel in which the bones of dead dinosaurs were buried.

On August 17, 1909, Earl Douglass, a paleontologist working for the Carnegie Museum in Pittsburgh, Pennsylvania, was walking along the small drainage channels of the Uinta Basin, searching for dinosaur skeletons. His search was rewarded. On that day he found eight still-articulated tail vertebrae of a herbivorous dinosaur called *Apatosaurus*, weathering from the rock. The excavation that followed revealed one of the most complete *Apatosaurus* skeletons ever discovered. Further excavation in the area over the next 75 years uncovered some 1,600 bones from 11 different dinosaur species. This rock outcropping later became known as the Quarry, and it became the centerpiece of the Dinosaur National Monument.

The Quarry is an uptilted slab of sandstone belonging to the Morrison Formation. Dinosaur remains have been found in this formation in a number of localities in western states. The rocks of the Morrison Formation were laid down as sediments about 150 million years ago, in the middle of the Jurassic Period, also known as the Age of Dinosaurs. The sediment in the Quarry area was sand and gravel from a fast-moving stream that flowed through the area. Dead dinosaurs were carried downstream and deposited in the river channel, where they were buried by rapidly accumulating sediments. Some of the dinosaur bodies were still intact; others were little more than scattered bones.

In the 150 million years that followed, the river disappeared, and the whole of what is now northern Colorado and Utah, including the dinosaur bone-bed, was buried under deep accumulations of sediment. The sand of the river channel solidified into rock, and the original bone material was replaced by mineral matter. Then the sedimentary rock containing the fossil bones was tilted upward by huge earth movements across the whole region. Eventually, weathering wore down and exposed the bone-bed, revealing the vertebrae at the surface for Douglass to discover.

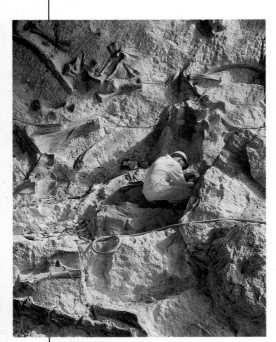

UNCOVERING DINOSAUR BONES IN THE ROCK WALL
The rock layer containing the dinosaur bones first discovered by Earl Douglass today forms one wall of the Quarry Visitor Center. Paleontologists continue to chip away at the rock to uncover the bones.

DINOSAUR NATIONAL MONUMENT
Around three-fourths of all the dinosaur bones found at the Quarry belong to the long-necked, long-tailed herbivores known as the sauropods. Apatosaurus *belongs to this family. It was 70–75 ft (21–23 m) in length and weighed about 37 tons.*

Page numbers in **bold** indicate main references and illustrations. Page numbers in *italic* refer to captions and illustrations.

ACKNOWLEDGMENTS

Author's Acknowledgments
Many people have worked very hard to make this book possible. Jane Laing has put in endless hours over many months planning, editing, and coordinating all aspects of the book. Margaret Carruthers has done a meticulous and much appreciated job of oversight on behalf of the Smithsonian, and Liz Wheeler of Dorling Kindersley has brought this all about. Christine Lacey, Miranda Harvey and Alison Gardner have done a superb job on design, and Jane Simmonds on editing. Gary Ombler and Linda Burgess have provided excellent new photography. Assistant Curator Monica Price and the Oxford University Natural History Museum have provided superb cooperation and access to their mineral collection, as has the Gemmological Society of Great Britain. The Diamond Trading Company have been very helpful with diamond pictures. Gaea Crystals of Wendover, Buckinghamshire and Mineral Imports of Teddington, Middlesex, have been generous in allowing the use of their commercial stocks for photography.

I would also like to thank Lilian Verner-Bonds for keeping me afloat, and Guy and Meriel Ballard for their patience throughout the 18 months it took to create the book. Finally, I would like to acknowledge Professors Malcolm McCallum, Joseph Weitz, Ernest Wolff, David Harris, and John Campbell, of the (then) Colorado State University Department of Geology whose teaching is the ultimate foundation of this book.

Dorling Kindersley and Grant Laing Partnership would like to thank the following people for their help in the preparation of this book: Monica Price and the Oxford University Museum of Natural History for providing access to over 250 mineral specimens photographed at the museum, and advice with aspects of the text; Doug Garrod and Lorne Stather and the Gemmological Society of Great Britain for providing access to, and advice concerning, more than 50 gemstones photographed at their premises; Mineral Imports, Teddington, for the loan of over 40 mineral specimens photographed for the book; Gaea Crystals, Wendover, for allowing photography at their premises of five mineral specimens featured in the book; R. Holt and Co. Ltd, London, for supplying gemstones photographed for pp.222-23 and 314-15; Greg Ohanian and Wilde One's, London, for providing access to Native American jewelry and some mineral specimens photographed at the premises; Ronald Bonewitz for the loan of mineral specimens and gemstones photographed for the book; Anne-Marie Bulat, Jasmine Burgess, Linda Burgess, Linda Dare, Nicola Dawtry, Miranda Harvey, Christine Lacey, Betty Laing, Jane Laing, Frances Pearl, Monica Price, Liz Statham, Jean Taylor, Ulrica Terje, Lilian Vernor-Bonds, and Liz Wheeler for the loan of jewelry and artifacts photographed for the book; Chip Clark from the American National Museum of Natural History, Smithsonian Institution, for his photographs from the National Gem Collection that appear in the book; Margaret Curruthers and Richard Efthim for their advice on the content of the text; Katie Mann and Ellen Nanney at the Smithsonian Institution for their liaison work; Chris Alderman at The Diamond Trading Company for assistance in locating photographs of diamonds and diamond mining; David Waters at the Oxford University Museum of Natural History for providing 34 photographs of thin sections for use in the book, together with identification advice; Neil Fletcher for supplying 40 location photographs; Helen Stallion and Mariana Sonnenberg for additional picture research; Miezan van Zyl for editorial assistance; and Anne Thompson and Marilou Prokopioum for design assistance.

Picture Credits

2 Corbis: © Jim Zuckerman b; © Jonathan Blair: t. 6–7 Corbis: Digital image © 1996 CORBIS; Original image courtesy of NASA: t. 8 Corbis: © Bettmann: cr. Science Photo Library: NASA: tr, Patrice Loiez/CERN: l. 9 Corbis: br, NASA: cl, tr, bl, bc. 10 Science Photo Library: Chris Butler: tr, European Space Agency: l. 11 Courtesy of Geo-Expeditions, www.geotoursafrica.com: bl, Science Photo Library: NASA: tr. 12 Corbis: tr; Digital image © 1996 CORBIS; Original image courtesy of NASA: bl. 13 Corbis: © Nathan Benn: bc, © NASA/Roger Ressmeyer: tl, © Roger Ressmeyer: cra; © Jeff Vanuga: tr; Science Photo Library: David Parker: tl. 14 California Institute of Technology Archives: br, Corbis: © Raymond Gehman: bl; Courtesy of Dr Sally Gibson, Dept of Earth Sciences, University of Cambridge: cl. 15 Corbis: © Jonathan Blair: tr, NASA: cr. 16 AIP Emilio Segrè Visual Archives, Gallery of Member Society Presidents: br; Geophotos: bl; Science Photo Library: Dr Ken MacDonald: c. 17 Corbis: © Tiziana and Gianni Baldizzone: c; © L. Clarke: bc; © Galen Rowell: br, tr. 18 Corbis: © Charles O'Rear: cr; Geophotos: bl. 19 Corbis: © Lloyd Cluff: cr; © Roger Ressmeyer; Geophotos. 20 DK Images: James Stevenson: tl; Corbis: bl; © Philippe Eranian: c, © Marc Garanger: br, © Sally A. Morgan; Ecoscene: cdb. 21 Corbis: William Whitehurst: br; Geophotos: t. 22 Corbis: © David Butow/CORBIS SABA cl, © Philippe Eranian: cr; Geophotos: tl; Dave Waters: br. 23 Corbis: © Roger Ressmeyer: cl, © Vo Trung Dung/CORBIS SYGMA: bl, © Galen Rowell: br. 24 Corbis: © Philippe Eranian: bl, © Layne Kennedy: cla, © Vo Trung Dung/CORBIS SYGMA; Jim Sugar: clb. 25 Natural History Museum, UK: br. 26 Corbis: © Ron Watts: r. 28 Corbis: bc, © Francesc Muntada: l. 29 Ron Bonewitz: bc; Corbis: © Galen Rowell: tl; Geophotos: bl, cr, bc. 30 Corbis: © David Muench: ca, cl; Geophotos: bl. 31 Corbis: © Tom Bean: tr, © Raymond Gehman. 32 Corbis: © Galen Rowell: b, © Jim Sugar: tl; Geophotos: c. 33 Corbis: tl, © Galen Rowell: crb, © Julia Waterlow; Eye Ubiquitous: cr. 34 Corbis: © David Muench: cl, © Michael T. Sedam: tr, © Paul A. Souders: bl, © Roger Wood: cb; Roy Starkey: tl; Dave Waters: br. 35 Ron Bonewitz: cl, bca; Corbis: © Bettmann: crb, © Kevin Fleming: t, © David Muench: cra, © Galen Rowell: tl; Geophotos: cr, cr, bl, br. 36 Corbis: © Hubert Stadler: br, Courtesy of www.Palagems.com: cl; Dave Waters: tl. 37 Corbis: © North Carolina Museum of Art: cb, © Roger Wood: crb; Geophotos: cb, tl; Dave Waters: tr. 38 © 2004 Smithsonian Institution: cl; Dave Waters: clb, tl, tr, bl. 39 Corbis: © Hulton-Deutsch Collection: cb, Geophotos; Dave Waters: clb. 40 Corbis: © Brenda Tharp: cra, © Raymond Gehman: cl; Geophotos: cr; Dave Waters: tl. 41 Corbis: © Hulton-Deutsch Collection: cr; Dave Waters: bl. 42 Corbis: © Roger Ressmeyer: tr, DK Images: The British Museum, London, UK: bl, bla; Geophotos: tcr, © 2004 Smithsonian Institution: br. 43 www.bridgeman.co.uk: Kremlin Museums, Moscow: tr; Museo del Templo Mayor, Mexico City, Mexico: ca; DK Images: Peter Hayman © The British Museum, bl, INAH: cl. 44 Corbis: © Michael St. Maur Sheil: tl; DK Images: Alan Williams, Courtesy of the National Trust: bl. 45 Lonely Planet Images: Gareth McCormack. 46 Geophotos: clb; Science Photo Library: William Ervin: cra, Masao Hayushi/DUNO: crb; Dave Waters: cla, tl. 47 Corbis: © Lowell Georgia: tl, © Barry Lewis: cr; Dave Waters: br. 48 National Geographic Image Collection: Richard Olsenius. 49 Alamy Images: r, Corbis: © Galen Rowell: b. 50 www.bridgeman.co.uk: Musee de la Presse, Paris, France/Lauros/Giraudon: br; © Gary Braasch: cra, © Wolfgang Kaehler: bl; DK Images: James Stevenson, Courtesy of the Museo Archeologico Nazionale di Napoli: cr, Dave Waters: cr, tl. 51 Corbis: cl, © Jay

Dickman: tl. 52 Corbis: © Jeff Vanuga: tl, © Ron Watts: b. 53 Corbis: cb, © Bob Krist: br, © Joseph Sohm; ChromoSohm Inc.: crb; Science Photo Library: Simon Fraser: tr. 54 Chris Gibson: tl, Science Photo Library: Martin Bond: tr, Rosenfeld Images Ltd: br; Dave Waters clb, cra. 55 Corbis: © Ric Ergenbright: tl; National Geographic Image Collection: Phil Schermeister: tr; Ron Bonewitz: clb. 56 Corbis: © Craig Lovell: tl; DK Images: Colin Keates, courtesy of The Natural History Museum: bl; Science Photo Library: Bernhard Edmaier: cla. 57 Travel Ink: Julian Parton. 58 Corbis: © James L. Amos: tl, © Bettmann: cla, © Hulton-Deutsch Collection: cr, © Kevin Schafer: tr, © Nik Wheeler: br; Dave Waters: cla. 59 Corbis: © Richard Cummins: tl, © Massimo Listri: br; The National Trust: Andreas von Einsiedel: bra; US Gypsum: bl. 60 Science Photo Library: Adam Jones: tl; Dave Waters: clb. 61 Corbis: © Jonathan Blair: tc, tr, cr, Stephen Kline: clb; Dave Waters: clb, tl. 62 Corbis: © Keren Su. 63 Robert Harding Picture Library: r. 64 www.bridgeman.co.uk: Victoria & Albert Museum, London, UK: bla; Corbis: © Tom Bean: tr, © Tibor Bognár: bl, Geophotos: cl, Chris Gibson: tl. 65 Corbis: © Jose Fuste Raga: t, © Otto Lang: cr. 66 Corbis: © Martin B. Withers; Frank Lane Picture Agency: b; © Buddy Mays tl. 67 Corbis: © Tom Bean. 68 © Christie's Images Ltd: clb; Corbis: © Martin B. Withers; Frank Lane Picture Agency: cr, © Enzo & Paolo Ragazzini: crb; Science Photo Library: Sinclair Stammers: tl; Dave Waters: cl. 69 Margaret Carruthers: cla; Corbis: © Robert Garvey: tc, © David Muench: clb; Dave Waters: tl, clb. 70 Corbis: © Francis G Mayer: br; DK Images: Peter Hayman © The British Museum: bl, © Judith Miller/Lyon and Turnbull Ltd: bra, Colin Keates, Courtesy of the Natural History Museum, London: cl, tr; Geophotos: tl. 71 Corbis: © Roger Wilmshurst; Frank Lane Picture Agency: cra; Science Photo Library: David Nunuk: crb. 72 Corbis: © Archivo Iconografica, S.A.: t; Getty Images: b. 73 Corbis: © Yann Arthus-Bertrand: tr. © Jonathan Blair: bl, © Denis Scott: br. 74 NASA: tl, © 2004 Smithsonian Institution: cra, br. 75 © 2004 Smithsonian Institution: br. 76 Geophotos: tl, bl. 77 Alamy Images: John C Doornkamp: tl; Corbis: © Galen Rowell: bc; Geophotos: ca. 78 Corbis: © Paul Almasy: bl, © Gary Braasch: ccr, © WildCountry: tr; www.dinodia.com: cl; Dave Waters: tl. 79 Corbis: © Ric Ergenbright: cr, © Robert van der Hilst: cr; Dave Waters: crb. 80 akg-images: Jean-Louis Nou tl, bl; www.bridgeman.co.uk: Private Collection cl. 81 Corbis: © Eric and David Hosking. 82 Corbis: © Tiziana and Gianni Baldizzone: cl, © Richard Klune: tl; Geophotos: clb; Dave Waters: tr, crb. 83 Science Photo Library: cb; Dave Waters: br. 84 ConstructionPhotography.com: ca; Geophotos: clb; Dave Waters: tl, cra. 85 Corbis: cl; Geophotos: tl, bc; Roy Starkey: tl; Dave Waters: cl, tl. 86 Corbis: © Gunter Marx Photography: cr. 88 Corbis: © Ludovic Maisant: bl, © Roger Wood: cl; Science Photo Library: Martin Land: tl. 89 Corbis: © Andrew Brown; Ecoscene: cl, © Ralph A. Clevenger: bc, © Kevin Schafer: t; Still Pictures: S. Compoint/UNEP: br. 91 Geophotos: t; The Australian Institute of Geoscientists. Photo by Roger B Cooper: bl. 92 Corbis: © William Whitehurst: r; Science Photo Library: WG: bl. 94 Corbis: © Ted Spiegel: br; Science Photo Library: Max-Planck-Institute for Metallurgy: cl. 95 The Natural History Museum, London: cr. 96 Corbis: © Jim Richardson: br. 97 Geophotos: br, bc. 98 Science Photo Library: Graham J Hills: tr. 104 www.bridgeman.co.uk: Bonhams, London, UK: tl; Corbis: © Bob Krist: cl; © 2004 Smithsonian Institution: bl. 105 www.bridgeman.co.uk: Ashmolean Museum, University of Oxford, UK: ca, cl; © The British Museum; Corbis: © Jeremy Horner: cr; © 2004 Smithsonian Institution: bl. 106 Corbis: © Bisson Bernard/Corbis Sygma: bl; The Diamond Trading Company: br; Mount Mica Rarities: cr. 107 www.bridgeman.co.uk: Egyptian National Museum, Cairo, Egypt/Giraudon: bcr; Corbis: © Anthony Bannister; Gallo Images: tr, © Michael S. Yamashita: tc, © Reza; Webistan: c; The Diamond

Trading Company: clb, bl; The Picture Desk: Art Archive: Dagli Orti: br. 108 Corbis: © Dean Conger: bl, © Charles O'Rear: tr; DK Images: © Judith Miller/N. Bloom & Son Ltd: cr. 109 www.bridgeman.co.uk: Ca' Rezzonico, Museo del Settecento, Venice: cr. 110 – 111 © 2004 Smithsonian Institution. 112 Corbis: © Burstein Collection: cr, © Joseph Sohm; ChromoSohm Inc.: cl; Werner Forman Archive: Statens Historiska Museum, Stockholm: c. 113 Corbis: © James I. Amos: cr, © Kim Sayer: clb; DK Images: Judith Miller/HY Duke and Son: cra; Courtesy of Geo-Expeditions, www.geotoursafrica.com: tl. 114 www.bridgeman.co.uk: Ashmolean Museum, University of Oxford, UK: clb, Egyptian National Museum, Cairo, Egypt/Giraudon: tr, Valley of the Nobles, Thebes, Egypt/Giraudon: cra; Corbis: © H. Armstrong Roberts: cb, © Bettmann: bc, © Mimmo Jodice: bl; Werner Forman Archive: National Museum of Anthropology, Mexico City: cla. 115 Corbis: © Lester Lefkowitz: t, © Denis Scott: c; © 2004 Smithsonian Institution: br. 116 www.bridgeman.co.uk: Egyptian National Museum, Cairo, Egypt/Giraudon: cl; Corbis: © Bettmann: bl, © Tibor Bognár tl. 117 Corbis: © Sandro Vannini. 118 www.bridgeman.co.uk: Bibliotheque Nationale, Paris, France: cl, The British Museum, London, UK: cl, © Brooklyn Museum of Art, New York, USA, Charles Edwin Wilbour Fund: tr, Museo de las Culturas de Oaxaca, Mexico/Banco Mexicano de Imagenes/INAH: tcr, Museum of Antiquities, Newcastle upon Tyne, UK: cr; Corbis: © Michael Freeman: clb; DK ImagesL Alan Hills and Barbara Winter © The British Museum: cl. 119 www.bridgeman.co.uk: The Fine Art Society, London, UK: c; Corbis: br; Science Photo Library: David Leah: tl. 120 Corbis: © Archivo Iconografico, S.A.: bl, © Gunter Marx Photography: tc; FLPA: Silvestris: tl. 121 Alamy Images: Christa Knijff; © Corbis: © Ludovic Maisant: cl, © Don Mason: tr. 122 Corbis: © Anthony Bannister; Gallo Images: tl, © Lowell Georgia: clb, © Ricki Rosen/CORBIS SABA; The Diamond Trading Company: br; © 2004 Smithsonian Institution: tr, cr. 123 The Diamond Trading Company: cr; Corbis: © Charles O'Rear; Crown © The Royal Collection © 2002 Her Majesty Queen Elizabeth II: tl; © 2004 Smithsonian Institution: tr. 124 Harold & Erica Van Pelt: American Museum of Natural History. 125 www.bridgeman.co.uk: Musee Antoine Lecuyer, Saint-Quentin, France: tr; © 2004 Smithsonian Institution: crb, br. 126 Alamy Images: Ethel Davies/ImageState: cal; Corbis: cr, © AINACO: clb, © George H. H. Huey: bcl. 127 Reg Grant: tl; Royal Cornwall Museum: bcr; Science Photo Library: Novosti: cr, Sam Ogden: ca, Charles D. Winters: tr. 128 Alamy Images: Rachael Bowes: tl; Science Photo Library: Steve Allen: tr, Mark Thomas: cra. 129 Corbis: © Craig Aurness: tl; Science Photo Library: Ben Johnson: bc. 130 AISA – Archivo Iconográfico S. A., Barcelona: cl. www.bridgeman.co.uk: Private Collection/Giraudon: cra; Corbis: Charles E Rotkin tl, © Alain Nogues/Corbis Sygma: ccr, Jacqui Hurst: cl. 131 Corbis: cra, © Matthieu Colin/Corbis Sygma: cr, © Roger Ressmeyer: cr, © Paul A Souders: tr; Geophotos: tl; Novosti (London): tl. 132 Corbis: © Richard T. Nowitz: cl; Geophotos: tl; Science Photo Library: Simon Fraser/Northumbria Circuits: tr; © 2004 Smithsonian Institution: r. 133 Alamy Images: Panorama Stock Photos: tl; www.bridgeman.co.uk: Louvre, Paris, France/Giraudon: cra; DK Images: Judith Miller/Sloan's: ccl; © 2004 Smithsonian Institution: tr. 134 Alamy Images: Christa Knijff. 134 © Christie's Images Ltd: ca; Corbis: © Bettmann: tr, © Eric and David Hosking: clb; © 2004 Natural Pigments LLC www.naturalpigments.com: cla; Reg Grant: clb. 135 Alamy Images: Rachael Bowes: tl, Bowmann/F1 online: tc; Corbis: © Charles Krebs: clb; DK Images: National Bank of America: tl; © 2004 Smithsonian Institution: tr. 136 Alamy Images: Robert Harding Picture Library: clb, Panorama Stock Photos: tl; www.bridgeman.co.uk: National Gallery of Scotland, Edinburgh, Scotland: bra; Corbis: tc, © Robert Maass: tr; © 2004

ACKNOWLEDGMENTS

Smithsonian Institution: cr. 137 Corbis: © Eric and David Hosking: tl; Geoff Dann © Dorling Kindersley, Courtesy of the Wallace Collection, London: ca. 138 Alamy Images: Pavel Filatov: cl; Corbis: tr, © Ludovic Maisant: tl; DK Images: © Judith Miller/Colin Baddiel: cr; Geophotos: crb. 139 Alamy Images: Leslie Garland/LGPL: tl. 140 Corbis: © Nick Rains; Cordaiy Photo Library Ltd: tl, © Brownie Harris: ca; Science Photo Library: br, Chris Knapton: crb. 141 Alamy Images: Natalie Tepper/Arcaid: clb, Andre Jenny: tl. 141 Corbis: © Lowell Georgia: clb. 142 Alamy Images: Leslie Garland/LGPL: cl; Corbis: © Charles O'Rear: clb; akg-images: clb; Alamy Images: Ethel Davies/ImageState: tr, Mediacolors : tl; Geophotos: clb. 144 Alamy Images: WilmarPhotography.com: br; Geophotos: cl. 145 Alamy Images: Bowmann/F1 online: tl, Van Hilversum: tc, J Schwanke: cr; Corbis: © Gerald French: clb, © Hulton Deutsch Collection: bca. 146 Jens C Andersen, Camborne School of Mines, School of Geography, Archaeology and Earth Resources, University of Exeter: cr; Corbis: cl. 147 Corbis: © Archivio Iconografico, S.A: tr, © Robert Holmes: tl. 148 Ron Bonewitz: tl; DK Images: Colin Keates, Courtesy of the Natural History Museum, London: bl; © 2004 Smithsonian Institution: cla. 149 Corbis: © Nathan Benn: br. 150 Ron Bonewitz: tl; Corbis: © Sheldan Collins: cra, © John Garrett: tr, © Araldo de Luca: clb; Michael Freeman: tl. 151 DK Images: Colin Keates © Natural History Museum, London, UK: cl; © 2004 Smithsonian Institution: cr, t; Harold & Erica Van Pelt: The American Museum of Natural History, gift of Mrs. George Bowen DeLong: br. 152 www.bridgeman.co.uk: Christie's Images, London, UK: br. 153 Courtesy John Harris, Gemlab: tc; © 2004 Smithsonian Institution: tr, cab, car, cbl, cbr; Harold & Erica Van Pelt: American Museum of Natural History: clb. 154 Ron Bonewitz: tl; Corbis: bl, © Frank Lane Picture Agency: clb; Science Photo Library: Mehau Kulyk: tr, David Nunuk: cl. 155 Alamy Images: Bryan and Cherry Alexander Photography: br; Corbis: © Michael Freeman: crb, © Richard Hamilton Smith: tl, © Roger Ressmeyer: tr; Science Photo Library: British Antarctic Survey: cra. 156 Corbis: © Richard Klune: bla; Reg Grant: tl; Sterling Hill Mining Museum: Maureen Verbeek tr. 157 Ron Bonewitz: tl; Crown © The Royal Collection © 2002 Her Majesty Queen Elizabeth II: c, tr. 158 Geophotos: cl; Science Photo Library: Photo Reseachers: tr; Sterling Hill Mining Museum: car, Maureen Verbeek: tl; Dave Waters: cb. 159 Corbis: © Hulton Deutsch Collection: cra; DK Images: © Judith Miller/H Bonnar: tr; Geophotos: tl; © 2004 Smithsonian Institution: cal, cla; Courtesy of the Trustees of the V&A: cla. 162 Alamy Images: Walter Bibikow/Jon Arnold Images: clb; © Bettmann: br, © Jason Burke; Eye Ubiquitous: car; DK Images: Colin Keates, Courtesy of the Natural History Museum, London; Geophotos: tl, crb; Science Photo Library: Arnold Fisher: cr. 163 George Hall: clb; © David Muench: clb; Geophotos: tl. 164 Alamy Images: Pavel Filatov: cb, Christa Knijff: tl; Corbis: clb, © Bettmann: cr, © Roger Ressmeyer: tr. 165 Corbis: © Gallo Images: clb. 165 Geophotos: tl, tc, cr; Ron Bonewitz. 166 Alamy Images: Pavel Filatov: tl; Corbis: © Sterling Hill Mining Museum: Maureen Verbeek: clb. 167 Corbis: © James L. Amos: bl, tr, © Bill Ross: br, © Paul A Souders: ccr, © Vince Streano: tl. 168 Alamy Images: Pavel Filatov: tr; Corbis: © Michael S. Yamashita: tr; Geophotos: clb. 169 Corbis: © Gianni Dagli Orti: c, © David Muench: tl. 170 Corbis: © Chris Lisle: crb, © Alinari Archives: bl; Geophotos: cl. 171 Alamy Images: Kevin Taylor: tl; Corbis: © Nick Rains; Cordaiy Photo Library: cl, © Fremont Stevens/Corbis Sygma: tc; Geophotos: tl. 172 © Christie's Images Ltd: clb, bc; Corbis: © Sandro Vannini: tl. 173 © The British Museum: cra; Geophotos: cr. 174 Corbis: © James L. Amos: br; © Bettmann: cr, cb; Geophotos: cl. 175 Corbis: © Dave G. Houser: clb, © Dewitt Jones: cr, © Alan Schein Photography: crb; Geophotos: tl. 176 Geophotos: cl, cr. 177 Alamy/Pictor International/ImageState: tl; Corbis: tr; Kevin Downey Photography, MA, USA: br. 178 Alamy Images: Tom Till: tl; Corbis: © Bettmann: cra; DK Images: Dave King, Courtesy of the University Museum of Archaeology and Anthropology, Cambridge; © 2004 Smithsonian Institution: crb, bl. 179 Alamy Images: Pictor International/ImageState: cl; © Christie's Images Ltd: c; Corbis: © Kevin Schafer: cl, © Michael S. Yamashita: cr; © 2004 Smithsonian Institution: bl. 180 Alamy Images: Markus Bassler/Bildarchiv Monheim GmbH: tl; DK Images: © Judith Miller/Barie Macey: tl; © The Wallace Collection, London: bl; © Smithsonian Institution: bcl. 181 Alamy Images: Mediacolors: clb, Noel Yates: tcl; Corbis: © Alinari Archives: clb; © Sally A. Morgan/Ecoscene: tl; Steve Sleight: crb. 182 Ron Bonewitz: tl; www.bridgeman.co.uk: Bibliotheque Nationale, Paris, France: cr; Geophotos: tl; DK Images: Colin Keates © Natural History Museum, London, UK: car. 183 Corbis: © O. Alamany & E. Vicens: tl, © Nick Rains; Cordaiy Photo Library: crb, © Sally A. Morgan/Ecoscene: tr, © Macduff Everton: clb. 184 akg-images: Erich Lessing: bl; DK Images: © Judith Miller/Freeman's: tr. 185 www.bridgeman.co.uk: Private Collection: br; © The British Museum: cl, c; © 2004 Smithsonian Institution: tr. 186 akg-images: cl; Corbis: © Antoine Gyori: tr. 187 Corbis: © Steve Raymer: cl. 188 Alamy Images: Witry Pascal: cl. 189 Alamy Images: Jacques Jangoux: tl; Corbis: © David Muench: cl; © Alan Towse: cra; Science Photo Library: Hank Morgan/University of Massachusetts, AT, Amherst:tr, US Navy: cl. 190 akg-images: Erich Lessing: bl; Geophotos: tl; Science Photo Library: cra. 191 Corbis: © Paul A Souders: tr; Geophotos: clb, tl; Courtesy Joe Marty. Photograph: Henry Barwood: bl; Jan McClellan www.designjewel.com: crb; © 2004 Smithsonian Institution: crb. 192 Alamy Images: Pavel Filatov: clb, crb; Corbis: © Danny Lehman: cr; Geophotos: tr. 193 Geophotos: tl, clb; © 2004 Smithsonian Institution: cr. 194 Corbis: © Nick Rains; Cordaiy Photo Library: tr; Reg Grant: tl; Geophotos: clb. 195 Art Directors/TRIP: N Rudakov: tl; The Natural History Museum, London: tl. 196 Corbis: © John Van Hasselt/Corbis Sygma: tcr, © Danny Lehman: cl; Heritage Image Partnership: The British Museum: bl; The Picture Desk: Art Archive: Dagli Orti: bl. 197 Corbis: © Dave G. Houser: cr, © Joseph Sohm/ChromoSohm Inc.: br. 198 Corbis: © Randy Faris. 199 Corbis: © Randy Faris: tl; © Ancient Art and Architecture: cr. 200 Corbis: © Nick Rains; Cordaiy Photo Library: tl; © Hulton Deutsch Collection: cr; Geophotos: clb; © 2004 Smithsonian Institution: cla. 201 Corbis: © Danny Lehman: tl; Geophotos: clb; © 2004 Smithsonian Institution: cb, crb. 202 akg-images: Erich Lessing: br; Geophotos: tl. 205 Alamy Images: Leslie Garland Picture Library: tl; www.bridgeman.co.uk: Iraq Museum, Baghdad, Iraq: car, Musee du Louvre, Paris, France: cra; © The British Museum: tr; Geophotos: cl. 204 Geophotos: tl. 205 Corbis: © Danny Lehman: cl, © David Turnley: tl; Geophotos: tl. 206 Corbis: © Tom Bean: clb, © Viviane Moos: crb; Geophotos: tl. 207 Alamy Images: Christa Knijff: tl; Corbis: © Peter Russell; The Military Picture Library: bl; Geophotos: cl.

208 Alamy Images: Terry Whitakker/Travel Ink: cl; Science Photo Library: John Howard: bc, bra. 209 Alamy Images: Tom Till: cl; Corbis: © Massimo Listri: tr; Geophotos: tl, crb. 210 Geophotos: tr; Science Photo Library: BSIP Dr Pichard T.: cr; © 2004 Smithsonian Institution: b. 211 Corbis: © Gallo Digital Image © 1996 CORBIS; Original image courtesy of NASA: clb, © Joseph Sohm/ChromoSohm Inc.: bl; Science Photo Library: NASA: tl. 213 Corbis: © Kevin Downey Photography, MA, USA: tr, tr. 214 Alamy Images: Stephen Saks Photography: tl; Corbis: © Kevin R. Morris: clb, © Charles O'Rear: br; Science Photo Library: Jerry Mason: tr, Maximilian Stock Ltd: bc. 215 Geophotos: tl, clb, cb; The Wellcome Institute Library, London: tr. 216 Alamy Images: Iain Farley: cb; Geophotos: © 2004 Smithsonian Institution: ca; Dave Waters: tc, tl. 217 Alamy Images: Leslie Garland Picture Library: tl; Geophotos: cl; Science Photo Library: NASA: cr, Peter Ryan: tr; © 2004 Smithsonian Institution: crb, bl. 218 Corbis: © David Muench: tr. 219 akg-images: Erich Lessing: cla; Ancient Art & Architecture Collection: tr; DK Images: Colin Keates © Natural History Museum, London, UK: br; Geophotos: tl; Science Photo Library: Sheila Terry: ccr; © 2004 Smithsonian Institution: c, cr. 220 Ron Bonewitz: tl; Corbis: © Charles O'Rear: crb; Geophotos: clb. 221 Corbis: © Dave G. Houser: clb, © Ludovic Maisant: cl; DK Images: Judith Miller/Dorling Kindersley/Joseph H Bonnar: bla; © 2004 Smithsonian Institution: b, tr; © 2004 Smithsonian Institution: cr. 223 www.bridgeman.co.uk: Bonhams, London, UK: tl; © Christie's Images Ltd: crb; Corbis: © Elio Ciol: cr. 224 Alamy Images: Robert Harding Picture Library: clb; Corbis: © Sheldan Collins: cl; Geophotos: tl. 225 Alamy: Gondwana Photo Art: tl, Jacques Jangoux: clb. 226 Ron Bonewitz: cl; Corbis: © Francis G. Mayer: br; Geophotos: tl. © 2004 Smithsonian Institution: c, cr. 227 Alamy Images: Mr Yogesh More/Ephotocorp cl; www.bridgeman.co.uk: Heini Schneebeli: c; DK Images: Dave King: tl © Judith Miller/Dreweatt Neate: crb; The Natural History Museum, London: tl. 228 Alamy Images: Tibor Bognar: clb, Mr Yogesh More/Ephotocorp: tl; www.bridgeman.co.uk: Musee du Louvre, Paris, France/Giraudon: clb; Ron Bonewitz: clb. 229 Alamy Images: Frantisek Staud: tl; www.bridgeman.co.uk: The Barber Institution of Fine Arts, University of Birmingham tc, Bonhams, London, UK: tr; Hermitage, St Petersburg, Russia: clb; Museum of Antiquities, Newcastle upon Tyne: bc; Ron Bonewitz: clb. 250 Ron Bonewitz: tl; © 2004 Smithsonian Institution: r. 231 akg-images: br; Tourist-Information Idar-Oberstein: bl. 252 Corbis: © Dave G. Houser: tl, © Paul A Souders: cr; © 2004 Smithsonian Institution: cra. 233 © 2004 Smithsonian Institution: cr, br, bc. 254 Alamy Images: Paul Shawcross: cr. 235 Ron Bonewitz: tl; © 2004 Smithsonian Institution: b. 236 Alamy Images: Witry Pascal: cl; Corbis: 237 akg-images: cl; Ron Bonewitz: tl; Corbis: © Blaine Harrington III: clb, © Bettmann: cr. 258 Alamy Images: Tom Till: cl; © Christie's Images Ltd: tl; Corbis: © The Cover Story: crb; Ron Bonewitz: clb; Courtesy of the Trustees of the V&A: Designer R Pearson. br. 239 Corbis: tl, © Ralph White: clb; DK Images: The British Museum: cra © Colin Keates, Courtesy of the Natural History Museum, London: br. 240 Alamy Images: Robert Harding Picture Library: bl, Tom Till: tr; © 2004 Smithsonian Institution: c, © Gavriel Jecan: tl. 241 Corbis: © The Cover Story: cra, © Wolfgang Kaehler: tl, © Hubert Stadler: cr; © 2004 Smithsonian Institution: tr. 242 Alamy Images: Christa Knijff: cl; Dave Waters: crb. 245 Alamy Images: Ronald Naar/ImageShop/Zefa: tl; Art Directors/TRIP: cl; © Christie's Images Ltd: c; Corbis: © Charles O'Rear: tr. 244 www.bridgeman.co.uk: Egyptian National Museum, Cairo, Egypt/Giraudon: cl; Corbis: © Reza; Webistan: tl; DK Images: © Judith Miller/Barie Macey: br. 245 akg-images: Erich Lessing: tl; www.bridgeman.co.uk: Bargello, Florence, Italy: br, Private Collection: tr. 246 © The British Museum: tl, cl, b. 247 DK Images: The British Museum. 248 Alamy Images: Christa Knijff: tl; DK Images: Alan Keohane: cl; Science Photo Library: br. 249 Alamy Images: Ian Wallace: cl; Corbis: © Bettmann: br. 250 Alamy Images: Mr Yogesh More/Ephotocorp: clb, tl, WilmarPhotography.com: tc; Derwent Water Systems, Matlock, UK: bl; DK Images: Alan Williams, Courtesy of the National Trust: b. 251 Alamy Images: Martin J Dignard: clb; Geophotos: tl, cb; Science Photo Library: Jeremy Walker: br. 252 Corbis: © Jacques Langevin/CORBIS SYGMA: tr, © Tim Thompson: clb; Science Photo Library: car. Jon Wilson: clb; © 2004 Smithsonian Institution: cl. 253 Alamy Images: Bowmann/F1 online: tl, Andre Jenny: clb; Corbis: © George D Lepp: cla; Science Photo Library: Astrid & Hanns-Frieder Michler: br. 254 DK Images: Alan Keohane: tl. 255 www.bridgeman.co.uk: Chapel of the Planets, Tempio Malatestiano, Rimini, Italy: tc; Corbis: © Ric Ergenbright: tl; Science Photo Library: John Beatty: crb, Alexander Tsiaras: cl. 256 © The British Museum: cr; Reg Grant: cl. 257 Corbis: © Raymond Gehman: cb; www.gemstonesgifts.com: cr. 258 Alamy Images: Pavel Filatov: tl; Corbis: © Roger Garwood & Trish Ainslie: br, © Michael S. Yamashita: bl; Science Photo Library: Dr Jeremy Burgess: cl. 259 akg-images: CDA/Guillemot: cr; www.bridgeman.co.uk: © Museum of Fine Arts, Houston, Texas, USA, Museum purchase with funds provided by the Museum Collectors: tr; Corbis: © Robert Estall: cl, © H. David Seawell: cb; Frank de Wit: tl. 260 Alamy Images: Pavel Filatov: tl, Jack Sullivan: crb; Corbis: © Danny Lehman: clb; DK Images: The British Museum: ca, © Judith Miller/Cooper Owen: cl. 261 Corbis: © Richard A. Cooke: tl, © Lowell Georgia: clb; DK Images: Alan Williams: clb; Ron Bonewitz: tl; Sterling Hill Mining Museum: Maureen Verbeek: cb. 262 Alamy Images: tl, © Stefano Bianchetti: cla, © Bob Krist: crb, © David Muench: cb; Ron Bonewitz: clb. 263 Alamy Images: Leslie Garland Picture Library: tl, Pavel Filatov: clb; Nigel Lacey: c; Courtesy www.ohiotoxicmold.com: tl. 264 Corbis: © Bowers Museum of Cultural Art, photo Don Wiechec: tc, © Pat O'Hara: tl, © Enzo and Paolo Ragazzini: tr; The Natural History Museum, London: cb. 265 Corbis: © Gianni Dagli Orti: tl, © Wolfgang Kaehler: cl, © Sandro Vannini: br, © David H. Wells: cr; Geophotos: tl. 266 Alamy Images: Mr Yogesh More/Ephotocorp: tl, Andy Christodolo/Cephas Picture Library: tl; DK Images: Kim Sayer: clb. 267 Alamy Images: Jacques Jangoux: tl; Corbis: © Sheldan Collins: br, © Jon Sparks: cl. 268 Alamy Images: Leslie Garland Picture Library: crb, The PhotoLibrary Wales: clb; Geophotos: clb. 269 Alamy Images: J Schwanke: tl; Corbis: © Paul A Souders: clb. 270 Corbis: © Roger Ressmeyer: bl; 270 Jenny Reakes: cl; Dave Waters: c. 271 Alamy Images: Bowmann/F1 online: tl; Art Directors/TRIP: cl. 272 Corbis: © Richard Klune: cl; Geophotos: tl, clb; Ron Bonewitz: tl; Science Photo Library: Michael Dunning: tc, Detlev van Ravensway: tr. 273 Science Photo Library: Alexis Rosenfeld: bcl; © 2004 Smithsonian Institution: cla, cl. 274 Alamy Images: Robert Harding Picture

Library: tl; www.bridgeman.co.uk: The British Museum, London, UK: bcl; Peabody Museum, Harvard University, Cambridge, MA, USA: bl; DK Images: Harry Taylor: bcl; Werner Forman Archive: Dallas Museum of Fine Art: 275 www.bridgeman.co.uk: Museo de America, Madrid, Spain: tr; DK Images: © Judith Miller/Sloan's: cl; © 2004 Smithsonian Institution: cr. 276 Science Photo Library: Chris Knapton: cr, Sheila Terry: bl. 277 Alamy Images: Pavel Filatov: tl; Ron Bonewitz: clb; © 2004 Smithsonian Institution: tr. 278 Corbis: © Jan Butchofsky-Houser: cl; Dave Waters: crb. 279 Corbis: © Nathan Benn: tc; Dave Waters: tc, crb. 280 Corbis: © Asian Art & Archaeology, Inc.: bl, © Royal Ontario Museum: clb, bc, © Tim Thompson: tl. 281 Kremlin Museums, Moscow, Russia/www.bridgeman.co.uk: tr; Corbis: © Lowell Georgia: tr. 282 The Picture Desk: Art Archive/Genius of China Exhibition: tl, b. 283 National Geographic Image Collection: The Xuzhou Museum, China/O. Louis Mazzatenta: tc. 284 Alamy Images: Martin J Dignard: tl; Corbis: © Richard Cummins: crb, © Blaine Harrington III: cl. 285 Corbis: © Hulton Deutsch Collection: tr, © Roger Garwood & Trish Ainslie: tl, © David Muench: clb, © Hubert Stadler: tr. 286 Alamy Images: P. S. Lahiri/Indiapicture: cr. 286 Geophotos: cl. 287 Alamy Images: Thaler Shmuel/Index Stock: cl; Geophotos: tl, cl; Division of Mines and Geology, California: cr. 288 www.bridgeman.co.uk: Ashmolean Museum, University of Oxford, UK: cl; Corbis: © Tom Bean: tl; Mount Mica Rarities: bl. 289 DK Images: cra, bc, br; © 2004 Smithsonian Institution: br; Alamy Images: Pavel Filatov: tl; Courtesy Steven Hoffmeyer, Hoffmeyer.com Photography: cr; Science Photo Library: US Dept of Energy: cl; © 2004 Smithsonian Institution: cr. 291 Corbis: © William A. Bake: c. © Bettmann: tr; Geophotos: tl, cl. 292 Alamy Images: Pavel Filatov: tl; Corbis: © Gianni Dagli Orti: tr, © Ann Johansson: cra; © 2004 Smithsonian Institution: bl. 293 www.bridgeman.co.uk: Bonhams, London, UK: crb, Courtesy of the Warden and Scholars of New College, Oxford, UK: c; DK Images: © Judith Miller/N. Bloom & Son Ltd: b; Royal Geographical Society, London: tr; © 2004 Smithsonian Institution: b. 294 Corbis: © Bob Krist: clb. 295 Corbis: © Paul Almasy: clb; © Mimmo Jodice: cb. 296 © Christie's Images Ltd: cr; Geophotos: clb; Ron Bonewitz: b. 297 Alamy Images: Pavel Filatov: clb, Helder Silva: crb; © Paul Almasy: tr © Charles Krebs: tl. 298 Courtesy of Dr Peter Bancroft: tl. 299 Ancient Art & Architecture Collection: cr; www.bridgeman.co.uk: Bonhams, London, UK: c; DK Images: © Judith Miller/HY Duke and Son: cl. 300 Alamy Images: Leslie Garland Picture Library: cl; www.bridgeman.co.uk: The British Museum, London, UK: bl; © Christie's Images Ltd: da; © 2004 Smithsonian Institution: br. 301 © Christie's Images Ltd: tr, cra, cbr; Corbis: © Nick Rains; Cordaiy Photo Library: clb; DK Images: © Judith Miller/Joseph H Bonnar: cb; Ron Bonewitz: tl; © 2004 Smithsonian Institution: b. 302 Alamy Images: Robert Harding Picture Library: clb, Witry Pascal: tl; © Christie's Images Ltd: tr, cb, cbl; © 2004 Smithsonian Institution: b. 303 Alamy Images: Robert Harding Picture Library: clb, Witry Pascal: tl; © Christie's Images Ltd: cla, cl. 304 Alamy Images: Malie Rich-Griffith: tl; Corbis: © Jim Sugar: bl. 305 Alamy Images: Dan White: br. 306 Alamy Images: Pavel Filatov: tl; © 2004 Smithsonian Institution: cr, crb; Courtesy of Dr Peter Bancroft: cr. 307 Corbis: © Bettmann: tr; DK Images: © Judith Miller /Goodwins Antiques Ltd: cr. 308 © Christie's Images Ltd: cr; Corbis: © O. Alamany & E. Vicens: tl; DK Images: Harry Taylor. tcr. 309 Corbis: © Bettmann: crb, © John and Lisa Merrill: tl; Jenny Reakes: clb. 310 Alamy Images: Jacques Jangoux: tl; Corbis: © Bettmann: bc; Sterling Hill Mining Museum: Maureen Verbeek: clb. 311 Alamy Images: Pavel Filatov: cb; Ron Bonewitz: tl. 312 Geophotos: clb, cb; Sterling Hill Mining Museum: Maureen Verbeek: tl. 313 Alamy Images: Jacques Jangoux: tcl; Profimedia CZ s.r.o.: tl, Jon Sparks: clb; Novosti (London): cb. 514 Alamy Images: Mediacolors: tc; Science Photo Library: David Nunuk: tl. 315 www.bridgeman.co.uk: Palazzo Vecchio (Palazzo della Signoria) Florence, Italy: br; © Judith Miller/Dorling Kindersley/Woolley and Wallis: cr. 316 akg-images: cl; Corbis: © Antoine Gyori: bl. 317 akg-images. 518 Corbis: br; Mary Evans Picture Library: br; Getty Images: bla. 319 Ron Bonewitz: tl; Science Photo Library: Sinclair Stammers: clb. 520 Science Photo Library: Andrew J Martinez: crb. 321 Ron Bonewitz: tl; www.bridgeman.co.uk: Galleria degli Uffizi, Florence, Italy, Giraudon: br, Heini Schneebeli: bl; DK Images: tr, cl, cla, cra, c, bra © Judith Miller / Dorling Kindersley / Lyon and Turnbull: bc. 322 Corbis: © Andrew Redpath: tl; Colin Keates © Dorling Kindersley, Courtesy of the Natural History Museum, London: tr; Courtesy of the Victoria and Albert Museum, London: tc; Courtesy of the IDNR: tr. 325 DK Images: Michel Zabe © CONACULTA-INAH-MEX. Authorized reproduction by the Instituto Nacional de Antropologia e Historia: br; SPL: Alexis Rosenfeld: cl. 524 Getty Images. 325 David Doubilet: br; The Picture Desk: Art Archive/The Bodleian Library Oxford: tr. 326 Alamy Images: Frank Chmura: tl. 528 National Geographic Image Collection: Michael Melford: tl; Science Photo Library: WG: cb. 329 Corbis: © Tom Bean: cl; © Layne Kennedy: bl, © Reuters: br; Science Photo Library: Sinclair Stammers: ca. 330 Corbis: © Derek Hall; Frank Lane Picture Agency: tl; Science Photo Library: James King-Holmes: br. 331 Corbis: © Chinch Gryniewicz; Ecoscene: b; Science Photo Library: tr, Martin Bond: cr, Astrid and Hanns-Frieder Michler: tl, Sinclair Stammers: cb. 532 DK Images: The Natural History Museum: cl, cr, crb, b. 333 DK Images: The Natural History Museum: ca, cl, c, tr, bc; Science Photo Library: cla. 354 Corbis: © Hubert Stadler: tl; DK Images: Photo Alan Keohane; Rainbow Forest Museum, Arizona: bl. 335 Corbis: © George H H Huey. 336 Corbis: © Hubert Stadler: tl; DK Images: The Natural History Museum: tc, crb. 337 Courtesy of Dr Peter Crimes: tr. 339 Corbis: © William A Bake: tr; Science Photo Library: Georgette Douwma: tl. 340 Corbis: © Jonathan Blair: bc; Colin Keates © Dorling Kindersley, Courtesy of the Natural History Museum, London tr. 542 Alamy Images: Frank Chmura: b. 343 Alamy Images: Robert Harding Picture Library: tl; The Natural History Museum: cl. 345 Corbis: © Derek Hall; Frank Lane Picture Agency: bl; DK Images: The Natural History Museum: tc. 346 Corbis: bl. 347 Science Photo Library: Matthew Oldfield; Scubazoo: tl. 548 Corbis: © Bettmann: tl; © James L Amos: cl; DK Images: The Natural History Museum: ca, cra, c, bl, br. 349 Corbis: © Anthony Bannister; Gallo Images: br; DK Images: The Natural History Museum: tr, c, bl, bl.

All other images © Dorling Kindersley.

For further information see: www.dkimages.com